JAMES VII

JAMES VII

DUKE AND KING OF SCOTS

ALASTAIR J. MANN

John Donald

First published in Great Britain in 2014 by
John Donald, an imprint of Birlinn Ltd

West Newington House
10 Newington Road
Edinburgh
EH9 1QS

www.birlinn.co.uk

ISBN: 978 1 904607 90 8

The publishers gratefully acknowledge the support of the Scouloudi
Foundation towards the publication of this book

British Library Cataloguing-in-Publication Data
A catalogue record for this book is available on request from the British Library

Typeset by Hewer Text UK Ltd, Edinburgh
Printed and bound in the UK by Bell and Bain Ltd, Glasgow

Contents

Illustrations

canvas by Pierre Mignard (1693–4). (Royal Collection Trust/© Her Majesty Queen Elizabeth II 2014)

13 Queen St Margaret, the medieval queen of Scots, a painting at the centre of the art collection at Saint-Germain. Oil on canvas by Nicolas de Largillière, 1692, National Trust, Sizergh Castle, Cumbria. (© National Trust Images)

14 The concluding lines of a letter from King James (in his own hand) to Cardinal Philip Howard in January 1691. (Stuart Papers, RA SP/MAIN/1/59; The Royal Archives © Her Majesty Queen Elizabeth II)

15 The Scots College in Paris in the Rue du Cardinal Lemoine. (From the author's collection)

16 The tomb of King James in the parish church of Saint-Germain-en-Laye. (From the author's collection)

17 The ceiling painting above the tomb in the parish church of Saint-Germain-en-Laye. (From the author's collection)

18 The plagues placed on the outer wall of the parish church of Saint-Germain-en-Laye. (From the author's collection)

19 King James's final words as printed (in Paris, 1702) on silk for Elizabeth, duchess of Gordon. (NRS, CH12/12/1546, Records of the Episcopal Church of Scotland, Episcopal Chest; Courtesy of the General Synod of the Scottish Episcopal Church)

Acknowledgements

This study has been one of long gestation and as such there are many individuals and institutions to thank for their patience and encouragement. Worthy of commendation are numerous archivists and librarians, including the staff of the National Archives of Scotland (now the National Records of Scotland); the Scottish National Library; the National Archives at Kew; The British Library; Dr Williams' Library; Bodleian Library, Oxford; Scottish Catholic Archives (visited at its spiritual home of Columba House, Edinburgh), and the Royal Archives at Windsor, where Allisson Derrett was particularly helpful. I am especially grateful to Lady Dunmore and John Douglas Stuart, 21st earl of Moray, for permissions to consult and quote from family papers. Particular acknowledgment is due to the late, ninth Duke of Buccleuch for granting permission to visit the Queensberry archives at Drumlanrig Castle and also to his then archivist Andrew Fisher for guiding me through the large collection. I gratefully acknowledge the gracious permission of Her Majesty Queen Elizabeth II to consult and quote material from the Stuart Papers in the Royal Archives. Additional permission for the use of pictures from the Royal Collection is also recognised and is specified, along with other permissions, in the separate list of figures.

Intellectual help has been provided by a number of current and former colleagues. A particular debt is owed to Professor Keith Brown at Manchester University, formerly of the Scottish Parliament Project at St Andrews University, for encouragement and guidance in ways mostly unbeknownst to him, and also to patient colleagues at Stirling University, led by Professor Richard Oram, who like many a student, have had to live with the long-term obsession of the biographer. My thanks to the School of Arts and Humanities at Stirling for sporadic but vital research time to complete the archival work and actual writing. I must thank Dr Mike Rapport for very accurate French translations. For assistance with the cost for research trips to Paris, Oxford and London I must thank the Strathmartine Trust for a generous grant. This publication has been made possible by a grant from the Scouloudi Foundation in association with the Institute of Historical Research.

The thanks owed to my family defeats calculation. My sons, Robert and Andrew, have looked on bemusedly over the years and have allowed me to keep my sense of humour. My mother Anna has encouraged with her genuine interest. As for my wife Lesley, she has had to put up with many hardships during the intellectual and practical journey that is the fate of the biographer. I love you all.

AM

The House of Stuart (1542–1807)

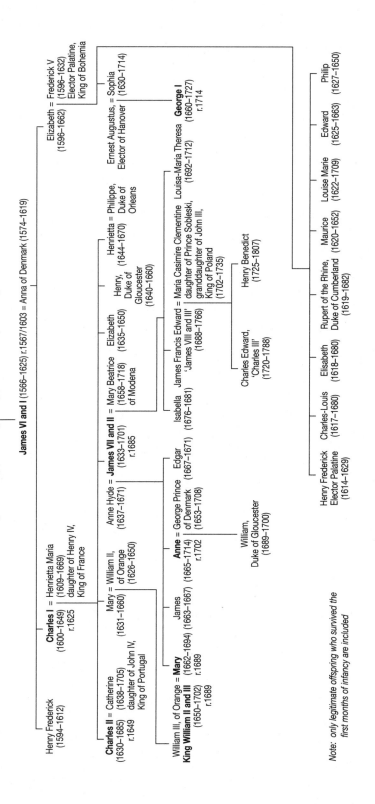

Henry Lord Darnley (1546–1567) = **Mary, Queen of Scots** (1542–1587) r.1542

James VI and I (1566–1625) r.1567/1603 = Anna of Denmark (1574–1619)

Henry Frederick (1594–1612)

Charles I = Henrietta Maria (1600–1649) (1609–1669) r.1625 daughter of Henry IV, King of France

Elizabeth = Frederick V (1596–1662) (1596–1632) Elector Palatine, King of Bohemia

Charles II = Catherine (1630–1685) (1638–1705) r.1649 daughter of John IV, King of Portugal

Mary = William II, (1631–1660) of Orange (1626–1650)

Anne Hyde = **James VII and II** = Mary Beatrice (1637–1671) (1633–1701) (1658–1718) r.1685 of Modena

Henry, Duke of Gloucester (1640–1660)

Henrietta = Philippe, (1644–1670) Duke of Orleans

Elizabeth (1635–1650)

Ernest Augustus, = Sophia Elector of Hanover (1630–1714)

William III, of Orange **King William II and III** (1650–1702) r.1689

Mary (1662–1694) r.1689

James (1663–1667)

Anne = George Prince (1665–1714) of Denmark r.1702 (1653–1708)

Edgar (1667–1671)

Isabella (1676–1681)

James Francis Edward 'James VIII and III' (1688–1766)

Maria Casimire Clementine = daughter of Prince Sobieski, granddaughter of John III, King of Poland (1702–1735)

Louisa-Maria Theresa (1692–1712)

George I (1660–1727) r.1714

William, Duke of Gloucester (1689–1700)

Charles Edward, 'Charles III' (1720–1788)

Henry Benedict (1725–1807)

Henry Frederick Elector Palatine (1614–1629)

Charles-Louis (1617–1680)

Elisabeth (1618–1680)

Rupert of the Rhine, Duke of Cumberland (1619–1682)

Maurice (1620–1652)

Louise Marie (1622–1709)

Edward (1625–1663)

Philip (1627–1650)

Note: only legitimate offspring who survived the first months of infancy are included

Introduction: A Contested Reputation

James VII of Scotland and II of England (1633–1701) is one of the most controversial historical characters of the early modern period. He is a reference point for historical assessment in a range of thematic fields including, to mention but some, the Restoration of the British monarchy from 1660, the 'Glorious Revolution' of 1688/9, the fiscal-military state, the European Nine-Years War (1689–97), the 'age of absolutism', the Ancien Regime, and the beginnings of Jacobitism as it unfolded from 1689 to 1746. Perhaps it is for this reason that some of his biographies creak under the weight of the task before them and why no Scottish life has so far been attempted.

The study of King James is not merely multi-faceted but quite perplexing. Too often chapter titles such as 'rise and fall' and 'study in failure' are suggested by a life with many fits and starts. As we shall see, he achieved an almost unbroken string of military and naval successes from 1652 to 1672, although in contrast to later reverses and humiliations. To quote a tepid comment from James's autobiography – which survives through J. S. Clarke's *The Life of James the Second* (1816) and is the nearest thing we have to a memoirs, based as it is on a manuscript compilation of his own writings – 'his life was made up of mortifications and crosses, so even the few satisfactions he had, were seldom without a mixture of disappointments'.[1] This seems astonishing for a handsome and dynamic young prince who served with distinction in the wars of continental Europe, and who on his return to Britain in 1660 promised a continuing and brilliant military career. In the horns of such a dilemma we see his life played out as 'contested reputation', bringing forth exaggeration and polarisation. Contemporaries and post-mortem commentators each have their own reasons to condemn or commend: Revolution men versus Jacobites, Presbyterians versus Episcopalians, Protestants versus Catholics, Whigs versus Tories, Empire historians, explaining the uniqueness and relative peace of British political reform, versus Thomas Paine and the upholders of European and American republicanism, and unionists versus republicans in the context of the modern island of Ireland.[2] There is also much scope for speculation.

Had James not survived his brother Charles II (1630–1685) his reputation would have been secured as an honourable military man and not as a Catholic monarch with perceived and sometimes stumblingly real inclinations towards absolutism.

There is, however, some consensus among Whig and Tory historiography on the scale of James's political shortcomings, with differences focusing on where weaknesses developed or our subject's personal motivations. These commentators, who look more to parliaments and the Crown respectively, often arrive at similar conclusions by separate paths. The contemporary Whig historian Bishop Gilbert Burnet, an Anglo-Scot who focused mostly on English affairs, led the accusation that James sought to undermine the English constitution in a drive for absolute power. The Revolution that followed this was therefore a constitutional rebalancing. Lord Macaulay, the nineteenth-century grandee of English history, took this same line, as did Trevelyan and others into the twentieth century. Meanwhile, the eighteenth- century historian Edmund Burke, mostly Whig in politics but Tory in much of his history, stressed religion in combination with constitutionalism. James's Catholicism led to a crisis and the Revolution was necessary only to correct that misalignment and, yes, to put back in place Parliament, but also the central role of 'right kingship'.³ Recently the early Whig line has been reactivated but transformed into a double revolution. The manipulation of the system arose, or a bureaucratic modernisation and 'modern revolution', with the imposition of the Catholic faith and arbitrary government being the objectives, and then this was followed by the revolution that removed King James. This counters the revisionist consensus of the twentieth century which argues, not only the conservative nature of the Revolution, but also that James's intolerance over religion has been greatly exaggerated, in some cases deliberately. In this study, however, the result of revolution will be set aside to bring centre stage James's intentions in his own lifetime, and in particular with regard to the kingdom of Scotland. Nonetheless, the Scottish historiography tradition, out of 300 years of Presbyterian historicism, concludes the Revolution was indubitably religious in nature, and much less a constitutional event. The work of P. W. J. Riley, still the most detailed published account of Scottish politics under William and Mary, brings up short the Presbyterian victors, from the contemporary Robert Wodrow to David Hay Fleming in the twentieth century, with secular motivations and cynicism pervading the actors of the day and (mightily) the historian as well.⁴ As this biography reveals, however, elite groups in early modern Scotland exercised both political and religious motivations in equal measure, as did James himself.

While there are no existing Scottish biographies of King James, those of him as king of England are numerous and provide a firm foundation. One remarkable tour de force of the mid twentieth century is F. C. Turner's biography which sparkles with detail, brilliant analytical moments but a familiar Whig-like prejudice. Turner also bridged the two phases of James's life. His seeming transformation, hinged at 1685 when he became king and moved from energetic and competent man to hesitant and increasingly feeble individual, is put down to a 'degeneration' thesis. A sudden deterioration in health was the cause. James's 'crisis' therefore was not merely about religion or even psychology. Maurice Ashley followed Turner's line, coupled with a re-evaluation of James's bright and dynamic youth. In both not only Scottish details but those of the second exile are seen as insignificant. Typical is this statement from Turner 'From Christmas day 1688 . . . until his death . . . the life of James II has very little . . . interest'.[5] The best single-volume English life remains John Miller's *James II: A Study in Kingship* (1989), first published in the late 1970s, where both the animation of events and characteristics, and the more extensive use of archival material, are ground-breaking. Yet Miller's study contains almost nothing on Scotland, and is also limited by the requirement of a constitutional appraisal. Amongst shorter biographies, and offering the most concise all round, three kingdoms and colonial introduction, is W. A. Speck's *James II: Profiles in Power* (2002), whereas others such as those by Testa and Mullet are doggedly English and ignore the second exile as well. The most recent grand exploration is the two volume life by John Callow (2000–04), and while these volumes will be too metaphorically insistent for some tastes, and oddly perfunctory over his period as king, the scale of this study is vast. An impressive effort has been made to place in centre ground the colonial, military and economic aspects of James's English career.[6] Importantly, and convincingly, Callow rejects the 'degeneration' theory: the same man was the dashing young prince as the defeated old king, and the seeds of James's failures were planted in the period of his youth.

Restoration studies also offer a rich mixture of material relevant to any reassessment of King James. The surveys of Miller, Seaward and Hutton on the English Restoration are fertile territory but the most detailed three kingdom investigations are Tim Harris's two volumes on the Restoration (2005) and the Revolution (2006). Scottish historians can only admire his painstaking effort to look where they have not. Some examinations are more cross-sectional. The late Kevin Sharpe's *Rebuilding Rule 1660–1714: The Restoration and Revolution Monarchy* (2013) provides his typically provocative and brilliant rendering of the political culture during these transitional phases.[7] Also, in the last decade several essay collections have brought both comparative and more forensic, drilled-down studies, and some of these are misleadingly titled, such as Hutton and Pincus's *A Nation Transformed: England after the Restoration* (2011) which is not only English in content. As for the biographies of James's brother, Hutton's *Charles II; King of England, Scotland and Ireland* is outstanding, while Antonia Fraser's life is very useful as an honest, entertaining and thoughtful study, but focused mostly on England.[8] Jacobite historiography, meanwhile, is also extensive and more Scottish-centred, though not as full for James as for the many post-mortem rebellions. It is a measure of how Jacobitism was launched as a cause with James's death, an event recalling Mary, Queen of Scots's words before her execution – 'in my death is my beginning'. The

Jacobite mix is certainly intoxicating, but Edward Corp's many studies of the exiled court are absolutely essential, and structured introductions come from the surveys of Lenman and Szechi, providing much needed contextualisation.[9]

Until recently Restoration Scotland has been something of black hole in terms of scholarship. It has not been subjected to the intensive re-evaluation and revisionism of the union of 1707, although some such union studies, like that by Allan Macinnes, are rooted in a century of connectivity. General Union of the Crowns studies, by Gordon Donaldson, William Ferguson and Keith Brown, provide a starting point, and before we reach 1660 David Stevenson on politics and John Young on Parliament set the scene. Once we get to 1660, however, we find that much of the best material remains unpublished.[10] Doctoral theses by Ronnie Lee (1995), Derek Patrick (2002) and Kirsty McAlister (2003) are fine studies of, respectively, Scotland's Restoration, particularly the economic and military aspects; the Revolution and the impact of electoral politics in the 1690s, and of James and politics from 1679 to 1686.[11] Parliamentary history was the driving force behind Patrick and McAlister, and in fact this has become a vibrant research area, stemming from the Scottish Parliament Project (SPP) at St Andrews University, and outputs of the editors and collaborators of the online *The Records of the Parliaments of Scotland to 1707* (2008–). Gillian MacIntosh's *The Scottish Parliament under Charles II, 1660–1685* (2007) and three edited volumes of essays emanating from SPP are testament to that. The second of these collections has important essays (by MacIntosh, Mann and Patrick) on the period 1660 to 1690 which are of great significance to this study. Recent essays have expanded on the parliamentary theme by discussing James's attitude to the Scottish Parliament and the political elite. But in addition to the distinctly parliamentary focus we must add Clare Jackson's lively study of Restoration royalism, Allan Kennedy's remarkable exploration of the Restoration Highlands and the key historiography of the Restoration Covenanting movement.[12]

Bringing all this together, with an array of archival material, what is the plan for this volume? James will be discussed from birth to death as a prince of Scotland, although not without recognition of the other two kingdoms and continental interactions. The progress of the chapters is chronological but the content within each is interwoven and cross border. The main axis of orientation for this discussion, however, will be a line drawn or cord stretched between James and the kingdom of Scotland. In this sense this work is not designed to be a full history of the period from 1633 to 1701, or of Scotland from 1660 to 1701, only a biography of the life and times of James, duke of Albany, who succeeded to become King James VII and II. It is a remarkable story that changed the history of the British Isles and especially that of Scotland.

CHAPTER I

The Making of a Prince

SECOND SON OF A SECOND SON

L ate at night, on a cold winter's evening in November, a son, the second prince of Scotland, was born. One day he would be king. Charles, the new son of James VI and Queen Anne of Denmark, was born at eleven o'clock at night in the year 1600 in the royal apartments of the abbey palace of Dunfermline. The following morning the king rode hard from Edinburgh to Dunfermline to congratulate his wife and to hold his new child. As he departed the capital three pieces of ordinance were shot from the Castle to announce the birth and as a brief expression of public joy. There may have been 'no bonfires and no bells' but there was contentment in the land and especially within the political community.[1]

Appointments were quickly made for the child's immediate care: Margaret Stewart, Lady Ochiltree, was to be governess with a Jean Drummond as wet nurse and Marian Hepburn as 'rocker'. However, this positive start was soon disorientated by tense negotiations over the timing of the baptism ceremony. The context was the complex and strained relations of the royal parents. Proposals, supported by Anne, to delay the baptism until the following spring, by which time the king of Denmark, her brother, and the duke of Brunswick, her brother-in-law, could be present, were rejected by both king and council in favour of a seemly, early and less costly baptism. And so, on 23 December 1600, Charles was baptised at Holyrood Chapel and Palace and proclaimed 'duke of Albany, marquis of Ormonde, earl of Ross and Lord Ardmonach', the first new-born given the title Albany since, as a baby, his father inherited it from his own father Lord Darnley in 1567. The dukedom was not, in fact, formally granted to Charles until 1603, only two years before his English title, Duke of York. But on a cold day in December 1600, the ceremonial choreography was both prompt and very deliberate. The 'gossips' or godparents were representatives from the French court and the countesses of Huntly and Mar. Henri, 'Prince' of Rohan carried the boy, wrapped in a golden robe, into the chapel and there the ceremony was carried out by David Lindsay, bishop of Ross. A crowd of hundreds gathered outside the palace as trumpets were sounded and cannons roared. Queen Elizabeth's secretary Robert Cecil was informed that thereafter 'The banquet was great' and 'the haill canons of the castell wer tuo severall tymes discharged' after the feast, but this was not the magnificent celebration for the birth of Henry, duke of Rothesay, the heir to the throne, which took place at Stirling Castle in 1594.² Notwithstanding the love of parents for offspring, to hereditary monarchy the insurance of a second heir could not match the ecstatic relief at the arrival and survival of a first born male. Although Charles would have time enough to grow used to the idea of becoming king on Henry's death in 1612, it was as if, from the beginning, it was just not meant to be.

Charles's son James Stewart, later James VII and II, was in effect the second son of a second son and another insurance policy which in due course, with the failure of his brother to produce a legitimate heir, had to be redeemed. Younger sons succeeding were common enough for the royal houses of Europe – England's Henry VIII and Scotland's James I, for example – but what was more unusual was that James succeeded in his fifties, at the age of fifty-one. James was, in fact, the third surviving child after his brother Charles and sister Mary, and the third but second surviving son (Charles James, duke of Cornwall having died at birth in 1629) of King Charles and his French Queen Henrietta Maria. He was born, like his father, at eleven o'clock on a cold winter night, at St James's Palace in London on 14 October 1633. His mother was twenty-four and his father thirty-three and apparently at the height of his political authority in England and Scotland. James, 'a goodly, lusty child', who compared well with his older brother Charles, was welcomed by public acclaim as throughout London and England bonfires were lit and church bells rung.³

The new prince was named James in memory of his grandfather, a symbolic and unionist gesture to and for England's partner in the Union of the Crowns. James's birth was also celebrated in Scotland but in muted fashion. On 25 October the town council of Edinburgh issued an order that 'bonefyres and fyres of joy be sett furth by all inhabitants' but the records of the Scottish Privy Council indicate no official celebratory activities and surviving diaries are quiet on the subject.⁴ This is not so surprising: the Scottish tradition, as seen following the birth of James VI and Prince Henry, was to view such a birth as a private matter but the baptism as an opportunity for public rejoicing. However, as with James's brother Charles, the formal celebrations in London would be a largely though not entirely English affair. James was christened at St James's on 24 November and the duke was carried into the chapel by the court favourite and lady of the bedchamber Elizabeth Grey, countess of Kent, assisted by the Lord Privy Seal, Henry Montagu, first earl of Manchester and James Stuart, fourth duke of Lennox, the most senior Scottish noble. The involvement of Lennox has echoes of James VI and I's insistence that Ludovic, the second duke, led the procession at his Westminster coronation in July 1603. In 1633 the three godparents, or sponsors, were all Protestants: the king's sister Elizabeth, the widowed Queen of Bohemia; her eldest son Charles Louis, prince of Palatine, both in exile in the Dutch republic; and Prince Frederick Henry, the prince of Orange. As they could not attend, substitutes took their place: Mary Fielding, marchioness of Hamilton, wife of James Hamilton, the third marquis and Charles's chief advisor on Scottish affairs, for the Queen of Bohemia; the Lord Treasurer Richard Weston, earl of Portland, for the Prince Palatine; and Thomas Howard, earl of Arundel (a Protestant convert but supporter of the Catholic Queen's interest at court) for the prince of Orange.[5] When the ceremony was complete, appropriately, York herald stood at the door of the antechapel and pronounced to the people the child's name and style as duke of York, though he was not formally created so until 1643. Remarkably, his Scottish title as duke of Albany was not formally conferred until July 1659 when the exiled Brussels court of his brother Charles sought to raise family morale by conferring the title. The failure to grant this dignity under the Great Seal of Scotland before the Civil War is a strange omission and reflects badly on Charles's handling of Scottish affairs and sensitivities, but also helps explain why, even in Scotland, James was some-times referred to as duke of York. He was confirmed, however, in December 1660 as taking precedence 'over all the other dukes' of Scotland.[6]

The christening was an event with diverse religious implications. All three godparents were Protestants. The ceremony was carried out according to Protestant rites, in spite of the strong Catholic beliefs of James's mother. In fact neither mother nor father attended the ceremony, and James was presented to his parents after the event. The christening was unashamedly Anglican with no Scottish element. It was presided over by William Laud, archbishop of Canterbury, assisted by Richard Neile, archbishop of York and Richard Corbet, bishop of Norwich. All were high Anglicans and Laud was at the height of his influence with the king as he promoted Arminianism, focusing on free will and rejecting the central Calvinist doctrine of predestination, and an agenda of liturgical and ritualistic conformity for the churches of England and Scotland.[7] While religious formalities of the chris-tening would not have seemed too alien to Scottish Presbyterians, the pomp and grandeur of the English bishops would have reminded Scots of the controversial coronation ceremony for Charles I held in Edinburgh just six months earlier. Even some moderate Presbyterians in Scotland could not distinguish between English bishops and Catholics and when James was still a little boy such strongly held views helped create the context for revolution.

Religious sensibilities were also evident in the court in London. It had been clear since Charles I's marriage to Henrietta Maria in 1625 that she would act as a protector of English Catholics and magnet for visiting envoys from Catholic Europe and Rome. The terms of their marriage contract made it clear that she should offer such protection and Charles went along with this, even though, as with his father, his own, personal Protestantism was never in serious doubt. Nevertheless, in the days after James's birth 'astonishment' was expressed that the queen had persuaded the king to agree to a Catholic wet nurse, one Katherine Elliott, and that, after much debate about an appropriate oath, Charles agreed the nurse could take the same 'ordinary oath of fealty' as that taken by Catholic priests attending the queen. However, the baby boy was too young for this to be any kind of factor in developing his subsequent religious beliefs.[8]

There has been much comment by historians of the deliberate efforts of James VI to keep his now Catholic wife Anne of Denmark from the upbringing of his sons Henry and Charles. There is no denying that James wished his sons to be correctly advised on matters of religion, but both Scottish and English traditions emphasised separation of the young heirs from the king and queen for reasons of security and personal safety. Equally the affairs of state and of the bedroom were not perhaps appropriate for the upbringing of younger children. Charles I was brought up in Stirling Castle under the guidance of the dowager countess of Mar and her son John Erskine, earl of Mar, both committed Protestants. For a period of over seven years Charles's son James joined his elder brother and sister in their own 'children's' court at Richmond Palace, and also in the fate of being brought up separated from their parents. Callow is correct to mock the image of the 'close knit' family as suggested in the cosy group portraits of Van Dyck. But although Charles and Henrietta Maria were not attentive parents, it was hardly fashionable to behave so in the royal courts of Europe. That does not mean, however, that James was in his first few years brought up in a cold and unwelcoming environment, and Gilbert Burnet's claim that James was overlooked does not match known facts of his upbringing between 1633 and 1638.[9] When in London this family court located itself at St James's Palace or Somerset House.

While some individuals seem to have carried out indeterminate roles as governors, such as Elizabeth, Lady Hatton and Henry Jermyn (the elder), the infant James was mostly put in the hands of his brother's Protestant governess and governor, Mary Sackville, countess of Dorset and the elderly William Seymour, first marquis of Hertford, a bookish man rather than a playful, surrogate uncle. As well as monitoring the work of the nurse, the countess ensured that a 'rocker' was on hand to push James's cradle, including one Mary Godbolt who received £150 for her pains in January 1636, and ensured that over £2,600 was paid to various tradesman for work carried out for the duke's nursery and rooms in the two years up to December 1635.[10] More formal play was well provided for in the form of instructors in dancing, archery and fencing. Also, James, Charles and Princess Mary were joined by George and Francis Villiers, the two sons of George, first duke of Buckingham, Charles I's old favourite, who were brought to the bosom of the king's family after their father was assassinated in 1628. Informal play, both outdoor and indoor, was therefore lively enough.[11]

As for formal education, details are slim, especially in the early years. James seems to have educated himself in the 1640s and 1650s wherever he happened to be located, and more by experience than through reading. He was something of the mature student, especially over religion. Yet some formal education was provided intermittently to James and his elder brother by Brian Duppa, the moderate bishop of Salisbury, at the recommendation of Laud, and the royal physician William Harvey. The academics Broughton and Croucher, fellows of Oxford colleges, joined Duppa as James's tutors in his days at Oxford between 1644 and 1646. There and in The Hague in 1648 he was taught handwriting and French, in which he became fluent, by the Frenchman Massonett, and James also developed a fondness for music, showing some skill as a guitar player from his teenage years. In general, he seems a reluctant scholar, though probably no more than his brother Charles. We cannot say that an inadequate or incomplete formal education facilitated James's later political embarrassments to any degree. Turner's comment that James's English style was 'undistinguished and pedestrian' merely reflects the literary qualities of a number of European princes and some intellectual snobbery on the historian's part (see Plate 14).[12] As a linguist he was fairly skilled – when the wealthy prospective match Anne Marie Louise, duchess of Montpensier, contrasted her impressions of the two brothers in exile she concluded that James (then fifteen years old) was 'very pretty, with a good face and fine figure, and of fair complexion; [and] he spoke French well which gave him a manner preferable to that of his brother'.[13] Although somewhat humourless compared to Charles, James was not a physically or socially unattractive young man. Burnet's often quoted words that '[James] was much neglected in his childhood, during the time he was under his father's care' is also, notwithstanding the political crisis from 1638 onwards, something of an exaggeration as far as social education is concerned. The provision of dancing, fencing and archery masters confirms that. Nevertheless, in keeping with the traditions of the period, the king and queen were not regularly involved in the day to day activities of their children.[14]

THE NORTHERN KINGDOM UNDER THE FATHER

When James entered the world in the winter of 1633–4 political storm clouds were beginning to build over Scotland. The then 'happy' state of his English kingdom, as not too convincingly suggested by Ashley, had certainly no relationship to the Scottish position, but in any case, not using parliaments was storing up future trouble on both sides of the Border. Eight years before James's birth, his father inherited from James VI and I some difficult foreign policy and financial circumstances, in Scotland and in England, yet at least the churches in the two kingdoms were in reasonable shape and in a condition of relative deference to royal wishes. For Charles I, however, leaving well alone or doing nothing was not an option. In spite of his Scottish birth, and the slight Scottish lilt inherited from his father, Charles was an Englishman preoccupied with English interests. Nevertheless, he proved proactive in Scottish affairs and wasted no time in removing, or sidestepping, the old regime of aging retainers and privy councillors. Some of his reforms seemed entirely sensible but, as James would learn later, a failure to communicate intentions and to explicate policy hampered the reform process.[15]

One of Charles's first objectives was to break the overlap between the Scottish Privy Council and the Court of Session to ensure that only qualified judges served. This looks like a rational effort to improve the court system, but Charles and his ministers moved too fast, upset nobles, some of whom were extraordinary lords of session with the associated pensions and status, and, of course, this weakened the options for patronage at a time when the Scottish elite needed to be won over. Then, in 1626, King Charles created a 'committee of war', including the Catholic Robert Maxwell, earl of Nithsdale, which in effect by-passed the full Privy Council. This, it was feared in Scotland, was to prepare the nation to make a full and costly contribution to a renewed war effort in Europe and it created not a little resentment. In fact, for a spell Maxwell, whose brother John had been executed for murder in 1612, had to remain outwith Scotland to avoid his creditors. Charles's reliance on such dubious characters did not help matters.[16]

As well as attacking the system, Charles appeared to abandon the advice offered by experience and wisdom. Thomas Hamilton, earl of Melrose, James VI's favourite and the Secretary of State, was demoted; John Erskine, earl of Mar, James VI's friend and Treasurer, was ignored; and the Chancellor Sir George Hay of Kinfauns was bullied. The notion of continuity, as seen with James VI and I's reliance on Elizabeth I's minister Robert Cecil from 1603 to 1608, was set aside. Charles appointed William Graham, seventh earl of Menteith, as President of the Council and Justice General in 1628. Although Menteith had no large network of support in Scotland, he managed the Privy Council well enough before scandal removed him from office in 1633. Some casualties are inevitable in the politics of any period, although Charles I, like James VII, did not have the same capacity for character judgment as James VI and Charles II. In fact, Mentieth was finally disgraced for asserting his claim to the ancient earldom of Strathearn, and also letting slip the idea that his blood was more royal than the king's, being a descendant of the second marriage of Robert II. This case would, as we shall see, have unexpected associations with an event in James's life in the 1690s. But now the evidence against Menteith was gathered by his political enemies and his case confirmed a nobility divided and that Charles would not necessarily come to the defence of his ministers. Such circumstances did not augur well for Charles I's coronation parliament in the summer of 1633.[17]

Charles faced some expected political difficulties as a result of unpopular European wars that required English and Scottish taxation, although the focus of elite opposition in Scotland before 1633 centered on his plans for a revocation scheme. Only months after succeeding his father, Charles used his prerogative power to impose his revocation ideas, and an act of Privy Seal was announced in July 1625 to that effect. Acts of revocation were common in Scotland, whereby a

king or queen could, before twenty-five years of age, revoke all grants of land made
during a minority. James V and James VI did this, though Mary, Queen of Scots
was forced to abdicate before she reached twenty-five years. Charles's plan to
recover such lands were, to many nobles and some lairds, questionable in law
because he was revoking grants made by his father, and he was seen as an opportunist being so close to twenty-five years. The fact that his father enforced an act
of revocation at the end of his minority was viewed by some as irrelevant, and
theoretically Charles's plans concerned land rights over secularised church property dating as far back as the 1540s. The plans caused much alarm, especially
among those whose estates were former church lands, and the fact that Charles's
favourite George Villiers, duke of Buckingham was behind it all, allowed him to
become the target for criticisms with a populist feel: English interference in
Scottish affairs.[18]

The revocation scheme was an exercise in the social engineering of land tenure.[19]
The purposes were to increase church income through the regular teinds tax, with
a percentage going to the Crown; to liberate heritors from feudal dependence on
the old nobility; to abolish heritable offices and so freeing up avenues of patronage,
and to alter the nature of feudal tenure to benefit the Crown, such that land would
be granted back to existing freeholders with the Crown as the superior. It was a
convoluted promise of jam tomorrow but to some, including leading privy councillors, it all appeared so arbitrary, and for most it was badly presented, and there
was even some talk of rebellion in 1626 and 1627. It was as if James VI's old
patronage system was to be destroyed. However, after intense lobbying, and a
convention of heritors that met in spring 1627 and rejected teind plans, a commission for teinds was set up which began an unsatisfactory Crown retreat. Although
it was agreed to compensate landlords, and to set prices for heritors to buy out
superiors, resentments at interference continued, and there was a lack of cooperation over land valuations. Even though the Scottish Parliament eventually ratified
the revocation in 1633, it was a disaster for the Crown, bringing in little income,
and creating perceptions of Crown weakness and of arbitrary government. James
might well have learned from his father's errors if not for his own tendency, when
king himself, to 'keep digging' when in trouble.

The death of Buckingham by assassination in 1628 and government concessions over the revocation offered some opportunity for political calm, though
Buckingham was an irritation rather than a major player in Scottish politics.
However, Charles's religious prescription for Scotland prevented a new opportunity for good will to break out. By the mid 1630s, ten of Scotland's fourteen
bishops were on the Privy Council and it was a long time since so many bishops
had been added. These clerics were bound to obey the Crown and replaced
nobles with independent views but also with a handle on the condition of their
localities. When the Scottish Parliament finally met in June 1633 the bishops
were viewed as voting fodder in support of Crown policies. In fact from 1627 to

1633 Crown managers had attempted to appoint sympathetic county sheriffs as electoral agents and, subsequently, tried to have elected 'approved' shire commissioners ('commissioner' being the term for elected members as opposed to nobles attending by right or bishops by appointment) who could be counted upon to support Charles's reforms when Parliament was finally convened.[20] Charles's management of shire elections would be imitated through James VII's efforts in the 1680s to manipulate municipal elections in England and to impose burgh provosts in Scotland. James's attempts to control elections to the Scottish Parliament were certainly nothing new.

Relations between Charles I and his English Parliament broke down irretrievably in 1629 and a Scottish parliament offered Charles a chance to show England what could be achieved, and James became a firm believer in this Anglo-Scottish approach. The difficulty, even with a 'managed parliament', was that the manner in which Charles handled opposition in Edinburgh brought into clear focus an unprecedented assertion of royal authority. After his coronation, the conclusion of the 1633 parliamentary session, and a brief royal progress to Linlithgow, Stirling, Dunfermline and Falkland in the first four days of July, Charles hurried back to his pregnant bride in London, confident in the success of his efforts in Edinburgh. Charles's 'success' had been over religion. Until now the Scottish clergy wore black gowns and at Charles's coronation in London, John Spottiswoode, Archbishop of St Andrews had refused to wear the extravagant vestments of an English bishop. However, the 1633 parliament passed a new act linking the power of the king to dictate clerical apparel with a restatement of the royal prerogative. In other words, to oppose the dress code question could be construed as treason. There was heated debate, even before the Lords of the Articles, the drafting and managing committee of Scottish parliaments, which presented the proposals. When the vote in the house took place, Charles famously destroyed much remaining good will by sitting in the chamber and noting down those who opposed him. Some still could not in conscience vote in favour of Anglican dress for the clergy and protested at the combined vote. Noble leadership of dissent was open, particularly through John Leslie, sixth earl of Rothes, John Campbell, Lord Loudoun and James Elphinstone, Lord Balmerino – but they were punished for their pains. Loudoun, for example, had his earldom cancelled. Balmerino, after being involved in an attempt to prepare the Haig Supplication, an attempt to criticise royal policy but dressed in loyalist language, was for his temerity tried and found guilty of treason in 1635. Constitutional opposition seemed impossible. Even though in 1636 Balmerino was eventually pardoned, the political damage to Charles was irreparable.[21] Would his sons Charles and James behave in this manner?

Between 1633 and 1637 Charles I could not see the dangers ahead. The weak Scottish government of bishops and James Hamilton, third marquis and later first duke of Hamilton, along with the out-of-his-depth Scottish Secretary William Alexander, earl of Stirling in London, provided insufficient direction and advice. As with his son James, ministers too often told Charles what he wanted to hear, rather than what he needed to know. After the chancellor Sir George Hay died in 1634, Charles turned to the archbishop of St Andrews, John Spottiswoode as chancellor, an obedient and aging cleric of sixty-eight years. Anti-clericalism increased among nobles and lairds as Spottiswoode, a relative moderate, struggled to implement the religious policies of his king who was egged on by the Arminian William Laud. The appointment of the fellow Arminian William Forbes in January 1634 to the newly created bishopric of Edinburgh increased anxiety in and around Edinburgh.[22] It was even feared that abbeys would be reintroduced.

Charles's policies of liturgical conformity were emphasised in England and Ireland as well as Scotland. The enforcement of the Thirty-Nine Articles of the Church of England in Ireland in 1634–5 suggested the same could happen in Scotland.[23] The high pomp of the 1633 coronation visit left Presbyterians with few doubts. Charles announced that a new prayer book would be introduced. This would neither be the English Book, which Laud wanted, nor the draft worked out in 1618 under James VI. The Scottish bishops did what they could to produce a Scottish text, but Charles insisted on aspects of ritual and numerous saints days which were entirely at odds with the Scottish Church. Charles added a proclamation prescribing the text by royal authority rather than by Church authority. James VI would have used the General Assembly yet Charles saw no reason for such niceties. The 1636 Book of Canons made no mention of presbyteries, and now the 1637 Book of Common Prayer replaced preaching with ceremonial. The book was 'foreign' even in appearance: old black letter like pre-Reformation Catholic Bibles, not the roman type used by Geneva Bibles and Scotland's Reformation texts. The whole thrust of policy was alien to Scotland's post-Reformation traditions. It was, as Maciness has suggested, an attack on a nation anxious over self-determination and feelings of provincialism since 1603.[24] The fact that Charles had a Catholic wife who openly encouraged the Mass and Catholic conversions also heightened the tension. Thus Charles's supremacy was absolute as expressed from the parliament of 1633, and not 'managed' as was James VI's style of paternalistic monarchy. And so, opposition grew, settled on fears for religion, property, tax, free speech and the erosion of ancient privilege.

In July 1637 the famous riot took place in St Giles Cathedral as the New Prayer Book was read from the pulpit by the unfortunate dean of the cathedral. This protest was, however, engineered by noble opposition more than a spontaneous grassroots reaction. Before long, opponents of royal policy would gravitate to signing the National Covenant.[25] This, a traditional type of bond, set radical Presbyterian conservatism versus Caroline authoritarianism and episcopacy (church government by bishops). Charles's failures to control Scotland were certainly managerial at elite level, and also from a more popular and widely based reaction to a range of novel policy initiatives and directions. Nevertheless, his greatest error was that while he attempted to create a court party of supporters, he alienated too many Scots at the top of Scottish society. James VII's father attempted to do too much with too few essential supporters, a lesson for James himself. The birth of a second healthy royal son must have had little relevance to most of Scotland's political community in the immediate years after the events of 1633. Yet with reinforced confidence from the birth, Charles presented an even greater threat to the established order, as was more widely feared when James's own son was born in the summer of 1688.

As a little boy James could have had little or no understanding of his father's mishandling of the Scottish crisis of 1638–41 as the shuttle diplomacy of James, marquis of Hamilton, and King Charles's military expeditions in the Bishops' Wars of May to June 1639 and August to September 1640 failed to bring Scotland's new Covenanting government to heel. Both the Treaty of Ripon of October 1640, and the subsequent session of the Scottish Parliament the following summer, ended this phase and confirmed the shift of authority from king to Parliament. Symbolic of this royal reversal was when in the parliamentary chamber in Edinburgh in 1641, with Charles attending in person, the king suggested he would be prepared to indicate royal assent (by touching acts with the sceptre as was the Scottish procedure) to legislation passed in 1639 and 1640, only to be quickly told that all these acts were already law and required no royal, ritualised imprimatur. This was not 1633. That Charles proceeded to plan a dubious and unsuccessful *coup d'état*, known as the 'incident', through which the parliamentary leaders Archibald Campbell, marquis of Argyll, and Hamilton were to be assassinated, confirmed he was not to be trusted, especially as it appeared the loyal servant Hamilton was to be targeted. News of this plotting bemused many moderate Covenanters.[26]

A CHILDHOOD AT WAR

Charles's difficulties, as would James's in the future, were of three kingdoms, not one. Over a decade of 'thorough', the Crown's campaign of administrative restructuring to improve efficiency, had, in the years of Charles's personal rule, created growing resentment in England and Ireland as well as Scotland. The chief impact of this resentment was the collapse in relations between the king and the English Parliament and political attacks on his chief counsellors, especially Laud and Thomas Wentworth, Viscount Strafford. The former was just as hated in England as Scotland for his divisive religious policies, and the latter so successful in controlling Ireland for the king that many Scots and English feared he would lead an invading Irish army to aid his master. While Charles attempted to prepare for the farcical First Bishops' War without the political risks of a new English Parliament, he was forced to call it to attempt to finance the second war. However, the short parliament of April/May 1640 refused to provide the necessary taxation and so Charles had to muddle on raising money where he could. This process led to rumours, not all unfounded, that the king was seeking aid from Spain and Rome, and had an overreliance on the personal wealth of Catholic nobles. The fund-raising activities of James's mother Henrietta Maria and her Catholic circle merely encouraged the impression that war against the Scots was counter to the reformed religion common to both kingdoms. Ironically, after the debacle of the Second Bishops' War, Charles was forced to call the English Parliament again to help meet the financial terms of Ripon and the subsequent Treaty of London. The Covenanter army (some 18,000 strong) occupied much of northern England and waited to be paid for the privilege – Scottish military success had fatally undermined royal power. Now in the winter of 1640/41, the English Parliament, with the connivance of the Covenanter leadership, used the Scots military menace to break yet further the power of the king. Charles felt forced to concede the arrest of Laud and Strafford and the execution of the latter followed in May 1641. The Irish Catholic rising in late 1640, in the name of the king though without his approval, merely confirmed that Charles depended too much on those both Puritans and Covenanters regarded as beyond the pale. Also, decisively, the City of London soon declared itself for Parliament. In the Restoration period James was to recognise the importance of cultivating good relations with the merchant interest of the English capital and had some success in this regard.[27]

During this period, before the English Civil War commenced in 1643, James continued to spend most of his time at Richmond, with spells in the summer months with his mother and sometimes his father at Oatlands Palace in Surrey. However, when rioting broke out near Richmond in 1640, the children, including James and his brother Charles, were moved to Whitehall to be near the king, before Prince Charles and his father took up residence at Hampton Court Palace. The king's failed and disastrous attempt in January 1642 at arresting five members of the Commons, including John Pym the 'opposition' leader, marked the beginning of a period of family disruption and intensive preparations for civil war. This *coup d'état* had exactly the same result as the Scottish 'Incident', the alienation of some as yet uncommitted of the Lords and Commons. The king concluded that London was no longer safe for the royal family. The following month King Charles arranged for Prince Charles to meet him at Greenwich before they both travelled to York, his new headquarters. The other children were transferred to the comparative safety of St James's Palace but, perhaps to better disperse and secure the royal line, James was returned to his own court at Richmond and under the protection of William Seymour, marquis of Hertford. In spite of attempts by Parliament to force Hertford to confine James to Richmond, in March Hertford escorted him to York to join up with his father. As if normality was restored, James's arrival was greeted with bonfires and ceremonial, which included his investiture with the Order of the Garter. Yet one of the characteristics of this period of phoney war was the continuation of family affairs. At Oatlands in July 1640 James's younger brother Henry, duke of Gloucester was born and the family gathered there for the christening two weeks later, at which James and the other children processed into the chapel for a service taken by Laud. Also, in November 1641, before the City of London came down on the side of Parliament, when King Charles returned from Scotland he was greeted with pageant, and some rejoicing by the City and people of London. The three eldest children, including James, joined the king in his triumphant entry by coach. Such display confirmed the capriciousness of the people but also enforced the delusion King Charles had concerning the 'successes' of his period in Scotland. In constitutional terms the 1641 session of the Scottish Parliament was a humiliation, not a series of concessions on which the retaking of royal power could be grounded.[28]

Not long after James's arrival at York his father employed him on a mission for the royal cause, an adventure the young prince would never forget. This mission was part of the arms race in the months before the English Civil War commenced. On 22 April 1642, only a month after his arrival at York and at only eight years of age, James was sent by his father to Hull to help secure the town, and more especially the arms and munitions stored there. Parliament had already instructed the governor of Hull, the MP Sir John Hotham, to keep the town for Parliament with a view in due course to transferring the arms to London. Charles realised the significance of the port following its use as a depot in the Scots wars, and also the need to acquire the munitions. James, accompanied by about fifty or so guards, servants and nobles, including his cousin and godfather Charles Louis Elector Palatine, then twenty-five years of age, was allowed entry into the town by Hotham. Charles calculated that the governor could hardly refuse the king entry the following day. However, although James was politely handled by Hotham, and was entertained with a fine dinner, when James told his host that Charles planned to enter the town the next day to dine with them, Hotham found himself pressured by the parliamentary garrison, and a few fellow MPs who happened to be in attendance, to bar Charles's entry. Charles then found himself forced into humiliating negotiations to get James and the others released from the virtual house arrest in which they had been placed. James was released after two days and was reunited with his father at York. Given that only a few weeks before James had been provided with a small bodyguard for protection, to expose him as a potential hostage was extraordinarily risky and could have ended badly. Later James would recollect the risks involved and the 'ill management of the whole affaire'. He judged that had an unexpected visit taken place, or a more violent plot been enacted where Hotham was seized and even murdered, most in the town would willingly have fallen in with the king. As it was, a disillusioned Hotham, who with his son attempted to find some middle ground between the two sides in the war, was in January 1645 'to receive his due reward and to lose his head' at the hands of an English Parliament that had him arrested for negotiating with the enemy.

Hotham's hopes for some kind of compromise were as anathema to James, looking back, as it was to the English Parliament in 1645. James also never forgot his first brush with imprisonment or that violent means rather than diplomacy should often be a first recourse.[29]

Over the next few months, with his sons Charles and James in tow, Charles moved around the Welsh marches, the Midlands and Yorkshire in search of arms and recruits, and finally in late August raised the royal standard at Nottingham to signify the declaration of war. At first recruits were slow to gather but the arrival of arms from Holland, arranged by the queen and delivered to the Humber, in the shadows of Hull, by a stalwart Scottish sea captain called Strachan, encouraged recruitment, as did the retinues promised by some of the nobility. In his memoirs James goes into great detail on Strachan who 'ran such hazards' to deliver his cargo in his boat *The Providence* and was forced to beach his vessel. In a typical reflection on the mysteries of the Almighty, James linked the name of the boat to the fact that after the Restoration it returned to royal service. However, such individual sacrifice for the royal cause was also mixed with the jealousies amongst the assembled officer corps, and the erratic behaviour of some of his father's commanders. This instilled in James the need for unquestioning obedience within the chain of command. The rivalry between General Robert Bertie, earl of Lindsey and his protagonists Patrick Ruthven, Lord Ettrick, later earl of Forth and Brentford, and Prince Rupert of the Rhine, Charles's nephew, illustrates the point. Ruthven, a Scot and professional soldier, had served in the army of Sweden for almost three decades and reached the rank of major general. Such participants confirm that by no means all Scots who experienced fighting for the great Protestant prince Gustavus Adolphus, such as the Covenanter general Alexander Leslie, sided against Charles and his sons.[30]

Ruthven, Lindsey and Rupert were all in action for the royalists at the first major action of the Civil War, the Battle of Edgehill fought near Warwick on 23 October 1642. Although only just turned nine years old, James was present at this inconclusive affair. In spite of his frightening experience at Hull, this was his first witnessing of open warfare and the boy was mightily impressed. Later looking back, always spellbound by the courage of his native countrymen and even those who were his enemies, James summed up the draw that unfolded before him: 'the naturall courage of English men . . . prompted them to maintain their ground, though the rawness and unexperience of both partys had not furnished them with skill to make the best of their advantages'. When King Charles felt the need to move forward to encourage the beleaguered royalist foot, he ordered that James and his elder brother be taken to a safe distance out of harm's way, and, after others refused to leave the field of battle, Sir William Howard and a detachment of King's Pensioners were ordered to secure the princes. This task was completed in two stages, but not before they were nearly captured by a body of enemy cavalry. James's own account of these exciting events confirms his view of it as a soldier's experiencing first blood. His father regarded it all somewhat differently. James remembered the deaths of General Lindsey, and the Scots noble George Stuart, Lord D'Aubigny, younger brother to James Stuart, fourth duke of Lennox and first of Richmond, and the Scot Lieutenant Colonel Monro, but reflected on the affair with gusto. However, his father immediately regretted the death of friends and the unsatisfactory outcome with competing claims of victory. Not listening to Prince Rupert's pleading to launch a full attack on London, as the Parliamentary army retreated north, Charles made a gloomy advance only as far as Oxford where he determined to make his political and military headquarters. Later James criticised his father's timidity and the failed opportunity to take London and 'put an end to the warr'. Nonetheless, it was Oxford, a strategically convenient town now an odd mixture of academic cloisters and exercising troops, which was to become James's home for the next three years.[31]

In February 1647, with King Charles a prisoner of the English Parliament in Northamptonshire (having been handed over by the Scottish Covenanters) and James a prisoner in London, the father got a message to James pleading with him to 'ply his book more and his gun less'. Moderate behaviour was a sensible precaution in the difficult circumstances of 1647, yet this was also a general criticism of James's attitude to studies in his youth. When in Oxford he clearly preferred to exercise his sword in the practice yard to his pen in the study. Natural youthful excitement at tales of daring mixed with a strong sense of boredom and resentment at not being as involved as his father and his elder brother. Some hunting, a pastime which became an obsession in later life, only partially relieved the frustration. He did experience his first parliament when the royalists convened their own alternative assembly in Oxford from January to April 1644, though both James's level of attendance and the nature of the deliberations are lost to us with the records. However, James's character was at this stage formed less by inaction than by isolation. When reflecting on the 1650s it was the contemporary statesman Clarendon who stated 'never little family was torn into so many pieces' and for James this was true before exile. James's father and mother came and went, the latter on various missions to obtain arms and support from the Continent, and also in June 1644 to give birth to James's youngest sister Henrietta-Anne in the apparent safety of Bedford House, Exeter, before almost immediately, in her weakened condition, departing to the safety of France and leaving the new-born princess behind. Her governess Lady Dalkeith managed to smuggle the princess to France in July 1646. Meanwhile, James's younger brother, the duke of Gloucester, was a prisoner in London. Typically, when King Charles took the Prince of Wales on the unsuccessful effort to relieve Reading in April 1643, James was left behind at Oxford. In March 1645 Prince Charles was given command of the royalist force in the west based at Bristol, as Charles unwisely separated his forces. Unfortunately, by the autumn the royal army was in retreat before the English Parliament's New Model Army, and in September Bristol was lost. Exactly a year after his arrival in Bristol, Prince Charles, accompanied by his servants and Sir

Edward Hyde, fled abroad on a boat to the Isles of Scilly and then Jersey, before finally joining his mother at Saint-Germain near Paris, the royalist cause in ruins. During all of this James remained at Oxford, encouraged by his father to keep up the morale of the garrison. The one moment of potential relief for James was when he and his brother accompanied their father on the abortive siege of Gloucester in August and September 1643. However, while vain efforts were made to build under-mines and tunnels – they were swept away by a downpour of rain – James and Prince Charles were placed in nearby Matson House for their own security. When the parliamentary garrison at Gloucester took heart on hearing that the earl of Essex was soon to relieve them, the king lifted the siege, sent his sons back to Oxford and prepared to meet Essex in the inconclusive Battle of Newbury. The prize of returning to London remained elusive. As they began their journey back to Oxford either James or his elder brother are supposed to have asked their father when they could go 'home' to London, and an encouraging answer could hardly have been forthcom-ing. Indeed, the Gloucester and Newbury affairs pointed to a level of irresolution which infuriated a defiant queen and later left James utterly bewildered at the behav-iour of his father and his generals. The duke was more a mixture of his father and his mother than he ever realised.[32]

In spite of the failure to advance to London, 1643 had been a successful year for Charles's forces. However, in the summer and autumn of 1643 news circulated in Scotland and England of Charles's scheme or 'plot' to bring an Irish Catholic force to the mainland, a move that horrified most members of the parliaments of Edinburgh and London. The duke of Hamilton's efforts to encourage a moderate party in Scotland were severely hampered and his attempt in early 1643 to neutral-ise the 'Scottish factor' by the Cross Petition, signed by many nobles advocating trusting the king and keeping out of the English Civil War, was now roundly condemned. Indeed, nothing was more likely to unite Puritan and Presbyterian in common cause than the prospect of a Catholic invasion, and the result was the signing of the Solemn League and Covenant in September 1643 by the English Parliament and the Scottish Covenanters, a bargain by which Scottish military aid would be offered in exchange for English pay and closer religious uniformity. With crusading zeal the Covenanters wished to export Presbyterianism to England and Ireland. The difficulty was that the English Parliament was only marginally inter-ested in this unionist agenda and was divided on the involvement of the Scots in their English war. In the end, however, they were able to sign up because the treaty was couched in vague terms with expressions such as 'according to the word of God' and Charles's forces were doing worryingly well. The Scots accepted qualifi-cations, confident that their faith and military strength would give them an important role in any final peace. James viewed all of this as definitive proof that Presbyterianism was inconsistent with monarchy.[33]

In January 1644 General Alexander Leslie, earl of Leven, led over 20,000 Scottish troops into England to aid its Parliament in the war against the king. This was a decisive move which tilted the odds against James's father and resulted not only in the defeat of Charles at Marston Moor in July 1644, which saw the capitulation of the north of England, but also, by buying time for the English Parliament to commission the New Model Army, the eventual loss of the Midlands at Naseby in June 1645 and the west at Langport the following month. In retrospect James viewed actions such as Marston Moor and the second battle of Newbury (October 1644) as entirely avoidable reverses. It was all down to poor leadership and tactical incompetence, and generally he had a poor impression of the military abilities of his father and his commanders.

Nevertheless, one commander he and his father both admired was James Graham, first marquis of Montrose. Montrose's Scottish campaign from September 1644 to September 1645, which began as a response to the Solemn League and his disapproval at Scotland entering the English Civil War, was an astonishing series of victories that contrasted with the declining fortunes of Charles's English forces. As a young teenager James will have read with enthusiasm George Wishart's account of Montrose's campaign which was published in Latin and English in London, The Hague and Amsterdam in the 1640s and 1650s. In September 1648, when fifteen years of age, James wrote to Montrose from The Hague reassuring him of personal support and encouraging him to further efforts for his father. Since his defeat and exile in September 1646, Montrose had been wandering Europe half-heartedly looking for commissions from crown princes, but really waiting his chance to rejoin the Scottish theatre. James's letter was delivered by another royalist, military Scot Sir William Drummond of Cromlix, who had served as a captain in the Scottish army in Ireland from 1642 to 1648, and who was now, after a brief spell abroad, returning to Scotland to support the Engagement, the plan to restore Charles I through Scottish military aid. Drummond was an example of the loyalist soldiery whose companionship James so enjoyed, and was the ideal go-between. But loyalism could come at a price. James knew later that, for reasons of practical politics, his brother had to abandon Montrose to his fate. After giving the marquis a commission in 1650 to land a royalist force to engage the Covenanters, when a chance arose Charles II restarted negotiations with the enemy for his Scottish restoration. When in March that year Montrose paused in Orkney before landing his force in Caithness, he received from Harry May, one of James's servants, the compensation of letters confirming his award of the Order of the Garter. James dispatched this from Jersey where his brother had appointed him governor. Less than two months later Montrose was to be captured and executed in Edinburgh, declaring at the scaffold his adherence to the National Covenant and also his king. James found such a conflation practically and philosophically impossible, even though almost all of the Scottish nobility, Hamilton as well as Montrose, had signed the Covenant, and it was the philosophical foundation of the movement. Nevertheless, Montrose the martyr played an important part in the Restoration culture of neo-royalism which characterised the

1660s and 1670s. His Edinburgh state funeral in May 1661, where his body was reassembled along with his embalmed heart, was a very grand affair, with the coffin carried by no less than fourteen Scottish earls. This belated event not only salved the guilt of Charles II, but also was the greatest ceremonial reminder in Scotland of the renewed primacy of loyalty. Many years later in his fatherly 'Advice to his Son' (1692), James would instruct him to trust none in Scotland but the 'antient loyal familys', and the likes of Hamilton and Montrose, who gave their lives for his father and brother, were members of this indomitable group.[34]

In the early hours of 27 April 1646 King Charles slipped out of Oxford in disguise and made his way north to Newark to surrender to the Scots army. All possibility of military aid for Oxford had dissipated and Sir Thomas Fairfax and the New Model Army were drawing ever nearer. James was left alone with the king's councillors, most of whom were ignorant of their master's plans. James lamented later, with a morbid tone of resentment, how '[my father] had it once in his thoughts to have carryd [me] along with him, but did not'.[35] Over the past six months various schemes had been considered to get James to safety, including sending him as an envoy to Ireland to encourage royalist forces there, and then away to France to join his mother, outcomes which James himself would have supported, though none came to fruition. Indeed, James had good reason, at least for now, to feel his father had abandoned him.[36] Meanwhile, James and the Oxford garrison awaited their fates. The New Model Army had besieged the city at various times in the last twelve months, but this was the first time there was no hope of relief. In fact it took nearly two months of negotiations before Oxford was surrendered to Fairfax, in effect ending the First Civil War, and during this period the general handled the whole affair with commendable moderation. The terms of the surrender were of particular significance to James. While his cousins Prince Rupert and Prince Maurice, Rupert's brother, were allowed to go into exile on the Continent, James was too valuable a property not to be secured by the victors. His current governor Sir George Radcliffe was instructed by the English Parliament to bring James to London and place him in the care of the moderate Presbyterian Algernon Percy, earl of Northumberland, who already had charge of James's siblings Elizabeth and Henry. Oddly, Percy and James already had a technical relationship. The post of Lord High Admiral fell vacant on the death by murder of the duke of Buckingham in 1628 and Charles I took his time to make a new appointment. He admired the enterprise and ambition of young Percy and wished to bind him to the court although in time began to doubt, with good cause, his political inclinations. A compromise was reached in 1638 which ensured Crown control of the fleet where Percy was made Lord Admiral, though not for life and at his majesty's pleasure, and under no less a Lord High Admiral than the four-year-old James, duke of York. This was but a quiet and peripheral beginning to the duke's subsequent long association with the English navy.[37]

A month after the official surrender of Oxford on 24 June 1646, Radcliffe delivered James into the hands of Percy at a rendezvous a few miles outside London. James's existing servants were dismissed, including a dwarf with whom the duke had developed a close attachment, and were replaced by a more reliable group of attendants under Percy's close instruction. James was then conveyed to the congenial accommodation provided for his 'imprisonment', St James's Palace, the place of his birth, at which he was reunited with Elizabeth and Henry. He would remain there for nearly two years. These may not have been happy times but nor were they months of persecution, and James reflected in his memoirs and in a letter to Percy's son on his father's death in 1668, the great kindness and consideration shown by the earl and his wife.[38] Although we cannot discount a bond of mutual respect between the duke and his new governor, a mixture of self-interest and pressing political imperatives also account for Percy's treatment of the boy. With King Charles in the custody of the Scots and the Prince of Wales abroad, James was then the most senior member of the royal family in the possession of the Westminster Parliament. Looking to the future, Percy was conscious that fate might one day see James succeed to the throne and little purpose was to be gained from alienating James and his younger brother and sister. Equally, Percy was under pressure from Westminster to hold James fast as a potentially more malleable candidate for the throne. The importance of James in this respect was emphasised when in August and September 1646 the idea circulated that a stubborn Charles could be deposed and replaced by a more compliant James. Not surprisingly, King Charles reacted with anger when he heard of this suggestion. The idea re-emerged in spring 1647 as the Army Council and House of Commons struggled for control, and the latter pressed for Charles to be removed, the Prince of Wales disinherited and James installed as king.[39]

Although barely fourteen years of age, by the winter of 1646 James determined, in spite of his humane treatment, to escape from his captors as soon as possible. He was, moreover, counselled to do so by his father. Father in Newcastle and son in London were in regular communication by letter, sometimes in cypher. The king was behind the first escape attempt in the winter of 1646/7 but it was discovered. The next serious attempt in early 1647 was also thwarted when a letter in cypher between son and father was intercepted when disguised as a note to James's brother-in-law William II, prince of Orange. A committee of the Lords and Commons interrogated James at St James's Palace and pressed him to deliver up the cypher key. To begin with he stubbornly refused to cooperate, claiming that he had burnt the cypher. However, when he was threatened with incarceration in the Tower of London by an exasperated Commons, James's resolve crumbled, he apologised and handed over the key which confirmed the plan to escape. The fact that James was ill, suffering from an ague or fever from late January until the end of March, accounts for some of his erratic behaviour and his swift capitulation.[40]

In one sense the need to escape was reduced when his father was yet again near at hand. In January 1647 King Charles was handed over to the English Parliament by the Scottish army at Newcastle. The Covenanter government, of which, as James noted resentfully in his memoirs, 'the Marquis of Argyle was the chief', had agreed to this in exchange for £400,000 sterling to pay the Scots army, though only half was paid. However, the sum agreed and the schedule of negotiations shows that the Scots were much more concerned to get Charles off their hands than to obtain the highest financial settlement. Essentially, it became impossible to take Charles back to Scotland without an agreement being struck with the English Parliament, and nothing that his Scots captors could say or do would persuade Charles to accept the terms on offer. Charles's return to Scotland without agreement might even result in war between the kingdoms. Meanwhile, Argyll, not a republican by choice but a believer in British confederation, was dispirited that a compromise could not be struck that preserved king and Covenant, and the likes of Hamilton and his brother William, earl of Lanark, were horrified that the Scottish Estates in Edinburgh agreed to hand over Charles, but at the same time could come up with no alternative solution. Therefore, almost exactly three years since they had entered England, on 30 January 1647 the Scots army left Newcastle to return home leaving Charles in the hands of English commissioners.[41] These commissioners included Percy himself, who was then able to report to the father on the welfare of the royal children, including James.

The agreed place for Charles to take up residence was Holdenby House in Northamptonshire, and this was his home for four months. However, as relations deteriorated between English Commons and Lords and the New Model Army, and the political atmosphere at Westminster polarised between Presbyterian and Independent (congregationalist) factions, Charles was in early June 1647, fatefully and notoriously, taken into custody for the army by Cornet George Joyce. He was delivered to its headquarters at Newmarket and, after talks with army officers, to house arrest in a series of great houses of army supporters in East Anglia and Hertfordshire. As he moved from place to place at the behest of the army, Charles requested, through General Fairfax, that his children be allowed to come to him, and in early July James, Henry and Elizabeth were escorted to meet him at Maidenhead, before spending two days in his company at Caversham House, near Reading. There Charles greeted his children with 'paternal joy'. It was over a year since James had seen his father and much longer for his siblings. In spite of this joyous family gathering, it was not until late August, when Charles was moved to Hampton Court, that the children saw their father regularly. While the English Parliament insisted that the children remained at St James's Palace in the care of Percy, their governor allowed them to visit their father two or three times per week over the ten-week period he was held there, and sometimes they used his own Syon House for these family gatherings.[42]

The Hampton Court meetings were of deep significance to the children and especially to James. Percy, an art collector himself, realised this and commissioned Sir Peter Lely to render these meetings in a series of romanticised oil paintings, and so the iconography of Stuart dynastic continuity was perpetuated (see Plate 1). These audiences were part of probably the first and certainly the last period in which James had intimate discussions with his father. At these the king imparted three clear messages, two of which James lived up to. Firstly, he was to escape to the Continent and his mother as soon as possible. The impasse in negotiations over the army compromise, the heads of the proposals, and wild talk from some of their supporters in Parliament that the king should be brought to justice, focused Charles's thoughts on securing his family. Secondly, James and his siblings were instructed to show due obedience to their older brother Charles. If the king was incapacitated the future lay with the Prince of Wales. Thirdly, Charles counselled James to hold fast to the doctrines and teachings of the Church of England.[43] As a fourteen-year-old, it is not surprising that James showed little interest in religious affairs, but in fact over the following decade there is no evidence that he was especially attracted to anything other than Anglicanism. Indeed, at the time and in retrospect, James viewed the revolution itself as political more than religious. Therefore, while he grew to despise the 'popular party' in England and the 'Presbyterians' in Scotland, it was his father's second instruction about obedience to his elder brother that was of most importance. This is on account of his assessment of his father's failings and eventual fate. Loyalty to monarchy and the Stuart dynasty was what mattered to James. Whereas his father had shown courage in attempting to defend this aspect of the traditional social order, at key moments he had been indecisive and made concessions when none were necessary. When James became king himself he would grow to realise that fixing a broken relationship with the political classes was not so easy to accomplish.

After various schemes and false starts, in April 1648 James succeeded in making his escape from St James's Palace. For this he had much to thank the English Presbyterian Colonel Joseph Bampfield who was behind the plan. Bampfield was yet another religious 'opponent' whose loyalty the duke understood in military rather than religious terms. Subsequently their relationship would be soured. Throughout his life James found the monarchism of Presbyterianism incomprehensible. Bampfield's role is, nonetheless, confirmed in James's own and other accounts of his escape, and the impression is given of a complex plan with many participants; and yet, as Callow suggests, the relative freedom that Percy gave to James, in and around St James's, makes it possible that the earl was deliberately turning a blind eye.[44] Either way, the details of the escape were to become part of the iconic narrative of the Stuart story, encapsulating the personal bravery of the family and the loyalty and sacrifice of its servants. From less auspicious events such as Charles's slipping out of Oxford in disguise in 1646, to Charles II's dramatic escape after the defeat at the Battle of Worcester in 1651, myths and reality about these excitements became almost indistinguishable. Following the Restoration both Charles II and James encouraged the proliferation of these stories of derring-do, including commissioning Samuel Pepys to record some of them.[45] On

20 April, according to James's own account, when playing hide and seek with Henry and Elizabeth, James hid before slipping away through the garden to meet up with Bampfield, who furbished James with a temporary disguise. A coach took them part of the way, before for safety they proceeded on foot down to the Thames. There they took a boat to the house of a surgeon Low near Tower Bridge, where James was clothed by Bampfield's fiancée Anna Murray with a dress she had made to the required size. In this new disguise, accompanied by Bampfield, James made his way to a barge at Billingsgate which would take them to Tilbury-Hope, where a Dutch vessel of seventy tons was waiting for them. Although the bargemaster became so suspicious that they had to take him into their confidence, he agreed to take them, lights extinguished and in silence, past the blockhouses that guarded the river and to the waiting vessel. There a small group of companions had assembled to help the duke, and they began the journey across the North Sea to Flushing. Entering the harbour there, after an uneventful crossing, the crew suddenly feared the presence of an enemy frigate, and they moved up the coast to come ashore at Middelburg. The next day James took a boat to Dort before sending Bampfield to report his arrival to his sister and brother-in-law, the Prince of Orange, who came down to meet him in what was a joyful reunion.[46] Ten days after his escape from St James's Palace, James was at The Hague and now, not yet fifteen years of age, a new factor in the complex rivalries of the exiled royalist community.

As James sailed into exile he must have contemplated the position of his father left behind in England. During James's youth the backdrop was a complex and bemusing cocktail of high politics, military affairs, and treaty negotiations with the parliaments of three kingdoms. Nevertheless, much of what preoccupied James in the light of the Civil War years to this point were not affairs of state but affairs of the person. In particular, his experiences as a prisoner, however well handled for much of the time, made their mark. The plight and demeaning treatment of his father left him disgusted at the disloyalty of many of his fellow countrymen. These impressions would leave him in later life totally intolerant of disloyalty and, when threatened with revolution himself, paranoid about the dangers of losing his liberty to his enemies. Yet these characteristics do not make him without comrades or without personal bravery, as will be seen in his conduct in the twelve years of exile which now stretched out before him.

CHAPTER 2

Exile and Military Life, 1648–1660

'SAVING' THE KING AND STRIVING FOR INDEPENDENCE

Once in exile, the fifteen-year-old duke began almost immediately to show impatience to act in support of his father's interests, and to his frustration the opportunities were all too rare. James was not a patient youth. Many hours of powerlessness during the Civil War had seen him develop a temper that could suddenly explode. One incident during his confinement at St James's Palace shows that even as a young teenager he could combust. When a servant let out the news that his father, having escaped from Hampton Court to the Isle of Wight in November 1647, had merely became a prisoner yet again, this time at Carisbrooke Castle, and that same servant rebuked the boy for cursing the news, James grabbed a long-bow and would have killed the man but for being physically restrained by others present. Percy was alarmed at this show of petulance, and although it was the only such incident during his governorship of the duke, it nonetheless confirms James's occasional short fuse.[1]

In spite of the sense of desperation felt by James, the royalist situation back in his father's three kingdoms was in the winter of 1647/8 going rather better than expected. While Charles's Lord Lieutenant of Ireland, James Butler, marquis of Ormonde, had negotiated peace in that kingdom (though this had included giving up Dublin to the English Parliament to avoid it falling into Catholic confederate hands) and royalist uprisings were soon occurring sporadically in South Wales, East Anglia and other parts, King Charles had at Carisbrooke in December 1647 signed the Engagement, his last gamble at regaining his kingdoms.[2] This deal was struck after three months of discussions with the representatives of the Estates of Scotland, the chancellor John Campbell, earl of Loudon, and the earls of Lanark and Lauderdale. With this deal, the Scots promised, after secret meetings with Ormonde to ensure the delivery of Irish support, a military intervention on Charles's behalf in exchange for a three-year trial of Presbyterianism in England

and suppression of the Independents, those congregationalists who rejected inter-ference by church courts as well as by kings. Scottish Covenanter nobles and soldiers such as John Lindsay, earl of Crawford-Lindsay and Colonel John Middleton (later earl of Middleton) saw a chance for political redemption – later James expressed his hearty approval as both monarch and God welcomed such returning to the fold. In 1647 and 1648, however, it was the disunity of the Covenanters which made the Engagement possible, and that same disunity that delivered its failure. The likes of Crawford and Middleton were the political supporters of the Engagement who were stripped of power in the aftermath of its military defeat, but who were rewarded for such sacrifice at the Restoration of the monarchy.

Nonetheless, the nine months between the signing of the Engagement by Charles and defeat at the hands of Oliver Cromwell offered renewed hope for royalists in the three kingdoms and in exile, and James began to focus on his own contribution to what became the second English Civil War. When he arrived at The Hague, however, he also needed to orientate himself within the exiled commu-nity. He required some form of court, promoting and managing his interests, and his saviour Colonel Bampfield set about helping him create his own household, within the wider court of his sister Mary and her husband the Prince of Orange, at their palace of Honslaerdyk, near The Hague. James remained at The Hague throughout 1648 and this made him both practically and politically semi-detached from his brother and mother based at Saint-Germain, though the political atmos-phere he was detached from was hardly one of unity.

Since the Prince of Wales's arrival in Paris in June 1647 two distinct factions had developed within exiled royalism. Prince Charles's group were mostly moder-ate royalists or 'old cavaliers', led by the likes of Hyde, Ormonde and Sir Edward Nicholas, Charles I's secretary. They favoured concessions to the English and Scottish parliaments and the 'old English' of Ireland to bring about a three king-dom solution to a three kingdom problem. Meanwhile, Queen Henrietta Maria's faction, or the 'Louvre' group as they became known, led by Henry, Lord Jermyn, John, Lord Colepeper and Sir John Berkeley, were more inclined to foreign inter-vention aimed at a refashioned authoritarian and pro-Catholic monarchy. The exiled community comprised of these factions is often mocked for the pettiness of its squabbles but there is little doubt that, bereft of more profitable activities, numerous courtiers with too little money and too much time on their hands wiled away the hours in backstabbing and futile subterfuge. It is small wonder that for most of his period of exile James favoured action in preference to intrigue. Nonetheless, there are interesting parallels with James's policies four decades later. When Charles I was in the hands of the Scottish army in 1646–7, the queen's faction favoured concessions to Presbyterianism in Scotland and England along with the relief of Catholics in Ireland and elsewhere.[3] These were policies James himself would unsuccessfully implement when he became king. Furthermore, although James had little time for religion or the close attentions of his mother for most of his years in exile, it was from her household that most of his long term servants came, and so they helped mould his attitude to kingship and authority and, to a degree, to religion as well. The 1640s and 1650s were formative years for James in politics as well as in military affairs.

Sooner than James could have hoped, an opportunity presented itself for him to take the fight to the enemy. In late May 1648 a squadron of the parliamentary fleet stationed off the Downs off the coast of Kent defected to the royalist side, and in early June anchored at the inlet before Hellevoetsluis, south of Rotterdam. To begin with, six ships arrived but this rose to some eleven vessels when their commander William Batten appeared with his warship, though this total would later be halved as some defected back to the English Parliament. Clarendon (Hyde) suggests the romantic notion that the sailors arriving in May were anxious to be led by James in deference to his formal and childhood commission as Lord Admiral of England. In reality, the motives for the seamen's rebellion was a mixture of genuine renewed royalism, loyalty to their commander Batten, himself a Presbyterian, and importantly, resentment at arrears of pay and excessive naval discipline. If any individual was to command them or impose a commander it would, of course, be the Prince of Wales. Nonetheless, when James at The Hague heard of the fleet's arrival he made his farewells to his sister and husband and straightways rushed to Hellevoetsluis, sending word to Prince Charles that he also should come to this fleet as soon as possible. When James arrived he was warmly greeted by the naval officers but his own servants, including Bampfield, looking to forward their own interest through their master, pressed on the seamen that James should command them and Bampfield himself persuaded James to appoint Lord Willoughby of Parham as vice-admiral (and effective commander), a man with no experience. It was at this point that some of the sailors protested their preference for the command of James rather than Willoughby, the latter having previously served the English Parliament, and a fresh wave of argument ensued. Charles arrived in the nick of time to stop the squabbling and to impose his own solution which engendered feelings of resentment and disappointment in his younger brother. Charles dismissed the troublesome Bampfield from his brother's service, retained Willoughby, and along with Prince Rupert, who had initially been invited to attend the fleet by James, took command himself. Thinking it best to keep the small fleet busy, Charles led them on seven weeks of inconclusive manoeuvres, culminating in a near sea battle with the earl of Warwick's parliamentary fleet which, being a trap, Charles fortunately withdraw from having run out of provisions.[4] During all this, for the sake of security, James was left behind and returned to The Hague, dispirited and unemployed.

If these weeks were not militarily effective they were certainly politically divisive. The small fleet represented a clear opportunity to support the Engagement and the various royalist risings throughout parts of England and Wales, but

Charles's courtiers and the naval command, and even regular seamen, were divided on the best way forward. Rescuing the king from Carisbrooke, engaging Warwick in battle, relieving the royalist army now at Colchester and sailing to Scotland to progress negotiations with the Scots competed for attention. Into this mix came John Maitland, earl of Lauderdale, arriving on board Prince Charles's ship off the Downs on 10 August (see Plate 3). He was appointed by the Engager regime in Scotland to negotiate support and terms with Charles and to 'invite the prince thither in name of the whole kingdom' to lead their efforts to re-establish the king. Lauderdale's instructions included completing an embassy to the French court to both explain the Engagement and to 'crave assistance . . . of money, arms and ammunition', and also to deliver letters to the queen, to The Hague and to James.[5] The Scottish Estates fully understood that providence might deliver James as heir or king and that he must be brought into the bosom of the project. This, however, was the first official indication by the Scottish Parliament that James might be a factor in any settlement concerning Scotland.

The meeting between Charles and Lauderdale was a personal and diplomatic success. Charles agreed to lead the Engager army in its campaign in England, and not to bring with him those who were anathema to the Covenanters, and while in their company to adopt their form of worship. More significant, in the long term, was the fact that Charles and Lauderdale quickly became intimates, much to the jealousy of Hyde and Charles's other courtiers. As news spread amongst the small fleet that Charles was likely to be bound for Scotland via Berwick, some seamen, alarmed at being abandoned by their prince, even threatened to throw Lauderdale overboard. Charles calmed matters and secured his new companion. The Scotsman's directness appealed to the prince.[6] Strangely, although Charles's brother also preferred frankness he and Lauderdale never became close. In fact it was the close relationship of trust and the loyalty of Lauderdale to Charles which would explain James's support for Lauderdale in the 1660s and 1670s rather than any personal chemistry.

On the sound advice of Sir William Batten, the fleet being short of supplies, Prince Charles agreed to return to Hellevoetsluis rather than to engage the enemy as advocated by Prince Rupert and the more hot-headed officers. The plan was for Charles to return to The Hague to prepare for the journey to Scotland. However, when they landed on 4 September word reached them confirming vague rumours – after a slow progress through England since early July, the duke of Hamilton and the Engager army were catastrophically defeated by Cromwell at the Battle of Preston on 17–19 August. For Charles the Scottish adventure was now unwise and incapable of success. In Edinburgh a coup had replaced the Engager government led by Lanark with Argyll's party and the Kirk. The personal and military intervention of Cromwell secured the new government and they sent word to Charles that he was no longer welcome.[7] However, it was not out of strength but from a position of weakness that Argyll and his allies came to terms with

Cromwell, and so kept out for a time an admittedly unwilling English army of occupation. Independents and Presbyterians were always strange bedfellows and in time natural ideological divisions would come to the surface. At the same time it was the chronic divisions within the Scottish political community which hampered both the Engagers and the Kirk Party under Argyll. In 1648–9 exiled English courtiers expressed doubts over the Engagement because of 'Argyll and the preachers', yet equally Lauderdale had made it clear to Prince Charles that the Engagers would under no circumstances have truck with their old enemy Montrose. Lauderdale often expressed the view that Montrose was a brutal monster and completely sympathised with Argyll following the depredations his clan and family had suffered at the hands of Montrose's army and its Irish contingent, even though his belief that posterity would never forgive Montrose proved false.[8] Loyalism to the crown in Scottish party politics came in the differing colours of Argyll, Hamilton and Montrose, and to a level of complexity James as duke or king found very hard to comprehend. James viewed Montrose as the best type of hero, a military martyr. But at the Restoration, when the royalist cult of Montrose was ritualised in his great state funeral, Lauderdale was forced to suppress his hatred of the romantic hero.

His options now reduced, Charles moved on from Hellevoetsluis to The Hague where James resided with his sister. There Charles was persuaded over the next few months to embrace an Irish campaign facilitated by the fact that soon the Confederate Catholics would agree a treaty with royalist forces under Ormonde, who himself returned to Ireland in September 1648 having spent several months in Paris arguing for an Irish campaign. The depleted fleet, reduced in numbers by defections, costly to maintain and a diplomatic embarrassment to the States General of the Dutch republic, was eventually sent there in January 1649 under the command of the capable Prince Rupert. The commissioning of Rupert by Charles was bitterly resented by James who saw himself as the natural choice by rank and through office, he being titular Lord High Admiral. When offered the chance to accompany the fleet to Ireland under Rupert, James declined.[9] Rupert's seniority in age and experience was irrelevant to the impetuous duke. The strong evidence for these basic and peevish emotions has not prevented some questionable speculation with regard to Ireland. It has been suggested that James revealed his 'prejudice against that country' when he refused his brother's offer. However, while it is true that James favoured an action nearer to the south of England and the prospect of securing his father from house arrest, command of the fleet would have seen him happy enough to do his duty. Any dislike he felt for Ireland, Scotland or parts of England, for that matter, would develop later and there is little sign of anti-Irish sentiment in the teenager. For James it was personal and the question of who would command the fleet was just one aspect of an intermittently strained relationship with his older brother during the years in exile. There was no comfort for James in the fact that, like the Engagement, the Irish initiative was also doomed to failure, with first the parliamentarian Colonel Michael Jones and then Cromwell defeating the royalist Irish alliance in Ireland in the late summer of 1649.[10]

Since his arrival in exile James felt like a package passed around at the whim of his mother and brother. As well as the question of the fleet – and even during discussion over that, he had been for some weeks sent to Rotterdam to avoid infection as his brother contracted smallpox – there was the need to agree the composition of James's household. Colonel Bampfield was sidelined, firstly by Prince Charles from any discussions over the fleet when it first arrived at Hellevoetsluis in June 1648, and secondly by Henrietta Maria generally who, exercising her right to control her young son's domestic environment, offered Bampfield the minor post of groom of the bedchamber. This Bampfield spurned, departing to take up a shadowy life as a republican spy and remaining in exile at the Restoration. Although later James grew to see the sense in removing 'a man of a turbulent and intriguing head', at the time he resented 'being used as a prisoner and not trusted with him selfe'.[11] The queen increased this resentment further when she named, in the absence of Charles I's appointee the soldier John, Lord Byron, her own favourite Sir John Berkeley as James's governor, a man James initially disliked but with whom he developed a close friendship. According to the Scottish exile and royalist Sir William Bellenden, all contact with James was now controlled: 'Barklay [is] plasid in such a trost that be order from S. Germins non is to speake with [James] bot in his presence. The yong sweet duc is much trobled and growes melanchole upon it'. Bellenden went on to extol the virtues of James as 'a most intelligent hopefull Prince' who at least had others '[to] mak him daylie act things not unbefitting him'. These others included Thomas Killigrew, an intelligent groom of the bedchamber, who became one of the Restoration period's most successful playwrights and theatre managers, and the clever Scot William Murray, earl of Dysart, a busy emissary between Charles I, Henrietta Maria and a range of Scottish politicians. Bellenden also recounted Berkeley's hatred for the Scots, no doubt brought on by the humiliating Bishops' Wars in which he fought for Charles I. There is even a suggestion that this might prejudice the young duke against those of the northern kingdom.[12] By the end of 1648 James had also been joined by a new secretary Sir Henry Bennet, the future earl of Arlington, his Anglican chaplain Dr Richard Steward, and intermittently by the queen's great favourite, the Catholic Henry, Lord Jermyn. Jermyn was first cousin to Sir John Berkeley and emphasised James's mother's control, but also how James would learn, as a counter-balance, to use his elder brother to ensure a certain level of independence. By February 1649, however, it was widely known that Berkeley and James were at loggerheads, to the extent that the former had reported James to his mother.[13]

In spite of the failure of the Engagement, when he returned to Scotland Lauderdale attempted to rescue an agreement between former Engagers, the Kirk Party and Prince Charles, and he was encouraged to this end by the likes of Jermyn who, out of pragmatism, had supported the Engagement and a rapprochement with Scottish Presbyterians. Nonetheless, in late 1648 Prince Charles could see that Ireland presented the best opportunity. He now considered sailing to Jersey, still in royalist hands, as the island represented a good point of departure for the Irish theatre. It seemed that both brothers would sail as James had returned to The Hague before Christmas on account of his brother's better health. As Prince Rupert and the small royalist fleet set sail for Ireland, Lauderdale conversely, finding himself too politically compromised as a major architect of the Engagement, went into exile and sailed back to Holland. Then on 22 January Ormonde wrote to Charles to invite him to come to Ireland to lead a new offensive to restore his father.[14] However, eight days later an event occurred that completely changed the political dynamics.

While Charles remained at The Hague, James came under pressure from his mother to go to her at Saint-Germain. James's petulance over the question of the fleet and disagreements with his older brother, let alone his governor, had been reported to her and she concluded he needed a guiding hand. He was still only fifteen after all and had not yet reached the point where he could ignore or sidestep her interference in his affairs. Also, he had not seen his mother for almost five years and, not unnaturally, she desired to see her son. James was instructed then to travel in December and so, shortly after the festivities of Christmas were at an end, he left The Hague for Paris 'with a small train', dismissing some minor servants and avoiding creditors thanks to the temporary intervention of the States General and the Prince of Orange. Travelling via Brussels and reaching as far as Cambrai, his mother sent word to him to delay his arrival on account of the civil discord of France's first Fronde Civil War. The eight-year-old Louis XIV and his court had taken flight to Saint-Germain, as the Paris *Parlement* rebelled against taxation imposed by the chief minister Cardinal Jules Mazarin. In response, in January a royal army under the great French general Louis, Prince de Condé, laid siege to Paris for King Louis. In such circumstances it was neither safe nor diplomatic for James to appear. James's situation came to the attention of Archduke Leopold-Wilhelm, governor of the Spanish Netherlands, and he sent word that the duke could reside at the Abbey of Saint-Amand which involved a short backtracking on his route. There, waiting for instructions from his mother, James was 'nobly entertain'd' by Benedictine monks for some three weeks. He came to close quarters for the first time with a Roman Catholic community at worship and appeared to enjoy the experience. Eventually, on 29 January he got word from his mother to meet her in Paris, and five days after they met in the city, in spite of the precarious security situation. It was there on 9 February that both, from the mouth of Lord Jermyn, heard the news that on 30 January Charles I had been executed by the Army and Rump Parliament of England. The shocking details had been delayed in reaching them due to the siege of Paris. It seems that Charles was found guilty of being 'a tyrant, traitor, murderer and public enemy' and a week after the execution the Rump declared English monarchy illegal.[15]

Jermyn struggled to tell his close intimate Queen Henrietta Maria that her husband was dead and her reaction we know to have been the expected distress of a widow. Prince Charles, now, of course, titular King Charles II at the age of eighteen, burst into tears on hearing the news at The Hague on 4 February. The reaction of James may seem a puzzle. We have no evidence that he was immediately very emotional. In his memoirs and other writings he fails to dwell on the subject and appeared to internalise his reaction. This is not, however, an especially unusual way to cope with trauma. In time he showed he was never comfortable with the religious martyrdom subsequently claimed for his father by the Church of England. Yet he was certainly deeply affected in the medium and long term. His father's execution was for James not a religious act but the ultimate treason – a despicable attack on natural order. In spite of the pressure he was put under to remain in the Church of England out of his father's martyrdom, he was never to accept this rationale, or that indeed his father had any authorship or connection to the publishing of the bestseller *Eikon Basilike*, first published in 1649, in which Charles was portrayed as a martyr to his faith. James was convinced that Dr John Gauden was the author, although for historians there is a strong case for some level of royal collaboration. What is more revealing is the vehemence with which he corrected Gilbert Burnet on this question in 1673.[16] For James, then, the murder of his father was a personal and a dynastic assault, not a religious matter. That sense of personal slight is seen not only in his later hatred of republicans and Covenanters but in his support for a plan to assassinate Cromwell in 1655. This was a plan proposed by Catholic royalists and as such would have been catastrophic to the interests of King Charles II in securing broad Protestant support for a Restoration. Fortunately, Charles and his council appear to have ignored the proposal, though James would return to assassination as a solution to political problems four decades later after he was deposed by William of Orange.[17]

A BROTHER NOW A KING

For the first few months of Charles's reign he lingered at The Hague considering his options. His servants were emboldened by their master's new status and encouraged the new king to ignore the pleadings of his mother to come to Paris and take her advice on the course of their affairs. Charles and his council made the decision to embark on a diplomatic offensive. They hoped to use monarchical revulsion at the execution of the late king to garner logistical, financial and military support from the crown heads of Europe. This saw privy councillors like John Lord Colepeper and Sir Edward Hyde redeployed as ambassadors, in their cases to Russia and Spain respectively, in an exercise that brought sympathy and promises not to recognise the new English republic if little concrete support.[18] That these ambassadors were forced to use their own funds, or borrow money where they could, added to the atmosphere of desperation that characterised the whole exercise. All began to focus on the only remaining domestic options – Scotland and Ireland.

While Ormonde and Prince Rupert did what they could to make progress in the Irish theatre, Charles and the Scottish Covenanters re-established lines of communication. On 5 February 1649 the Scottish Estates had declared Charles II king in its 'Proclamation of Charles the second king of Great Britane, France and Ireland', and by so doing, the Kirk Party now in power was in breach of its post-Engagement alliance with the English Parliament. The execution of Charles I was, more importantly, a betrayal of the Covenant and so religion and loyalty to the Stuarts conflated. There was therefore almost universal disgust in Scotland at the fate of the late king, 'now removed by a violent death' according to the Scottish Estates, yet it was essential to the Covenanters and their kirkmen to get reassurances on religion before Charles could be welcomed with open arms.[19] With this in mind, and to ensure that the new king signed the Covenant, in March a deputation of commissioners was dispatched to The Hague led by John Kennedy, sixth earl of Cassillis, and the lawyer George Winrame of Libberton and several clergy, including the diarist Robert Baillie.[20] Meanwhile at home, spurred on by outrage at the king's execution, a brief royalist insurgence known as Pluscardine's Rising (led by Sir Thomas Mackenzie of Pluscardine) forced General David Leslie to take decisive action in February and April around Inverness and Atholl. Simultaneously rumours flew around that ex-Engagers and the great enemy Montrose were planning an invasion.[21] It was in these circumstances that the commissioners arrived to negotiate with Charles, he with few options and they anxious to hold firm under external threats that could ignite yet again a major Scottish civil war. To focus minds at home and abroad, the royalists George Gordon, marquis of Huntly, and James, duke of Hamilton, were executed in Edinburgh and London respectively, the former unlucky to be made an example of over the Pluscardine affair when he was a prisoner at the time and not directly involved himself. He was the first noble to be executed in Scotland since the revolution.[22]

James, completely excluded from the deliberations, twiddled his thumbs in Paris when the Scottish commissioners held talks with Charles. It was in these months that his relationship with his mother began to deteriorate, driven on by the chronic bickering between his servants and those of the queen. This would get worse before it got better. Meanwhile, after two months, the talks with the Covenanters broke down over Charles's inability to give adequate assurances over religion and the composition of his retinue if he came to Scotland. A particular sticking point was Charles's unwillingness to promote a Presbyterian religious settlement outside Scotland, something agreed to by Charles I in the Engagement. The commissioners therefore returned to Scotland empty-handed. Charles had listened to the advice of Montrose, who had appeared in person, and the Scots Lord Napier and Lord Sinclair, backed by much English royalist opinion present, to look to Ormonde and to use a Montrose-led force to invade Scotland, rather than reach an agreement under such terms. With differing motives, the ex-Engagers Lanark (now the second duke of Hamilton) and Lauderdale, both also present, argued that Charles should sign the Covenant, but their advice was politely rejected. The ex-Engagers' prejudice against Montrose saw them leave every room he entered in spite of Charles's pleadings for them to work together.[23] As it transpired, their division was a fatal weakness for both the preservation of Scottish independence and the royal cause.

Sending Montrose off to negotiate with foreign powers and to raise an army, and determined soon to make his way to Ireland, in July 1649 Charles relented and joined his brother and mother at the Louvre in Paris. Soon the two brothers would set up court together at Saint-Germain. There James saw his brother also fall out with their mother, as the king, not taking his own advice, regularly walked out on her whenever she interfered too much in matters of state. Charles realised that her influence on the affairs of her father had often been destructive of the royal cause. The Queen Mother regularly showed herself impervious to political realities. For example, she now recommended that both Charles and James go to Ireland but convert to Catholicism before departing, without comprehending the broad base of royalist support and the inevitable fallout in England and Scotland. Again Charles and James ignored this suggestion, although later the mother's weak political judgment was visited on the younger brother.[24]

In spite of the initial warm welcome on his return to France afforded to Charles by the French Queen Regent, Anne of Austria, and the boy King Louis XIV, it soon became clear that two royal brothers short of money were something of an embarrassment to a French royal family troubled by civil war and war with Spain. Consequently, although letters from Ormonde warned of the need to delay Charles's arrival in Ireland until more information was gained on the Irish campaign and an assessment made of the large force under Cromwell that the English Commonwealth was despatching, Charles determined to sail for Jersey.[25] The island was still in loyalist hands and its advantages as a point of embarkation to the British Isles had been considered the year before. Therefore, in late September Charles, James and their two households, all dressed in the black of mourning, set sail for Jersey from Countainville on the French coast aboard frigates provided by the Prince of Orange. It was intended that James would travel with Charles to Ireland and, to underscore this before departing, James was confirmed in his position as Lord Admiral. After an enthusiastic welcome by the islanders and the royalist bailiff and lieutenant governor of Jersey Sir George Carteret, the brothers were accommodated in Elizabeth Castle at St Helier. Carteret then showed considerable skill in finding provisions for the combined households of about 300 people, as well as three coaches and horses and the dogs the brothers used for hunting, a popular diversion before fears of attack from republicans encouraged more cautious entertainments. Staying occupied became a problem, especially for James.

Charles may have had an inkling of this. Before leaving France he purchased the governorship from Lord Jermyn (who had inherited the post from his father) and gave it to James.[26] While Carteret no doubt did all the work, James, nonetheless, had some authority on the island. Charles's attentiveness to the needs of his brother is to be admired.

The duke and his elder brother were joined in Jersey by a panoply of servants. For James, his secretary Henry Bennet, who he heartily disliked; his chaplain Dr Richard Steward and his governor Sir John Berkeley attended. To this group were added Sir Edward Herbert, the Attorney General, who became a close confidant of James; Lord Byron, the soldier guardian appointed to James by Charles I and who later joined the duke on his first campaign with the French royal army, and the brothers' childhood friend George Villiers, duke of Buckingham.[27] While Charles remained with his brother he could prevent these councillors filling James's head with unhelpful feelings of resentment at his lot, but in a few months Charles would depart leaving a frustrated James behind.

As winter approached on the island of Jersey and before Charles left, it became clear that the Irish adventure had stalled. News arrived in late autumn that Cromwell had reinforced the parliamentary forces in mid August following Ormonde's defeat to a smaller force at Rathmines two weeks before. Charles had no option but to reopen negotiations with the Covenanters and Argyll, although he had maintained communication channels with Argyll and other leading Covenanters with suggestions that he night make concessions. Now the king agreed to meet their commissioners at Breda and signalled a willingness to take the Covenant and protect Presbyterianism. This came about after a divided Scottish Estates eventually despatched the lawyer George Winrame to negotiate with the king in exile, after settling on clear instructions in August. Winrame had travelled via Holland, unaware as he was that Charles had relocated to Jersey. However, this gave the lawyer the opportunity to persuade exiled English Presbyterians to offer support and for a few to accompany him to Jersey. Winrame and his delegation arrived at St Helier on 6 December. While Winrame had been on the Scottish committee of estates since 1643 and had been elected shire commissioner for Edinburghshire in the parliaments of 1644–7 and 1648–51, he had also been a friend and associate of the late marquis of Hamilton. Winrame was a man of compromise in a sea of rigid conscience, and James described him as 'a very loyall gentleman'.[28]

Although it must have seemed to Sir George Carteret and the islanders that Jersey was awash with courtiers, the reality was that full privy councillors were thin on the ground and as negotiations commenced Charles had to drum together a group to offer him advice. To a sprinkling of existing councillors, such as Ralph Lord Hopton and Robert Long, were added by informal invitation a number of individuals who happened to be present, including Sir Edward Nicholas; Thomas, Lord Wentworth; Henry, Viscount Wilmot (later earl of Rochester); Henry, Lord

Percy; Sir John Berkeley and Byron. James, who admittedly had only just turned sixteen, was effectively excluded from the talks, a situation he strongly resented. After much heated debate, tempered by the conciliation and rationalism of Charles and Winrame, the bad news from Ireland pressed Charles and his advisors to agree to negotiations with Scottish commissioners at Breda on 15 March 1650.[29]

On 13 February, Charles departed for Breda, via France and a few weeks with his mother, he and James leaving each other's company in much emotion. Since the execution of Charles I the capacity of family members to enact tearful departures seemed to have increased. The boys' mother, however, continued her 'austere carriage' with regard to her sons, while in the realm of high politics she held out the hope of shaping any political settlement that might develop. According to Clarendon, Henrietta Maria, who we must remember did not have good relations with the historian, had come around to approve of the Scottish negotiations, not because she preferred 'the glory of the Church of England before the sordidness of the Kirk of Scotland, but thought it the best expedient to advance her own religion (Catholicism) that the latter should triumph over the former', but whatever her motives, this appeared the only game in town.[30] As for James, he neither approved of the terms offered by the Scots or the decision to go to Breda to negotiate a treaty. Indeed, he appears to have been quite irritated by the whole process, as much, no doubt, by his lack of involvement as in the outcome itself. Once Charles had departed, somewhat petulantly James even dismissed from his household Berkeley and Byron on account of their voting in favour of negotiations.[31]

Before Berkeley was dismissed he was, however, sent to follow Charles and to make suggestions that his master went into service with Prince Rupert on the high seas, a proposal that would have had the young James swallowing his pride. Rupert was now at Lisbon, his Irish adventure over, maintaining himself through privateering. Charles would have none of it though and it was clear that James's career for the coming months was as governor of Jersey. So while Charles and the Scottish commissioners completed their negotiations at Breda in March and April 1650 – and the two sides in mutual delusion claimed a covenanted king had made an agreement with a loyal Scottish Estates – James festered in Jersey and had his head turned by members of his household, including Sir George Radcliffe, who saw that their best chance of future preferment lay with the young duke.[32]

In fact James was well out of the situation in which his older brother found himself – forced by necessity, so not to halt the momentum of his restoration plans, to sign in late June the National Covenant and Solemn League. This he did at the last minute while anchored off the coast of Scotland at Gartmouth, near Buckie on the Moray Firth.[33] Four weeks before, the great royal servant the marquis of Montrose was executed by Charles's new allies. This remarkable state of affairs was on account of Charles's mixed messages to the marquis, either to hold off or put military pressure on the Scottish Estates during negotiations. Charles's messenger on Scottish affairs Sir William Fleming had been dispatched too late with various contradictory instructions to the marquis, and arrived in Edinburgh just in time to witness Montrose take his punishment with great dignity. He also handed over a letter to the Estates in which Charles disowned Montrose.[34] The marquis was a victim of high politics, and must have known this was possible when he was initially asked to transport his force from Orkney to the mainland. Other officers of Montrose's force were also captured after their defeat on 27 April at the Battle of Carbisdale bordering Ross and Sutherland. David Leslie's troops were Montrose's nemesis yet again, though this time under Archibald Strachan who within a year would himself change sides and become republican. One of Montrose's officers executed with him was Major General Sir John Urrie [or Hurry] of Pitfichie, a former Covenanting commander who had made a career of changing sides and, for this reason, was executed with little regret. From Lauderdale to Argyll most of the Scottish elite approved of this justice, especially for the 'traitor' Montrose, even though such nobles abstained or kept their opinions to themselves for fear of damaging the agreement with Charles.[35] As for James, who from afar admired Montrose as a soldier and loyal servant, he found the whole affair, and the behaviour of his own brother, quite deplorable.

The lack of speedy and accurate information on the fate of Charles was very troubling for James, however, both as a loyal brother and as heir to the throne. While he kicked his heels on Jersey, occupying himself with hunting, sailing and the minutiae of the island's affairs, those closest to him egged him on to return to The Hague or Paris to make his own mark on events, and, if necessary, disregard the instructions of his mother and brother. Moreover, initial reports of the deal struck by Charles with the Covenanters, especially those referring to the removal of loyal supporters from the king's presence, and the setting aside of Anglicanism, left James feeling vindicated in his rejection of the idea of talks in January 1650. He and his mother could agree on this point – she was similarly horrified at the concessions Charles was forced to make. Nonetheless, by August James slowly understood that his brother had to rely on erstwhile enemies. As back in Scotland Argyll toiled to maintain unity between a reluctant king and a Kirk Party that was appalled at the ungodly populism that saw many Scots welcome the 'return' of their king, James sent a letter of encouragement acknowledging the marquis's 'very considerable' contribution to the cause of his brother. Unfortunately ten days later, on 3 September, Cromwell decisively defeated the Covenanting army of David Leslie at Dunbar, the godly forces badly weakened, in quality if not numerically, by the purges insisted upon by the radical Kirk Party leadership, headed by the likes of Archibald Johnston of Wariston and clergy such as Patrick Gillespie.[36] The ramifications of this defeat were unclear and James, unable to contain himself, quickly set sail for Paris and his mother's court.

James and his mother were not close and there is plenty of evidence for their mutual dislike of each other from James's return to Paris.[37] More generally, James's psychology developed in the context of a father who was stiff and reserved and a strict mother who wasted no time in comparing him unfavourably with his older brother Charles. The affect on James of this dysfunctional family was to make him as reserved as his father and as humourless as his mother. It could also occasionally lead to a crisis of confidence when the pressure was on. However, in September 1650 approaching seventeen years of age, he was imbued with the stubbornness of youth and deliberately ignored his mother's advice. In this he was encouraged by his 'uneasy family' of servants, as Hyde described them, and in particular Sir Edward Herbert, the English Attorney General, and Sir George Radcliffe.[38] In the last few months these men had suggested to James an odd scheme to go to Brussels and offer himself to the service of Charles, duke of Lorraine, in the hope of not only 'good council but assistance to make it effectual' – that is, much needed money to rid himself of dependence on his mother. Herbert and Radcliffe put forward the idea that Lorraine's circumstances in some way mirrored those of James for he too had his lands removed and was forced into exile. However, Lorraine was not only an ally of Spain but an enemy of Louis XIV, and so the whole proposal was an acute embarrassment to Henrietta Maria who relied on the French court and the goodwill of Louis's ministers to continue in Paris.[39] Undeterred James travelled to Brussels in early October, arriving there on the thirteenth of the month. He spent two months in the company of Lorraine without obtaining more than polite hospitality and some much needed, if minimal, funds. The Spanish government was unimpressed with the visit as it was anxious not to upset its new allies, the recently declared Commonwealth of England, and it soon became clear to James that being a soldier for the duke was not an option. A final proposal was made by James's party that he marry Lorraine's illegitimate daughter from his liaison with Madame de Cantecroy; yet the plan was unanimously rejected by Lorraine, Henrietta Maria and Charles himself in Scotland, who had been kept informed of his brother's erratic behaviour. Charles wrote to James instructing him to return to Paris, obey his mother and reduce his household, though he understood his brother's frustration. The combination of military inactivity, impecuniousness and squabbling courtiers made it difficult for the young duke to work out a coherent role for himself.[40] Inaccurate rumours that Charles had died at sea or under mysterious circumstances after Dunbar merely added to the anxieties of all the exiled community and especially of James. Even when it was clear that Charles was safe and arranging an invasion of England James could hardly be placated.

The Brussels affair having run its course (provoking hardly a mention in his memoirs), James determined to move on to The Hague to the court of his sister Mary and the Prince of Orange and not back to Paris. Yet the princess took her instructions from her mother and urged James to go to the Louvre. Moreover, two events at his sister's court made less attractive the company of a fretful brother. The Prince of Orange died suddenly of smallpox in early November and within a month a posthumous son, also William, was born to Mary. This is the child who three decades later would become James's nemesis. Immediately, though, from a political perspective, the death of the great Stuart ally made a visit by James to The Hague less attractive as the States of Holland now gave full vent to their republican sympathies, and soon would begin treaty negotiations with ambassadors of the English Commonwealth. Temporarily, James moved to Rhenen in Gelderland and spent Christmas at a house owned by his aunt Elizabeth, the exiled Queen of Bohemia, Rupert's mother. But family affairs were foremost on James's mind, for when at Brussels, he heard the tragic news that in October his fifteen-year-old sister Elizabeth had died at her father's old prison of Carisbrooke Castle. Therefore, as soon as his mother relented and gave her permission, in mid January 1651 James quickly travelled to The Hague to give his respects to his sister and to catch first sight of his new baby nephew. This sibling idyll did not last long as the appearance of Commonwealth ambassadors at The Hague made it necessary for James to move his small court to Breda. There he held out until early May before finally writing to his mother to ask her to formally invite him back to Paris. He was now desperate, having run out of funds and without means to keep his servants with him and under his control. Charles had written to him demanding James dismiss Killigrew and Radcliffe from his service and obey his mother. Finally in June, after Sir Edward Hyde was dispatched to Breda to reorganise his financial and personal affairs, finding the duke's entourage 'in all confusion imaginable', James made his way back to his mother's household at Saint-Germain, where the Queen Mother had retreated away from fresh violence from the 'Fronde of the nobles' around Paris.[41] When mother and son were reunited at the palace of Saint-Germain, both made great efforts to be warm-hearted and, for a short period at least, to set aside recriminations.

Throughout the spring and summer of 1651 Henrietta Maria and James continued to wait anxiously for news from Scotland. Cromwell's victory had not produced a definite outcome and Leslie was able to retreat to Stirling and reorganise his remaining forces. Since the defeat at Dunbar, however, Charles grew increasingly frustrated at continued attempts by the Kirk Party to further purge the army at a time when every able-bodied soldier was required regardless of whether they were Engagers or had taken the Covenant. Wariston and like-minded Covenanters meanwhile blamed the defeat on an ungodly army, not chronic disunity. When in late September 1650 the committee of estates ordered the removal of many of Charles's servants and friends, Charles reacted by agreeing to a 'secret' coup d'état on 3 October. On the very day of the defeat at Dunbar, Charles wrote to Sir Edward Nicholas in Holland requesting that the Prince of Orange arrange for a boat to be placed offshore or docked at Montrose in case he needed to make his flight abroad: removing himself completely was another option if he was to finally lose all confidence in the Covenanter leadership. The plan for the coup, however, was to arrest the purgers and, using loyalist noble and Highland support, institute a royalist takeover. But this attempted coup, known as 'the Start', was stillborn on account of the indecision shown uncharacteristically by Charles and more usually associated with James. In the end, as confusion reigned and contradictory messages to rise or stand down reached the 'rebel' commanders, Charles was detained by a troop of Leslie's horse while hiding in a remote farmhouse in Glen Clova in Angus the day after the planned rising.[42] So ended yet another of those conspiratorial fiascos so common to the Stuarts since the outbreak of hostilities in 1638.

In a letter to Nicholas, Charles ranted about the 'hypocrisy' of the Covenanters and how this comforted him in his commitment to the Church of England. For him anyone who was not a pragmatist must be a hypocrite, a curious definition when we reflect on the fate of his brother. Nevertheless, for now Charles continued to cooperate with those of the 'hypocritical' party. Indeed, once he had apologised to the committee of estates for his actions he emerged in a much stronger position. The committee realised they had pushed him too far, given that the monarchy was the fountain of their legitimacy, and they moved to pardon those involved and to place Charles closer to the business of the committee and of government. Within a few weeks the leading 'rebels', including the Engager General John Middleton and senior royalist noble Lewis Gordon, third marquis of Huntly, eldest son of the executed marquis, had laid down their arms and signed a treaty with Leslie. Huntly's estates and title, forfeited at his father's trial, were reinstated by the Scottish Parliament. Conversely, the radical Kirk Party members saw 'the Start' as proof of Charles's perfidy and soon a 'remonstrance' was forthcoming from the Western Association, formed in October 1648 to coordinate the military and religious effort of the Covenanting western shires, outlining his 'errors' and the infection of ungodliness that had proliferated since Charles's arrival.[43] With Scotland now fragmented militarily and politically into royalists in the north and east, the Western Association in the south and west, Argyll and clan Campbell in the West, and the Kirk Party in the centre, disunity was more evident than ever as Cromwell's army struggled to control Edinburgh, the Lothians and various strongholds in the centre. However, both Cromwell and Charles could be said to have gained from the next event in this unstable situation – the rash attack on a detachment of English troops at Hamilton by the Western Association's commander Colonel Gilbert Ker. As the committee of estates threatened to replace Ker for his hesitancy in fighting for an 'ungodly' king, on 1 December, in an attempt to show his metal, mistakenly thinking it a small detachment, he attacked an English force twice the size of his own and was swiftly defeated and captured. The collapse of the forces of the Western Association meant that the Kirk Party had no choice but to turn to the officers and men of the Engagement and the recent abortive royalist coup. The ideology of a war of patriotism, to rid Scotland of the English, began to take precedence over a war of religion. Therefore, in spite of the clergy and the commissioners of the General Assembly now splitting between 'resolutioners' who supported a patriotic war and a strong minority of 'protesters' who adhered to the

tenor of the Western remonstrance and the continuation of the Act of Classes of
1649, which excluded all but the most rigid Covenanters from public office and
the army, the road was now set for a 'new' army to be created for King Charles to
lead into England.[44] All that was required was to formalise the relationship between
monarch and kingdom.

In the surreal context of an invading republican army occupying much of
Scotland, and after agreement by the Scottish Parliament the month before,
Charles's coronation ceremony took place, as tradition demanded, at Scone near
Perth, on 1 January 1651. This was the constitutional rite of passage never experienced by James VII of Scotland. On 28 December, however, the parliament
remitted 'to the comittie of estaitt to tak the duik of York, his condition, to consid-
eratioune, and quhat advyse is to be givin to him' not only due to Charles's known
concern for his brother's behaviour, but also because the coronation of one brother
focused minds on the succession in the right of the other, given, of course, the
dangerous nature of the time. The ceremony itself and the immediate aftermath
delivered mixed messages.[45] While the young King Charles had to stomach,
though it seems with some bravado, a ceremony couched in terms of the National
Covenant, Kirk Party radicals had to watch on as more and more cavaliers participated in political and military affairs, and the army became committed to the
restoration of the Stuarts in their three kingdoms. Indeed, by the time Parliament
convened in May 1651, the Kirk Party was in full decline. In early June the Estates
repealed the Act of Classes of 1646 and 1649 and made illegal support for the
Western remonstrance. The General Assembly of the Kirk that met in St Andrews
and Dundee in July split asunder as 'Protesters' walked out rejecting the newly
confident royalism and what they saw as a dilution of the religious cause.[46]
However, the preparations of the army were hampered by more than some disgrun-
tled clergy. Shortages of supplies and resources, the difficulties of recruiting as
English troops harried to west and east, and Argyll's refusal to commit his clan to
an invasion of England that was motivated by political rather than clear religious
reasons, meant that overall the size of the main Scottish army never exceeded
about 14,000 men. Therefore, when finally the stalemate was broken and Cromwell
engineered the destruction of 4,000 Scottish troops at Inverkeithing in Fife on 20
July, and overran the county before taking the surrender of Perth, so shutting off
access to reinforcements and supplies from the north, Charles and his advisors
took the decision to invade England before the army disintegrated. In effect, out
of weakness and desperation Charles's army of restoration entered England and
soon met its defeat at the Battle of Worcester on 3 September. Exactly a year since
Dunbar, Cromwell defeated Charles with a force which outnumbered the Scots
more than two to one, Charles's hoped-for flood of English royalist recruits not
materialising. Yet in the only particularly life-threatening military engagement of
his life, Charles showed much courage in his actions with the Scottish army. When
all was lost he escaped from the field and embarked on his celebrated six weeks,

skulking in disguise across the southern counties of England, before eventually departing for the Continent by boat from Shoreham in Sussex on 14 October. The unfortunate English peer James Stanley, seventh earl of Derby, who had held the Isle of Man for Charles and his father, was captured and executed, but not before giving Charles information on the Catholic network of Shropshire and the Penderell family who had helped him in similar dire straits, and who were so vital in concealing the king in his 'wonderful deliverance' in the immediate aftermath of the battle.[47]

The impact on those others Charles left behind, the newly asserted royalist leadership of Scotland, was catastrophic. Most of the leadership was captured or killed. The second duke of Hamilton, like his brother after Preston, gave his life for his master, dying of his wounds. Other leading Scots, notably Leslie, Lauderdale and Middleton, were imprisoned, though Middleton escaped from the Tower of London in his wife's clothes in January 1652. Leslie and Lauderdale were not so fortunate or inventive but at the Restoration all three benefited from the gratitude of Charles and his younger brother.[48] For Charles, the whole experience of the past sixteen months was of despair, disappointment and defeat. Worcester brought a humiliating conclusion to an extraordinary thirteen years, a golden age of Scottish military assertiveness. But in the end the Scots had shown themselves incapable of delivering the restoration of their own royal dynasty, and Charles retained a distrust of Scottish initiatives for the next decade, an unheeded lesson for later Stuarts in 1715 and 1745. Charles also developed a lifelong aversion to Presbyterianism, and in this he and James encouraged each other. Neither fully understood the extent to which Presbyterianism was a broad 'church'. Later this would lead them to the kind of hypocritical approach to practical politics which the older brother so disparaged in others.

James, Henrietta Maria and other exiled royalists felt a mixture of shock and relief when news reached them that Worcester was a catastrophe but that Charles had escaped. When Charles returned in October, full of stories of his adventurous flight and expressing hatred for Scottish and English Presbyterians, the latter for failing to rise in his support, he found his brother and mother barely on speaking terms. Indeed, diminishing prospects ensured that faction fighting returned to those surrounding mother and sons, and as Hyde put it, '[the] vanity of our friends trouble us little less than the vices of our enemies'. James's own lack of prospects and money was acute and his mother deliberately withheld what help she could offer out of her French pension in order to keep him in line. James left Paris to meet his brother at Magny before king and queen mother were reunited at the Louvre, no doubt to put his side of things. However, Charles now had the same difficulties. As Cromwell and the English army consolidated their position in Scotland, and the Isle of Man and Channel Islands were overrun, domestic options were exhausted and efforts turned to financial survival and the cultivation of diplomatic alliances against the republic. Charles ignored or dismissed those most strongly in favour of the Breda treaty with the Covenanters, such as John Lord Colepeper and George Villiers, duke of Buckingham. Few senior Scots were in exile to incur the king's wrath, and his Scottish physician Fraser was forgiven on account of his excellent medical skills.[49] It was as if the treaty had never been – an aberration – and Charles's attitude to Scotland's Restoration Settlement of 1660 would be dictated by his selective memory over what had been agreed.

A SOLDIER OF FORTUNE

While from the winter of 1651/2 Charles looked for a diplomatically acceptable and financially viable location for his court, with some impatience James returned to the idea that a military commission was his best means of security and independence from his mother, as well as 'making himself fit one day to serve the King his brother in a useful capacity'. In Hyde's words, 'there need be no spurs applied to inflame the duke, who was most impatient to be in the army'. Staying put was not in any case a viable solution. His French hosts, the Queen Regent and her minister Mazarin, in spite of James's personal popularity with some French at court, were unwilling to finance further a diplomatic liability who was merely the next in line to a king who was king of very little indeed. Fortunately for James, with the help of Hyde, Charles and Henrietta Maria were brought round to the idea that he could enter French royal military service in the Fronde civil war against the nobility, which he did in April 1652, initially as a gentleman volunteer but soon as a fully commissioned officer.[50] James set out with his intimate Sir John Berkeley, who had promoted the scheme for some months, and Colonel Robert Werdon, who like Berkeley had served under Charles I. As they departed, James and his party were given practical assistance by his brother, who not only lent him some horses but also participated in the deception of pretending to go hunting so as to avoid being discovered in their true purpose by their uncle Gaston, Duc d'Orléans, who had control of the Paris area and was a Frondeur and enemy of Mazarin. James would join the French royal army commanded by one of the great generals of the age, Henri La Tour d'Auvergne, vicomte de Turenne, Marshal of France, then located at Chartres to the west. He and this Huguenot general would develop an intimate friendship, akin to father and son yet in a military setting, and in his own military memoirs James is seen to idolise his commanding officer.[51]

One event as he journeyed to Chartres shows James both as fortunate and an asset to his new superiors. En route he stopped at Corbeil, a neutral town in the civil war, and was able to persuade the inhabitants to not only let him enter but to declare for the Queen Regent. Soon Turenne was able to occupy the town and both the boy Louis and his mother moved their court there also, rewarding James with a little money and much needed supplies.[52] This was a fruitful beginning to James's career with the royal army of France and with Turenne in particular. What we know of this career is largely conveyed by James's own military memoirs, a somewhat dull, flat and laboured affair, which reveals his obsessions with fine detail rather than the overall political significance of events in the French theatre. The memoirs, repeated closely but not exactly in the relevant years of the 'Jacobite' *Life*, does not even provide much of a glowing picture of James in action. The blandness of the account in comparison with other passages in the *Life* suggests less editorial tampering and more the authentic voice of James himself.[53]

James fought six campaigns from 1652 to 1658 in what were the most enjoyable years of his life, secluded from financial, family and political pressures. These were mostly summer campaigns necessitated by the difficulties of finding forage for armies in winter, so in these months James returned to the company of the exiled court and particularly his brothers and sister. In four of these campaigns he served under Turenne with the French army of Louis XIV – from April 1652 to January 1653, June to October 1653, July to November 1654 and August to November 1655 – the first of which was part of the Fronde civil war between the royal army and that of the rebel princes, and the others against the Spanish whose commanders included that other great French general of the time, the Prince of Condé, who had not become reconciled to the Queen Regent and Mazarin. Surprisingly, in the other two campaigns – from June 1657 to January 1658 and from April to September 1658 – James fought with Condé for the Spanish army of Flanders against France and Turenne. This followed Charles II's treaty with Felipe IV of Spain in April 1656, sandwiched between the Anglo-French treaties of October 1655 and March 1657 agreed by Cromwell and Louis XIV's government. Allies and enemies swapped places with remarkable regularity in the military theatre of mid seventeenth-century Europe. But although James may seem like a mere soldier of fortune, such changes of allegiance could be entirely honourable and in keeping with the gentlemanly conduct of continental warfare that James so admired. Also, kicking his heels at court was not a preferred option. In the winter of 1655/6 when difficult negotiations were taking place with Charles, Mazarin and Cromwell on where James could be commissioned, one suggestion of the Italian Mazarin was captain general under the Italian Francesco I d'Este, duke of Modena, who commanded the French, Savoyard and Modena forces at Piedmont. James was delighted to comply with a suggestion that enabled him to continue 'acceptable' military service, though the Spanish phase of Stuart diplomacy from 1656 to 1660 necessitated he serve with Spain, a partnership which was seen by Charles as the best hope for an assisted restoration in the British Isles.[54] The Piedmont option had other advantages – his aunt was Françoise Madeleine d'Orléans, duchess of Savoy, sister to Henrietta Maria. Yet the fact that his uncle Charles Emmanuel II, duke of Savoy, was infamous for the recent persecution of Italian Protestants would in any case have made such an adventure unwise for the heir to the thrones of Protestant England and Scotland. Almost two decades later, however, the family ties with Italy would grow stronger when in 1673 James married his second wife

Maria Beatrice Anna Margherita Isabella d'Este, Mary of Modena, granddaughter of Francesco, duke of Modena, and a Catholic.

James's reputation and qualities as a military and naval commander are debated, but his military memoirs and supplementary detail from other contemporaries confirm that in the 1650s he was a man of action who frequently risked his life. In July 1652 during an attack on a barricade at the Battle of Faubourg Saint-Antione near Paris, James witnessed at close quarters hand-to-hand fighting in the streets as Condé's army of the princes 'ply[ed] them with their shott as thick as haile'. Starting his role as reliable eyes for his short-sighted commander, James accompanied Turenne throughout the engagement, and both were exposed to periods of close fighting with James's gentleman of the bedchamber, Colonel Weldon, being seriously wounded when standing next to his master.[55] At the Battle of Arras in August 1654, a successful action to raise the Spanish siege of the town which commenced the month before, James showed his skill and bravery as a cavalry officer when risking his life to rescue a fellow officer and, at a key moment in the battle, rallying the horse and foot of the left wing when word circulated that Turenne had been wounded. James also had considerable responsibilities, and suggestions that he was a mere aide-de-camp do him a total injustice. James was certainly young, not yet eighteen years old, when he fought his first campaign, yet it was not especially unusual for noble sons to fight at such a tender age. It is true that in 1652 and 1653 he spent time delivering messages to divisional commanders, dangerous work in itself, but by Arras he was a lieutenant general of horse and even before, he took command of various detachments. In the wake of Spanish and royalist defeat at the Battle of the Dunes near Dunkirk in June 1658 James was charged with commanding and holding the coastal town of Nieupoort, east of Dunkirk. He was a member of the council of war for the French in 1655 and for the Spanish in 1658. In November 1655 Turenne briefly left James commanding the whole French army while he was away at the French court and Don Juan, governor of the Spanish Netherlands, also left James in command of his army at Dunkirk in late 1657. Therefore, setting aside the exaggerations in his military memoirs, such as the various stories of why the enemy respected him so much, they would not fire on him; the post-Restoration hagiography that idealised him as a romantic knight, and the fact that Lord Berkeley, an experienced soldier, attended the duke at all times, a reputation for personal bravery and military efficiency has the ring of truth. Contemporaries of various hues commented on his service – Hyde that he 'showed extraordinary courage and gallantry' at his first engagement at the siege of Étampes in 1652; Ormonde that he was 'brave' in 1657, and even a republican spy that he was by 1653 'much esteemed in the French army and hope[d] by the time to fight for his countries as he is forced now to do so for his bread'. Such was his reputation in the 1650s that when the commander-in-chief in Scotland, General Monck, contemplated intelligence reports that the royalists planned a Spanish-backed invasion of Scotland in October

1656, he believed James would be in overall command.[56] In the end this invasion failed to materialise and the first time that James led a field army into battle was the fateful Battle of the Boyne in 1690.

Militarily, James became the most experienced prince of England since Henry VIII and of Scotland since James IV. He served as a commander of horse with the French and of foot with the Spanish. In his military memoirs he comments on tactics, siege techniques and the performance of generals. He also reveals his attitude to the various nationalities who served with or under him. While the French and English (on either side) could do no wrong, the Irish are portrayed as quick to retreat and unwilling to obey commands, while the Spanish are lazy and their officers too complacent.[57] Scots, on the other hand, with the exception of some individuals, are not often reflected on by James, and this perhaps indicates that he often considered them with the English, even though they had a distinctive presence in both the French and Spanish armies in which he served.

Scottish service in the French army had a long tradition sustained by the Auld Alliance. This service dates back to the 1440s when the elite hundred-strong *garde écossais* became the personal bodyguard of the kings of France. This stemmed from Scottish support for France during the Anglo-French Hundred Years War (1337–1453). While the Scottish Reformation of 1560, French Wars of Religion (1562–98), Union of the Crowns of 1603 and anti-Protestantism of Louis XIII and his chief minister Cardinal Richelieu made French service less palatable for many Protestants, it has been calculated that more than ten thousand Scots served in the French army between 1624 and 1642.[58] Although many of these were Catholics, after the outbreak of the Bishops Wars (1639–40) and the English Civil War in 1641, service in the French army became more attractive for royalists whatever their religion, particularly as the position of Charles I deteriorated by stages in the British Isles, from Marston Moor in 1644 to the king's execution in January 1649.

When James began his service with the French two Scottish infantry regiments were active with him, the 'regiment of Douglas', as it was known, and a now expanded *garde écossais*, plus one Scottish cavalry unit, the *gens d'armes écossais*. Scottish Catholic officers are seen to exhibit significance beyond their numbers. The first of these regiments was originally raised for Swedish service by the Haddingtonshire laird Sir John Hepburn, but transferred to the French in 1634, when Hepburn, a spirited Catholic officer, fell into dispute with the Protestant Swedish court and King Gustavus Adolphus, the great champion of Protestantism in the Thirty Years War (1618–48). The regiment took the name Douglas when Lord James Douglas became commander in 1642. After Lord James's death in 1647 he was succeeded nominally by his younger half-brother Lord George Douglas, though in effect his other brother Archibald, twelfth earl of Angus, took command until his death in 1656, with George serving in the French court and receiving a military education. After Angus's death, George Douglas, who later would become first earl of Dumbarton and commander-in-chief in Scotland in

1685, then took personal command and, unlike his brother, was no mere figure-head and was actually in the field with the regiment. This Catholic officer became very popular with both Charles II and James. His influence as an recusant army chief in Scotland was, however, somewhat diluted by his remaining in England in the 1680s after his regiment was formally disbanded from the French service in 1678, and was reformed, not for Scotland but on the English establishment as the 1st Royal regiment of foot (Royal Scots). Throughout the 1650s the Douglas regiment fought with the French army and with much bravery with James at the Battle of Faubourg Saint-Antione and at the Siege of the Castle of Ligny, both in the 1652 campaign against Condé and the Fronde princes.[59]

The *garde écossais* had a slightly less tortuous history of command. The regiment was formed in Scotland in 1642 by James Campbell, earl of Irvine, half-brother of the Covenanting leader Archibald Campbell, marquis of Argyll. In April that year the Privy Council, confirming his commission granted by Charles I the month before, stated that 4,500 men, an optimistic target, should be raised for French service under Louis XIII, and by the end of the summer the regiment was in France. Irvine died in 1645 and his command passed to the Presbyterian Sir Robert Moray. Moray was to have an eventful life, including a year as an imperial prisoner in Bavaria in 1643–4, being a founder member of the Royal Society attending its first London meeting in 1660, and a major figure in Scottish Restoration politics, but he also served in France under Hepburn in the 1630s and by 1642 was lieu-tenant colonel in Irvine's new regiment. Although he was therefore the logical successor to Irvine in 1645, the complex nature of Scottish politics saw Moray commit most of his time in London and Edinburgh, attempting to negotiate the best possible deal for a restoration and Presbyterian settlement, and neglecting his recruiting responsibilities. In the end he was forced to resign in 1650 and was replaced before 1653 by Andrew Rutherford, subsequently earl of Teviot, a Catholic who commanded as lieutenant colonel. Rutherford had distinguished himself in French service in the 1640s, including at the Battle of Lens in 1648 under Condé which secured Paris from Spain and the Empire. Subsequently, Rutherford remained loyal to the French monarchy during the Fronde and served under Turenne.[60] When James, duke of York, joined Turenne's forces in 1652, Rutherford was one of his comrades in arms and their close relationship helps explain the latter's elevation to the peerage as Lord Teviot in 1661 and then as earl in 1663. The first of these elevations came with his regiment's final amalgamation with the Douglas regiment in 1661, and his brief appointment as governor of English-held Dunkirk the following year when he successfully negotiated its sale back to the French.

The earliest of the Scottish units active in the 1650s was the *gens d'armes écossais*, a mostly mounted force which dated back to the 1620s, when it was revived from an earlier manifestation by the Catholic George Gordon, earl of Enzie (later the marquis of Huntly executed for treason by the Covenanters in 1649) with a co-religionist Andrew Gray, seventh Lord Gray, as lieutenant from 1624.[61] Gray appears to have served in France in the 1620s and 1630s, but thereafter spent most of his time in Scotland and England, while Enzie returned to Scotland in 1637 to become head of his family on his father's death, only to be cast into the turmoil of the revolution. Gray's French service was intermittent in the 1640s and early 1650s. Although banished from Britain by the Covenanters' committee of estates in 1645, he was still in Scotland the following year. Also, at least twice before, in 1638/9 and 1643, he was in Scotland attempting to recruit Scots for his French regiment. In spite of the difficulties of recruiting during periods when soldiers were in demand elsewhere, he proved remarkably successful, especially at recruiting fellow recusants. One report suggests that in 1638 the *gens d'armes écossais* consisted of 1,200 men, nearly 60 per cent of who were Catholics. Eventually, in the early 1650s Gray was back in French service yet he was soon persuaded in 1655 by Charles II and James to step aside in favour of the Calvinist Frederick Herman, comte de Schomberg, subsequently one of the great European commanders of the period, who became captain lieutenant of the *gens d'armes écossais,* now a regiment of horse and foot, in October 1652. Schomberg was, like James, a protégé of Turenne and his command of the *gens d'armes écossais* and promotion to lieutenant general in 1655 was in recognition of his valour and command ability shown in the various campaigns from 1651. Since 1652 he and James has been comrades in arms under Turenne at the siege of Étampes (1652), siege of Rethel (1653), the relief of Arras and capture of Le Quesnoy (1654), and fighting at Landrecies, Condé and Saint-Ghislain (1655). James had considerable respect for Schomberg's martial qualities and confirms in his military memoires that Schomberg was injured at Étampes, as he was at Ghislain, and, in spite of James's personal bravery, as a professional soldier Schomberg certainly put himself in harm's way more often than the duke. Schomberg went on to develop a close relationship with Charles II, both in exile and in the 1660s and 1670s, as he would do with William of Orange in the 1680s. After the Restoration James cooled his relationship with the commander on account of the latter's religious convictions, and according to Burnet viewed him by 1673 'as [effectively] a Presbyterian and an unfit man for [his] purpose'.[62] James's assessment of Schomberg proved accurate, though the latter was hardly to blame for the nature of European religious politics. After becoming a 'Huguenot' exile from France, following Louis XIV's rescinding of the religious compromise the edict of Nantes in 1685, Schomberg was appointed commander of William's Irish campaign of 1689–90, and this simply shows how William, Louis XIV and James had succeeded in polarising the officer corps of Europe. The Nine Years War (1689–97), for which the British Revolution of 1688/9 was an aperitif, was certainly geopolitical and on one side anti-French in nature, but it was also viewed by many participants as being as profoundly religious as the Thirty Years War in the first half of the century.

The Battle of the Boyne in 1690 was not, however, the first time that James and

Schomberg had confronted each other in battle. At the Battle of the Dunes near Dunkirk in June 1658 they also found themselves on opposite sides. Since Charles II's treaty with Spain of April 1656, following on from Cromwell's alliance with Louis XIV the previous October, efforts had been made by Charles's commanders and diplomats to recruit six regiments into Spanish service, to forward the new policy of a Spanish-supported restoration. James, along with a number of the officers and regular troops, switched from French to Spanish service and assisted the recruitment drive. The plan was for 6,000 to be raised but James, who was to be their field commander, only had some 2,000 in June 1658. The majority of these were Irish troops who in fact dominated four of the regiments, including the largest under the titular command of the marquis of Ormonde and the actual control of Colonel Richard Grace, a man whose honourable conduct was especially admired by James. Even the force known as the Duke of York's Regiment was predominantly Irish. However, as well as the mostly English King's Own Regiment and duke of York's life guard of fifty to a hundred troopers commanded by Charles Berkeley, nephew of Sir John Berkeley, there was one solely Scots regiment to be commanded by Lieutenant General John Middleton, with Sir James Hamilton as lieutenant colonel.[63] Since the execution of Montrose, Middleton was certainly the most senior Scottish officer on the royalist side and yet Charles had deployed him to Poland and Danzig in September 1656 with a view to raising money from Scottish merchants and persuading Scots in Swedish service, particularly those in Lord William Cranston's regiment, to leave and join the Spanish initiative.[64] Therefore, in Middleton's absence the command of the regiment was given that same year to James Livingston of Kinnaird, Viscount Newburgh, originally its lieutenant colonel.

Newburgh was yet another Scottish army officer with impeccable loyalist credentials. After plotting with others in the late 1640s over various unrealised schemes to bring Charles I to safety, he fled to exile in 1650 only to return with Charles II and to join in the defeat at Worcester. Like the king, Newburgh was able to escape to the Continent and then took on the role as go-between, as Charles kept contact with the dispersed band of Scottish royalists, and so became a chief advisor on Scottish affairs. In this sense, and having shared the Worcester debacle, Newburgh was more Charles II's man than James's. Nonetheless, even before Worcester and a diplomatic career thereafter, Newburgh had developed as every bit the soldier, a hot-headed individual who frequently became involved in duels, the first in Paris when he was only sixteen years old. By the 1650s both his military experience and bellicosity made him an ideal commander for Middleton's regiment, and Charles and James had been impressed enough with his service at that time to reward him at the Restoration with an earldom, a place on the Scottish Privy Council and the position of Vice-Admiral of Scotland. The fact that his stepson Charles Stuart, sixth duke of Lennox and third duke of Richmond, had in 1660 inherited the titles and positions of the dukedom on the premature death of his cousin, including being hereditary High Admiral of Scotland, enabled an appointment based on high favour and nepotism. At least Newburgh proved more conscientious than his stepson in attending Scottish Council meetings. He was also one of a small breed of courtiers who sat in both the Scottish Parliament, as a member of the noble estate, and the English Parliament, as elected member of the House of Commons, representing Cirencester. Also, more fittingly and with the approval of James, from January 1661 to 1670 Newburgh was appointed captain and then colonel of the elite king's bodyguard or troop of life guards, a force that remained on the Scottish establishment until 1709 when it became part of the British Horse Guards regiment under the name the 4th Horse Guards.[65] Although the formation of this troop by Newburgh came in 1661, it actually dates back to a decade before when in 1650 Charles II commissioned a life guard under Alexander Montgomery, sixth earl of Eglinton, with Newburgh as lieutenant colonel. It was this life guard that Newburgh commanded at Worcester and so we see underlined the attempts by James and his older brother to maintain military continuities, and to reward loyal martial servants. Newburgh, therefore, was a member of the 'new' officer caste of Scottish nobility which at the Restoration had the earl of Middleton at its head.

As the Franco-Spanish conflict intensified in 1657–8, few Scots were left with the French army and the 'regiment of Douglas', the *garde écossais*, and *gens d'armes écossais* were set aside, individuals either defecting or taking no part. Some like Andrew Rutherford did not abandon French service, although there is no evidence he fought at the Battle of the Dunes. Schomberg, before the battle itself, recruited a fresh German regiment which he commanded at the Dunes along with the second line on the French left wing. In fact, the French insisted that the Cromwellian force of six thousand or so were all English, even though a few Scottish officers served, such as Sir Bryce Cochrane who had fought for the Covenanters but had come under the influence of General George Monck, the Cromwellian commander in Scotland. Indeed, their commander-in-chief at the Dunes was the Scot Sir William Lockhart of Lee, Cromwell's ambassador to France who had negotiated the Anglo-French treaty. At a time of heated diplomacy and James's difficult decision to enter Spanish service, James reports that at Clermont in 1656 he and Lockhart almost came face to face in an embarrassing coincidence at the Hotellerie de la Poste in the town. But when James later recalled the defeat of the royalist-Spanish alliance at the Dunes, it was Lockhart's regiment of English troops that he so admired showing their 'great eagerness and courage' as they charged the Dunes and soon overran his own force. As for Lockhart himself, he certainly had a mixed record, although at a time when many Scots could claim the same. In the 1640s he was a loyalist who as a young man distinguished himself in the French army, and went on to support the Engagement in 1648. However, slighted by Charles II in 1651, when his offer to march with him into England was not taken up, he then cooperated with

Cromwell and even became a member of the Cromwellian Parliament in London. Nevertheless, Lockhart returned to the royalist camp at the Restoration, being protected by General Monck who effectively delivered the Restoration. Indeed, in the 1670s Lockhart became a shire commissioner for Lanarkshire in the Scottish Parliament, Charles II's ambassador to France and also was appointed Lord Justice Clerk. Essentially, for Charles perhaps but for James especially, it was the soldierly qualities of Lockhart that appealed, as well no doubt as his straying from the path yet ultimate return to the fold.[66]

In his military memoirs James describes in great detail the disposition of the pro-Spanish troops in the summer of 1658 as the Battle of the Dunes drew near. The battle was a set piece and it and the preamble were of major significance to James, his reputation and his brother's cause. Before this James's service for the Spanish from June to December 1657 produced no major actions as, especially in July and August, the Spanish forces marched purposelessly around, with James as commander of foot, in an area from Mons to Calais. In September some action came at Mardyke west of Dunkirk, where firstly the French successfully laid siege to the coastal fortress, and then the Spanish under Don Juan, with James, Charles and Ormonde in attendance, made a half-hearted effort to retake the fort which, now in English hands, was protected by guns from Cromwell's ships. This was one of those rare occurrences where Charles risked his own life, and when news came that Ormonde's horse was shot from under him when next to the king, Hyde wrote to his young master cautioning him against taking excessive risks. The skirmish futile, the Spanish army then returned to Dunkirk and remained there with James as commander before the order came to disperse to winter quarters on 1 January 1658. This saw James return to winter at Brussels and at Bruges and Antwerp in the company of his widowed sister and elder brother.[67]

When in late May 1658 news reached Brussels that the French had begun to besiege Spanish forces at Dunkirk, Don Juan, the Prince of Condé, and the other commanders agreed to relieve the town by land, and by 3 June the Spanish allied army was deployed on the dunes north of Dunkirk faced by the Anglo-French forces of Turenne and Lockhart. Out of perhaps fewer than fifteen thousand in the Spanish army, James was commander of two thousand English, Scots and Irish forces in five regiments formed into three battalions: Charles II's English regiment of foot and George Digby, earl of Bristol's Irish regiment combined under Lieutenant Colonel Thomas Blaque; the Duke of York's Regiment of Irish under Donough MacCarthy, Viscount Muskerry; and thirdly, Ormonde's regiment of Irish under Richard Grace combined with Newburgh's regiment of Scots under Major Sir William Urry. Urry was the younger brother to Major General Sir John Urry who was executed with Montrose in May 1650. William was a staunch royalist and not as prone as his brother to changing sides and in 1651 he joined the Northern royalists under Middleton in the incident know as 'the Start' before the Battle of Worcester and the subsequent conquest of Scotland by Cromwell. In the 1660s Urry became a major and captain in the king's Scottish foot guards and was involved in efforts to suppress Covenanting. He was yet another of that band of returning soldiers who fared well at the Restoration under Middleton's patronage.[68]

While it appears Newburgh was not on the field of battle at the Dunes, there is no doubt that Urry was and also James himself and his younger brother Henry, duke of Gloucester. When battle was joined on 4 June the Spanish allies had the advantage of the high ground, but that did not stop a relentless attack by Cromwell's redcoats. James marvelled at the uphill assault by Lockhart's men who, led by Major General Thomas Morgan, took the high dunes from Spanish veterans. Also, as the conflict continued and the Spanish allies strained before the onslaught, James led his life guards of English, Irish and Scots cavalry on repeated charges, risking his own life and also witnessing Henry have his sword struck from his arm, and his captain Charles Berkeley being wounded. In the end the victory for Turenne was complete as perhaps six thousand Spanish allies were killed or captured, compared with a mere 10 per cent of that number for the victors. The royalist battalions under Blaque and Muskerry were destroyed, and only that of Grace and Urry, which had been held in reserve in any case, was able to leave the field intact, though some of the soldiers were also captured. Less than half of James's 2,000 men left the field. Ten days after the battle, Dunkirk surrendered to Turenne and was given over to Cromwell as agreed in the Anglo-French treaty, and for the next few months Turenne's army, seemingly invincible, captured much of south west Flanders and it became clear to King Charles II and King Felipe IV of Spain that their alliance was incapable of delivering their respective objectives.[69] The Spanish solution was dead in the water and for Charles and James there seemed no other practical means to promote a restoration.

The remaining Spanish forces dispersed northwards to garrison various towns still in their control and James and the surviving royalists were given the task of holding the port of Nieupoort. There James, first in dual command with the unpleasant Spanish General Alonso, Marquis de Caracena, who James disliked, and then on his own, held the town for three months from skirmishing French forces, whose momentum had been temporarily slowed by news that King Louis had been taken ill with fever. Then, while at his post, news came to James in early September that God had moved to support the Stuart cause in a way that opportunistic diplomatic and military alliances had not. Cromwell had unexpectedly died and James, being at his own request relieved of his post on 11 September, made for Brussels to the court of his brother to join those exiles considering the implications of divine providence.[70]

Unbeknownst to James this departure was a watershed for quite another reason. His Spanish campaigns of 1657–8 were to prove his last in the European theatre, and the loving care he took in writing and preserving his military memoirs of the 1650s, and in ensuring the rendering of the text in French in 1695–6 and gifting it to the nephew of Turenne, Emmanuel-Théodose de la Tour d'Auvergne, Cardinal de Bouillon, show these to be the happiest days of his life.[71] The companionship of comrades and opponents, like Charles Berkeley, Newburgh, Rutherford, Condé, Lockhart, Schomberg and his beloved Turenne, confirm this in the mind of the soldier prince. This was underscored by the portrayal of James himself in his military memoirs and autobiography. James is not merely depicted as a brave solider, a frankly realistic and convincing picture, but also as a heroic and virtuous figure respected by friend and foe alike. The reaction of the French and English to James's service for Spain is the triumphant highpoint in this idealised image of the 'perfect' European prince. James recounts how in 1657 at the siege of Mardyke, French officers recognised him from a distance due to the large greyhound that accompanied him at all times, and how before long they had asked for a parley with him, and when they did so in large number, the Spanish officers with him looked on askance as the enemy fraternised with James out of respect for his reputation as a soldier. Soon after, the English commander John Reynolds, on seeing 'the civilities which the French took pleasure in showing the Duke of York when they found an opportunity of speaking with him', also wished to meet with James. Working through Newburgh his desire for an interview was met, and Reynolds was able to express his compliments and admiration for James, even though they were fighting on different sides. Some of these details are clearly exaggerated, at least in tone, and the notion that Reynolds was signalling a desire to switch sides, as James suggests, is somewhat fanciful for a Cromwellian loyalist, yet these events confirm James's wish to embrace the image of a soldier of virtue, and also the great store he placed in self-publicity. His own writings may be vital sources for the study of his life but are also unashamedly works of personal and family propaganda.[72] As for his particular reflection on the Battle of the Dunes, while it is too strong to say that he was obsessed with killing rather than with the bravery of the combatants, it is reasonable to conclude that James was less concerned with the sacrifices of the common soldier, and more to apportion blame for defeat than was Turenne in his account. Victors, of course, have the luxury of generosity, if they wish to deploy it. Turenne confirmed that the enemy commanders, including James, 'behv'd themselves very well', though they too were 'obliged to fly with the rest'. In particular, he was impressed with the fortitude of the enemy cavalry, some of whom were commanded by James.[73] Behind the myth there was a man.

FROM DESPAIR TO UNEXPECTED TRIUMPH

When James arrived in Brussels at his brother's side, there was great excitement at the prospects, with Cromwell dead and the perceived likelihood of republican division and confusion. Unfortunately it soon became clear that the transfer of power to Oliver's son Richard had passed remarkably smoothly, at least initially.

Those same conservative tendencies that might have welcomed a return to monarchy were initially happy enough to opt for the status quo under the Protectorate. Matters therefore turned again to promote some form of internal rebellion to encourage decisive foreign intervention, but in an atmosphere of military and financial exhaustion where Spain and even France needed a pause in hostilities.

The prospects for Stuart restorations, either in the 1650s or the 1740s, were ever compromised by the merry dance of continental support. Yet support at home was also difficult to galvanise and talk was cheap amongst royalists in the three kingdoms. Since the Battle of Worcester, the English Rump parliament, the army and Protectorate council had controlled England so effectively that royalism was almost totally eclipsed. A royalist conspiracy or society known as the 'Sealed Knot' (though sometimes the 'Select Knot' or 'Secret Knot') had been given royal approval since late 1653 and took shape early the following year. James was too busy on the battle fields of Europe to be involved in communications with this group, and that task was left to Hyde and Charles himself. But this society was as deeply divided on tactics as the exiled court, and as it split into factions, minor and futile uprisings took place in the summer of 1654. Further divisions led to the royalist Penruddock rising in Dorset and Wiltshire in March 1655, led by Colonel John Penruddock, the swift suppression of which was easily achieved, even though the perceived royalist threat encouraged Oliver Cromwell to introduce district rule by major generals.[74] Meanwhile in Ireland, the severity of army rule and the appointment of Henry, younger son of the Lord Protector, as Major General and Lord Lieutenant of Ireland from 1655 to 1659, delivered submission from that island.

In Scotland discontent with occupation by a foreign army and its regime, cooperated with by Argyll, encouraged a groundswell of support for a royalist rebellion from early 1653. Even Argyll's son Lord Lorne, a young Presbyterian who while abroad had grown strong royalist tendencies, became associated with a mainly Highland and old royalist group of nobles, many of whom had supported or sympathised with the 'royalist Covenanter' factions of Hamilton and Montrose. In November 1652, as James was engaged in the siege of Bar-le-Duc with Turenne, his elder brother received in Paris a messenger from Angus MacDonald of Glengarry who had set himself up as leader and spokesperson of various disaffected clans, loyalist certainly, but also driven to rebellion out of material necessity. After a few months of hesitancy and debate on how to handle this news, and reflecting on the fact that the English army in Scotland under Colonel Robert Lilburne had been depleted to fight the First Anglo-Dutch War (1652–4), commissions were sent to William Cunningham, eighth earl of Glencairn, to command a rebellion until Middleton, Charles's commander-in-chief in Scotland, could land in person. Glencairn had written personally confirming his willingness to serve and being a Lowlander, he seemed an ideal candidate to secure the widest possible support.[75]

By the summer of 1653 a full-scale revolt had developed led by Glencairn, Lorne, Glengarry and Alexander Lindsay, first earl of Balcarres, and Lilburne and his officers struggled to contain the rebel force which, by the end of the year, was raiding as far south as Carlisle.[76] However, at no time did the royalist force number much more than five thousand. Estimates of their numbers were exaggerated by the English officers looking for their superiors in London to provide more resources, and by the royalists themselves to encourage support from the exiled court. The Jacobite disease of imagined support was to be a Stuart malady of long standing. Certainly when Middleton arrived in February 1654 he was very disappointed with the progress of the rebellion and the size of his force, as were his new comrades with the few score soldiers and supplies he had brought with him. Initially, however, the arrival of their commander boosted the morale of the rebels, although Middleton then became aware of the chronic divisions that had affected them. This was brought into sharp focus when Glencairn and Middleton's second in command, Sir George Monro, fought a duel leading to the latter's serious injury, and Glencairn severing his own retinue from the main army. But it was the arrival of Monck to take up overall command in Scotland that transformed matters decisively in favour of the English occupiers. The Dutch War being over, Monck was given greater financial and manpower resources by London, and he now added the last piece of the suppressive jigsaw – legal measures, emerging from the Instrument of Government and Ordinance of Union under the Protectorate, to strangle sympathy and support within the civil population.[77]

In the early summer of 1654 Monck's regiments began a pursuit of Middleton's forces aided by a second detachment of troops under Thomas Morgan, who later at the Dunes would fight so admirably under Turenne. In a three-month period of counter-marching and criss-crossing the Highlands from Argyllshire to Aberdeenshire, Monck and Morgan chased Middleton until Morgan caught him and defeated his forces at Dalnaspidal near Loch Garry in Northern Perthshire on 19 July. Middleton's remaining forces were scattered and crucially lost hundreds of horses to the enemy. Subsequently, Monck carried out a severe campaign of harassment of the rebels and torched the countryside that offered them food and material support. This coupled with the atrocious winter of 1654/5 persuaded most to surrender on terms, and even the most ardent of royalists such as Glencairn and John Mackay, Lord Reay, had capitulated by May 1655, and the rebellion was over. Middleton himself, though wounded at Dalnaspidal, was able to avoid capture and fled for the Continent again in April, where in Cologne he briefed Charles on the debacle.[78] Middleton lingered just long enough in Scotland to hear of the abortive Penruddock rising in England, and to give his remaining comrades permission to surrender under the best conditions possible. All the letters of encouragement that Charles had sent from 1652 to 1655, including promises to come in person and even patriotic plans to secure the honours of Scotland from Dunnottar Castle and bring them away to safety, were inadequate without the actual arrival of the king and a foreign army. When he left Paris in April 1654, Charles may have asked James to manage his English affairs if he was to decide to enter Scotland again, but Hyde knew well that Charles was reluctant to repeat the debacle of 1650/1, and expose himself yet again to the insolence of Scottish Presbyterians. Charles's attitude to these 'fanatics' is seen in his treatment of the loyal Balcarres. This royalist Covenanter was in April 1654 one of the first to go into exile as the Glencairn rising faltered. Since then, he had joined Charles's court and, along with Newburgh, provided expert advice on Scottish affairs. However, when in March 1657 Charles heard that Balcarres had initiated a plan to draw up a declaration in Scotland that insisted Charles uphold the Covenant and appoint someone other than Middleton (now an Episcopalian) as commander for any future rebellions, he was dismissed and banished from court.[79] Yet in practical terms Charles was proved correct: Scottish Presbyterianism was no more likely to deliver a restoration than, as it turned out, a treaty with Spain.

In Brussels, in the aftermath of James's final Spanish campaign and the death of Cromwell in September 1658, the two brothers and the court debated how to take advantage of improving prospects. But the smooth transfer of power to Cromwell's son, and continental preoccupations with Franco-Spanish peace talks that opened by the end of the year, ensured a waiting game of almost twelve months before any concerted action to restore the monarchy by force. The six depleted royalist regiments were soon reconstituted and James was ready to do his part as commander-in-chief, but kings Louis and Felipe and their great ministers Mazarin and Don Luis de Haro had other fish to fry, even though the Spanish gave Charles a little money to tide him over the winter. Charles's great hope was that out of a peaceful Catholic Europe there might emerge a more focused and unified effort to restore him to power. In addition, communications were reopened with the royalist 'Sealed Knot' society through John Mordaunt, the young brother of the earl of Peterborough, and in February 1659 Charles authorised a new conspiracy – the 'Great Trust' – intended to unite English Presbyterians with the 'Sealed Knot' in a new, broad-based grouping.[80] Then in April and May 1659, the Protectorate ran into trouble at last. The Third Protectorate Parliament (27 January to 22 April) showed loyalty to the Protectorate, yet in April an army coup forced the dissolution of this assembly and reinstated the old Rump parliament of mostly republican individuals. During May, the Protectorate was abolished and Richard Cromwell was forced to resign. On hearing this news, Charles encouraged the new conspiracy to rise up, though yet again there were divisions and some of the 'Knot' would not cooperate. Nevertheless, he and James moved to Calais and Boulogne respectively, with the objective of finding ships to transport them separately to England once a rebellion was fully underway. When the rebellion came in July and August, it was not conveniently on the east coast, providing a safe landing for the royal brothers, but to the west. This was a Presbyterian, royalist affair led by Sir George Booth, which, although wide geographically and spreading to Cheshire, North

Wales and Lancashire, was quickly put down by the army under General John Lambert at Winnington Bridge, Cheshire, on 19 August. Before news of the defeat came to him James took that chance to meet his old master Turenne at Amiens and was offered, on behalf of Charles, Turenne's own regiment and the remaining *gens d'arms écossais*, as well as weapons, food and transports. Even though the bad news from England made these offers redundant, James was pleased that his relationship with Turenne was cordial despite the fact they had recently fought on opposite sides. The duke departed with a small loan for his trouble. Soon he was back in Brussels while the new setbacks spurred Charles to rush to Fuenterrabia, east of Bilbao, to witness the treaty between Louis and Felipe, known as the Peace of the Pyrenees, signed 7 November (New Style (NS)).[81] Being present gave Charles the opportunity to claim tenuous linkages between his restoration and Continental peace. At least he obtained a further sum of money from Spain, although certainly no indication from the Spanish or the French of any willingness to plan an invasion.[82] Peace also meant an end to the profitable campaigning of his brother James who, unable to pay his troops, meet his debts and envision any prospects for the future, cut a despondent figure in Brussels and Bruges over the coming months. His need to rely on Charles for money did not help matters.

James put it succinctly when he described that in early 1660 'the hopes concerning England [were] now reduced to the lowest ebb'. The 'Knot' collapsed under the treachery of one of its own associates, Sir Richard Willis. Nevertheless, James's own reputation as a military man who had fought with and against the great generals of his age, Turenne and Condé, made him a convincing beneficiary and bringer of patronage, the latter on account of his ability to attract the service of English, Irish and Scottish soldiers and, of course, seamen. This was confirmed when the Spanish made the remarkable offer to appoint him High Admiral of Spain or *Principe de la Mare,* a position normally kept within the Spanish royal family and close relations. Although James was titular High Admiral of England, for someone with little naval experience, a foreigner and a Protestant, this looks an astonishing appointment, although it is fairly clear that it was seen as honorific and was accepted by James, with Charles's approval, for the associated prestige and pension rather than a likelihood of command under fire. Spain was, however, still at war with Portugal. In the end James's willingness to accept the post was surely out of financial desperation as well but also, as Turner suggests, a sign that he 'contemplated permanent exile' as a mercenary. A suggestion that the duke of Gloucester could take the position instead was not taken seriously by the exiled court or the Spanish.[83] James was fortunate that his good relations with de Haro compensated for the mutual animosity between himself and Caracena, recently made governor of the Spanish Netherlands instead of the dismissed Don Juan.

News emanating from England in the winter of 1659/60 did not appear especially optimistic for Charles and James. The Rump Parliament and the republican army had cooperated uneasily until Booth's rising had been defeated and then divisions crystallised around who would command the army, whether it should be replaced by a militia and the purging of supporters of the Protectorate. The army officers in England would not accept this and the lack of movement on their own agenda of reforms, and forcibly dissolved the Rump in October. However, it became clear over the next few months that Monck in Scotland would not accept this dissolution. Put plainly, although driven more by practical rather than philosophical considerations, he could live with rule by protectors or kings or parliaments, but not by army officers, and he soon gathered his forces to march southwards. It appeared to Charles and his court that Monck might have had his eye on the ultimate prize to be the new Cromwell, yet from late 1659 he began hesitant negotiations with Charles through the good offices of Sir John Grenville, a king's man who had been a clandestine intermediary for royalist plotters, governor of the Isles of Scilly for Charles and his father, and, importantly, was a cousin of the general. But some, including James, thought that Lambert was just as likely an ally as Monck. There had been royalist communication with Lambert since his dismissal by Cromwell in July 1657, and even a proposal that James marry his eldest daughter.[84] Either way James remained convinced until late April 1660 that a restoration by force of arms was the only certain and honourable way to secure royal objectives.

Monck's army finally entered England on New Year's Day 1660 and, joined by the great Model Army General Sir Thomas Fairfax, who had come out of retirement, began a slow march to London to take control of a confused situation. His slow pace allowed opposition to melt away as even the popular Lambert could not convince enough men to oppose him. Having arrived in London in early February, Monck initially supported the Rump but soon also added those purged in 1648, which included a number of royalist Presbyterians rather than republicans.[85] Then remarkably, after Grenville visited Monck in March and delivered letters of encouragement from Charles, Monck in turn indicated his terms, and then engineered the calling of free elections and the dissolution of the Long Parliament which had first sat in 1640. This paved the way for a new royalist Convention and the restoration of the House of Lords and the monarchy. All that was required of Charles by Monck was that he relocate away from Spanish territory to Breda, and proclaim a declaration that offered a general pardon and amnesty for actions against the crown during the Civil War and Interregnum; accepted the claim of the army to arrears of pay; recognised the importance of taking advice from a free parliament, and agreed a degree of religious toleration. Thus the Declaration of Breda was created, a document seen to deliver more constitutional reassurance for England than Scotland's Breda declaration of 1650 offered to the restoration in the northern kingdom.[86] Hyde's pen was behind the blitzkrieg of letters from Charles to almost any member of the English Parliament or army and naval officer whose influence might smooth the Restoration, as also in the drafting of the 1660 declaration. Men who had fought against Charles I over religion held out hope from the words:

we do declare a liberty to tender consciences, and that no man shall be
disquieted or called in question for differences of opinion in matter of
religion, which do not disturb the peace of the kingdom.[87]

Nevertheless, these words were meticulously drafted by Charles, Hyde, Nicholas,
Ormonde, and James, no longer excluded from affairs. Those Presbyterians returning to Westminster who hoped for a Presbyterian church and a restricted monarchy
were to be disappointed. Their ideals were swept aside in the clamour to participate in a festival of royalism. Essentially though, as many a modern general election
rejects the unpopular party in power, delight at the return of monarchy was
drowned out by relief at the end of the republic with all its military rigour and
religious prudery. In terms of James's character, as it would develop in middle age,
this was extremely ironic.

When the autumn 1659 invasion plan petered out, James returned to Brussels
in December – he remained there for six months, one of the longest periods of
time in years he had been at court with his brother.[88] The long absences on military
campaigns kept him a little removed from the jealousies and jostling for position
at court. His return with his small, impoverished entourage reactivated some old
animosities that had begun a decade before. The court had three major internal
and interrelated problems other than prosecuting the diplomatic and military
effort and struggling with mounting debts and poor liquidity: the composition of
Charles's court, James's household and relations within the royal family. The last of
these involved the Queen Mother, Mary, and her two older brothers, but ironically
one of the most explosive arguments concerned young Henry, duke of Gloucester.

In 1649 Henrietta Maria had tried, unsuccessfully, to persuade James and
Charles that the best means to achieve a restoration was for them both to convert
to the Catholic faith before a planned invasion of the British Isles through Ireland.
Up to 1660, and indeed until her death in August 1669, she favoured linking her
family to Catholic Europe, especially France, by diplomacy and by marriage, but
also by planting her faith within the family. Charles and James were unimpressed
with her proselytising and supported each other over this. Both understood the
political disaster that would befall them if they adopted a religion anathema even
to the moderate Protestants of England and Scotland. During their period of exile,
the religious beliefs of James (to be considered later) and of Charles were not
dramatically swayed by experiencing occasional Masses or the hospitality of various French monastic houses. Curiosity should not be confused with willingness to
convert. Also, too much should not be read into Charles's letters to the papacy
seeking money in exchange for the promised toleration of Catholicism if his family
was restored. There is, of course, some dispute over the extent of the brothers'
interest in Catholicism during the 1650s but, as Hutton convincingly argues, one
piece of evidence appears incontrovertible. Charles's instructions in 1658 to the
Irish Catholic Sir Richard Bellings, who was secretly negotiating support from

Rome through Charles Stuart, tenth Seigneur d'Aubigny (who later became Duke of Lennox and Richmond), the exiled French Cardinal de Retz, with whom Charles had various conferences, and Cardinal Francesco Barberini, 'Protector of the three Kingdoms at the Court of Rome', confirm that Charles would 'neither [through] conscience or discretion' convert but nor would he 'incline to persecute Catholikes or Catholik religion'.[89] There is no evidence from the decade that James thought of converting either, and his loyalty to his brother's insistence on this point would have prevented such an action in any case. But one of the biggest family disputes concerned their mother's attempt to convert James's younger brother Henry in late 1654 when he was fourteen years old. Henry was with his mother in Paris while Charles and his court had moved to Cologne; leaving the boy behind proved unwise. In October Henrietta Maria suddenly dismissed the boy's Protestant tutor, and placed Henry in the abbey of Saint-Martin at Pointoise, under her confessor, the English exile Walter Montagu, second son of the Earl of Manchester and abbot of Nanteuil, to facilitate his Catholic education. Henry resisted but when Charles heard about it, he reacted in fury writing to his mother, Lord Jermyn and Henry saying that they would never see or have contact with him again if this was allowed to continue. James had been asked by Charles to specifically watch out for such interference by their mother when he went to Cologne in July, although James was in the field with Turenne from July until November and when he returned his mother refused him permission to speak alone with Henry. Ormonde was despatched to remove Henry to Cologne and then to the safekeeping of their sister Mary at The Hague. Lord d'Aubigny's 1658 prescription for the catholicising of the royal family included the observation that the forbidding of Henry's conversion had severely damaged Charles's cause in the eyes of Rome, and the fact that his sister Henrietta-Anne was being brought up a Catholic in Paris by their mother made all wonder at his stubbornness. However, although Charles made some effort to secure his little sister as well, he insisted that the religion of the three brothers was another matter, and all three were united in remaining Anglican throughout the 1650s. Their sister Mary was shocked at 'this great misfortune that is likly to fall upon our family'. The relationship of the Queen Mother to her sons and eldest daughter could be strained but this was certainly a low point. More generally, this is seen in the fact that when Charles met his mother at Saint-Colombe in December 1659 when returning from Fuenterrabia, they had not seen each other for six years. It was at this meeting that Charles reacquainted himself with his little sister Henrietta-Anne, now fifteen, and began a decade of close and affectionate correspondence, regardless of religion. Charles sometimes called her 'Minnete' as a term of endearment and appeared to exclude others from this intimate world, including James.[90]

The question of the composition of James's household also raised itself again from time to time, especially when he returned to court between military campaigns. In the field, Sir John Berkeley, Charles Berkeley and young Henry

Jermyn (from 1656) were his constant companions, but this grouping was not popular with Charles and his advisors. Religion was not particularly the issue, for although Jermyn was a Catholic, like his uncle Lord Jermyn, the Berkeleys were not, in spite of contemporary rumours to the contrary. Although Mary and Charles had been devoted siblings since 1648, with James part of their circle and Mary doing all she could to help the brothers' financial plight, tensions increased when in April 1656 Charles struck his alliance with the Spanish. The Spanish Netherlands and the Dutch Republic were, after all, implacable enemies. For once Mary and her pro-French mother were on the same side of the argument. Furthermore, James was initially very unhappy over the Spanish initiative as it was agreed without his involvement and left him, if he entered Spanish service, in the position of opposing his mentor Turenne, 'one of the men in the world [he was] most obliged to'.[91]

Charles in turn was angered at James's claim that he had already agreed to serve with the French and it would be dishonourable to jump ship. Then James stated that he would only change his mind if an actual commission was forthcoming from the Spanish. Charles promptly insisted that his brother abandon his commitment to the French and attend him in Brussels as soon as possible, or in Bruges, which became from May the headquarters of the exiled court. However, James lingered in Paris throughout the summer unwilling to give up his French pension and his chance to serve again with his hero. Charles then sent Sir Henry Bennet, still nominally James's secretary but who had just assisted Charles in setting up in Bruges, to bring James to the court. Initially James refused. He had grown to despise the bombastic Bennet who he regarded, with justification, as being completely of his brother's interest. Sir George Radcliffe was also back again in Paris trying to ingratiate himself with James and agreeing too readily with Bennet. James suspected Bennet and Radcliffe of designs on removing those he most trusted, the Berkeleys and Jermyn. So it proved, when Bennet hinted heavily that Sir John Berkeley was not welcome at court and should be dismissed. James ignored this – when he eventually travelled to Bruges in September he took Berkeley with him much to Charles's irritation. By now, Hyde, Bennet and Bristol (at the time Charles's most important councillor as a Spanish linguist and expert) set about with gusto undermining Sir John. James's favourite was certainly unlikable. The slur developed was that Berkeley, building on diplomatic contacts with the Army established in the late 1640s, had been communicating with the enemy in England, and was also encouraging James to set up his own party to challenge Charles. Mary, who had been in Bruges since November, took James's side, feeling he was being harshly dealt with and unjustly excluded from decisions made by the king and Hyde. Yet before long, her brother was ordered by Charles to dismiss Berkeley. This James appeared to do in January 1657. However, finding that resentment at these threats to his independence had mastered his loyalty, he and his inner circle fled in haste from Bruges two days later, met up with Sir John and left the Spanish Netherlands for Holland, with a view to skirting by land or sea back to France and French service. Mary claimed no knowledge of this wild scheme but Charles himself was astonished and appalled at this turn of events. Not only was unity in the family vital but James's military reputation and loyal soldiery was essential to the Spanish initiative. His brother was needed at his side for diplomatic as well as family reasons. Ormonde and other courtiers were swiftly despatched to try to locate James, and Charles and Hyde went into overdrive composing conciliatory letters. James wrote to Charles from Zulestein near Utrecht, where he had taken up lodgings, to explain his loyalty and that he would sacrifice 'all interest but that of [his] honour', and that was the point. When in late January James dictated the terms for his return, in a stark eleven-point list of complaints and five-point list of conditions, including a demand for respect for his person by Charles's court, respect for his servants, the reinstatement of Berkeley, removal of Bennet from his household and most important, direct communications with Charles if problems arose rather than working through intermediaries, Charles conceded to all his demands, other than insisting that Berkeley delay return for a month. Soon James was back at Bruges; Bennet was conveniently sent to Madrid as ambassador to Spain (though Charles was already of a mind to do this); Berkeley was, after submission to the king, made a peer which calmed his wilder plans for self-aggrandisement; and even Bristol, Berkeley and James developed a *modus vivendi*. As for Turner's claim that 'nothing could save James from swallowing the very bitter pill of selling his sword to Spain', the confirmation soon of his appointment as lieutenant general and his command of six Irish, English and Scottish regiments soon added sweetness.[92]

In the course of 1657, then, relative peace broke out among the factions at court, although significantly, James and especially Charles had learnt important lessons about communication and consultation within the family. That did not, of course, stop occasional rifts over other matters. For example, on hearing that in early 1658 Mary had become infatuated with the charms of young Henry Jermyn when he and James visited her at Breda, Charles gave unwelcome advice to send him away, which she soon did. However, his sister thought that such public criticism was unnecessary over a small domestic matter and was peeved at her brother's interference. Mary, like James, was determined to exercise independent judgement, as seen in early autumn of 1657 in her welcoming, much to Charles's displeasure, of the discredited Balcarres to her court, and her making his good wife a lady-in-waiting. It is also of interest that even the duke of Gloucester took James's part in his dispute with Charles in 1656/7.[93] It seems that the family authority exercised by Charles needed the restoration of monarchy in his kingdoms before compromise could be achieved between willing siblings and a less censorious Charles.

In the years leading up to the Restoration Sir Edward Hyde dominated the royal court and this was emphasised by his appointment as Chancellor in January

1658. Nicholas, still secretary, was respected but less influential and matters were mostly decided between Hyde, the grandee Ormonde and the young king. Bristol was rewarded for his success in the Spanish negotiations of 1656 by being restored to the post of senior Secretary of State which he had under Charles I, but his conversion to Catholicism ended that position and his influence in 1659. From the resolution of the Berkeley affair, however, James became, when not at war, part of this inner circle – Charles would not make again the mistake of excluding him. In Scottish affairs though, Charles turned to Middleton and Newburgh, although of course the latter was prone to aggressive behaviour and duelling. Middleton had received his earldom in 1656 and had carried out a range of embassies to Danzig, Poland, Brandenburg and Saxony from 1656 to 1658, but by 1659 he was back at court as chief Scottish advisor. He had, since they met in 1652, come under the influence of Hyde, both politically and religiously, and represented a strong and at times resentful Episcopalian interest. Newburgh had signed the Covenant in 1651 but was no more inclined to be restricted by its tenets than Middleton or Charles. The eclipse of Balcarres removed a Presbyterian interest from the court which was not replaced. If the likes of Lauderdale or Crawford-Lindsay had been in exile rather than prison, they too would have found it difficult to maintain a Scottish Presbyterian interest at court in the face of Charles's animosity, encouraged by Hyde. Ironically, as the negotiations took place over a restoration in early 1660, English Presbyterian support was seen as crucial by Charles and the court. Overall, in spite of the efforts of a few wilder spirits, like the Irish Jesuit Peter Talbot who promoted a Presbyterian and Catholic agenda in England with James at the head, by now the court was more united than at any time since 1649.[94] Queen Henrietta Maria, Lord Jermyn and the 'Louvre' group were emasculated by the Spanish alliance, and when that too failed, they never recovered the initiative. Charles, with James by his side, was fully in charge of policy.

There has been much written about the immorality and extravagance of the exiled court and contemporaries such as Ormonde and Hyde despaired at Charles's 'immoderate' and 'vulgar' conversations which increasingly dominated his social interaction.[95] But some courtiers, such as the Irishman Theobald, Viscount Taaffe, seem virtually to have acted as royal pimps for the king's various amorous adventures, of which there are too many to estimate with accuracy. Famously, the 'very handsom' Lucy Walter, as James himself described her, who was the mother of James Scott, duke of Monmouth, Charles's oldest illegitimate son, was Charles's mistress, and was so on and off for three years from 1648 to 1650. However, his first mistress was perhaps Marguerite Carteret in Jersey in 1646, and his first sexual encounter was probably with his former nurse, Lady Christabel Wyndham, the year before when he was fifteen years old.[96] For James, the first sexual encounter is not so easily traced. He was in exile from fourteen to twenty-six years of age and it would not be unusual for a young courtier, let alone an active soldier, to seek the solace of the various entertainments that Paris or Brussels could offer. In fact,

James was never as heavy a drinker as his brother, but his sexual appetite was probably equally as developed in these years in the company of men like Charles Berkeley or Henry Jermyn.

The most significant liaison established by James when in exile was with Anne Hyde, eldest daughter of Sir Edward Hyde, Charles's chief minister. Anne left England with her mother and siblings in 1649, when she was twelve years old, and from then until at least 1653 they lived mostly in Antwerp, with occasional visits to Brussels.[97] In 1652 Anne visited for the first time the court of Mary at The Hague and, making an impression, two years later became at the age of eighteen one of her maids of honour. A year later, when Mary visited her mother in Paris, Anne met James for the first time. His unwillingness to join Charles in the Spanish Netherlands may in part have been due to his early fascination with Anne. But when James moved to the royal court in Bruges and Brussels he was able to make regular visits to court Anne, and in November 1659 at Breda, they had contracted with each other to marry. While the secret contract remained just that, Henrietta Maria had already, out of her hatred of Anne's father, pressed Princess Mary to dismiss Anne. In this she was unsuccessful as she was in one of her missions in England after the Restoration intended to break the relationship between Anne and her son. By then James was, after Charles, the prime candidate for a major European wedding to the benefit of the family, the succession and, as the Queen Mother saw it, a revival of her Catholic and pro-French policies.[98] As it was, by the spring of 1660 Anne discovered she was pregnant through James before she embarked with the royal party for London. When there, pressure grew on James to make a decision on whether to marry her formally and declare her his wife, or to label her a mistress, which perhaps his duty to his family dictated. Hyde himself was appalled and would have preferred the status of 'mistress' to, from his own perspective, the politically dangerous 'royal wife'. At first James begged his brother to approve the wedding and, though reluctant for reasons their own mother would understand, he relented. Therefore, at midnight on 3 September 1660, a mere six weeks before their child was born, they were married secretly by James's Anglican chaplain James Crowther with as witnesses Thomas Butler, sixth earl of Ossory, son of Ormonde, and Ellen Stroude, one of Anne's maids. Then, remarkably, James changed his mind and began to 'deny that he was [already] married', or that an original contract had been struck between him and Anne in 1659. Charles Berkeley, Henry Jermyn and several of James's circle, if the exiled Frenchman Philibert, comte de Grammont, is to be believed, took it upon themselves to spread tales that she had warmed their beds as well as his, and so was not a suitable wife for a prince – the child could not certainly be attributed to their master. As all seemed lost for the wedding to be accepted, with Hyde and Henrietta Maria still implacably opposed, and Mary also seeing James as foolish, an ashamed Berkeley admitted his falsehoods and Charles finally stepped in and insisted the marriage be recognised. We can conjecture his reasoning as a combination of expecting decent treatment for the girl and humour at his brother's predicament, but Charles's perception that James was genuinely fond of Anne cannot be discounted, and nor can his realisation that the one shaft of truth illuminating the affair was Anne herself. Even Henrietta Maria came around, a letter from Mazarin warning her not to alienate the king and his court with any more outraged tantrums which would hinder more important diplomatic objectives. An offer by Hyde to manage her debts also sweetened the pill. By January the new duchess of York was presented to the wider court and Hyde was soon made earl of Clarendon. It had been a difficult period for the royal family as well as the Hydes – the duke of Gloucester died of smallpox in the previous September and his sister Mary, who had come to London to do honour to Charles and also to press him to support the claims of her young son William, did likewise in December.[99] Both deaths were sudden and unexpected, and James and Charles were especially distressed at the passing of Henry, cut off in his prime at only twenty years, and the Queen Mother at the death of her daughter, in spite of their differences. It was a season for tragedy and farce. In May, Anne and James's baby son, named Charles, duke of Cambridge, died at barely six months old.

When the elite norm was not to marry below station but to set up mistresses comfortably and move on, this whole affair of James's first marriage was without doubt a contemporary scandal. Importantly, the circumstances point to a lifelong weakness of James when presented with conflicting loyalties, and also his willingness to accept too readily unwise advice from well-meaning and loyal friends and courtiers. These characteristics would become more dangerous for James as his preoccupations moved from soldiering to the world of politics. Soon after the wedding, James continued his womanising, he having, as Grammont's biographer described it, 'quieted his conscience by the declaration of his marriage, thought that he was entitled, by this generous effort, to give way a little to his inconstancy'.[100] In this respect, he lived as the other princes of Europe, including his brother Charles and soon enough his cousin, Louis XIV.

Charles's transformation from titular king to Louis's of reigning sovereign was achieved with remarkable swiftness. In Scotland Thomas Morgan, who had been sent back to Edinburgh by Monck to command forces there, kept order as the transfer of power took place. Monck had in November at Edinburgh and in December at Berwick convened two assemblies of shire and burgh representatives to discuss the changing political situation in a Scottish context. The talks were inconclusive and Monck had to break off and make his march southwards, but one clear sign from these meetings was the resurgent position of the nobility who, being allowed to participate, dominated the shire elections and took control of negotiations. Monck agreed that a third assembly could gather again in Edinburgh on 2 February to draw up grievances and priorities, yet, unhappy with the vacuum in the absence of Monck, in April the nobles convened a meeting without his authority. While noble domination was again reflected in the electoral process, general frustration was evident in the beginnings of frantic communication with senior Scots in London.[101] Meanwhile the Scots cleric James Sharp, a moderate 'resolutioner' Presbyterian who had come to terms with Monck, was in London from February when the general took control of the city, and, pushing at an open door, pressed for the release of Scottish prisoners. Soon Lauderdale and Crawford-Lindsay were released and reporting to loyalists in Edinburgh galvanised by Glencairn. In April Charles wrote from Brussels to encourage Lauderdale – 'I am very glad you are at liberty, and in a place where you can do most service', and shortly after Sharp was on a boat to Breda to see his king with a letter of recommendation from the earl and a briefing from Monck. Lauderdale soothed English Presbyterian sensitivities, writing reassuringly to one of their leading clerics Richard Baxter – '[Charles] the elder brother I know to be wise and just . . . [James] I am confident is not what it seems he is by his enemies reported to be', and with some success, even though it became clear that proceeding on the basis of the Solemn League and Covenant was impossible. The Presbyterians in London blinked and it was all over. Lauderdale soon followed Sharp to Breda, and on to The Hague to renew his friendship with Charles. In Edinburgh an assembly met in February and agreed to send a noble-dominated group of commissioners to London. However, the next month they found it increasingly difficult to make headway on Scottish grievances and representation in decision making, and when, as a holding measure, Monck agreed in early May to set up an army council in Edinburgh under Morgan and three colonels, with a small appointed judiciary the majority of whom were English, a full restoration settlement in Scotland seemed a long way off.[102] The temporary executive was approved of by Charles and would administer Scotland until August. Although Scotland had begun the revolution against monarchy, it would be in England where it would finally be brought to an end.

On 8 May 1660 the Convention Parliament in London, convened two weeks before, declared Charles rightful king since 1649 and the death of his father – both houses the week before had voted unanimously for the restoration of monarchy. By 14 May the English fleet under Admiral Edward Montagu, who in spite of his Cromwellian past could like Monck see the practical benefits of a restoration, was anchored off the coast of Scheveningen near The Hague. Representatives of the army, including Fairfax, of the Westminster Parliament, the City of London, as well as various foreign ambassadors and a small band of Scots leaders and opportunists, made their way to The Hague where the States General had put on a week-long festival of celebration in honour of Charles and his family. Then on 22 May, James himself experienced his own symbolic restoration and one of particular poignancy. He came aboard to inspect the fleet, and was welcomed as Lord High Admiral by Montagu, his captains and a gun salute – on 16 May Charles had formally reconfirmed James's naval status. James sat with the commanders and Montagu's secretary, Samuel Pepys, from whom a vivid account is rendered, and confirmed the arrangements for sailing to England the following day. The next morning Charles and his brothers rode to the quayside through tens of thousands of well-wishers and then were rowed, along with the Princess Royal, the Prince of Orange and the Queen of Bohemia, who would disembark before sailing, out to Montagu's flagship. The vessel was called the *Naseby*, although that day it was renamed the *Royal Charles,* and later the figurehead of Cromwell was hacked off to help expunge the past.[103] On the morning of 25 May, after breakfast, the former exiles disembarked at Dover and were immediately met by Monck who, calm in a sea of frantic rejoicing, was not merely greeted warmly but treated like a father figure by the three brothers. Charles and his entourage travelled to London via Canterbury, Rochester and Blackheath where the army was drawn up by Monck for royal inspection, perhaps also to remind the Stuarts of who had delivered them back to power. They could have proceeded with more haste yet on 29 May, in inspired choreography, Charles entered London on the day of his thirtieth birthday to the acclaim of huge crowds, church bells and more deafening ordinance. It took seven hours to get to Whitehall and the royal party were quietly bemused by the marvel of it all. The diarist Sir John Evelyn, a former exile, recorded his own reactions to Restoration day: 'I stood in the strand, and beheld it, and blessed God: And all this without one drop of bloud, and by that very army, which rebell'd'. For Pepys – another eyewitness – 'the shouting and joy expressed by all [was] past imagination'.[104] As for James, he had returned to the three kingdoms the most important individual after his brother, a status that was emphasised when only months later Henry died. In 1660 James was at least as popular as Charles and from the point of view of the succession, in England, Scotland and Ireland, a reassuring presence.

CHAPTER 3

Restored King and Duke: James the 'Careerist', 1660–1685

HOUSEHOLD AFFAIRS

W hile Scotland's elite, and especially the nobility, took as much control as they could of the political implications of the Restoration, the rejoicing that greeted the return of the king of Scots to British shores was demonstrably popular in nature. The testimony of the chronicler and Edinburgh writer to the signet John Nicoll shows this clearly. Nicoll's surviving diary, covering 1650 to 1667, graphically describes how on the proclamation of Charles's return on 14 May 1660, Edinburgh responded through 'ringing of bellis, setting out of bailfyres, sounding of trumpetis, roring of cannounes, touking of drumes, [and] dancing about the fyres'.[1] After this spontaneous rejoicing an official day of thanksgiving on 19 June was presided over by Morgan and the army council who, to the discomfort of many, lingered in Scotland for several months before the fate of the English forces was determined and the composition of the administration of Scotland was agreed upon in London. For that day in June, however, old animosities were set aside, and in Edinburgh:

> the Magistrates . . . and the Commoune Consell wer present, all of thame
> in thair best robis; the [chancellor's] great mace and sword of honor
> careyed befoir thame to the sermond, and throw the haill streitis as they
> went, all that day. And eftir the sermond endit, . . . [they] went to the
> Mercat Croce of Edinburgh, . . . and thair drank the Kinges helth, and his
> brether; the spoutes of the Croce rynnand all that tyme with abundance of
> clareyt wyne . . . And in the meantyme, quhyll thai wer thus feasting at the
> Croce, the haill bellis in Edinburgh and Cannogait did reing, the drumes
> did beatt, trumpettis foundit, the haill troupes on horsbak, and sodgeris on
> fute being also with in the toun at this tyme and upone service, with the
> haill inhabitantes, both men, wemen, and chyldrene, gave thair severall

volyes . . . at nycht thair wes bonefyres put outthrow the haill streitis of
Edinburgh, and fyre workis both thair and at the Castell of Edinburgh,
and within the Citidaill of Leith that nicht, in abundance, till eftir xij
houris and moir.[2]

Back in London Scottish matters could not have been further from James's mind.
While Charles, with the advice of Edward Hyde, Chancellor, key minister now
and, from April 1661, earl of Clarendon, set about forming administrations and
handling the tricky questions of indemnities, necessary but limited retribution
and church settlements in three kingdoms, James was preoccupied with household
and family. That James was focused on private not public affairs may be understandable given the long-awaited end to his years as a nomad, but it makes a
strange contrast with his contemporary image in royalist propaganda as the selfless
soldier and loyal brother. One anonymous 'life' published in 1660 extolled the
virtues of James's 'courage' and 'fraternal love' although these qualities were not
greatly deployed in public view.[3] Charles himself was no workaholic when it came
to matters of state. The assessment of George Savile, marquis of Halifax, that
ministers, including himself as privy councillor from 1672 and Keeper of the Privy
Seal from 1682 to 1685, had to 'administer business to [Charles] as doctors do
physic, [and so] wrap it up in something to make it less unpleasant', accurately
describes the king's temperament.[4] However, with Clarendon's guidance, Charles
understood that more commitment was required in the first few years of the
Restoration while satisfactory political settlements were embedded. Meanwhile,
for most of the 1660s James's approach to politics boiled down to supporting
whatever his brother did and taking advice from Charles's first servant, Clarendon.
This last aspect was a mixed blessing. By January 1661 it was common knowledge
that Clarendon was also James's father-in-law, and even though his wife's father
was the lightening rod for a political jealousy that claimed he was feathering his
own nest, James's association with the Hydes also came with some political difficulties, in part because there was now a new factor in court circles, his wife Anne.
While James suffered some humiliating jibes as a result of the farcical circumstances of his marriage to a mere commoner, the death of Henry, duke of Gloucester
in September 1660, leaving James the sole male heir, and the dignity with which
Anne conducted herself, soon saw James recover his own dignity and reputation.
Also, in that first year of reconciliation he became the natural focus for those royalists who wished a harsher line over Cromwellian collaborators. They resented the
inclusive negotiations adopted by Charles and Clarendon which brought some
Presbyterians and Cromwellian soldiers into the English government. Monck,
created duke of Albermarle in July 1660, was understandable, yet why so many
others? In this respect James was soon established as the leader of a high Anglican
and old loyalist interest, but this also reflected one of his lifelong character traits, a
tendency to be unforgiving. In the words of Burnet, James was 'a firm friend but a

heavy enemy, and [kept] things long in his mind and [waited] for a fit opportunity'. Paradoxically, in spite of this 'revengeful' quality, James retained an admiration for those who returned to the fold, though he would only 'receive an enemy upon an absolute submission' with no half measures. James had a complex personality but a black and white view of loyalty.[5]

As political negotiations were underway in England between Charles and the English Convention Parliament, with the Scottish elite in Edinburgh and London feeling semi-detached as even the settlement in Ireland appeared to be making more progress, James set up his new household. For most of the next quarter century, both the households of king and duke, the two 'families', lived at the palace of Whitehall. The labyrinthine complex of over 1,500 rooms offered adequate accommodation for both, as well as the smaller households of the respective wives and the many retainers, including several mistresses. When Charles stayed at Windsor Castle, seen as a safe, fortified place during security anxieties, James's entourage often followed, and did so on occasions when the king camped at Tunbridge in Kent to take the waters of the famous well. From 1666 the brothers began visiting Newmarket in Suffolk together to enjoy horseracing in the spring and autumn seasons for two to three weeks at a time, and frequently with their wives and numerous courtiers.[6] Visiting Scottish supplicants, advisors and officers of state, such as the primate of the Scottish Church or the Scottish Secretary, had no choice but to travel to Newmarket with the brothers and their retinues although, in the natural order of things, it was mostly Charles's wake which had to be scurried after. While from 1660 to 1685 James's political influence waxed and waned, Charles's remained constant. Newmarket was an opportunity for shared fraternal entertainment over horsemanship and horse ownership, even though James was always more interested, and obsessively so, in hunting than racing. Soon after Prince George of Denmark married his niece Princess Anne in 1683, Charles advised the new husband, in a typical bawdy moment, that the best way to cure his fatness was to 'walk with him, hunt with his brother and do justice on his niece' and as Charles was renowned for walking at astonishing speed, James for hunting with ferocious enthusiasm and both for their insatiable sexual appetites, poor George could only struggle in comparison.[7]

Diversions other than purely equestrian pastimes were also available at Newmarket, including hawking, cock fighting and, in inclement weather, the 'new' card game of basset, a Venetian creation brought over from France in the 1670s, and at which James's daughter Anne and second wife, Mary of Modena, were extremely accomplished. There James could, and as often as possible did, satisfy his obsession with fox hunting, and was always there at the kill when others had fallen from their rides or faltered because of the terrain. The brothers were both excellent horsemen. Also in the 1670s, with or without Charles, James often diverted southwards to Winchester, near Portsmouth and the fleet, where hare hunting with beagles, which Mary and Anne much enjoyed, stag hunting and 'hawkes every day' were common activities. But when not at Newmarket or Whitehall, James summered at St James's Palace, the place of his birth. In effect this was his official, business residence and some of his household remained there when he decamped to his apartments at Whitehall. To complete James's residential portfolio he kept permanent apartments at Hampton Court Palace and also used Richmond Palace, ten miles west as the crow flies from Westminster, as a country retreat. This Tudor ensemble was gifted to James by Charles in 1664 and became the nursery for James's children by Duchess Anne but was also where their two young sons, both dukes of Cambridge, died before their fourth birthdays.[8] Richmond Park, with its deer and game was a clear attraction to James but the acres of St James's Park were quite different. From the Restoration they became Charles's pet landscape project with artificial waterways and exotic wildlife.

James had also to create his own household. Unlike Charles, who at once, and generally throughout his reign, realised the need for an inclusive government and entourage which embraced loyalists and some of those tainted with the Interregnum, he could allow his prejudices full expression and appoint those servants who were with him in exile or those individuals conspicuous for military valour and sacrifice. Those companions who were part of his exiled court, such as Charles Berkeley and Henry Jermyn, pressed on James to not only have a household but to do so in the French grand manner, where the younger brothers of French kings had an establishment almost as large as that of the monarch.[9] James had first-hand knowledge of this from the household of Phillipe, Duc d'Orléans, brother of Louis XIV, who married his younger sister Henrietta-Anne in 1661. In fact, by 1662 James's household consisted of more than a hundred servants with an additional thirty or so for his wife. The numbers were supplemented following the death of the duke of Gloucester in 1660 after which the late brother's household servants were redeployed to those of his older brothers.[10]

James's relationship with his servants reflected his military background where commander and junior officers shared mutual respect, assumed common cause, and advice given upward was trusted as genuine. This was not conducive to practical efficiency in the management of servants. The Florentine philosopher and political neutral Lorenzo Magalotti, who toured northern Europe with Cosimo de' Medici, Grand Duke of Tuscany, and visited the English court in 1668/9, described James's connection to his servants with some perceptiveness:

> [James] has not much penetration into political affairs because his rough and impatient spirit does not let him stop for long to examine things, but makes him follow his first impulses blindly. Nevertheless, he is very often influenced by people, and once he has chosen [his servants] it is not easy for him to free himself from their sway; his mind is always like wax, ready to receive and retain indelibly every slight impression of their ideas, without considering whether these proceed from reason, or from

self-interest, or malignity or ambition. To everyone except these people he is inflexible, no matter if they come armed not only with reason, but with evidence itself.

Others came to have similar views. Clarendon, who knew intimately the behaviour of both princes and had little reason to flatter either, concluded that 'if [James] seemed to be more firm and fixed in his resolutions [than Charles], it was rather from an obstinacy in his will, which he defended by aversion from the debate, than from the constancy of his judgment, which was more subject to persons [his servants] than to arguments'.[11] The ironic position of a master who disliked debate but relied on the input of his close advisors, made life difficult for the majority of James's servants and encouraged a contraction to small-group advice, or government by 'cabinet' council, that in the 1680s would prove fatal for James's political fortunes in England and Scotland. Before then, however, the Restoration represented continuity in James's life, with servants treated as in the 1650s yet within the context of a larger household, extended patronage and apparently substantial financial resources.

Royal households, large or small, were arranged in a pyramidal hierarchy, a patriarchy working down from the head of the family to the likes of an attorney general, solicitor general and almoner, down to the most humble servant. In James's case, at the Restoration his most senior servants were Sir William Coventry, his secretary, who became a commissioner of the navy, but also left James's service in 1667 after his great power as an orator was deployed in the House of Commons to help remove Clarendon from power; Sir Charles Berkeley, groom of the stool, who left to become Charles's Keeper of the Privy Purse in 1662 and would subsequently die in June 1665 in the first naval action of the second Anglo-Dutch War (1665–7); Henry Jermyn, James's master of the horse before and after the Restoration, raised to the peerage as Lord Dover in 1685 when James came to power, and Richard Talbot, groom of the bedchamber, who led a colourful life as manager of James's mistresses, dynamic politician in Irish affairs and, like Jermyn, ennobled in 1685, in his case as earl of Tyrconnell in the Irish peerage. Of these four only Coventry stood out, not being Catholic and not being a comrade in arms of James's from the 1650s. The evidence for James predilection for Catholic soldiery is clear enough and his 'perceived' favouring of Irish over English was commented on by Pepys. However, another exception was the Protestant Sir Allen Apsley, a royalist soldier, distant relative to Clarendon and friend of John, Lord Berkeley, who became James's sole treasurer and receiver-general in 1666 after joining James's household just before the Restoration. Apsley, who ended his days a pious Anglican, became James's political manager in the Commons and stuck by his master over his marriage to a Catholic princess (1673), the English Test Act affair (1678) and Exclusion Crisis (1679–81), as a Whig parliament sought to exclude James from the English succession (controversies we will consider later).

Apsley's ability to negotiate with parties of various hues, which even allowed him to help his brother-in-law John Hutchinson avoid execution (he was one of the 'regicides' who signed the death warrant of Charles I), was seen by James as a particular asset. James's contact with such men planted in him a view of personal toleration in religion which he would not retain at institutional level from the 1680s. It also shows that he could retain effective servants, an ability associated more with his older brother. The man Apsley supplanted as James's treasurer was Sir Thomas Povey who had acted as Apsley's senior co-partner in James's financial affairs since 1661. Povey, though Pepys's friend, fellow enthusiast for things naval and for the Royal Society, the great scientific society founded in 1660, was described by the diarist as a man not 'fit to be in such [administrative] employments, and particularly that of a Treasurer' – Pepys and Povey remained friends but Povey and Apsley grew into bitter rivals in one of those confrontations that arose in James's household, from time to time, as he stuck too loyally by his servants. As a respected colonial expert and entrepreneur Povey was at least able to encourage James to look to colonial enterprises as a means to sustain prestige and increase revenue.[12] Advice was certainly plentiful, although before the 1670s James's councils and household lacked direct Scottish advisors, and yet the 'old' cavalier and Episcopalian interest in Scotland found him a willing supporter.

In addition to the senior players, James's household contained numerous minor servants who reflected the diversity of his preoccupations and the carefully choreographed grandeur of his 'family'. In 1682 his establishment contained a groom of the armoury, a gunsmith 'to keep [James's] guns and pistols in repair and maintain a horse to attend [him] in shooting', and various huntsmen who joined a 'secretary to the languages', chaplains, a physician, surgeon and apothecary, along with gardeners at St James's and Richmond and numerous pages and maids. For his daughter Lady Anne, then seventeen years of age, there was a guitar master and dancing instructor. James's equestrian establishment was extensive – in 1673 he had sixty horses in total including twenty-one coach horses and fourteen hunting horses – as were his packs of hunting dogs. A master of horse was also required for Lady Anne and Mary, duchess of York, and the marquis of Atholl's son Lord Charles Murray, made first earl of Dunmore in 1686, was so appointed to both in 1683 and 1685 respectively. All of this cost a considerable amount and although in the winter of 1677/8 the French ambassador Paul Barrillon d'Armoncourt, at the English court from then until 1688, praised James for an efficient household with 'servants paid punctually' and no debts, this was not the case a decade before.[13]

James had, however, been generously provided for since the Restoration. Ad hoc payments were made to him by the English Convention Parliament and subsequent Cavalier Parliament, including £10,000 on his return in 1660, a further £15,000 in 1661 and the huge sum of £120,000 in 1665 in thanks for his command and victories in the second Anglo-Dutch War. More important was his regular income which amounted to an annual allowance of £20,000 agreed by a loyalist parliament in February 1661. Various sinecures and revenue streams supplemented this regular allowance. These included the very profitable revenues from the post office, bestowed on James and his heirs by the Westminster Parliament in 1663, and which brought in an estimated £16,000 per year, and revenues from the wine licences and related excise profits which had brought in a similar annual sum since 1661. Income from land, mostly from forfeited republicans in England and the highly complex post-Restoration land-ownership situation in Ireland, supplemented this, as did some speculation in the money markets of London and Amsterdam. Nevertheless, a desperate Povey confided with Pepys in 1667 that James's expenditure, perhaps c.£75,000, was then 50 per cent more than his income, about £50,000. To address the shortfall Povey and Apsley led James's commissioners in various retrenchment schemes in 1662/3 and 1666/7. In the end only the dismissal of Povey, an economy drive led by Apsley, and the growth in income from James's post office and wine licences, brought the household finances to positive balance. One signal factor in this financial debacle was James's wife Anne. The duchess took a close and even controlling interest in her husband's finances but at the same time always protected her own large pension of near £5,000 per year. As Povey and Penelope, Lady Peterborough, informed Pepys, Anne was 'not only the proudest woman in the world but also the most expenseful' and did by 1669 'lay up, mightily, [with] jewels'.[14]

By the 1670s James's finances were on a much surer footing, the death of Anne in March 1671 no doubt speeding the process, though not as much as the fortuitous trebling of the post office revenue. Therefore, when James made his first visit to Scotland in November 1679 he could afford to transport to Edinburgh by coach more than a hundred members of his court. As hereditary Keeper of the recently renovated Palace of Holyrood, William Douglas, third duke of Hamilton (see Plate 4), had the task of accommodating James's extensive entourage there and in nearby buildings. This included, as well as James's second wife Mary, his master of horse, the Irish Protestant and soldier-poet Wentworth Dillon, fourth earl of Roscommon; his master of the robes, Colonel John Churchill, brother of Arabella, James's mistress from 1665 to 1678, who in 1702 became the first duke of Marlborough; and also his comptroller (since 1674) Colonel Robert Werden, a veteran of the Civil War, and father of James's secretary (since 1672) Sir John Werden, the former diplomat. This group included James's keeper of the privy purse, Colonel James Grahme, later of Levens, grandson of the Scottish peer James, first earl of Hartfell, who from 1671 to 1674 served under the Scottish Catholic Lord George Douglas, first as a captain in the French *regiment de Douglas* and then within the British Brigade formed to fight against the Dutch in alliance with Louis XIV. Along with this mixture of soldiers and Irishmen, of faithful servants so reliant on James's patronage, came as one of the duchess's maids of honour the twenty-two year old Catherine Sedley. This plain but witty girl supplanted Arabella as James's mistress in 1678/9 and would remain his sexual diversion for the next decade. Her reward was elevation to countess of Dorchester in 1686.[15] Searching, therefore, for a mistress during James's time in Scotland need go no further. As long as the faithful duchess travelled with her husband she, at first unwittingly, connived in his continued infidelity.

James did not, as is sometimes asserted, have almost no dealings with Scotland before 1679. It is true, however, that his concerns before then were not greatly financial. His Scottish title duke of Albany, confirmed through the Great Seal in 1660, was honorific rather than territorial and came with no estates or lands. James had no official residence in the northern kingdom and the Scottish Parliament granted him no personal privileges or revenues. Consequently, before 1679 his engagement with Scottish policy was abstracted and modest, beyond supporting the broad sweep of his brother's religious objectives, the promotion of loyalism and the work of crown ministers. Admittedly, James had some particular influence over Scottish commissions and appointments, yet his personal levers of patronage were limited in a Scottish context. Ostensibly he delivered a relatively neutral impact on Scottish affairs before he came north, something that could not be said of England and Ireland.

RESTORATION SETTLEMENTS

Ireland's was a particular and difficult restoration, not least because of the complexity of ethnic and sectarian interests and of land ownership. The heady mixture of Catholic, Protestant (Episcopalian and Presbyterian), native Irish and Old English complicated the management of Irish affairs and policy before, during and after the Interregnum. Many Protestants had taken the side of the English Parliament in the English Civil War following the violent Catholic Irish Rebellion of autumn 1641. In early 1649, however, royalists under Ormonde had succeeded in uniting Irish Protestants and Catholics against the Commonwealth, only a few days before Charles I was executed, but within a year Ormonde's army was defeated by Cromwell and opposition was brutally suppressed. In 1652 the newly created republic came up with an Act for the Settlement of Ireland intended to punish, generally by forfeiture of land, those anti-army elements and especially those who rebelled in 1641. This was an anti-Catholic measure – toleration under Cromwell never extended to Rome. The result of this process was that the amount of land in the possession of Catholics (over 70 per cent of the population) declined from 60 per cent in 1641 to less than 10 per cent by 1660. Catholic landowners rejoiced at the Restoration believing that the restitution of their lands would follow. But the trouble was that it was Protestants, and especially former collaborators with Cromwell like Sir Charles Coote, who, significantly, served under Monck, and Roger Boyle, Lord Broghill, who had facilitated the Irish Restoration. They, and those parliamentary adventurers who had acquired lands during the 1650s, felt they had legal right to their estates, particularly as they represented the key 'English interest' that managed Ireland. Consequently, Charles's promise to turn the clock back to 1641, evinced in the high optimism of the 1660 Declaration of Breda, was not merely difficult but impossible. Demands made on Irish land were double the acreage available. Nevertheless, Charles, with the advice of Ormonde and Broghall, made earl of Orrery in 1660, clarified Charles's Irish declaration of November 1660 with a new Act of Settlement of May 1662. In this three objectives were explicated: to return estates to Catholics innocent of the 1641 rebellion; to reward Protestants who had served with Ormonde and Crown forces before their defeat in 1649, and lastly to accommodate former soldiers and adventurers who should either keep the land they had acquired or be compensated for giving up some of it to those innocent of 1641. The 'court of claims' that was set up to deal with these objectives was inundated with thousands of cases and quite unable to cope. Then in 1665 the unpromisingly entitled 'Act of Explanation' sought to draw a line under the whole affair by declaring that soldiers and adventurers would lose a third of their land to enable a degree of estate restoration. No more claims would be considered. Catholics ended up with a third of the lands they held in 1641.[16] In short, other than a small band of elite individuals and royal servants, most were unhappy with the land settlement, and Catholics particularly so.

One of the reasons for the failure of Charles's Irish land policy was his generosity to his brother. After the Restoration, the easiest way to secure a satisfactory settlement in favour of James was to give him the land taken from the regicides in England and Ireland – no such approach was taken in Scotland. In April 1661 James was given, under his title as earl of Ulster, the Irish lands of the regicides Daniel Axtell, Miles Corbett, Henry Ireton, Edmund Ludlow and other prominent republicans who had profited in Ireland – in total nearly 170,000 acres. Others like Ormonde, Lord Lieutenant of Ireland from 1662 to 1668 and 1677 to 1685, also benefited from Charles's Irish gifts of land. In James's case, however, sympathy for Irish Catholics did not translate into benevolence for his hard-pressed tenantry. Their circumstances were not improved by the Restoration. A few months after Ormonde took up the post of Lord Lieutenant he wrote to Clarendon pleading with him to press James to take firmer control of his Irish affairs as his land agents were distressing poor tenants who would be 'absolutely ruined [with] their familyes' unless James 'undertook their protection'. The exploitation for profit continued throughout the 1660s, and while Charles reasserted his brother's right to his Irish lands in January 1668, the poverty of tenants and rent payers, of all religious denominations, was merely intensified by the Westminster Parliament's imposition of restrictions on the import to England of Irish cattle in 1663 and 1667.[17] James was not personally responsible for much of the policy with regard to Ireland, but he did nothing to alleviate the poor circumstances of his own tenants. In short, at arm's length and working through agents, he put his own revenue first. After years of exile in relative penury, this might be excused in a prince self-conscious about appearances, although the irony in polit-ical terms would become self-evident in the 1680s.

Increasing levels of post-Restoration discontentment in Ireland and the politi-cal consequences in London reflect the full extent of the three kingdom problem that dogged the Stuart monarchy since 1603. This related to economic matters, as seen in the protectionist legislation from the English Parliament in the 1660s; religious policy, as with efforts to re-establish the minority Episcopalian and Protestant church of Ireland in the face of Catholic and Protestant nonconformist resentment; and political affairs, where the management of Ireland depended on too many irreconcilable and competing factions. After a few disengaged months as Irish 'viceroy' by Monck, one of his 'rewards' for being the father of the Restoration, the choice of Ormonde as replacement was ideal, being that he was close to Clarendon, Charles and, by his loyalty, to James as well. His understanding of Irish business allowed him to govern inclusively, at least as much as his own Protestantism and directives from London would allow. Ormonde had the good sense not to press for an Irish 'Test Act' or punative 'conventicle act' which in their English and Scottish forms represented a Protestant and Episcopalian backlash. Ormonde was the great Anglo-Irishman and although he can certainly be accused of nepotism, self-interest, military unpreparedness and failed policy initiatives, his steadiness in the face of crisis made him an invaluable servant to the Crown. He handled with calm assurance events such as the attempted coup of early 1663 by nonconformist ministers and army officers led by Alexander Jephson and Thomas Blood, who resented the imposed church and land settlements and threatened to seize Dublin Castle. So, also, the Catholic conspiracy known as the Popish Plot, which broke in 1678 as an irrational scare over a supposed Catholic plot to kill the king and intro-duce popery, which soon evolved into the Exclusion Crisis, and unexpectedly propelled James into Scottish politics.[18] In the case of the Popish Plot Ormonde steered a cautious course which clamped down moderately on Irish Catholics yet without heating the atmosphere too much, while accusations of Catholic plots engendered panic through most of England. A fierce suppression of Irish Catholicism would merely have driven many Irishmen to the very extremes feared by Protestantism in all three kingdoms.

Ormonde's tenure as viceroy was interrupted, however, by an eight year period in the political wilderness. His association with Clarendon, coupled with a campaign against him led by Orrery, the brash George Villiers, duke of Buckingham, and covertly by Sir Henry Bennet, later earl of Arlington, Charles's secretary and in effect Clarendon's replacement, saw Ormonde removed in February 1669. What followed were three years of instability as first the morose, no-party man and former Presbyterian John, Lord Robartes, was made Lord Lieutenant. Although he favoured toleration he alienated too many and was dismissed after only nine months. As Bennet put it he was 'as weary of the Imployment as the Imployment [was] of him'. The replacement was John, Lord

Berkeley, formerly of James's exiled household, who for two years brought to the position intoxication with authoritarianism and an awkward association with Rome, having a Catholic wife and being seen as one of James's circle at the very time that the duke's Catholic conversion became common knowledge. Berkeley was replaced in turn in 1672 by Arthur Capel, earl of Essex, who governed in the practical and pragmatic style of Ormonde, but was removed by Charles on account of constant bickering between ministers. In fact Ormonde, Robartes, Berkeley and Essex all had to contend with those carping from the sidelines in Dublin and London such as Orrery and Talbot who bent the ears of the king and his brother over, respectively, the Protestant and Catholic agendas of Ireland. In the end Ormonde sensed in the final years of Charles's reign that he was becoming surplus to requirements. He was, though a high Tory himself, insufficiently robust in promoting supporters of divine-right monarchy, those royalists who from 1682 saw James as their natural leader. The death of Charles and the end of Ormonde's commission brought his lieutenancy to an end before he could be dismissed. The irony here is that it was James who secured Ormonde's reinstatement in 1677. The duke used all his influence to block a plan to make his nephew and rival, the duke of Monmouth, viceroy in Ireland. This would have raised him to an unacceptably high level of status in James's eyes at a time when the nephew was being spoken of as the best way to secure a Protestant succession.[19] It was Ormonde's dignity in adversity which even James admired. He was certainly 'the' Irish grandee, an Irish Lauderdale in terms of authority yet without the bravura cunning of the great Scot. Probably no Scottish politician had shown such widely admired qualities of integrity since Alexander Seton, earl of Dunfermline, James VI's Scottish Chancellor and High Commissioner to Parliament who, though a closet Catholic, was respected by all church parties and interest groups.[20]

If James's close involvement in managing Ireland in the 1660s and 1670s is to be doubted, so also is his engagement with English affairs. He was accused by some contemporaries of laxity when it came to state business, and by historiography of not attending sufficient executive meetings. James's position was a complex amalgam of duty and detachment. The observations of the Venetian ambassadors Angelo Correr and Michele Morosini, made in late 1661, appear to sum up James's attitudes and their general context:

> Twice a week his Majesty holds the Council of State, composed of many leading persons. Divers matters are discussed there but the greater part derive their substance from the opinion of the Lord Chancellor, and the same person sees that they are carried out. This minister, as has been said, possesses all the king's esteem and respect and at present seems the sole director of affairs. The better to consolidate his authority he has married a daughter to the duke of York, who bears him great respect. This prince applies himself but little to the affairs of the country, and attends to

nothing but his pleasures; but he is a young man of good spirit loving and beloved by the king, his brother, and he discharges the office of Lord High Admiral. He treated us with great courtesy and offered to go in person to the war against the Turk, if the opportunity should arise . . .[21]

The fact that the same ambassadors reported that Albermarle '[confined] himself to his private affairs, and [had] little desire for authority in public matters, only exercising it in his office of general of the military forces of the kingdom' provides clues as to James's own apparent reluctance to get too involved in state affairs. A war 'against the Turk' would have suited both men who became soldiers bored with inaction for the first few years after the Restoration. The likes of Prince Rupert could relate to these frustrations and during 1661 he travelled to Vienna on a diplomatic mission for Charles hoping to gain a general's commission in the imperial army against the Turks. Meanwhile, James and Albermarle were able to keep relatively busy with small policing actions, such as sharing in the suppression of the millenarian Fifth Monarchists rebellion of January 1661, when a small band of extremists led by one Thomas Venner briefly terrorised London to the cry of 'King Jesus!', in a futile effort to replace the monarchy with a godly regime. In fact, by the time these commanders arrived with a mounted force, the City of London militia and the royal guards had restored order, although the impact of the scare and other rumours of plots by republicans and sectaries led to a rethink on the need for a standing army. In the wake of Venner's Rising James pressed the English Privy Council and Charles to rescind plans to disband Albermarle's guards and as a result, a standing army of over 3,000 men was created, paid for by the king's ordinary revenue, consisting of two cavalry regiments – one of life guards under Albermarle and another of horse guards under Aubrey de Vere, earl of Oxford – and two infantry regiments of guards, one also under Albermarle's command, which from his death in 1670 became the Coldstream Guards, and one under Colonel John Russell, who fought under Rupert for Charles I in the English Civil War. The existence of even a small standing army made some uneasy in the English Parliament and the country, and even Clarendon could see the political dangers. However, James's persistence over military affairs shows he could be more energetic than his brother over some policy matters. But the truth is that he attended the Privy Council from 1661 onwards, once his personal affairs were more regularised, and especially when Charles was present, and also other committees, such as the more important Committee for Foreign Affairs, a private inner cabinet, as well as committees for the naval and military affairs and of trade and plantations.[22] In any case it is difficult to make a precise assessment of James's business commitment at court where so much was carried out via small ad hoc meetings and away from public gaze. While this suited Charles's inclination to the intimate and informal, it encouraged James to put too much store in small-group discussion.

With James intermittently by his side, Charles and Clarendon set about an

English settlement that encapsulated the political, financial and religious objectives of the Crown. To begin with an extended 'cabinet' of privy councillors was created which blended loyalists and former opponents, a policy which Charles genuinely supported out of a desire for reconciliation and practical politicking. As well as Clarendon continuing as Chancellor and James as Lord Admiral, Thomas Wriothesley, earl of Southampton, a loyal supporter of Charles I who 'retired' in the Cromwellian period, was made Lord Treasurer, and Sir Edward Nicholas, a servant of Charles II and of his father, was to remain principal Secretary of State, at least until October 1662 when intriguing led by his unforgiving nemesis Henrietta Maria saw him replaced by Henry Bennet. Meanwhile, as well as the unavoidable though wise appointment of Albemarle as Lord General, other 'collaborators' added to the administration included Sir Anthony Ashley Cooper, who became first earl of Shaftesbury in 1672, made Chancellor of the Exchequer and later Lord Chancellor; Cromwell's' admiral Edward Montagu, made earl of Sandwich in 1660, who was appointed Vice-Admiral under James; and his cousin and namesake Edward Montagu, earl of Manchester, the former parliamentary general, who became Lord Chamberlain. With the exception of James himself, this group favoured reconciliation and a settlement that would bring moderate Presbyterianism under the wing of a new and comprehensive church settlement. Unfortunately this would not be easy, in spite of the warm words of the 1660 Declaration of Breda with its promises of a general pardon and amnesty, the securing of Protestantism and 'liberty to tender consciences'. And then there was the question of the penal laws against Catholics, and Charles found himself reminded of his commitment to repeal these by some members of his court circle without ministerial briefs. These included Henrietta Maria, who returned to England for a few months in October 1660, and the Catholic earl of Bristol who endeared himself to the king, after his return from diplomatic duties, by throwing extravagant parties and at the same time setting up in opposition to the overbearing Clarendon.

Charles was not nearly as committed to the Anglican Church as his father or Clarendon, or even disposed to take much interest in the theological and liturgical nuances of the various branches of Protestantism. Indeed, in July 1680 Burnet witnessed a conversation between Halifax and Charles where the king stated 'he was of no church'.[23] This apparently flexible condition might be seen as ideal in delivering a Presbyterian settlement in Scotland and an episcopal one in England, which the Prince of Orange would come to in 1689, but was subsumed by the need to pursue the best means of achieving political order. Charles could see though that for England some form of inclusive episcopal settlement was necessary to embrace Presbyterian moderates. It was viewed by both chancellor and king as one of the best ways to secure loyalty to the monarchy and deliver political stability. However, Charles found that the Convention Parliament could not be easily managed on the issue of toleration.

The English Convention of 1660 had to wrestle with four main questions – the land settlement, the character of the national church, royal finances and agreeing a Civil War indemnity act. The greatest achievement of both houses, especially if we make comparisons with progress in Scotland, was their passing in August of a generous Act of Free and General Pardon, Indemnity and Oblivion. In this the competing interests of the two houses, and only occasional vindictiveness by Charles, saw just over thirty individuals exempted from pardon and of these, only a third, mostly regicides, were executed. In Scotland as well as in England, collective guilt was assuaged through the grim fate of a small number of scapegoats. But also in the summer of 1660 the Commons conceded the right of the king to lay the ground for a religious settlement. The result of this was the Worcester House negotiations, convened by the government and held at Clarendon's official London residence in the presence of the king, from which on 25 October a declaration was issued in favour of a modified and comprehensive episcopacy. Charles hoped that this would push the Convention into concerted action. Unfortunately, the following month a divided Convention rejected the plan with Episcopalians, encouraged by some in James's household, feeling that concessions diluted traditional Episcopalianism, while Presbyterians, many unwilling to go as far as the compromise in the first place, found it impossible to give more ground. When a further gathering of English clergy was convened in May 1661, the Savoy House conference, the attitude of the bishops and liturgical obstinacy of the Presbyterian divine Richard Baxter, who feared the generalised nature of the concession granted might be turned into liberty for Papists, underlined that a middle way was impossible. The talks ended in deadlock.[24]

In spite of his sympathy for loyal Presbyterians, Clarendon then went against his master's wishes and supported the Commons in rejecting a bill giving some measure of toleration to Independents and Quakers. In an Anglo-Scottish context this was no surprise. A new wave of Episcopalianism was evident in Scotland as well as England – only a few months before, the Edinburgh Parliament abolished all Presbyterian legislation passed since 1633. A royal 'victory' in Scotland may have contrasted with compromise in England but both settlements were unforgiving in nature. One of the weaknesses of the reigns of Charles and James was an inability to get the parliaments of London and Edinburgh to deliver the liberal religious policies they pursued. Restoration absolutist tendencies were therefore underscored in this regard and helped drive the brothers to summon parliaments only sparingly which, conversely, fed claims of arbitrary government. Meanwhile, the English 'Cavalier Parliament', with an overwhelmingly Anglican membership elected in March and April 1661 and not dissolved until 1679, and the first Restoration Scottish parliament, elected in November and December 1660 and dissolved in 1663, were certainly to deliver much that the Crown could have hoped for; but they were, in the long run, two highly unsatisfactory religious settlements. The legacy of intolerance inherited by James made it less likely that his own confessional objectives could be achieved by gradualist and non-confrontational means. In England in 1660/61 an opportunity was missed by the Crown. Later when in exile James would complain, as Charles did before him, that Clarendon spurned the chance to secure, before a docile parliament, a more fulsome English Restoration in terms of royal finances, toleration and royal prerogative. Through this he could 'have obtain'd such a Revenue settled upon the Crown as might have secured it for the futur from the attempts of factious Spirits, and such [subsequent] terrible calamitys', but chose not to. James puts this down to his father-in-law 'being a zealous Protestant', fearful of a king with Catholic tendencies; Evelyn to the Chancellor's desire to '[keep] up the forme and substance of things in the nation', and Burnet to the fact that Clarendon 'hade no mind to put the king out of the necessity of having recourse to his parliament'. In this sense Clarendon's mixture of 'ancient constitutionalism', as Miller terms it, and strong Anglicanism was a barrier to the policies of Charles and James and made him a liability.[25] Certainly some of those who replaced him in 1667 were not so wedded to the niceties of constitutionalism and mutual cooperation between Crown and English Parliament.

As far as Catholics were concerned Clarendon had no intention of initiating a wide toleration as feared by Baxter, merely royal discretion over the application of penal laws, but the same could not be said of Charles and James. The apparent inconsistency of Charles's behaviour confounds straightforward analysis. Typically, in 1660 to 1661 he displayed one face in private and another in public – in late 1660 reassuring his mother's lord almoner, the abbé Walter Montagu, who managed her chapel at Somerset House, that penal laws against Catholics would be lightly enforced, while giving assent to an act that from June 1661 made it an offence to declare the king a Papist or to suggest he 'endeavour[ed] to introduce popery'. The majority in the Cavalier Parliament viewed the oath of allegiance as non-negotiable and a just barrier to English recusants as well as Protestant non-conformists. But the return of bishops to the Lords in 1661 increased the atmosphere of Anglican authoritarianism and, encouraged by the reinstatement of bishops to the Scottish Parliament the same month, a new Act of Uniformity was passed in May 1662. This prescribed the new Prayer Book, required the renouncing of the Presbyterian Covenant and resulted in nearly a thousand clergy being forced to stand down. Charles took this setback to his toleration policy relatively calmly and before long asserted a dispensing power to loyal dissenters, and, of course, Catholics, through his first indulgence of December 1662 which suspended the Act of Uniformity. Yet within a few months, the second session of the Cavalier Parliament rejected this power and, with the Commons threatening to impose even harsher penalties, Charles backed off, and Bristol and Henrietta Maria had to accept that loose application of the penal laws, the status quo, was the best way to protect their co-religionists.[26] Informal means seemed the only possibility as events conspired against toleration in the 1660s and 1670s, with the likes of the Great

Fire of 1666, which with traditional neurosis many blamed on Catholic conspirators, and the confirmed conversion to Rome of James, increasing fears of the Catholic menace abroad and at home, especially within the royal court.

When Charles introduced a second English indulgence in March 1672, designed to calm Protestant nonconformity at a time when the third Anglo-Dutch War (1672–4) was about to commence, it was widely viewed as a device to free Catholicism. It not only licensed public worship for Protestant dissenters but also private worship for Catholics. Charles, with James's concurrence, was more comfortable with the latter given that dissenting Protestants in England and Scotland had engaged in various rebellious incidents in the 1660s, including the Pentland Rising of Covenanters in Scotland in late 1666, a skirmish which coincided with the second Anglo-Dutch War (1665–7) and, by implication, operated with the collaboration of Dutch Calvinists and their printing presses. In 1666 Archbishop Sharp accused the latter of delivering printed material into Scotland 'to bring people into a detestation of the king and his government'. In addition, as part of the Treaty of Dover of May 1670, a secret agreement between Charles and Louis XIV and concluded before the 'simulated' public treaty the following December, the ground was prepared for the latest war by agreement that Charles would declare his conversion to Catholicism in exchange for French subsidies, along with Louis's undertaking not to attack Spain, and to suspend his shipbuilding programme. However, until the progress of the conflict was evident, Charles took the view that the indulgence would have to stand alone as signalling relief for recusants. Yet remarkably, a year later, this indulgence also had to be withdrawn by the king when it was rejected by the Commons. This second policy reversal was forced on Charles and his ministers to obtain the supply (taxation) required to continue the war. James was one of those, along with Shaftesbury, Thomas Lord Clifford, the Lord Treasurer, and Lauderdale – a nonconformist sympathiser, a Catholic (with Clifford soon to convert), and an upholder of the prerogative – who pressed the king to sustain his dispensing power over religion above the needs of war. Charles rejected this course when even his ally Louis XIV thought pragmatism a necessity in the interests of the war effort. Charles attempted to dress up this volte-face as a magnanimous gesture but the affair was a humiliation. To compound this, to acquire supply he was forced by an increasingly anti-Catholic Commons to give assent to a Test Act in March 1673. By obliging office holders to swear the Oaths of Supremacy and Allegiance, to repudiate by declaration the doctrine of transubstantiation so dear to Catholics, as well as take communion from the Church of England, this act meant that Catholics were excluded from public affairs. The king's right to appoint whom he pleased was qualified. James's failure at Easter 1673 to take Anglican Communion aroused further suspicion at Westminster and in the country, and helped heighten the acute anti-papist tone of the English parliamentary debate. Then in June he, along with Clifford, resigned their offices, including James's position as Lord High Admiral of England, confirming the extent to which Catholicism had infiltrated the court at the highest level. The war with the Dutch had petered out into an unsatisfactory draw which, like the French alliance, became increasingly unpopular with the majority of English and Scots who found themselves allied with an old Catholic enemy against fellow Protestants. Charles had to signal to Louis XIV – an announcement of his own conversion was delayed indefinitely. James was appalled at this turn of events. To him it was the result of his brother's weakness and indecisiveness.[27] Ironically then, while court Catholicism increased, the prospects of a statute-based toleration for recusants was now less likely than it had been in 1660. For the remainder of the 1670s this became the defining context for popular and parliamentary politics. Meanwhile, in the context of relations with the English Parliament and the policy of toleration, the third Anglo-Dutch War was a disaster for Charles. From this point onwards James's prospects as an authoritarian monarch, never mind as a Catholic one, were severely disadvantaged.

The fall of Clarendon in August 1667 arose from the insistence from both the Chancellor's enemies at court and Parliament that someone take the blame for the debacle that was the second Anglo-Dutch War. Efforts to describe the campaign as an honourable draw were not convincing as seen in the concessions to the Dutch in the concluding Treaty of Breda. Yet the campaign had begun very well, with James leading the fleet in June 1665 to a comprehensive victory over the Dutch off Lowestoft. After various setbacks however, as engagements were inconclusive and new enemies gained with France and Denmark entering the war on the side of the Dutch, the final humiliation saw the Dutch fleet, taking the initiative to speed peace negotiations, sail up the river Medway in June 1667 and sink several ships, even towing away the flagship the *Royal Charles*. Both perceptions and growing evidence that corruption and misgovernment was at the core of an incompetent admiralty sealed Clarendon's fate – the chief minister had to go. These developments placed James in a dilemma. Clarendon was vulnerable, his morale depressed by the sudden death of his wife Frances in early August. While James had many reasons to resent the policies adopted by his father-in-law, especially those concerning the rights of Parliament, the status of Catholics and the Chancellor's initial opposition to the second Anglo-Dutch War, loyalty to his wife's father made him express support in councils, before his brother and in the House of Lords. Such were the difficulties from this that some of his own servants argued for Clarendon's removal, including Sir William Coventry, James's secretary, who swiftly left James's service. More significantly, the relations between the two brothers were soured as the king became frustrated at parliamentary tactics that looked as if they would save his chancellor. In the end the threat of impeachment before a committee of peers left Clarendon feeling he had little choice but to flee to exile in France. James took to his bed with a bout of smallpox towards the end of Clarendon's four-month ordeal, although the latter's despairing letter to Ormonde sums up his appreciation of James's loyalty – 'the Duke of York hath been and is as gracious to me as possible'.[28] Eighteen months of estrangement between James and Charles resulted from the affair.

AFTER CLARENDON

The legacy from the Clarendon years is referred to by historians as the 'Clarendon Code', a series of legislative measures that emphasised both royal and Anglican supremacy. This suited a secure English Restoration but in the long run was not necessarily ideal from James's perspective, and to be precise was not entirely of Clarendon's making. The 'code' consisted of four main pieces of legislation passed from 1661 to 1664 aimed at the forced comprehension or restriction of English Protestant dissent: the Corporation Act of 1661, aimed at purging local government of dissenters; the Act of Uniformity of 1662 which, as we have seen, forced Anglican obedience or resignation from the clergy; the Conventicle Act of 1664, designed to prevent religious meetings by dissenters after a small group of radicals rebelled in Yorkshire in October 1663, and the Five Mile Act of 1665, which banned dissenting ministers from proximity to their old parishes. Clarendon felt these measures were too severe and did what he could to moderate the penalties involved. Charles, however, was encouraged by the agreement in Scotland to restore bishops and in particular legislation in 1663 to restrict nonconformity, including the 'Act against separation and disobedience to ecclesiasticall authority', which punished Presbyterians for worshipping outside the episcopal church, and the 'Additional act concerning the declaration to be signed by all persons in publict trust', which imposed an oath against the Covenants by all in burghs subject to loss of trading privileges and right to sit on burgh councils. Charles's Scottish Secretary of State, Lauderdale, was assumed by all Englishmen to be behind these achievements. The conflation of Scottish and English policy is obvious, but significantly, the boldness of Lauderdale's successes in Scotland at the 1663 Edinburgh Parliament confirmed what was necessary to tackle nonconformity across the Border. It is small wonder that in the 1670s opposition leaders in England feared a 'Lauderdale code' would be visited on the English people and their own ancient constitution.

Once Clarendon was forced to take ship and flee to France, Lauderdale had a key role to play in the new English administration. This 'regime' is often termed the Cabal, an acronym from the first letters of the names or titles of the main five ministers – Clifford, Ashley, Buckingham, Arlington and Lauderdale – though not a coherent group, as the label misleadingly suggests. They did, however, share a rejection of the restrictive toleration favoured by Clarendon. From their different perspectives they desired the extension of toleration through the royal prerogative and, in as much as Catholicism could be embraced along with moderate Protestant dissent, a foreign policy that favoured France. Arlington was now the most powerful English minister as the senior Secretary of State, and Buckingham, until late 1673, closest to the king. Lauderdale meanwhile, with the end of Clarendon's interference, was not only to be supreme in Scottish affairs for the next decade, but was also much involved in English and international policy, especially through his membership of the Committee for Foreign Affairs. Clarendon's fall also finally ended the Scottish council in London. This had existed since autumn 1660, though it had been weakened since the dismissal of the earl of Middleton in March 1663, Charles's man in Scotland until then, who had used the committee's exist-ence to limit the London-based power of his bitter rival Lauderdale. From autumn 1667 Scottish policy now worked with a Scottish Secretary dealing directly with his king. Lauderdale's strong position over Scottish business is revealed by his deputy Sir Robert Moray in a letter to his master in September. This was just days after Charles sent the Secretary of State, Sir William Morrice, to collect the seals from the doomed Clarendon:

> It is [. . .] my clear judgement that you stick no more at the considerations
> have formerly prevailed with you, but frankly & without hesitation
> propose, advise & carry on. Whatsoever you judge fittest for the good of
> the King's service, please or displease whom it will below him. All mists are
> now cleared up. Nobody can make the King suspect your loyalty, your
> integrity, your affection to him, nor the candor of your professions as to
> things Ecclesiasticall as well as Civil.[29]

Nevertheless, Lauderdale was to have a more central position in English affairs than any English minister now had over Scotland – remarkably the tables had turned. That some historians have emphasised the duke's importance only in the Scottish sphere is an estimation which relies too much on the single, if surprising, fact that Lauderdale, in spite of his significance, was not initially privy to the secret Treaty of Dover of 1670. But most of Charles's intimate ministers and servants were also ignorant and remained in that condition. Suggestions that Lauderdale 'spent most of his time in Scotland' are inaccurate as he frequently attended the Committee for Foreign Affairs and from 1674, the English Privy Council.[30] His views were not, however, necessarily politically advisable for himself or his royal master. Lauderdale became one of the more hawkish foreign policy advisors and, in addition, promoted Scottish solutions to English problems when it came to religious policy, an approach which in due course increased English fears of the motives of the great Scot. Given the history of Anglo-Scots relations during much of the period, this was highly ironic.

One vital member of the Cabal administration, excluded from the acronym, was James himself and his advice was greatly respected by the king after the frosty period in their relations ended by May 1669. James retained his own business agenda. His main concerns were threefold: foreign policy, with its strategic and economic consequences; military affairs, both at land and sea, and more generally opportunities to express loyalty to his brother's policies, mostly with the advice of his father-in-law up to 1667, with the aim of underpinning royal authority and the family dynasty. The last of these was largely achieved through the management of the votes of his own group of MPs in the Commons, coordinated by Sir William Coventry and Sir Allen Apsley, and through James's regular attendance at the Lords. Nevertheless, relations between the two brothers fluctuated and could do so from the extremes of mutual resentment to tearful and mawkish affection. In the culture of personal monarchy that dominated the Tudors and the Stuarts, the political became interwoven with sibling rivalry and family tension.

Since the John Berkeley affair in 1657, relations between the brothers had been fairly good. For example, while certainly Charles had been firm, he was also sensitive over the fiasco surrounding James's marriage to Anne. Some of this sibling harmony was displayed in public. Clearly this was the case over Charles's English coronation at Westminster Abbey, on St George's Day in April 1661. The magnificence of James's robes was surpassed only by those of his brother and the duke was therefore symbolically rendered as second in the realm and heir apparent. But also when London was devastated by the Great Fire in the first week of September 1666, the brothers cooperated and showed, in Evelyn's words, 'extraordinary vigilanc and activity'. They rode together around the City issuing instructions, distributing money to encourage the efforts of those fighting the fire, ensuring demolition took place and dismounting to join in the work. This was a public relations dream for both after their reputations, for different reasons, had suffered since 1661. It also cemented their brotherly bond. Nevertheless, the fire, when coupled with the outbreak of Great Plague in the summer of 1665, which especially affected London – as is so vividly described by Pepys and which forced the Court and Parliament to transplant themselves to Oxford – and the ill fortune that bedevilled the war against the Dutch, pressed down heavily on public morale. This helped embolden the government's critics.[31]

Charles had no consort at the time of his coronation when in Anne, James had a new and frequently pregnant wife – this was a source of fraternal tension. Efforts at finding a bride for Charles had been occasionally entered into during the years of exile, but after the Restoration, both the death of the duke of Gloucester and the muddle, and, for some, scandal, of James's marriage to a low-born bride, recommended a fairly swift negotiation over a suitable princess. The fact that Charles was already publicly in a liaison with his first major mistress, Barbara Palmer, neé Villiers, countess of Castlemaine, created duchess of Cleveland in 1670, with both titles awarded for her private intimacies with the king, made no difference. While Bristol made his usual and unsuccessful pitch for a Spanish connection and so a Spanish bride, Clarendon arranged for Charles to be betrothed to the Catholic Princess Catarina Henriqueta de Bragança, daughter of the late Juan IV, king of Portugal. Catherine, to use the anglicised form of her name, was eight years younger than Charles, and after negotiations concluded a promised dowry of over £300,000 and possession of Tangier in North Africa and Bombay in India, a marriage contract was signed on 23 June 1661. Catherine sailed for England the following April landing at Portsmouth in May 1662, before being officially married to Charles in two ceremonies, a private, indeed secret, Catholic ceremony and a public Anglican one, both conducted at the port.[32] The extended proxy courtship in Lisbon was partially on account of vain efforts to await Papal approval of the independent kingdom of Portugal and so elevate the status of the new bride to that of royal princess.

After an ambassadorial tug of war between Portugal and Spain, this choice of bride was not only a financial success, even though some of the dowry never materialised, but a foreign policy coup for Charles and Clarendon. Approval of the marriage came from Louis XIV, happy to see Portugal's struggle for independence bolstered by a defensive marriage treaty against Spain. Charles's mother Henrietta Maria strongly supported the match. After all the marriage in March 1661 of Charles's sister Henrietta-Anne to Louis XIV's brother, Philippe, Duc d'Orleans (known in France as 'Monsieur' and so she as 'Madame'), confirmed the pro-French policy of the restored monarchy. Also, the fact that Catherine was a Catholic was not of itself a problem, given the Romish proclivities of the wives of James VI and I and Charles I. The Protestant peoples of the three kingdoms had become accustomed to royal consorts with their own religious accoutrements of chapels, monks and confessors. Furthermore, Catherine lived up to the promise made by her ambassador Francisco Manuel de Mello, that she was not temperamentally inclined to flaunt her religion and was 'totally without that meddling and activity in her nature, which many times made those of that religion troublesome and restless, when they came into a country where another religion was practised'.[33] She never entered much into religious and therefore international politics as did her opinionated and interfering mother-in-law. However, the new queen's religion became more controversial when a general attack on popish tendencies of the court gathered momentum from the late 1660s.

Charles had genuine affection for Catherine in spite of his continued infidelity. He never, as James grew to in old age, viewed the existence of his many mistresses as a moral impediment to a loving relationship with his spouse. His reactions on meeting her for the first time – her 'face is not so exact as to be called a beauty, though her eyes are excellent good . . . [and] . . . she has as much agreeableness in her looks altogether, as ever I saw' – confirm she was no beauty like Barbara Palmer, but not unpleasant in appearance, and his admiration for her conversation and wit were qualities that Charles looked for in all his female companions. In another respect, however, Catherine failed to achieve the success of the king's many mistresses and the duty of consorts of the Stewart line going back to Robert II in the fourteenth century – the production of children. She was not barren as Clarendon's political foes argued and had various pregnancies, suffering miscarriages perhaps in 1666, certainly in 1668 and probably also in 1669, yet her practical barrenness became very central to James's prospects as heir apparent as well as, ironically, those of his Whig opponents.[34]

By 1669 several years of rumour had established credibility that Catherine's infertility was making Charles consider divorce in order to remarry. Such a divorce would clearly challenge James's right to succeed. Then in March 1670, and with unfortunate timing from James and Catherine's perspective, a particular case came to a head before the House of Lords. This was where John Manners, Lord Roos, sought a civil divorce from an adulterous wife, who had children from her lovers, in order to remarry and to secure the hereditary rights to the family earldom of Rutland for the legitimate offspring of his second marriage. Roos's wife and he had been in dispute since at least 1663, and in civil courts since winter 1667/8, but the dynastic implications of the case suddenly came into view in the early months of 1670. Speculation reached fever pitch, especially as Charles chose to attend some of the proceedings in person, showing a fascination for the theatre of it all. James saw the dangers and rallied his supporters in the Lords to contest those who appeared to front Buckingham's and Charles's views in favour of Roos. The group who supported the divorce strategy now included Arlington. He and Buckingham wished to counteract the possible threat posed by the duke, especially if he succeeded his brother, given their involvement in the fall of James's father-in-law Clarendon. In the end, James and Catherine narrowly 'lost' as Roos won, yet Charles soon made it clear he had no intention of divorcing the queen.[35] The king's motives in all this are obscure. Perhaps he was toying with his brother and letting the 'exclusionist' plans of Buckingham free rein before slamming the door shut. He also had a prudish, if hypocritical, side to his nature – the infidelity of a husband was one thing but that of a wife quite another.

Simultaneously with the divorce affair, another solution presented itself to court 'enemies' of James's interest, though it began earlier and proved disconcerting to Charles's Scottish administration. In August 1662 Henrietta Maria made her second visit to England since the Restoration, and this time James Crofts, Charles's illegitimate son by Lucy Walter, accompanied her. Charles had suggested he come over with her and quickly became fond of the boy, as indeed did his brother. Soon honours were lavished upon young James, including the dukedom of Monmouth. Charles also approved of the marriage of Monmouth to Anna Scott, heiress to the wealthy Scottish dukedom of Buccleuch, a match suggested to Charles in May 1661 by the girl's mother Lady Wemyss. They would be married at court with great pomp in April 1663 when they reached legal puberty, he four-teen and she twelve years of age.[36] But before then, young James's illegitimacy led to some speculation as to whether his children could succeed to his new wife's estate. Remarkably, finding no help under English law, in October 1662 the king summoned Sir John Gilmour, Lord President of the Court of Session, to London to establish if any precedent under Scots Law, especially concerning the natural sons of James V – including Mary, Queen of Scots' half-brother, James Stewart, earl of Moray – could be used to legitimise young James. Scotland's code proved no more yielding than that of England, yet Gilmour was able to assure the king that the boy could pass on his estate provided he did not die intestate and had lawful issue. Charles was delighted and it is easy to see why, from the arrival of the popular young prince, he was regarded as a rival to his uncle James with, as it often appeared, Charles's imprimatur.[37]

This legitimacy question was but one aspect of a controversial Scottish legal problem which bubbled away from November 1662 to October 1663. Charles was to put pressure on the legal profession, his ministers and Estates of Scotland to change a private entail through act of parliament, something he was entitled to do with his own property but not that of a private individual. This related to the Buccleuch estate which Anna's mother wished to prevent from passing to the next heir, John Hay, earl of Tweeddale, through his wife, Anna's aunt via her father. This would have been convenient for Tweeddale as some link to the Buccleuch estate, by marriage or inheritance, would wipe out a huge debt he owed to Anna's late father. Meanwhile, Charles desired, with the same result sought by Anna's mother, for the estate to pass to Monmouth should Anna die without heirs, and that the marriage contract be couched in such a way that there be no possibility of subsequent legal challenge. Prompted by the indomitable Lady Wemyss, Charles began this whole business as early as January 1662 when he asked Lauderdale to query the original entail as it related to Anna's deceased older sister. On making initial inquiries, Gilmour expressed to Lauderdale the vain hope that 'as it is his Majesties just inclinatioun not to interpose in privat processes depending befoir the Session, so it may be expected [he] will be pleased to suffer and allow justice to have its owne cours'. In any case, legal opinion in Scotland throughout 1662 and 1663 was united in viewing Charles's proposal as illegal. In particular, the suspension of the right of private appeal, as stated in an act of 1592 and confirmed in the 'Act regarding *salvo jure cujuslibet*' of 1606, was seen as a fundamental encroachment. However, as Lauderdale was preoccupied in the summer 1663 with both managing the session of parliament in Edinburgh in a trouble-free manner and in handling the climax to his political rivalry with Middleton, and Gilmour and Chancellor Glencairn began to fear they would lose their positions without a positive result, in early October the Estates were persuaded to pass an 'Act and ratification of the contract of mariage betuixt the duke and dutches of Buccleuch' in the terms favoured by the king. Tweeddale, for wise political if not sound financial reasons, absented himself from the vote. In all of this James encouraged his brother strongly – it was a matter of prerogative for the duke. But such an early example of the Crown playing fast and loose with private rights was alarming for Scottish lawyers and landowners alike – some questioned whether anybody's property could now be secure and some with long memories remembered the reign of Charles I. These events confirm that both brothers were equally prepared to stretch the law in the royal interest when they deemed it necessary. To further muddy the waters, back in London, Pepys reported rumours in autumn 1662, only six months after Charles married Catherine, that young Monmouth was legitimate and that when in exile, the king had married Lucy.[38] The rumour mill went into overdrive as soon as Lucy's son arrived at court. James was not impressed.

'DANGEROUS, FALSE AND FLATTRING CREATURES'[39]

Taken in the context of her husband's stubbornness not to divorce her, and James's obstinacy over sticking by his conversion to Catholicism once it became common knowledge, Catherine's procreative failure was one of the most significant catalysts of the long-term Restoration crisis. Meanwhile, James found a surprising ally in his efforts to assert his rights and to counter ideas of divorce or of the elevation of Monmouth – the countess of Castlemaine. Although the royal mistress had helped defeat Clarendon, she had no desire to see the status of her own children by Charles diminished through a challenge to James's right to succeed. James found during 1670 his stature as heir apparent reaffirmed and his relations with his brother much improved.

Lurid sexual liberalism is one of the most regularly commented upon aspects of the Restoration court with Charles at its head. The countess of Castlemaine was only one of many with whom he had an extramarital relationship and resultant illegitimate children. Notwithstanding the exaggerated sexually charged atmosphere portrayed by some contemporaries, such as Louis XIV's sometime ambassador Philibert, Comte de Grammont, or as passed down to us via the private musings of Pepys, there is no denying the hedonism of the king's circle. Charles sired from seven different mistresses at least thirteen or fourteen natural sons and daughters, with all but four of these being born since the Restoration and all but six conceived since his marriage to Queen Catherine in May 1662.[40] This impressive total includes only those who can be identified with certainty and who reached maturity. James had fewer natural children yet certainly as many mistresses, and had a busy decade in the 1660s in particular. Some were able to resist James's advances, including in 1662 and 1663 Elizabeth Hamilton, 'La Belle Hamilton', sister of Anthony Hamilton, author of the memoirs of Grammont; and most notoriously, Frances Stuart, 'la belle Stuart', later duchess of Lennox and Richmond, who from 1663 to 1667 held back both James's and Charles's best efforts. But if we exclude his early relationship with Anne Hyde, James's affairs followed thick and fast from the Restoration – Goditha Price (1660–1), one of the first four maids of honour to duchess Anne; Anne Carnegie, countess of Southesk (1660–1), daughter of William, second duke of Hamilton; Elizabeth Stanhope, countess of Chesterfield (1662–3), Ormonde's daughter; Arabella (1665–78), sister of John Churchill, and Margaret Brooke, Lady Denham (1666), wife of Sir John Denham, the poet and MP, came in quick and sometimes overlapping succession. Other than a brief infatuation with the widowed Susan, Lady Bellasyse (1671), who James viewed as a potential second wife after Anne's death before Charles gave his veto, and a scandalous relationship with a 'commoner' in Mary (Moll) Kirke, daughter of George Kirke, groom of the bedchamber to Charles – she was sent from the court in 1675 having acted simultaneously as mistress to various courtiers while being married herself – Arabella became James's regular mistress. With this slender and somewhat plain companion, considering the voluptuous taste of the day, he had four natural children from 1667 to 1674, all given the Fitzjames surname, including most famously James Fitzjames, duke of Berwick, the great soldier who would become a marshal of France. Anne was initially furious at her husband's activities and then became resigned, taking solace in heavy eating. In fact James continued his relationship with Arabella until she was replaced by Catherine Sedley in 1678. James had several children by Catherine but only their daughter Lady Catherine Darnley reached maturity. By the time James travelled to Scotland in 1679, with Catherine in tow, their affair had begun.[41] It was a typical development in the sexual dynamics of the Restoration court – the majority of the mistresses of James and Charles were either already or would become maids of honour to their respective wives. Their royal households were the recruiting grounds for this promiscuous sisterhood.

The character of Stuart Restoration politics was highly personalised in a manner more intensely joined than in the reign of Charles I and even compared to the 'court of favourites' culture established by James VI and I. Influence was dictated by opportunity for regular contact and audiences with the king and his brother. Courtiers, placemen and supplicants jostled for position and chances to make their case in the presence of the king. This was made more difficult for Scots resident in the northern kingdom for whom absentee monarchy and distance from London was a political as well as a practical hurdle. It was in this context that the influence of mistresses developed greater political significance for Scotland as well as England.

Charles had two mistresses who gained political significance, the countess of Castlemaine and her replacement in the king's affections, Louise-Renée de Kéroualle, daughter of the French count de Kéroualle. Louise first met Charles in 1670 when she was maid of honour to 'Madame', Charles's sister Henrietta-Anne. That May it was she who, on behalf of Louis XIV and with Louise in attendance, conducted the successful negotiations with her brother over the secret Treaty of Dover. She returned to Versailles in triumph but died unexpectedly soon after. Both Charles and his cousin Louis were profoundly shocked at the sudden death of the popular 'Madame' who was only twenty-six years old. In his memoirs James records 'the great surprise and grief of the royal family', but seems more concerned with her ill-advised involvement in creating a treaty that quickly brought warfare against the Dutch, which through financial necessity made the Crown too dependent on Parliament, than reflecting on his own feelings for his sister. James did not have the sentimental attachment to 'Minette' felt by his brother. Soon though, French eyes turned to securing the treaty itself. Noting Charles's desire that Louise become a maid of honour to Queen Catherine, and seeing the opportunity to place a French spy within the court in London to ensure the treaty was fulfilled, the French king gave his approval to Louise's return to England. By autumn 1670 she was located at court and, within the year, in close intimacy with the king. Following on from the birth in 1672 of her only son by Charles, Charles Lennox, who became duke of Richmond and Lennox, in 1673 Louise's status was confirmed with her elevation to duchess of Portsmouth.[42]

After Charles and Barbara fell out in 1663 over his obsession with 'la belle Stuart', Pepys records the nature of their reconciliation – she again 'command[s] the King as much as ever, and hath and doth what she will'. Yet neither Louise nor Barbara had consistent influence over Charles and his ministers. While in 1662 Barbara helped secure the appointment of Arlington and Charles Berkeley, earl of Falmouth, as Secretary of State and Keeper of the Privy Purse respectively, she also coordinated the opposition campaign to remove Clarendon in 1667. She had a stormy relationship with her kinsman George Villiers, duke of Buckingham, but mediated between Buckingham and Charles when the former was temporarily imprisoned in the same year. Also, when James returned to favour in 1669 she supported him and became a close confidante of Duchess Anne. But both her elevation to duchess of Cleveland in 1670, and the arrival of Louise at court the same year, represented the beginning of the end for her position as a political heavyweight. In one respect, however, she continued thereafter to represent a particular policy direction – under the influence of Henrietta Maria she converted to Catholicism in 1663 and, once replaced in Charles's affections, developed a pro-French outlook, even living mostly in France from 1676 to 1682 while tending to the education of her children.[43]

In contrast, Louise began her time at court as clearly Catholic and pro-French, though her political alliances meandered. Arlington's tendencies to be pro-Spanish and pro-Dutch, as architect of the 1668 Triple Alliance between the English, Dutch and Swedes aimed at containing French military successes in the Spanish Netherlands, made Louise his natural political enemy. Arlington took a Dutch bride and was related to the Prince of Orange. However, he also found himself serving his master during the secret negotiations over the Anglo-French Treaty of Dover, and saw the political advantages of placing Louise in Charles's path. In spite of Arlington's Francophile veneer, in 1673 the new mistress switched support to the new Lord Treasurer and rising star, Thomas Osborne, Viscount Osborne of Dunblane in the Scottish peerage, and later earl of Danby and duke of Leeds in that of England, who had also become close to James. Danby's support for more naval expenditure and some mitigation for Catholic army officers and members of the duke's household, all victims of the English Test Act that year, saw to that. Louise liked that Danby paid her pension on time. Thereafter, with her closeness to the king, she was until 1679 a recognised conduit for patronage, and also of regular audiences, often in her chambers, between the French ambassador and Charles on the subject of a new treaty. Initially it failed to materialise.

Louise's special status over foreign policy was, though, interrupted by the Popish Plot of 1678 and the Exclusion Crisis of 1679 to 1681. Monmouth or James to succeed was the apparent choice. These events saw her break with Danby and ally herself with the new Secretary of State, Robert Spencer, earl of Sunderland, a remarkable 'professional' politician who, without the religious conscience of most, became a key figure in court affairs for the next two decades. In 1678 James was rightfully worried about the Plot being near him when the duchess's secretary Edward Coleman was arrested, tried and executed for a secret correspondence with Rome and Paris in which the duke was closely involved. But as the byzantine details of the Plot emerged in 1678/9, and fears intensified of a Catholic succession and of 'popish and arbitrary government', Louise at first supported James against those who pressed Monmouth's credentials. However, when in June and November 1680 the exclusionists, led by the earl of Shaftesbury, brought before the grand jury of Middlesex charges of recusancy against James and of prostitution and French agency against Louise, she switched to their party and supported Monmouth. The fact that Charles quickly halted the proceedings made no difference. Louise's remarkable change bemused the French and James, who felt 'played', but not necessarily Charles. Although her volte-face was no doubt carried out for fear of her immediate predicament, as well as stored up resentment that in recent years James's wife Mary had shown some partiality for the king's new mistress Hortense Mancini, duchess of Mazarin, Louise made all her moves with Charles's knowledge.[44] Barrillon, the French ambassador, wrote to his master expressing puzzlement at the king's 'secret and impenetrable' conduct at this time. Charles was notoriously difficult to read. At times he appeared willing to concede all to Parliament, pressing James 'strongly to take the Protestant tests' and convert back to Protestantism, as he had pleaded in 1672 and 1673, out of sheer exasperation with his brother's religious convictions. As he later declared to Barrillon, explaining the political expediency of agreeing to the marriage of James's daughter Mary to the Prince of Orange in 1677, 'It is my brother, the Duke of York's conduct, that has given rise to all these suspicions. All the jealousy and passion which people have in this country against the prosperities of France, comes from the Duke's declaring his religion.' Charles may have hoped that James would yield at last. But as the Exclusion Crisis abated, all returned to the condition of 1678, especially for Louise. During 1681 her chambers at Whitehall regained their significance as the venue for Anglo-French negotiations. In March a new secret treaty was agreed with the French promising a large pension in exchange for abandoning the pro-Spanish alliance, evident in the treaty signed the previous year, and Charles's dispensing with the English Parliament for three years. The crisis had seen three English 'exclusion' parliaments summoned from March 1679 to March 1681. At each the opposition grew bolder in drafting and submitting bills to exclude James from the succession. Charles summoned the last of these parliaments to the royalist stronghold of Oxford in early 1681. When his final offer of regents – a regency of William and Mary acting as a check on the Catholic proclivities of James as king – was rejected, emboldened by the French pension agreed only days before in the last of his secret French treaties, Charles suddenly dissolved Parliament to the consternation of the opposition.[45]

By now the pejorative labels 'Whig' and 'Tory' had gained acceptance with their derivations from Scottish Presbyterian rebels of the 1640s and Irish Catholic cattle thieves. Over the next six months, Charles and the loyalists took revenge on Shaftesbury and his party in a 'Tory' reaction to the Exclusion Crisis led by Charles himself. By the end of the year Louise was reconciled to James and lent her weight to those pressing for his return from exile in Scotland after his effective stewardship of the session of the Scottish Parliament that summer. During 1682 Louise engineered the return of Sunderland to the government in spite of his career-threatening vote for exclusion in 1680.[46] Even the threat from her rival Hortense had subsided. Although Hortense was the most beautiful of Charles's main mistresses, her embarrassingly liberal sexuality and lesbian tendencies, and her insignificance at a time of political crisis, saw Charles turn back to the bosom of Louise.

The extent to which the great mistresses were a factor in Scottish Restoration politics is less tangible. The direct as opposed to indirect involvement was minimal, especially for Castlemaine. Before 1681 all hung on the relationship of these women with Lauderdale himself. As Castlemaine became an enemy of Clarendon, with whom Lauderdale had an awkward association – and was glad to see the Englishman depart given that he interfered with his Scottish fiefdom even after Middleton's removal in 1663 – the Scottish Secretary was not negatively affected by the Chancellor's fall from grace. The countess, therefore, developed little interest in Scottish affairs in spite of the fact that, according to Burnet, she disliked Lauderdale on a personal basis.[47] At least he was one of Charles's ministers who had the intelligence to match her caustic wit. Her conversion to Catholicism in 1663 made it almost impossible for her, had she wished it, to activate a Scottish interest or party around the immovable object that was Lauderdale, and while her rival Clarendon was Chancellor in England, Scottish Episcopalians looked to him and the English bishops for succour and support.

Reflecting back in his confessional 'Advice to his Son', written in 1692, James commented not merely on the political dangers of powerful mistresses, but also their heavy cost to the public purse – 'what care they took to enrich themselves' with their desire for 'great titles' and 'great establishments'. All Charles's and James's mistresses participated in this process of enrichment. In 1673, for example, Barbara, duchess of Cleveland attempted to avail herself of various properties and associated revenues in Ireland, although Essex, the then Lord Lieutenant, successfully resisted Charles's plans to give her the official residence of the 'viceroy' just outside Dublin.[48] Scotland was also seen by Louise, duchess of Portsmouth, as a source of occasional riches, especially after Lauderdale's regime ended. In this respect there are several reasons why 1680 to 1681 was a watershed. Lauderdalianism, as played out from 1663 to 1680, was both efficient and venal. The Secretary's grip on the Scottish administration, through a tightly-managed communication conduit from Edinburgh to London, saw a level of control unmatched by his successors once he resigned his post of Secretary of State in September 1680. Equally, the royalist reaction after the Exclusion Crisis had its particular impact on Scotland, although exclusion never took on the level of political and parliamentary controversy seen at Westminster. William, duke of Hamilton, and his party, who had opposed Lauderdale and developed common cause with Shaftesbury and the English Whigs, played a quiet game when James presided over the Scottish Parliament in 1681, and before 1686 mostly distanced themselves from plots and conspiracies. As part of the 'reaction', the Scottish episcopacy was rejuvenated, and Covenanting was redeclared the common enemy as the so-called 'Killing Times' unfolded between 1681 and 1685, and the perse-cution of field preachers and field meetings intensified. Also, the make-up of the Scottish administration became less a matter of those in favour with Charles, and more those supported by James or, as an alternative, those who could get the ear of the king through intermediaries, such as the royal mistress. While Charles left James to become the main man of Scottish affairs from the winter of 1680/1, the latter did not achieve the monolithic control of a Lauderdale. As never before, Charles's preference for private advice and counsel was now visited on Scotland and the 'reaction' in the last years of Charles's Scottish reign brought with it a new wave of political infighting. Meanwhile, the duchess of Portsmouth's financial prospects in Scotland were increased by the retirement from political life of the two strongest women in Scottish politics since the Restoration – Elizabeth Murray, countess of Dysart, Lauderdale's second wife who he married in early 1672 and who, James was convinced, outshone all in greed and corruption, and Anne, duchess of Hamilton, wife of the third duke, a pious Protestant who, with her husband, would return to prominence in 1688.[49] As for Louise, like all the royal mistresses, her main concern was to secure the fortunes of her offspring and in her case her only son by Charles, the duke of Richmond and Lennox. By 1681 this boy was nine years of age and Louise looked to opportunities to gain the titles and prestige afforded to Barbara's brood.

Although Louise had promoted the final return of James to court in 1682 after his Scottish exile, and in the summer that year John Paterson, bishop of Edinburgh wrote to the new Scottish Chancellor Sir George Gordon of Haddo, that Louise was 'truelie a friend to [James]', by the autumn of 1683 some Scottish ministers were growing concerned at her interference in Scottish affairs. John Drummond of Lundin, recently made Treasurer Depute and one of the new men popular with James, deplored the fact that not all matters were channelled through the duke.

While Louise was in Paris for several months in 1682, James did what he could to persuade Charles to exclude her from affairs north and south of the border but to no avail. Ironically, Louise and James agreed over a reshaping of the post-Lauderdale administrative structure in Edinburgh which would now operate through a closed group or secret committee, excluding from influence the extended Privy Council.[50] With this in mind, Louise was building her own support networks. Another new favourite who came to James's attention during his months in Scotland was Middleton's son, Charles, second earl of Middleton, who impressed the duke with his honesty and soldierly qualities, having served in Flanders against the French in 1678. In September 1682, and after James's recommendation, the earl was made joint Scottish Secretary with Alexander Stewart, fifth earl of Moray, Lauderdale's replacement, a novel arrangement that would create difficulties and a new phase of political rivalry in the 1690s. But in late 1682, Louise very swiftly gained the confidence of Middleton and employed his good offices to secure the interests of her servants and retainers. More particularly, when members of the secret committee, led by William Douglas, duke of Queensberry, the Treasurer, and James Drummond, earl of Perth, the Justice General and Lundin's older brother, decided to depose Haddo – the Chancellor of humble origins had been raised to the earldom of Aberdeen but cut an isolated figure with only James for support – they paid Louise £27,000 to secure her help in persuading Charles to carry out the dismissal. Middleton and Lundin, who travelled to London, were both deployed to help with this mission while James, uncharacteristically given his general loyalty to servants, did nothing. Middleton's reward was Louise's help in obtaining in August 1684 the post of English Secretary of the northern department when Sydney Godolphin was made Lord Treasurer, with Lundin becoming the new Scottish joint secretary and Perth the new Scottish Chancellor. Later in 1686, after Queensberry himself had been removed from power and the Drummond brothers began their vice-like grip on Scottish affairs that would last until the Revolution, Queensberry appealed to the Privy Council for reimbursement of £27,000 'of incident charges and expenses on intelligence'. However, when an outraged Hamilton discovered this was for a bribe paid by Queensberry and Perth to Louise to facilitate the removal of Aberdeen, he made sure the appeal was rejected.[51]

James also found it difficult to refuse Louise's desires. Given his long-held military patronage in Scotland, in 1681 she was to browbeat him into placing the governorship of Dumbarton Castle in the hands of her son Charles. She pressed unsuccessfully for the lucrative command of Edinburgh Castle as well. But for Louise, events in Scotland suggested other revenue streams. Along with smaller sums of money paid to her to 'oil' the machinery that delivered to individuals various civil and military commissions, there was the question of forfeited estates and the prospect of additional land to add to the dukedom of Lennox.[52] Following the scrupling of Archibald Campbell, ninth Earl of Argyll, to take without explanation the oath resulting from the Scottish Test Act of 1681 (of which more later), and his subsequent trial for treason and escape into exile, the forfeiture of his estates appeared to offer rich pickings. Then after details of the Rye House Plot emerged – a wild plan in 1683 to ambush and murder Charles and James near Newmarket – a small band of Scots suspected of involvement were transferred to Edinburgh to face trial. There Scotland's more liberal approach to the use of torture to gain evidence was seen as 'convenient' by the royal brothers. This regime meant that suspects could be imprisoned for as long as necessary while evidence gathering took place and even, with clearly questionable legality, if they were acquitted. One such high-profile case was that against Sir Hugh Campbell of Cessnock, whose trial took place in March 1684, and Louise had high hopes of having his forfeited estates transferred to her son. Campbell was a strong Presbyterian and, since the 1660s, a regular suspect for 'fanatical' activity and supporting conventicles. However, his prosecutors failed to make a case for his involvement in the Rye House Plot and also over their fallback position, participation in the 1679 Covenanting rebellion that culminated in the Battle of Bothwell Brig near Hamilton, the event that precipitated Lauderdale's demise. Eventually, having been detained in prison for over a year in spite of his acquittal, Campbell confessed when the evidence of others, gathered under torture, was brought to bear. He was then forfeited. Unfortunately for Louise, James had replaced Charles on the throne by then and she was no longer able to cash in on political favour. Also, although Argyll was forfeited back in 1681, once his creditors were satisfied, Charles decided that most of his estate should be passed to his son and not dispersed. Meanwhile Lundin, made viscount of Melfort in April 1685 and earl of Melfort in August 1686, was granted some of the confiscated Argyll estates and parts of the lands forfeited from Sir Hugh Campbell of Cessnock.[53] Both winners and losers emerged from this spate of real-estate opportunism.

Although the duchess of Portsmouth was to be disappointed from 1680 to 1685, there is a strong sense of Scottish ministers under pressure to satisfy her demands, as seen in the ultimately futile assurances given to her by the Drummond brothers that Cessnock's forfeiture could bring rewards. As for this age of political mistresses, of which Louise was a high point, the accession of James brought it to an end. No evidence has yet been found that James's mistress Catherine Sedley, countess of Dorchester, became as politically significant in Scotland. After eighteen months of apparent 'abstinence' on taking the throne, showing a moral example to others and encouraging Catherine to spend time in Ireland, James recommenced their affair on her return in August 1686. Going to his mistress after hunting was common. He was perhaps encouraged to do so by his senior Anglican ministers, in particular Henry Hyde, second earl of Clarendon, and Laurence Hyde, earl of Rochester, who, claimed the likes of Sunderland, sought to counter Catholic influence at court through Catherine's Protestantism. It was a tactic their great father, the old Chancellor, would have understood but found distasteful. Yet if this was their plan, it had no impact. In spite of her engagement in Jacobite conspiracies with the Hydes and other loyalists from 1688, Catherine was never permitted to interfere in high politics, in all three kingdoms, in the way that Charles indulged both Barbara and Louise. In this respect at least, James learnt from his brother's political if not his sexual weaknesses. From his accession to the Revolution, James arranged numerous meetings with other unidentified women, either at his closet at Whitehall or at St James's. If he wished to construct an edifice of guilt there was plenty of building material.[54]

Charles, it seems, took pleasure in mocking James's taste in 'plain' women, and famously informed Burnet that he was sure his brother's mistresses were 'given him by his priests to do penance'. Given the beauty of some of those mistresses, such as Lady Denham, this seems a casual jibe of fraternal mockery, even though Catherine Sedley once declared, with her own brand of delicious humour, that 'it cannot be my beauty [that attracts James] for I have none; and it cannot be my wit, for he had not enough to know that I have any'. More important, though, to our comprehension of James's personality is the nature of his sexual appetite, not the 'quality' of his paramours. His sullen and aggressive sexuality is starkly but convincingly described by Magalotti: 'In his inclination towards sensuality [James] is the opposite to [Charles], since he cares little for the more innocent preparations for tenderness, and longs for the occasion for the release of a vicious brutality'. This assessment from the 1660s finds James a frustrated man of action – the soldier itching for active service, the obsessive hunter of foxes, as well as 'the most unguarded ogler of his time', as one fascinated contemporary described his attitude to women. Writing in the 1690s in his private papers of devotion, James placed his failures and God's judgments upon him squarely with his sins of the past, and especially those 'voluptuous pleasures'. That he retained an insatiable appetite for sexual gratification after his sincere conversion to Catholicism meant he was both appalled by his condition, yet able to live with it because of his faith and the ministrations of his priests.[55] The link between his desires and his confessors was more direct than Charles could have realised in a momentary aside made in the 1660s.

CATHOLIC PRINCES

One of the strangest aspects of the relationships between Charles and James and their respective mistresses was their personal religion – while Barbara and Louise were or became Catholics, Arabella and Catherine were Protestants. Nevertheless, the convergences between Anglican loyalism and Catholic pragmatism make these contrasts less stark, especially when belief in the extension of royal power was a common denominator. The religious proclivities of Charles and James themselves are quite another matter and clearly of enormous significance.

Although some contemporaries cast doubt on the truth of Charles's deathbed conversion to the Catholic faith, historiography accepts its veracity. Put simply, there were too many witnesses, including the trusted Protestant earls of Bath and of Feversham, although the precise significance of the conversion event in February 1685 is open to question. The testimony of Father John Huddleston, the English priest and Benedictine monk who sheltered Charles after the defeat at Worcester and so aptly was on hand, as part of the Queen's household, to perform the last rites and deliver a safe haven for Charles's soul, is the most credible given that it is shorn of imaginative detail. The deployment of contemporary or near contemporary forgeries, particularly by Catholics seeking to make capital from the late king's conversion, has, however, muddied the waters. For himself, James was ever inclined to believe what he wished to believe, and his impressions of his brother's interest in Catholicism confirms this facet of his character, a hopeful zealot in the face of the perplexing indifference often shown by the more sceptical Charles. The relevance of Charles's early brushes with Rome while in exile can be discounted, his robust rejection of his mother's attempts to convert the duke of Gloucester making his position clear. He also conformed to the Church of England throughout his reign. Additionally, James put far too much store by Charles's apparent willingness to convert in 1669 during the secret negotiations with Louis XIV. This was part of a diplomatic, money-making and essentially secular strategy which in Scottish terms reminds us of Mary, Queen of Scots's unconvincing 'promise' to Pope Pius IV that she would deliver a counter-reformation in Scotland in exchange for a papal pension. Our admiration must be with Pope Pius's refusal and Charles's financial success rather than with Mary and Louis, in spite of the latter cementing Charles to the French interest. In 1669 Charles's own tactics seem devoid of emotion. With French help he wished to prosecute a war against the Dutch to avenge the indignities of the Medway debacle of 1667. Yet if we are to believe James's account in his memoirs, in January 1669, after making his intentions known to his brother the month before, Charles confessed in tears, before Arlington, Clifford, Lord Arundel and James, his fervid desire to embrace the Church of Rome. In the context of a secret treaty with a large French pension, where in return his conversion was 'promised' at some time in the future, and also given James and Charles's admiration for a French monarchy with the financial means to eschew parliaments, this makes sense from 'absolutist' and bargaining standpoints, but hardly in terms of personal faith. Setting aside the supposed emotion, the fact of the January meeting can be believed, although the agenda more likely concerned the negotiating value of a royal conversion not, judging by Charles's later behaviour, some spiritual watershed.[56] James, however, not being temperamentally suited to dissembling when it came to religion, was now even more encouraged to declare his own Catholicism to the wider world, and in an unrestrained manner that, given the political dangers, much annoyed Charles. After the king's death, James did his best to elevate his brother's conversion to that of a wondrous event in which he took a leading role. Distinctions between truth and fabrication became blurred. James's so-called 'discovery' in Charles's cabinet of two papers in his brother's own hand defending the primacy of the Church of Rome has the historian puzzling. Were they merely copied out from other sources and so not reflective of Charles's own views? Neither have been discovered in their originals and nor are they composed in Charles's style, and so, although James showed copies to Pepys in autumn 1685 and in 1686 published the texts as 'evidence' of Charles's true feelings, their authenticity must be doubted.[57] Nevertheless, the very fact of Charles's conversion was a great comfort to the new king, as well as being central to a campaign to promote Catholicism and an agenda of religious toleration in England and Scotland from the autumn of 1685.

James's own conversion is just as certain in fact but much less so in precise timing. In part this is because of his failing, especially seen in his memoirs, of reading events backwards and placing disproportionate significance in early experiences. This predetermination was true of his personal religion where he sought to explain how God mapped out his journey from ignorance to the path to salvation. Thus the story related by James to Burnet in 1683, of a meeting with a nun in a monastery in Flanders in the 1650s, became a point of departure. The nun 'desired him to pray every day, that if he was not in the right way, God would bring him into it; and . . . the impression of these words made on him never left him till he changed'. There is, however, no corroborating evidence that James showed any inclination to embrace Catholicism before 1668/9 in spite of the close proximity before that date of a small band of Catholics within his own household and entourage. Indeed, one of the reasons for the extreme political reaction when his conversion was widely known was the fact that it appeared a complete volte-face for someone who since childhood had accepted the religion of his father and had married into the Hyde family, the great defenders of Anglicanism. This, naturally, increased the sense of betrayal by some of those royalists who had suffered for his father in the struggles of the 1640s and 1650s. As it was, encouraged by his brother's apparent interest in conversion and what he believed was his own scholarly and rational re-analysis of the significance of the Church of Rome, James appears to have converted in early 1669. He was probably received into the Roman church by the English Jesuit Joseph Simons, formerly Emmanuel Lobb, with whom he confided about the prospect, ultimately impossible, of obtaining papal dispensation to continue outwardly as an Anglican. To this extent James tried briefly to avoid the consequences of his decision. But the leaking of his public declaration came on in slow stages – although keen to declare himself in 1670 in the context of the Treaty of Dover, James only stopped attending Anglican communion in 1672, but continued, without taking the sacrament, to attend Church of England services until Easter 1676. His final refusal to attend led to another breach with his brother who well understood the 'unnecessary' political implications. In fact, James did not make a public declaration of his faith until 1685, yet his position was well known long before 1676.[58] As a result of the Test Act of March 1673, which compelled office holders to take the sacrament according to the Church of England, James felt forced to resign his commission as Lord High Admiral. Such an action from someone so committed to the navy and with a not inconsiderable reputation as a naval commander underlined publicly his new religious persuasion.

James's conversion can be explained in experiential, intellectual and personal terms. The rational approach to his reflections, as confirmed in his papers of devotion of the 1690s, concerned two strands of thought. The first of these saw a rejection of the anti-Catholicism so prevalent in England since Elizabethan times. James '[had] became sensible by experience, that [he] had wrong notions given [to him] of the Catholic Religion, and they are not guilty of several things they are falsely taxed with'. It was 'devine providence' that took him abroad for twelve years in the 1640s and 1650s and provided an antidote to that 'prejudice to Catholike Religion' which had been drummed into him.[59] The loyalty of Catholics, in England, Scotland and Ireland, and even the impressive religious devotion of French and Spanish comrades in arms in the 1650s, was evidence of their innocence of malicious charges. The second aspect was his consideration of the respective merits of the Church of England and Church of Rome. The key argument for James was infallibility, an idea which sat comfortably with his desire for certainties, whether it be in military matters, politics or, in this case, faith. He began in the 1660s to enquire into the reason behind the Reformation and the break from Rome. But each time he sought to understand and seek reassurance from the work of Protestant divines, such as Richard Hooker and especially Peter Heylin's *Esslesia Restautara; or the History of the Reformation of the Church of England,* published in 1661, he became more convinced of the spurious motives behind the Reformation, as first the polygamist Henry VIII and then illegitimate Elizabeth sought for worldly reasons to use the church to achieve personal objectives. Elizabeth had, he felt, clearly succeeded unlawfully while conversely Mary, Queen of Scots was a legitimate heir. This was not the only occasion where James expressed his personal and deeply felt pride in the Stewart dynasty. But in the context of religion with the Protestant churches that proliferated at the Reformation and afterwards, which had seen 'our lands . . . over run with diversities of sects', apostolic authority and so infallibility had ceased, in spite of the arguments put forward by Anglican bishops, divines, his own chaplain Richard Steward and his father-in-law that it continued through the reformed episcopacy. Luther and Calvin had undermined Christendom.[60] Thus, in rather an unsophisticated way, James concluded that the only true church was that of Rome.

James could be impressed by the religious convictions of others provided they were loyal to the crown. This respect extended to some pacifist Quakers, such as the Englishman William Penn and the Scot Robert Barclay, with whom James became familiar from the 1670s, if not to beyond-the-pale covenanted Presbyterians.

When some of his closest comrades and family members showed a preference for Rome, he became even more convinced of the role of divine providence in shaping his own belief. In addition to delighting at his brother's secret inclinations, two other conversions encouraged James to embrace his new faith. In late 1668 it became known that his mentor and friend Turenne had converted. This seemed remarkable given James's experience of the great general's strong Protestantism when they were comrades in arms. More significant was the conversion of James's wife Anne. She had been brought up in high Anglican tradition, although she became much more devout than her father and brothers. While the precise timing is unclear, she was received into the Roman church probably at sometime before or by the winter of 1670/71.[61] Charles insisted on absolute secrecy, his own awareness of political priorities being seen in his firm resolve that James's daughters Mary and Anne be strictly brought up in the Protestant faith. This policy decision was to have fateful consequences for James.

Historians are divided over whether it was James or Anne who took the leading role in their change of faith.[62] Known discussion between James and his brother and the resultant chronology suggest James took the lead. However, if we are to believe Anne's own explanatory declaration, published by James in the autumn of 1686, it seems she began to share her doubts with close confidants in late 1669, probably simultaneously with her husband's change of heart. Also, her precise justifications for challenging Protestantism are identical to those stated by James in his later devotional papers.[63] Therefore, either they gave mutual support to each other in a shared period of intellectual and spiritual reflection, or her declaration itself was one of those stylised, perhaps even falsified, accounts so prevalent in the campaign to secure toleration for Catholics. To some degree we must speculate. Nevertheless, given that James was impressed by the views of those at hand, was forced to rely more on the political and personal counsel of Anne after the fall of Clarendon, and that she became renowned at court for Christian devotion, it is highly likely that she was a major force behind his conversion. In this respect Clarendon's desperate appeal to James in 1668/9 to prevent his daughter turning to Rome becomes even more forlorn. From exile in Montpellier in France he pleaded with James:

> when those whispers breake into a noise & public persons begin to report
> that the Dutchesse was become a Roman Catholique, when I heare that
> many worthy persons of most unquestionable devotion to your RH are not
> without some feares & apprehensions of it, & that many reflections are
> made from thence to the prejuduce of your RH & even of the Kings
> Majesty himself, I hope it may not misbecome mee, at what distance
> soever, to cast myself at your feet & to beseech you to looke to this matter
> in time, to apply some antidote to expell the poison of it.

For a year Anne was also sent occasional disbelieving rebukes from her father but to no avail.[64] Clarendon, like Charles, understood the political dangers in his daughter's conversion let alone that of his son-in-law. He also felt a touching regard for his daughter's spiritual welfare though he proved to be no more successful in shaping her devotions than was James with his daughters Mary and Anne.

After some months of illness, probably as a result of breast cancer, Anne Hyde died on the last day of March in 1671. She endured the weakening factor of pregnancy, giving birth to her eighth child the month before – a daughter, Catherine, who died before the year was out. Conflicting accounts exist of the exact circumstances of Anne's death as with the fact of her conversion – but that aspect is indisputable.[65] In spite of whispers her secret was kept safely for now. Nevertheless, the upsurge in anti-Catholicism which subsequently engulfed England from 1672 had more significant catalysts than rumours of the duchess's religious convictions. Setting aside the secret Treaty of Dover, the open treaty with France against the Dutch brought a very unpopular war where Charles's predominantly Protestant kingdoms sided with a Catholic power against confessional brothers. A naval conflict was one thing, though under James's command it was inconclusive with heavy losses on both sides. That the supporting French naval contingent included two senior commanders of the Protestant religion gave some comfort to Lauderdale as he reported events to Scotland. Yet when in the summer of 1672 the French land army overran five of the seven provinces of the Dutch Republic, popular fears grew that the expansion in the power of Catholic France would threaten Protestant England and Scotland. The Declaration of Indulgence granted by Charles in March that year, a measure aimed at reassuring dissenters and also allowing Catholics to worship unhindered in their own homes, quickly backfired and was seen as a reflection of the increasing Catholicism of the court. The withdrawal of the indulgence by Charles in March 1673 and reimposition of penal laws against recusants, came after great political pressure from an English Parliament which set conditions for agreeing further supply to pay for the war, and also resulted in the Test Act which would lead to James's resignation from his positions of authority. That Charles's 'Catholic interlude' ceased, or that his secret agreement to promote Catholicism and convert himself was suspended, *Catholicite* as the French ambassador termed it, was not enough to salve a sense of broken trust that gripped many in the House of Commons.[66] When in 1672/3 it became common knowledge that James was Catholic, only one final element was required to complete this cocktail of Protestant fear.

Only a few weeks after his wife had died, James began the search for a new bride. In 1671 he made a secret promise to marry the commoner Lady Bellasyse but was forced by Charles to retrieve the promise. Charles made it clear he would not sanction another marriage to a lowly bride and that James's 'choice' must be made with international diplomatic considerations. There being no suitable French candidate, Charles looked to the house of Habsburg, a dynasty with the two main branches of Spain and Austria. Perhaps they could then be dissuaded from aiding the Dutch in the coming war. This would, of course, mean a Catholic wife. With this in mind, Claudia Felicité, daughter of Archduke Ferdinand Charles of Innsbruck was pursued during 1672 with the approval of Leopold, Holy Roman Emperor, yet in March 1673 the Empress Margaret Theresa died and the widower Leopold promptly married Claudia himself. James and his agent Henry Mordaunt, earl of Peterborough, with Louis XIV acting as matchmaker and promising a dowry for an agreeable candidate, then considered a bewildering selection of princesses and duchesses with French connections. Peterborough practised frantic shuttle diplomacy between the cities of continental Europe. Papal approval was essential, as well as a dispensation to marry given that James was still attending Anglican services, and reassurances that a Catholic princess in England would be able to worship unmolested. Time was of the essence. The Westminster Parliament was due to convene in October 1673 and James was anxious to resolve matters before the possibility of a hostile House of Commons that might prevent him from marrying a Catholic. The princesses of Württemberg and of Neuberg were first proposed and then rejected. James's last option appeared to be one of the two Italian princesses of Modena and after intensive negotiations, and an incomplete process of papal approval which annoyed the Vatican, the younger princess, the pious Mary Beatrice Eleanora, was married to James by proxy at Modena in late September. A mere two months later she landed at Dover and married the duke in person. She was 15 and he 40 – it proved a love match. But the immediate political consequences were seen between the proxy ceremony and actual weddings. A vote opposing the marriage was passed in the Commons within days of Parliament reconvening 'praying the King that the pending treaty of Marriage between the Duke of York and the Princess of Modena be not further proceeded with'. The Commons was ignored, yet the journey to the Exclusion Crisis had begun. For those Protestant parliamentarians who were alarmed at the 'Catholicite' of the court and the threat of arbitrary rule, as personified in the monarchy of Louis XIV, their fears were surely justified. While practical limitations still prevented Charles or James from achieving absolutism in the French manner, the theoretical objective clearly existed. As one witness to the negotiations over the secret Treaty of Dover put it, the overall objective was to 'labour to introduce into [the three] kingdoms the Catholick Religion and reassume by degrees absolute power'.[67]

The English high Anglican response to the circumstances of James's lapse from the Church of England is summarised by John Evelyn's observations in March 1673 when, for the second year running, James failed to take, as was the custom, Anglican communion with the king at Easter:

[This being] within a day of the Parliament sitting, who had lately made a severe [Test] Act against the increase of Popery, gave exceeding grief and scandal to the whole nation, that the heir of it, and the son of a martyr for

the Protestant religion, should apostatize. What the consequences of this
will be God only knows, and wise men dread.[68]

According to Evelyn, James continued to attend the royal chapel until three
years later when, recording his absence, the English court diarist declared the
'infinite grief and threatened ruin of the nation'. What then of the view from
Scotland? Burnet's claim that by 1670 none of the political class in Scotland,
other than Lauderdale, knew of James's interest in Catholicism is an exaggeration, although when it became common knowledge we would expect the
predictably negative response. Presbyterian distaste at James's conversion was
certainly evident. The radical Cameronians, the followers of the field preacher
Richard Cameron, urged in their *Sanqhar Declaration* of 1680 that war be
declared on Charles for his 'tyranny' and betrayal of the Covenant, and on James
for his 'repugnant' popery. Before then less extreme Presbyterians like James
Kirkton, an ousted minister who rejected the imposition of bishops after the
Restoration, tied together the events of 1672 to 1673: 'The Dutch warre was
unsuccessfull, [while] a popish interest prevailed. The Duke of York married the
Duke of Modena's daughter, highly to the advantage of the papists'.[69] Kirkton
became bitter about the level of persecution meted out to those who could
merely see what was before their noses. In order at this time to display their 'zeal
against popery', the Scottish government, he informs us:

> bored the tongue of a wretched fellow for speaking truth, in saying the
> Duke of York was a papist; and by this a man may see in what a case
> Scotland was, for either our governours were falsely informed, and if so,
> that was bad; or if they were truely informed, than they were very unfaith-
> full, and that was worse; for the duke declared afterward, that indeed he
> was then a papist, and had been long before.

Kirkton's outrage was taken up later, when it was much safer to comment, by the
more moderate cleric and church historian Robert Wodrow, yet until the Exclusion
Crisis was in full swing in England, and James arrived in Scotland in 1679 as part
of his 'second exile', the correspondence and diaries of Scottish politicians and
episcopate suggests little concern with the personal faith of the king's brother.[70]
The typically sanitised church court records are no help to the historian. But
certainly Presbyterian sympathisers, like Sir William Scott of Harden, the Border
laird and victim of fines for nonconformity, consumed the latest printed pamphlets
from London that criticised court Catholicism, and foresaw a foreign army as the
only means of its establishment, and the marriage of the 'Glorious Pair', as one
hagiographic verse labelled James and his new Italian wife. Much private and
Protestant Scottish alarm would have concurred with Andrew Marvell's satirical
poems that decried a prince 'Who still doth advance the Government of France,

With a Wife and Religion Italian' and had 'the Turk in his head and the Pope in his heart'. Nevertheless, three main reasons can be found for the lack of anxiety in Scotland: firstly, there were too few Catholics in the northern kingdom to cause widespread alarm; secondly, most Scots in the political classes genuinely believed the sincerity of Charles's repeated assurances that he would protect the reformed church, and thirdly, the then political crisis in Scotland was not built around fear of popery but the suppression or accommodation, alternately, of Presbyterian nonconformity. Yet from March 1673, driven by English priorities, anti-recusancy measures were given disproportionate priority in Scotland. The same month that the English declaration of indulgence was abandoned by Charles, proclamations were issued in Scotland as well as England demanding the oath of allegiance be taken by army officers and that penal laws against Catholics be enforced. By the end of 1673 the Privy Council in Edinburgh was instructing bishops to prepare comprehensive lists of papists in their dioceses.[71] Meanwhile, Scotland's own political circumstances demanded a simultaneous crackdown on nonconformity. Attempts at establishing a general 'Accommodation' to bring dissenting Presbyterians into the orthodox church, as promoted by Robert Leighton, formerly bishop of Dunblane and now archbishop of Glasgow, and his protégé Gilbert Burnet, had mostly failed. Moreover, complete failure characterised their efforts to convene a national synod to iron out differences and advance a form of primitive episcopacy. Having too much to lose, Sharp and the other bishops made clear their opposition. With this Lauderdale turned to more oppressive measures. He was compelled to this position by pressure from his political rivals, Hamilton and his 'party', and also from the danger posed to both order and his reputation for effective stewardship by a potential split in the orthodox clergy. Equally, given that the Scottish parliament of 1672 was called to finance the third Anglo-Dutch War, and the context was pervasive Dutch propaganda and stark recollections of the alarming eruption of the Pentland Rising during the previous war, suppression of dissent appeared a sensible policy. This was an approach to which Charles and James agreed, given the desires expressed to Parliament for the session of 1673. Soon Leighton retired to England in disgust, summing up attempts at compromise, including his own, as 'a drunken scuffle in the dark'.[72]

In the meantime, that more earnest scuffle, the third Anglo-Dutch War, continued. In the summer of 1672 James took command of the fleet and, in the thick of the action, on two occasions had to change flagships as his own vessels were sunk. In spite of James showing commendable bravery under fire, no way could be found to turn these engagements into some kind of qualified victory. A year later two inconclusive naval engagements took place in the summer. These were presided over by Rupert who had replaced James as commander. Six months after that, the unpopular war was over. The termination of hostilities with the Treaty of Westminster of February 1674 – as Charles found himself refused further money by the English Parliament and facing new enemies as the Dutch Republic and their new stadholder the Prince of Orange were joined by Spain, the Holy Roman Empire and Denmark against the French – marked a watershed in English and also Scottish political life. In England the Cabal disintegrated. Shaftesbury, unable to bring Charles to secure a Protestant succession by admittedly drastic means such as annulling James's marriage, was dismissed as Chancellor and, with Buckingham, who fell out with Arlington and also lost his offices, joined the 'country' party in the Westminster Parliament. Clifford had to resign on account of his Catholicism and soon committed suicide, distraught at the turn of events. Arlington continued as secretary until September 1674 but was a spent force. The only survivor who remained in office was Lauderdale. In Scotland the parliamentary politics of 1672 to 1674 had shown that opposition to his polices and personal rule had built from a faction in 1669 into a recognisable party.[73] In England, meanwhile, his durability became increasing associated with arbitrariness and the excesses of corrupt government. Buckingham, Shaftesbury and others had stored in their collective memory banks those instances where in council Lauderdale made bold aggressive statements to encourage his master to deal summarily with opposition. It was a simple strategic calculation to label Lauderdale as a Crown agent provocateur who deployed policies that subverted privilege and outraged a growing sense of representativeness in the parliaments of England and Scotland. Before long he was even seen as an agent of Catholicism which, perhaps more than any other charge placed at his door, shows he was misjudged by contemporaries. Nevertheless, the fact that James was back as the king's constant advisor, once Charles cooled his anger at the 'unwise' confirmation of his faith, markedly increased fears of 'popery and arbitrary government'. Inevitably, in England Lauderdale was associated with this fear and from 1674 his removal became the focus of greater Anglo-Scottish cooperation amongst opposition politicians.

RESTORING SCOTLAND

Lauderdale never understood the religious intransigence of Duke James. The Scottish Secretary supped from the same philosophical vessel as Charles which imbued them both with a deep-rooted religious pragmatism. This made Lauderdale ideally suited to the role of Crown man in Scotland. While perhaps best fitted to this task when Charles focused on Scotland, what of those periods when James did so? Indeed, was James concerned much with Scotland in the period between the Restoration and when, in the flesh, he arrived in Scotland in 1679?

The initial phase of the Scottish Restoration rested mostly on the foundations of the close personal relationship that developed between Charles and Lauderdale, though others also took a hand. Once the English army commissioners were finally replaced by the remaining members of the old committee of estates appointed in 1651, matters could turn to the make-up of Charles's Scottish administration. Its composition as created in the late summer and autumn of 1660 suggests that Lauderdale's counsel of caution was heeded. A broad-church grouping was commissioned mixing soft and hard Covenanters with Engagers and old royalists who had suffered for their loyalty. Yet the political map was not quite as balanced as it seemed. Lauderdale himself was made Scottish Secretary resident in London, although, given his earlier career as an ambassador for the Covenanting regime, not to universal acclaim. Middleton was appointed commander-in-chief in Scotland, although more significantly Lord High Commissioner to the Scottish Parliament (the position made necessary by the absence of the monarch since 1603), which would meet on the first day of January 1661. In fact, Middleton was the natural appointment as the most senior surviving officer from the unsuccessful campaigns of the 1650s, but it was more than his personal sacrifices and soldierly qualities that ensured his appeal to Charles and James. Although he fought with Montrose in the first blush of the Covenanting revolution, he turned vengefully against his former ally when Montrose's royalists killed his father in 1645. Subsequently, however, Middleton developed a profound hatred of Presbyterians. This followed his excommunication and public penance in the winter of 1650/51, at the instigation of James Guthrie and some radical Covenanting clergy, who were determined to rebuke him for involvement in the Engagement of 1648 and various royalist insurgencies over the following two years. Charles meanwhile found his own view propelled in the same direction by political events. If Burnet is to be believed, on meeting with Lauderdale in 1660 Charles, with characteristic understatement, declared that Presbyterianism 'was not a religion for gentlemen'. But in spite of various indulgences and efforts to bring English and Scottish nonconformity a degree of freedom of conscience in the 1660s and 1670s, by the 1680s Charles's own loathing for presbytery was given full vent as, from 1681 to 1685, he encouraged a crackdown on conventicles in both England and Scotland. In Scotland, it was these infamous years that became known as the 'Killing Times'. Indeed, after the English exclusion parliament of early 1681, Charles frequently recalled his humiliating ordeals at the hands of the Kirk Party in 1650 and 1651, and increasingly associated all nonconformity with republicanism and the days of Cromwell. This was a view James held long before, even though for short-term political reasons he occasionally had to promote policies of toleration as duke and as king. For James it was simple: Presbyterians were 'bitter enemies to Monarky'.[74] Therefore, a confirmed Episcopalian like Middleton, who fell under the influence of the Anglican Clarendon, was in 1660 an ideal High Commissioner in Scotland as a religious settlement within the Union of the Crowns required astute navigation towards episcopacy. So for James, loyalty to the Commissioner chosen by his brother was added to loyalty to his father-in-law.

The other senior members of the Scottish government commissioned in 1660 included the Presbyterians John Lindsay, earl of Crawford-Lindsay, retaining the position of Treasurer, and John Kennedy, earl of Cassillis, now Justice General, who reflected the split in Presbyterianism given that the former supported and the latter, an Argyll man, opposed the Engagement. Crawford-Lindsay, like Lauderdale, had been imprisoned for almost a decade in various English prisons, ending his confinement at Windsor Castle. Also, the old Engager, Hamiltonian and royalist insurgent, the earl of Glencairn, was appointed Chancellor in recognition of his sacrifices and periods of confinement in the 1650s. John Leslie, earl of Rothes, an Engager who was captured at Worcester who had his estate sequestrated by Cromwell and became a personal favourite of King Charles, was made President of the Council. Yet another Engager and captive William Keith, earl Marischal, was made Lord Privy Seal, with the thanks of his sovereign and the Scottish Parliament for doing his bit, with the help of his wife, to preserve the honours of Scotland during the 1650s. The new Lord Advocate Sir John Fletcher and new Clerk Register Sir Archibald Primrose had survived the Cromwellian period, the former as a criminal lawyer and the latter in spite of having his estate sequestrated for being at Worcester. Both were allies of Middleton and this helped secure their appointment.[75] These lairds, so anxious for preferment, were no different to the likes of the earl Marischal who was virtually bankrupt by 1660. The entire political class, and not merely the nobility, viewed the Restoration as an opportunity to regain dwindling prestige and financial security. Nevertheless, the royalist backlash in Scotland at the Restoration was essentially a noble and, as a rejection of the confessional politics of the previous two decades, secular reorientation. This 'anti-clericalism' guided, to a greater or lesser extent, most of Charles's ministers, regardless of their confessional backgrounds, although division still broke out. In the longer term, Charles's reliance on an assortment of self-interested, jealous and at times feuding nobles contributed to the capriciousness of his Scottish regime before 1679. Appointment on the basis of loyalty rather than ability did not help, as James would discover to his cost when he became king himself.

Charles's objective in Scotland from 1660 to 1662 was, in parliamentary and institutional terms, to turn the clock back to 1633. This was the year of Charles I's coronation parliament in Edinburgh, one of the authoritarian high-water marks of Stuart government. In England, although the son was unable to achieve a total restoration of his father's monarchy, some of the constitutional reforms of 1641 stayed in place. The king's royal prerogative courts, the Star Chamber and Council of the North, were not revived, and the English Triennial Act of 1641, which denied the power of the king to dismiss the Westminster Parliament for indefinite periods, was retained although amended in watered down form in 1664. In other words, the English Parliament was irrevocably altered by the upheavals of the Civil War.[76]

The Restoration in Scotland was, however, ostensibly more complete. In just over two years, from the May 1660 formal proclamation in Edinburgh of the king's return, Privy Council, Parliament, judiciary and finally a refashioned epis-copacy had been restored to their pre-revolutionary status. Admittedly the political influence of bishops was curtailed, with only the two archbishops sitting on the Council, though this became three from 1678 to 1687 as a favourite of James's was added, John Paterson, bishop of Galloway, then of Edinburgh and finally arch-bishop of Glasgow from 1687. When bishop of Galloway, he was allowed to reside in Edinburgh for want of appropriate accommodation in his own diocese, and being at hand, he became one of the most regular council attendees. He chaired various sub-committees and particularly those of the council Committee of Public Affairs investigating cases against conventiclers and radical Covenanters, and so was behind the 'Killing Times' as much as any conscientious army officer. But between 1660 and 1662, reflecting majority noble and Crown concerns, the Covenant was abruptly set aside and the Kirk placed under clear civil authority, with the king at the head. Lay patronage was revived, the means by which vacan-cies to clerical cures were filled through nomination by secular landed patrons. Notwithstanding, this reinvention of episcopacy was an exercise in pragmatism where zealots of *jure divino* episcopacy or presbytery were simultaneously disap-pointed. Philosophically the Scottish Restoration church was in the image of Charles rather than James, the would-be zealot. The authority of Scottish bishops was placed over the existing structure of kirk sessions and presbyteries, and the liturgical engineering of the 1630s was not repeated, as acts that once imposed English-like rituals, such as the Five Articles of Perth, gathered dust and were not enforced. In 1662 the 'Act concerning such benefices and stipends as have been possest without presentations from the lawfull patrons' was passed in Parliament and, as such, 'collation' of bishops (examination and confirmation) was added to 'presentation' by patrons. As Donaldson has described it, 'it was a restoration of the moderate Episcopalian regime of James VI's middle years without the ritual-istic accretions and the arbitrary interference'.[77] The impact was that 270 ministers, a quarter of the total, were forced to demit office for not having episcopal presenta-tion and collation. However, the lack of a *jure divino* ideological spine weakened Scottish Episcopalianism as an independent institution and made it more commit-ted to and reliant on the Crown's agenda of authority and order. Consequently, for much of the period in which Middleton, Lauderdale and James influenced or managed Scottish affairs, they were able to work with the Scottish bishops directly, or in James's case also through the influence of the English episcopate indirectly, to underpin Crown authority in the northern kingdom. In the meantime, in spite of the return of royal prerogative and of loyalist bishops to the chamber, in tone the Scottish Parliament was nevertheless irrevocably altered. The controlling and management parliamentary committee the Lords of the Articles returned, much to James's approval. In the 1690s, reflecting back on his experiences in Scotland and offering advice to his son, he declared:

> The constitutions of the [Scottish] Parliament . . . are very good, and ought not to be altered, especially that of the lords of the Articles, for by that

means a Parliament can do no great harm, and I have observed, that those who had a mind to be troublesome and to have it in their power to be so, endeavour'd to take that great prerogative from the Crown.

Nonetheless, after the Restoration there were longer parliamentary sessions and more resistance to rubber-stamping measures proposed by the Articles, a body which, following the tightly managed sessions of 1621 and 1633, was as a constitutional grievance dispensed with by the Covenanters, as it would be abolished after the Revolution of 1688/9. From 1661 the batching of measures became, for voting purposes, restricted to uncontroversial matters, such as ratifications related to private rights. Also, while there was little immediate sign in Edinburgh of the kind of organised opposition which began to appear at Westminster from the first day of the Cavalier Parliament, as factionalism grew in the course of the 1660s, fertile ground was prepared for opposition parliamentarians to deploy a collective political memory.[78] This recalled the representative legacy of the 1630s and 1640s, and the constitutional settlement of 1641, and yet was a secular and constitutional parliamentarianism, a culture shorn of much of the narrow religious context of the previous two decades.

As High Commissioner to Parliament Middleton was charged to deliver policies on five fronts: to reimpose the royal prerogative; to raise supply; to navigate the complexities of an act of indemnity or of oblivion, a pardon related to the rebellion against Charles I; to explore a church settlement and preferably one that appealed to moderate Resolutioners, like Sharp, and sidelined Protestors, leading to the reintroduction of Episcopalianism; and lastly, to find a means to annul the legislation of the Covenanting period which, of course, underpinned Presbyterianism. The parliamentary instructions Charles gave Middleton excluded mention of the Church, however – a clear sign that in this contentious area the king was listening to the warnings of Lauderdale to move by stages. The first two of the five objectives were achieved with minimal difficulty when the Estates convened in January 1661. Royal prerogative was re-established by acts that confirmed the king's authority to appoint his own servants, members of the Privy Council, military commanders and justiciary, the summoning and dissolving of parliaments, and control of the militia and treaties. This was supported by a new oath of allegiance to be taken by all members which, with its wording declaring the king 'soverign only supream governour . . . over all person and in all causes', left Cassillis and a small band of Presbyterians unable to take it without reassurances that the Church was not included. They promptly walked out of the Estates and into the political wilderness. The addition in the 1662 session of a declaration of public trust further excluded those without 'sound principles and entire loyalitie' from public office, and emphasised the extent to which the Covenanter's culture of oath taking had now been turned against opponents of resurgent monarchy.[79]

James viewed this statutory restatement of Crown authority as essential and yet it conflicted with his life-long held philosophy, expressed in 1667 before his own political crisis related to his faith took hold, that his brother should '[not] bring into Parliament things wherein his majesty, alone, was able to give relief'. This encapsulates a shared fraternal dilemma – a reluctance to summon parliaments but the necessity of doing so – and was certainly evident over taxation where, every bit as much as for England, approval by the Scottish Estates was a constitutional requirement. The cost of the Scottish establishment certainly could not in a direct manner be supplemented by a French pension. In 1661, however, the second objective was achieved when a compliant Scottish Estates granted Charles an annuity for life of £480,000 scots raised solely from customs and excise duties.[80] The movement from the Cromwellian cess or land tax to duties on consumption and imports relieved a hard-pressed nobility.

Two policy matters were held over to the next session in 1662. The precise nature of the religious settlement remained unclear as legislation confirmed a 'holding pattern' which allowed the continuation of kirk sessions, presbyteries and synods but declared Charles's intention in due course to settle the government of the church in a way 'most agreeable to the word of God, most suteable to monarchicall government [and to] the publict peace'.[81] However, fears that Presbyterianism would be supplanted by Episcopalianism came clearly into view when the question of annulling the legislation of the 1640s and 1650s was tackled. Secondly, the delay in passing an act of indemnity gave the Crown time to reflect on what punishments were practical or desirable given Charles's wish to build common support and also his concern at how punitive measures might be viewed in England before the political temperature was more predictable. Nevertheless, it left the Estates behaving meekly in the face of uncertainty over the terms of a future act of oblivion. So, most parliamentarians found themselves 'willing' to consider how to annul the legislation of the Covenanting period, while smaller minorities positively welcomed the move or protested strongly at the 'betrayal'.

Annulling this legislation was administratively Charles's most complex objective of the 1661 session. In January and February 1661 the Lords of the Articles set about considering the backlog of legislation and although some initial progress was made, with acts annulling the convention of 1643, condemning the delivering up of Charles I to the English Parliament in 1647 and approval of the Engagement of 1648, it became clear that the committee could not navigate the entire legislative morass and remove all elements that restricted the royal prerogative. The solution was one of breathtaking simplicity – the 'Act rescissory' passed on 28 March 1661 which swept away the entire, public legislative programme from 1640 to 1648, essentially turning the clock back to 1633, and in the process annulling all the statutory foundations of the Presbyterian church. This was coupled with the 'Act concerning religion and church government', passed on the same day, and it left the final settlement of Church government to the king's discretion. The way was paved for the reintroduction of episcopacy.[82]

The origins of the 'Act rescisory' are uncertain but Thomas Sydserf, formerly bishop of Galloway, the last remaining member of the Caroline Scottish episcopacy and the only one to regain episcopal office, this time as bishop of Orkney, appeared to be the first to propose this single-bullet solution. Sydserf composed a memorial on the subject for the king's information in late 1660 and it seems likely that it circulated amongst government ministers and Episcopalian sympathisers before the Estates assembled in January the following year. Burnet and James Sharp's accounts of the circumstances surrounding the act both confirm that it was at first raised in the committee the Lords of the Articles, probably in jest by the Clerk Register, Sir Archibald Primrose, or in Sharp's words, 'by way of ralliery [mockery] with [the Presbyterian] Crafurd', though they do not identify the original source. However, in its recommendation to 'by ane Act annull all Parliaments and Assemblies held since the year of 1637' and also to maintain a standing army, discipline the clergy, eject those who would not accept the authority of bishops and not to call general assemblies, Sydserf's memorial so closely follows royal policy over the next two years as to be its template. It closely followed the preferred agendas of Charles, Clarendon and James himself, when the latter championed the Anglican interest favoured by his father-in-law. Ironically, whereas Sydserf argued that to allow Presbyterianism to continue in Scotland would merely encourage the 'discontented party' in England, Charles initially favoured caution lest much needed Presbyterian support in Westminster would be lost. As it was, the new cavalier ascendency in the House of Commons ended that fear and, although Middleton exceeded his instructions, the positive outcome much pleased the king. James marvelled at what could be achieved with bold parliamentary management but he and his elder brother failed to note that at least forty individuals voted against the act. These malcontents, led by the duke of Hamilton, pondering the forgotten sacrifice of his father-in-law, the first marquis of Hamilton, were especially outraged that the sessions of 1641 and 1648, when, respectively, the late king was present, and the Engagement in support of Charles I was agreed, were wrapped up in this comprehensive annulment.[83] In this sense the Scottish Restoration settlement was not the unbridled constitutional success story for the Crown that is sometimes portrayed. The inherent weaknesses of regal union not only remained but were made more pronounced.

Middleton's objectives in March 1661 were to achieve a fulsome restoration of the royal prerogative and also to wound Lauderdale, his main political enemy, although how did that leave James? In many ways the history of Restoration Scotland is understood through the career of Lauderdale and so James's engagement with Scotland must in large part turn on his relationship with the Secretary. That did not mean that James agreed with all the policies Lauderdale deployed for Scotland in Charles's name, notwithstanding that loyalty to his brother's wishes came before every consideration except James's personal faith. Yet before Middleton's fall from grace in 1663, it was not clear to James in

whom Charles placed the most trust. Attempts by Middleton and his supporters to paint Lauderdale as a closet Presbyterian – though he was undoubtedly
committed to presbytery in the 1640s and 1650s – tapped into James's prejudice against the Scottish Presbyterian clergy, and he did not feel the need to
moderate his opinions an account of a personal friendship like that which
Charles shared with the Secretary.

One of the main difficulties for Commissioner Middleton, based mostly in
Edinburgh, was that Lauderdale was located in London, close to the ears of the
king and James. Clarendon supported the idea of a standing committee to be set
up in London to advise the king on Scottish affairs, and when the commission
for the Scottish Privy Council was agreed in February 1661, a London sub-committee was formed consisting of whichever Scottish privy councillors were
present, plus six Englishmen – Clarendon, Albemarle, Ormonde, Edward
Montagu, earl of Manchester, and the two English secretaries of state. Once Sir
Henry Bennet was made one of these in 1662, he regularly attended over Scottish
business. It would be an exaggeration to say, though, that this represented
English domination, and mostly the Scots outnumbered the English at these
meetings, and it should not be forgotten that since 1603, Scots, generally six in
number, had also been commissioned to the English Privy Council. Form
mattered less than the policy but nevertheless in 1661, for practical, personal
and even patriotic reasons, Lauderdale was very unhappy with this revised
arrangement.[84] Middleton thought the new London council a good idea for the
very reason that it would restrict Lauderdale and he could rely on Clarendon, a
fellow Episcopalian, to keep him informed of developments.

It is sometimes argued that James was not a particularly conscientious partici-
pant in the committees of state such as the English Committee for Trade and
Plantations, where his attendance was rare in spite of his colonial interests, or the
full English Privy Council, particularly following the English Test Act of 1673,
after which he only attended by invitation and on specific business. For Scotland,
however, such criticism is unfounded. In his first period of exile in Edinburgh,
from 24 November 1679 to 17 February 1680, James attended every single meeting of the Scottish Privy Council once Charles commanded in early December
that he could attend without taking the oath of allegiance which was inconsistent
with his Catholic beliefs. In his second period, from October 1680 to May 1682,
other than two months back in England in spring 1682, he is recorded at nearly
120 council meetings. Indeed, attendance at the Privy Council in Edinburgh
increased by 50 per cent when James was present in person. Wider participation
was encouraged by the presence of a royal prince as well as respite from the domination of Lauderdale.[85]

James's own engagement is also found when Scots matters were considered in
London. When in November 1679 he was advised by Lauderdale and the Scottish
Privy Council to take the oath of allegiance before taking his seat on the Edinburgh

Council, James declared in irritation that he had never been expected to take such an oath when 'satt in the Scots Councell at Hampton Court' and had participated in Scottish business. He was present at the Scots council in March 1661 when Middleton's report on the possibility of the restoration of bishops and the annulment of all Covenanting legislation was discussed. James supported Middleton's approach and also the decision in the summer of 1661 to restore episcopacy at the next session of Parliament, in contrast to Lauderdale's continued caution to move slowly. Lauderdale was not 'wholly Presbyterian' as some commentators and Middleton clearly thought, for he had his monarch's understanding of political expediency when it came to religion. However, his great concern was to bolster his master's and his own authority, while keeping the peace, and that involved accommodating as many as possible of the existing clergy in a new church settlement. Nevertheless, Middleton won the day and Charles signalled his desire by a proclamation issued by the Scottish Privy Council in September 1661 restoring 'right governement by bishops' and so 'better harmony' with the churches of England and Ireland. The following May, at the next session of the Scottish Parliament, bishops were brought back into Parliament by an act passed on the first day and by the end of the month a full restoration of episcopacy had been enacted. Middleton's policy had therefore been successful, as least ostensibly. Yet on the ground, opposition remained strong and recruitment of the fourteen bishops had been a serious problem for Sharp, the new Archbishop of St Andrews. In all of this James may have taken Middleton's side out of loyalty to his new Anglican father-in-law and his brother's wishes, but also out of his clear hatred of nonconformity. It is problematic to see James as someone who embraced toleration in the 1660s given that he could not distinguish Protestant nonconformity from republicanism. As it was, most of the Scottish nobility agreed with Middleton in any case. They did not realise, any more than Lauderdale and Middleton, that the return of episcopacy would prove, in Brown's stark words, 'the fundamental blunder of the restored monarchy'.[86] Unfortunately, royalist Presbyteriansim, which would have garnered support from moderate Resolutioner clergy and also Sharp, was not entertained. Not for the first or last time, Scottish problems could not be solved with English solutions.

The Middleton versus Lauderdale rivalry continued during and after the 1662 session of parliament and was played out in the convoluted scandal known as the 'billeting affair'. This arose from the insertion of the last piece of the Restoration jigsaw, the Act of Indemnity. Lauderdale, as much as anyone, was keen that this was secured, at least to offer the many Scots who signed the Covenant the same level of reassurance which the English had been given by their Act of Oblivion passed in August 1660 – the first, not the last, part of the English Restoration settlement! Middleton and his supporters adopted an extraordinary scheme to have Lauderdale and his senior men, such as John Hay, earl of Tweeddale, and Sir Robert Moray, excluded from public trust and removed from office. Firstly, they got Charles to agree that there could be twelve exemptions from the Act of Indemnity. At a meeting in London of the Scottish council in June 1662, held during the 1662 session of the Scottish Parliament, a nervous Lauderdale argued against this measure. However, Sir George Mackenzie of Tarbat, Middleton's spokesman and a young lawyer on the rise, persuaded Charles, James and the council that this merely followed the precedent set by the English act where the regicides were excluded from indemnity. In the second stage, when later in the summer the Edinburgh Parliament came to consider the act, Middleton and his group came up with the unprecedented idea of a secret ballot to select the twelve. When in September Charles discovered, through Lauderdale, that the Secretary himself had been named by this means, he was furious at this interference in his power over his own servants. Middleton was eventually summoned to London in February 1663 to explain his actions and, before a combined Scots and English council and the royal brothers, Lauderdale made a speech which, according to Mackenzie of Rosehaugh, was 'the great masterpiece of his life'. This, coupled with new evidence of other financial infelicities perpetrated by Middleton, ended his political career by the following May.[87] As some level of compensation, and in lieu of his respect for an old soldier, James helped Middleton obtain various small military commissions around London and in 1668 the governorship of Tangier.

In the Restoration settlement years of 1660 to 1663, Charles included his brother in much decision-making related to Scotland, and so James attended various key meetings of the Scottish council in London. However, several lessons were gained by both Lauderdale and James from this period of Crown success and Scottish ministerial division. For Lauderdale, the London council had to go and it did. By August 1663 Sir Robert Moray, Lauderdale's deputy left in London while his master and Rothes, Middleton's replacement as Commissioner, were in Edinburgh, reported that Charles 'doeth the business of Scotland not onely alone but with pleasure'.[88] The fall of Clarendon in 1667 was then the second stage in a decoupling of English ministers from direct influence in Scottish business. This did not end the informal lines of counsel so favoured by Charles, and James continued to be consulted on Scottish affairs, even after his conversion to Rome became common knowledge. Notwithstanding his reliance on Lauderdale, over Scotland, Charles favoured informality with a large coterie of advisors, while Lauderdale, and later James, developed a taste for less informality and reduced numbers of senior personnel. Indeed, from 1663/4 and especially from 1667, after which Lauderdale was both Secretary and parliamentary Commissioner, the Scot became wedded to government through a handful of individuals. James appears to have been impressed with this approach. In the years 1664 to 1678 a series of paired 'ministers' supported Lauderdale – Archbishop Sharp, who managed the refashioned episcopacy while Rothes as Chancellor remained in Edinburgh, from 1664 to 1667; John Hay, earl of Tweeddale, in Edinburgh with Sir Robert Moray moving between the capitals as required, from 1667 to 1672; Charles Maitland,

Lauderdale's younger brother and Treasurer Depute, running affairs in Edinburgh with Alexander Bruce, earl of Kincardine, treasury commissioner and confidant of James, travelling the administrative axis, from 1672 to 1674; and finally John Murray, first marquis of Atholl, Lord Privy Seal in Edinburgh, and the privy councillor Archibald Campbell, ninth earl of Argyll, who had seen his family fortunes recover since the Restoration under the patronage of Lauderdale.[89] Ironically, while we can marvel at the length of Lauderdale's term in office, each of these triumvirates collapsed under the weight of the Secretary's capriciousness, the interfering attitudes of his second wife, the countess of Dysart, and, more significant from a political perspective, the periodic rejection by the likes of Tweeddale, Kincardine and Atholl of the more extreme policies aimed at the repression of Protestant nonconformity. In this respect these three came to agree with the duke of Hamilton, and there is no greater testament to the sense of alienation Lauderdale engendered than that fact. It also became clear that a man who trusted no one could not himself be trusted. We might therefore understand that for good, even wise, political reasons, James never considered himself close to Lauderdale.

A PRINCE OF SCOTS

The conduct and policing of religious policy in Scotland after 1662, and for the remainder of Charles's reign, consisted of a bewildering oscillation between repression and conciliation towards Presbyterianism. In some senses Lauderdale's policies were moderate and no compulsion with regard to liturgy and ritual was attempted, although moderates could complain that the General Assembly never met during the reign. As for Lauderdale, tactical shifts towards indulgence or repression were made depending on the political threat posed by opponents like Clarendon, and the Scottish opposition leader Hamilton. Indulgences, or amnesties for nonconformist clergy, were declared in 1669, 1672 and 1679, this last time under authority of the duke of Monmouth, and these measures were successful in bringing some sheep into the fold, but not in extinguishing long term resentment.[90] This was the context in which James's views of Scottish church government entered the stage.

In what could be described as the cavalier phase in his engagement with Scottish politics, from the Restoration to the mid 1670s, James's interest in Scotland centred around three issues – the health of Scottish episcopacy, and two more careerist aspects, the prospects for Scottish economic affairs and the nature of the military establishment.[91] The overriding context, as always, was loyalty to his brother's policies. But his concern for the religious government of Scotland was something of a mixed blessing for Lauderdale and indirectly also for Charles, given that it encouraged inconsistency. James was, of course, a key player in the High Anglican party in England, close to most of the English bishops led since 1663 by Gilbert Sheldon, Archbishop of Canterbury, and to Clarendon himself. James became in faith a Catholic but in politics always an Episcopalian, wedded to crown-controlled church structures. Even though Lauderdale had at the 1663 session of the Scottish Parliament, with Rothes as High Commissioner and himself in attendance, delivered on his promise to secure episcopacy and attack conventicles by legislative means, the more intolerant English bishops remained concerned at the precarious status of Scottish bishops and, as they saw it, insufficiently rigorous efforts to suppress nonconformity.[92]

The key to James's links to Scottish episcopacy was his relationship with Sheldon. In general Sheldon disagreed with enforcing severe penalties against loyal English Catholics, but more specifically supported in council and the House of Lords James's plans to rebuild the navy in 1666, to defend Clarendon in 1667 and to oppose the Roos divorce case in 1670.[93] More importantly for Scotland though, Sheldon encouraged Sharp to embrace episcopacy, then from 1663 pressed for harsher measures to tackle Presbyterian field meetings, especially in the volatile south west of Scotland. From 1664, when the hawkish Alexander Burnet was elevated to the archbishopric of Glasgow, his shrill warnings aimed at the court in London made Sheldon and James even more anxious for a sustained policing effort. To them, the Pentland Rising of November 1666, a spontaneous combustion borne out of this general feeling of discontent and, particularly, exasperation at the arbitrariness of religious fines, merely proved that Burnet was correct.[94] Lauderdale was able to push most of the blame for the rising on to Rothes and Sharp, leading to the archbishop's political eclipse for six years, but he now realised that Burnet had to be removed. However, even though he engineered Burnet's resignation in 1669 and persuaded Charles to grant the carrot of the first indulgence the same year, James, Sheldon and the English bishops had to be placated with a more rigorous stick, and Lauderdale delivered at the 1670 session of the Scottish Estates the Conventicle Act (known as the Clanking Act) which threatened the death penalty for preaching at field meetings.[95]

The policy of conciliation continued when Leighton finally replaced Burnet in 1671, yet in spite of the second indulgence, Leighton's attempts at a grand accommodation and the convening of a national synod both failed, and were undermined by Sheldon. After Leighton's resignation Lauderdale was forced to turn back to Sharp and the High Anglicans, and even Alexander Burnet was reinstated to Glasgow in September 1674. The same year, fresh troops were deployed in the south west. By now Lauderdale was increasingly in alliance with Charles's new minister Danby, and he in turn, as a staunch Anglican, was close to Sheldon and therefore James, though it would require the Popish Plot of 1678 to bring James and Danby into greater political cooperation. Lauderdale's options for an independent religious policy were now more limited. In spite of the second indulgence, bringing perhaps eighty non-conforming clergy into the church, he found himself attempting to impose an episcopal settlement which could not be entirely achieved either by moderation or by muscle.[96] From 1674 Charles had opted for muscle having, against his natural instinct for toleration, his mind turned to this course by Sheldon and James.

At the convention of estates in the summer of 1678, the last meeting of the Estates under Lauderdale's management, a new taxation of £1,800,000 scots was voted to suppress conventicles. Local militias could no longer be trusted to maintain order in the affected regions, now expanding into Angus, Perthshire and more widely in Fife, and so the remarkable creation that year of the eight thousand-strong Highland Host (a militia force where a third were actually lowlanders) was the Secretary's last desperate effort to simultaneously defeat dissent and criticism from Hamilton's party. Hamilton and his close supporters even walked out of the chamber in protest at Lauderdale's autocratic procedures. Mocked subsequently by those who claimed their powerlessness in the face of a Crown majority and reduced power since 1673 when they forced an adjournment, they actually achieved their key objective of exposing the Secretary's tactics to his English critics.[97] But in Scotland the persecution merely intensified, and field meetings grew in size, leaders such as Covenanter preacher Richard Cameron touring the west in the tradition of John Knox. Then after troops and a large conventicle clashed at Lesmahagow in Lanarkshire in March 1679, and the brutal assassination by a group of radical dissenters of the 'turncoat' Archbishop Sharp near St Andrews the following May, a full Covenanter rising commenced. It achieved a surprise victory over government forces at Drumclog, also in Lanarkshire, though it was ultimately defeated at Bothwell Brig nearby in June 1679, where the duke of Monmouth defeated the rebels. Cameron met his death at the skirmish of Airds Moss in Ayrshire soon after, but the message of Covenanting continued through civil disobedience, printed protests and the efforts of exiles and their presses in Holland. Lauderdale's religious policy had failed and his time was up. In the end, however, the qualities of his administration mattered more than religion. The corruption of Lauderdale's regime, with its shifting political alliances, was now increasingly being seen as deep and widespread. His second wife, the countess of Dysart, was viewed as greedy and extravagant and his brother Charles Maitland of Hatton, who coined it in with a monopoly on the royal mint, was actually indicted. If contemporaries like Tweeddale are to be believed the degree of venality appeared to eat away at every aspect of public life. This, combined with an unfettered royal prerogative, weakened the reputation of Lauderdale himself.[98]

In spite of these concerns, James remained stalwart, probably more so than Charles, in his support of Lauderdale, particularly over his handling of the Hamiltonians throughout the 1670s. In December 1673 he wrote in angry terms to Hamilton demanding an explanation for his behaviour which had left his brother the king 'not well pleased'. In the summer of 1674 James publicly supported Lauderdale over his management of the difficult 1673/4 session, mocking the pretensions of Hamilton and his confederates, and reacted similarly to Hamilton's protests in 1678 at his 'ill-treatment'. Indeed, he wrote to Lauderdale congratulating him on the convention of estates of 1678 which 'so well finished his Majesty's affairs'. However, in June 1678, before the convention gathered and to Lauderdale's discomfiture, Charles had written to him with instructions to be careful not to give political opponents more ammunition to attack him and his master, and to treat Hamilton and his confederates 'wth all civility'.[99] For James, in the context of the exclusion campaign against him that was building in momentum and attempts since late 1673 by the English Commons to impeach Lauderdale which forced the Secretary into the arms of the English bishops, common cause could be felt for a loyal servant doing his duty while under threat from the enemies of monarchy.

One of the more surprising aspects of James's engagement with Scotland, where episcopacy was the preserve of most of the elite and presbytery of the popular majority, was as patron of Scottish episcopacy, in spite of his personal faith. James had good relations with most Scottish bishops on account of his support for measures to clamp down on conventicles. However, with the murder of independent-minded Archbishop Sharp in May 1679, and replacement by a chastened and acutely loyal Alexander Burnet, James was regularity consulted over episcopal reshuffles and university appointments. For example, when the candidature of Alexander Rose, professor of divinity, to be principal of Glasgow University was considered in 1684, it was subjected to his judgment, even though Rose's own uncle Arthur Rose, Archbishop of Glasgow, had made the nomination. James's prestige also increased in this regard in England when on Sheldon's death in 1677 he was replaced by the less ambitious William Sancroft. When Burnet also died in 1684, Arthur Rose replaced him as Scottish primate but, being a poor successor to Sharp and Burnet, he did little of political significance without the approval of Canterbury and James. The key Scottish political bishop was now John Paterson, bishop of Edinburgh, yet another member of James's circle.[100] It says everything for James's misjudgement of political realities once king that from such a promising foundation he was to alienate so many bishops on both sides of the Border.

James was also, more expectedly, the key patron for military appointments in Scotland and long before his arrival there in 1679. The condition of Scotland's small army had been a source of frustration for him since the Restoration. The disbanding of the standing army after the Pentland Rising of 1666 left about 1,200 men, including the garrisons at Edinburgh, Stirling and Dumbarton, and even when temporary regiments were raised, as during the Bothwell Brig rising of 1678 to 1679, it came to fewer than 2,800 foot and horse. Also, in spite of proposals for a new militia, at first agreed by the Estates in 1663 with the offer of 20,000 foot and 2,000 horse, which was worked on subsequently by the Privy Council but officially scaled back to an unfulfilled 5,000 foot and 500 horse in December 1679, the situation continued to present limited possibilities for military expansion and officer corps patronage. Much of the military provision of Scotland was theoretical rather than practical with the treasury unable to sustain even militia forces of reasonable strength. But that did not mean it was uncontroversial. The militia was to be available to Charles in 'any parte of his dominions of Scotland, England and Ireland for suppressing of any forraigne invasion, intestine trouble or insurrection' and Englishmen, especially the House of Commons, were deeply offended at what appeared a threatening measure in the spirit of Strafford.[101] Thus it was that Lauderdale, manager of the 1663 session and subsequent militia measures, and James, the man charged by Charles with appointing officers and who converted to Rome, came to be portrayed as agents of arbitrary government and a threat to English liberty.

In the various pieces of legislation intended to develop the militia plan, officers commissions were left to the king and for the most part to his brother, particularly after the fall of Middleton in 1663. This could involve very fine detail, such as the long list of military commissions he authorised in September 1678.[102] James also kept good relations with the Scottish officer class who he had come to admire from his experiences in exile in the 1650s, in spite of their varied confessional backgrounds. Amongst Catholics, in whom James took a special interest, was Andrew Rutherford, earl of Teviot, who had served in the 1640s and 1650s under Condé and Turenne, and at the Restoration, James ensured he was elevated to the peerage, and made governor of Tangier in 1663. Another Catholic of a younger generation was Thomas Buchan, later a Jacobite army officer. Buchan entered French service in 1668 and, during the Anglo–Dutch War from 1672–8, stayed out of the way fighting on the German front. James nevertheless directed him to enter Dutch service from 1678 to 1682 under Colonel Hugh MacKay of Scourie, before returning to Scotland to help John Graham of Claverhouse prosecute the 'Killing Times' of the mid 1680s. Later and more famously he attempted, with little success, to continue the counter-revolution started by Claverhouse (then Viscount Dundee) in 1689. In his lifetime, James paid special attention to Buchan and communicated with him at great length in the 1690s. However, the Catholic officer who rose to most pre-eminence was George Douglas, earl of Dumbarton. Dumbarton entered military service in the Douglas regiment with Louis XIV in the late 1640s and 1650s, as a Catholic less able to serve in Scotland or England. Although the regiment was briefly recalled in 1666/7, in the 1670s Douglas fought with Monmouth and the regiment *anglais* in the French army during the third Anglo-Dutch War, before his regiment was disbanded in 1678.[103] James made him commander-in-chief in Scotland in 1685 when the government faced the Argyll Rebellion. In fact, by now he was one of the key members of James's Catholic court 'party', supporting the policies of the Drummond brothers, Melfort and Perth. He advised James to flee in 1688 and himself died in exile at Saint-Germain.

Some Protestant officers came under James's wing. Former Civil War veterans included William Drummond of Cromlix, viscount Strathallan, and Thomas Dalzell of Binns, two individual friends with almost parallel careers. Both served under the Covenanters, in Ireland in the 1640s, the Engagement of 1648, at the battle of Worcester in 1651 (when both were captured but escaped) and the Glencairn rising of 1654, after which they ended up in Russia for ten years in the service of Tsar Alexi I. When they returned home in 1665, under Charles's command and James's advice, Dalzell was made commander-in-chief in Scotland with Drummond as his major general and they participated in suppressing the Pentland Rising in 1666, and then Dalzell was reappointed in 1679 until his death to deliver the 'Killing Times' and the crackdown after the murder of Archbishop Sharp. The Presbyterian historian Robert Wodrow saves some of his greatest invective for Dalzell's grim suppression of Covenanting. Meanwhile, Drummond ran into a few political difficulties including marrying a daughter of the great Presbyterian Archibald Johnston of Wariston, and also being one of those parliamentarians deputed in 1678 to complain to the king about the conduct of Lauderdale. Nevertheless, after Lauderdale's demise and on James's insistence, he was brought back in 1682 and as lieutenant general of all forces in Scotland, tackled the Argyll Rebellion of 1685, which brought the demise of the ninth earl of Argyll. Drummond was one of the group of nobles and officers who James put under pressure to convert to Rome, but he refused, although as his brother-in-law James Johnston memorably put it, he was 'a bad Christian but a good Protestant'. He and Dalzell were infamous for their 'Muscovite ways' and harsh military discipline.[103]

Two contrasting case studies perhaps sum up James's relations with Scottish soldiery, Sir James Turner and, most famously, John Graham of Claverhouse. Turner was a Covenanting veteran who began in Swedish service with Gustavus Adolphus before joining the Covenanters in 1640. He served in Ireland in the 1640s before returning to Scotland in 1648 to deal with Alasdair MacColla, Montrose's Irish ally. Again, like so many others, he served in the Engagement and at Worcester, where he was captured and escaped. At the Restoration James made sure he was appointed a major in the king's foot guards in Scotland, and in 1666 he was promoted before suppressing Covenanting in the south west with such ferocity that he helped provoke the Pentland Rising and was himself captured. Turner was blamed for the debacle and lost his commission. He was brought back into service, however, in the 1680s to help deal with the suppression of dissidents but resigned in 1686 after the Argyll Rebellion, dying at the Revolution, now an old man. Claverhouse like Turner was Protestant, married to a firm Presbyterian, and he also changed sides in his formative campaigning years. Claverhouse joined William Lockhart's regiment in France in a force commanded by Monmouth in the service of Louis XIV, under the overall command of Marshal Turenne, but in 1674 he changed sides and joined the Dutch and was in continuous service for three years. He then came to the attention of James who ensured he was given command of a troop of horse in Scotland in 1678, and was ordered to subdue the south-west from 1678 to 1679. Nevertheless, he was then summoned to London and for the next three years was a close companion of

James and Charles around London, Newmarket and Windsor. With James he travelled to Edinburgh, to and fro from Edinburgh to London, before going back to London with James in 1682–3. He kept regular company with the duke before returning to Scotland to serve during the 'Killing Times' and over the Argyll Rebellion. Subsequently at the Revolution, Claverhouse was one of those profoundly shocked at the decision of James to flee to France and not to stand and fight.[105] No military individual was closer to James from 1679 to 1689 than Claverhouse, though at the time, James assumed John Churchill, the brother of his mistress Arabella, was also his loyal protégé.

We can get a few insights into the nature of the relationships between James and these men. In 1700, while in ill health and only months before he died, with the instruction of his son in mind, James took time to pen a series of instructions on military deployment and readiness. Turner during his period of retirement had published in 1683 his *Military Essayes of the Ancient Grecian, Roman, and Modern Art of War*, a manual of warfare admired by James out of that same love of the ancient art. In the dedication to James, Turner describes the duke as a 'great master in the art of war', as well as thanking him for 'princely favours'. Claverhouse was also very loyal to James and is reported to have wept on news of his flight to France, but occasionally a reflection reveals a more complicated relationship between soldier and commander. In 1683 Claverhouse wrote to Queensberry and stated: 'The duek thinks the army his own province, and that he understands about the men and business of it better than anybody, and he has his owen maxims that it is hard to put him af'. James could be insufferably opinionated about soldiering. He admired military debate and the reflections of Turner and the like, but his own views were paramount.[106] All this reveals that the nature of James's relations with this soldiery and the Scots network was complex. Protestant officers were pressed to turn Catholic in the 1680s and Presbyterians were generally not trusted, unless expedience dictated, as was the case with George Monro of Culrian and Newmore, a Covenanting veteran called up by James in some desperation in 1688, but who hesitated before siding with Prince William. Notwithstanding, looking at these veterans and new men, Covenanters and continental adventurers, leads us to the conclusion that at times the overriding concern for James was not religious or political in his relations with soldiers, but in the fact of soldiering itself. He was also the most significant influence on the Scottish military in the Restoration period.

In this period James's military reputation hinged on his naval rather than his army career, but there was little scope for such adventures in the northern kingdom. However, he was appointed Lord Admiral of Scotland in the very year he resigned from the English equivalent on account of the English Test Act, and this left some possibilities for patronage as well as confirming the Exclusion Crisis was mostly an English affair. The Scottish post was facilitated by the death without heirs in December 1672 of the Scottish incumbent Charles Stuart, sixth duke of

Lennox and third of Richmond. In a personal maritime calamity, all too typical of his accident-prone life, Richmond died of the cold having fallen overboard while drunk off the coast of Denmark. Thereafter, with James at the helm, the Admiralty Court records of Scotland reveal him mostly obsessed with his right to wrecks and prizes from his Scottish jurisdiction rather than the building of ships. Indeed, his first dispute with Archibald, ninth earl of Argyll, came in 1677 over the case of a Spanish armada ship that sank off the Western Isles in 1588. The gold aboard, if it existed, James hoped to claim for himself as Lord Admiral. Yet the lords of session ruled against him and in favour of Argyll with his clear rights in the matter. To some it seemed a rather opportunist action and suggestive of James's acquisitiveness. The protagonists wrote to each other in friendly terms after the judgement, although the case did nothing to improve relations when they collapsed in early 1681.[107] Once in post in Scotland, James took the chance to appoint trusted royal servants to admiralty positions and notably, as vice-admiral or judge admiral, Alexander Bruce, earl of Kincardine, in 1673 and, on his death, John Murray, marquis of Atholl, in 1680. On James's succession, Atholl continued as head of the Scottish admiralty while James, in England and Scotland, kept for himself the two Lord Admiral positions. Before then, in spite of his Catholicism and in the aftermath of public sympathy following the Rye House plot of 1683, James returned in May 1684 to be de facto Lord High Admiral of England, although with Charles signing papers on James's advice. James did not, however, sit on his hands when it came to reforming the Scottish administration. Firstly, he refocused the efforts of the Scottish admiralty courts as the third Dutch War took its course, and then he advised his brother on new rules of admiralty that in July 1673 brought Scottish and English procedures into line, a measure of Anglo-Scottish convergence which would have pleased his father and grandfather. Finally, out of the council of trade chaired by James himself that advised the 1681 Scottish Parliament, James ensured that the jurisdiction of the Admiralty Court and its judges was made independent of the Court of Session with the 'Act concerning the jurisdiction of the admiral court', a statute which remained in place until 1830.[108] James had his impact on Scotland's peace-time business of the sea.

There were more significant proposals for Anglo-Scottish convergence than rules about seafaring. In echoes of the economic background to the union of 1707, in the late 1660s Charles II explored the union of England and Scotland as a solution to Scotland's economic grievances and his own government's perception of general political dangers north of the Border. In Scotland economic motives predominated. The English Navigation Act of 1660 meant the English market, and especially the plantations, had been legally closed to Scots and war with the Dutch, Scotland's major trading partner, made trading conditions worse. In early 1668 negotiations on a commercial union began but became bogged down in fine detail and English reluctance to give the Scots open access to the colonies, and were suspended in early autumn. Even before these negotiations began, Lauderdale had suggested political union as a solution to cure the economic rivalry which poisoned the regal union. Charles, therefore, at the prompting of Lauderdale, Sir Robert Moray and the great union enthusiast John Hay, earl of Tweeddale, switched to the objective of parliamentary union. Fears of disloyalty from Scottish Presbyterians during the second Anglo-Dutch War (1665–7), the Pentland Rising of 1666 and continuing conventicle activity, and the shock engendered by the attempted murder of Sharp on the High Street of Edinburgh in 1668 (eleven years before the successful second attempt) came together to give Charles reasons to adopt this policy, although there are few signs that he was particularly enthusiastic. In reality, few were on either side but, expressing loyalty to his brother's wishes, James supported Lauderdale's efforts to push the union agenda in the Scottish parliamentary sessions of 1669 and 1670. In the end, of course, the Scottish and English commissioners who met in London in October and November 1670 failed to reach an agreement. When all was apparently lost, Lauderdale was able to snatch victory from the jaws of defeat by playing the patriot. He made the spoiling and impossible demand that the Cromwellian model of a small number of MPs would not be acceptable to the Scots, and that the new parliament must accommodate all Scots members.[109] By now the secret Treaty of Dover had been signed which furnished Charles with greater financial independence from the English Parliament. Given that the treaty empowered him to meet any challenge from that quarter, and without the constitutional risks that union might involve, he now left the union project in limbo, neither undermining nor encouraging. Lauderdale was left to deliver the *coup de grâce*.

The political advantages to the Crown of a parliamentary union can be summed up in Tweeddale's comments in April 1668 – in time Scotland could become 'a citadel for his majesty's service'. A strongly monarchical union could be achieved, with a more awkward England made more manageable through the votes of loyal Scots in a union parliament. Thus Scotland would be a 'Trojan horse' for absolutism leaving, in James Kirkton's words, Charles 'as absolute in Brittain as the French king [in France]'. However, those Scottish cavaliers relieved at the failure of negotiations could turn this argument on its head. As Sir George Mackenzie saw it, the existence of two parliaments offered the chance that over the royal prerogative or obedience to the royal will 'one might always be exemplary to the other'. James's personal views on union supported this latter approach, in spite of his apparent enthusiasm for union from 1668 to 1670. His anti-unionism was strengthened by his experience managing the Scottish Parliament in person and the fact of the Williamite revolution, as is made clear in his 'Advice' of 1692. In this he states: 'Tis the true interest of the crown to keep the kingdom separate from England', and those who support union should be seen as 'weake men, bribed by some private concern'. If it was swallowed up by England, as in the time of Cromwell, Scotland as a 'great supporter' of the Crown would be lost forever.[110]

From the 1670s James adopted a 'colonial' vision of unionism under the regal union in which internal freedom of trade for the three kingdoms and the colonies, an imperial trading system, had priority over institutional convergence or even full economic union. It was this vision that brought together his apparently genuine, if generalised, concern for the economic development of the kingdoms, the key significance of naval power but also his personal income. This is seen in his investment and patronage of the new joint stock companies that traded the globe in the Restoration period. James became governor of the Royal Fisheries Company (1664), Company of Royal Adventurers Trading to Africa (1664) and Hudson Bay Company (1682) after their foundation in 1661, 1662 and 1670 respectively. While the fisheries struggled to become an effective challenge to Dutch competition, and the unaristocratic nature of the Hudson Bay Company suppressed James's interest, as it did that of the court other than the governor Prince Rupert, the Company of Royal Adventurers, rebranded the Royal Africa Company in 1672, had James's full attention. He and many investors believed in the potential riches of African trade in what was something of a gold rush. By the late 1660s, however, it was clear that for lack of known gold deposits and sufficient elephants, gold and ivory could not sustain this trade. James, then, more than any other proprietor, was thereafter responsible for a calculated switch to slavery linked to New York and the plantation market in the West Indies. He made substantial profits from this human misery. Yet it was in the light of all such joint stock experience, good or ill, that James supported a new Royal Company for the Fishery in Scotland established in the summer of 1670. This gave exclusive rights over all other Scotsmen to fishing around Scottish waters and off the coast of Greenland. Unfortunately it was even less successful than its English equivalent, and became a source of resentment by fishermen who were merely taxed by the company for every 'last' (or shipload) of exported herring, and was dissolved in late 1682. Nevertheless, James was also a great believer in a Scottish trading company to sit alongside the Elizabethan-founded East India Company, and suggested such a development in 1681. Early that year, under James's chairmanship, a Scottish Privy Council 'committee of trade' considered and approved a 'Memorial concerning the Scottish plantation to be erected in some place of America' submitted by Scots merchants. This made a strong case for a Scottish settlement in territories near English colonies not yet extensively populated, such as Florida and Carolina. The committee also took various measures to secure Scots trade from unwelcome overseas competition, and took this mercantilist agenda to the Scottish Parliament the following summer. As for James, he no doubt hoped to create a new source of revenue for the Crown. The East India adventurers had provided the royal brothers with extensive loans and gifts since the Restoration, many in lieu of renewed and expanded charters, and, from 1681 to 1688, an annual gift to the Crown of 10,000 guineas. James himself purchased £3,000 of stock in 1684 and was gifted £10,000 for a new charter in 1687. By now the Company had shown itself unable to keep out of the political divisions of the time, to the extent that many investors and ousted directors supported the Revolution against James. Under Sir Josiah Child's governorship, the Company had became too dependent on royal patronage and unwanted interference. It is therefore clear why James, though in exile, would have agreed with the creation of the Company of Scotland in 1695.[111]

James was able to convince the English Privy Council to allow Scots to share from the 1670s in the activities of the Royal Africa Company and Hudson Bay Company and to trade freely with New York, but his record over his own colonial schemes was mixed.[112] His proprietorship of his American colonies, the port and territories of New York – granted to him by his brother and taken by force from the Dutch in 1664 to be regained in 1674 after reverting back to the Dutch for two years during the third Anglo-Dutch War – was a sorry tale of authoritarianism, corruption, mismanagement and chaos. Fragmenting the lands of the southern territories, now named East New Jersey and West New Jersey, by dividing them up between favoured courtiers caused administrative chaos and endless disputes over land. Meanwhile, failure to grant representative assemblies depressed the means to raise taxation and at the same time created resentment, even amongst English settlers. Eventually in 1682, when it was obvious the previous year that taxation could not be raised without such a concession, James granted an assembly to New York, although after he became king, it met only one further time (a third session) before being dissolved in January 1687. The objective of increased taxation achieved, King James let the assembly wither and rejected a Charter of Liberties presented to him in late 1684. It was therefore in spite of these difficulties that he supported and authorised Scottish colonies in South Carolina (1682) and East New Jersey (1685).[113]

The Scottish South Carolina colony was a short-lived affair that found itself embroiled in political controversy. The project became linked to the Rye House Plot and because of this, some historians have doubted its credibility given that in the summer of 1683 a band of desperate Scots used gatherings of potential colonists and investors in London as a cover for plotting the demise of the royal brothers. It is true that a small number of potential proprietors became associated with the earl of Shaftesbury, who was not only the great English Whig grandee but one of the original English proprietors of Carolina. It was, however, to much earlier that the scheme owed its foundation. From a suggestion for a Presbyterian sanctuary first mooted by Sir George Lockhart of Carnwath ten years previously, the dissenters Sir John Cochrane of Ochiltree and Sir George Campbell of Cessnock declared by August 1682 that they had already made an agreement with the 'lords' of Carolina to acquire two counties for new settlers. These and other Covenanters were attracted to the opportunity to escape persecution as nonconformists, and to practice their religion unhindered. The involvement of stanch Covenanters like Henry Erskine, Lord Cardross, who became a South Carolina undertaker, confirms the confessional nature of the scheme, as also that they finally set sail under his leadership in July 1684. However, the plantation was always a well-planned business venture, with English proprietors in Carolina, and Scots noble investors and merchants, such as the Glasgow Atlantic trader Walter Gibson, envisaging substantial economic returns. It was ironic, of course, that James encouraged the Covenanters into exile for economic as well as political reasons because the instigators 'would carry with them the disaffected', and that Charles gave his formal approval to the English Privy Council in April 1684 enabling the departure of 'such rebels as appear penitent'.[114] When some departed on a ship captained by Gibson's brother they were a mixed band of ex-prisoners, hopeful Covenanters and believers in the prospects for a prosperous future. The Argyll Rebellion of 1685 then provided more 'penitent' colonists. Yet unfortunately the settlement had two weakening characteristics that in the late 1690s would impede the infamous Darien Scheme. Firstly, it was founded as a trading a colony where basic goods from Scotland could be exchanged with native produce, but with insufficient prospects for trade to the other American colonies. Also, and ulti-mately most significantly, the territory was claimed by the Spanish. Without the diplomatic flexibility or military strength to secure or defend the colony, two Spanish raids in the course of 1686 destroyed it and its main settlement Stuart's Town, a 'capital' not saved by being named in honour of royal patrons. The survi-vors of a community of perhaps a few hundred strong either fled to Charleston, where a Scots business network became well established in transatlantic and Caribbean commerce, or moved to other colonies including New Jersey.[115]

East New Jersey was a more successful effort after a group of Scottish associates were signed up in March 1683. This group was headed not merely by nobles and senior officers of state but individuals who from 1679 became intimate with James as duke and king of Scots. They confirm his key position as a patron of Scottish colonialism. For the East New Jersey plan both the confessional diversity and regional origins differed from Carolina, as Episcopalians and Quakers, as well as Presbyterian lairds, became proprietors and investors, mostly from the north east and south east of Scotland and not the Covenanting west. The contract of inden-ture by the duke, subsequently confirmed in letters patent by Charles II in November 1683, lists as the senior proprietors James Drummond, earl of Perth, his brother the Treasurer Depute John Drummond of Lundin, later earl of Melfort and, like Perth, a future Catholic convert, George Mackenzie, Viscount Tarbat, the Clerk Register, and Robert Barclay of Urie, the leader of the Aberdeen Quakers. The Quaker connection was crucial to the project's gestation period. Since the mid 1670s, James had begun in private to admire the passive religious toleration advo-cated by the English Quaker William Penn, given his own confessional circumstances. Penn recommended Barclay to James, and when Barclay visited other Friends in London in 1677 he had several audiences with the duke and pressed on him the plight of the dozens of Quakers imprisoned in Aberdeen the year before. While James could do nothing immediately, the Aberdeen Quakers were finally set free when he arrived in Edinburgh in 1679. Penn also interested

Barclay in colonial ventures, the letters patent for his own territories west of the Delaware (Pennsylvania as it became) being granted in 1681, and with Penn and other Quakers having holdings in West and East New Jersey and able to testify to the possibilities. By early 1683 though, George Haliburton, the new bishop of Aberdeen, was making renewed protests to the Privy Council in Edinburgh about Quaker activity in the North East, and Barclay saw a colony of sanctuary as a potential solution for his co-religionists. Equally important to his motivation, however, was his strong interest in agricultural improvement. This was very much a commercial plan, and being based on agricultural production in the fertile fields of New Jersey, it was built on firmer foundations than the Carolina initiative. Indeed, Barclay did more than anybody else to promote the Scottish colony, using his persuasive skills in speech and print, yet also gaining the ear of James. Barclay was appointed governor of the enterprise, though he accepted only on condition that he never crossed the Atlantic himself. Two of his brothers made the journey. It is ironic, nevertheless, that Barclay and the Presbyterian George Scot of Pitlochie found themselves advocating transportation to the new colony for Quakers, and especially the Covenanters swelling east coast prisons in 1684, and more intensively the following year after the Argyll debacle. The Privy Council responded by granting various commissions of transportation. In the period from 1684 to the Revolution, therefore, perhaps seven hundred Scots had settled in East New Jersey, some willingly and some by force, to add to those who had moved over from South Carolina. Up to a hundred prominent Scots became investors, in part encouraged by royal involvement in the enterprise.[116] After 1690, however, emigration declined but due as much to the death of Barclay that year as to the absence of James himself.

To Scotland's struggling mercantile interest and frustrated parliamentarians these colonial schemes of the 1680s represented a chance to circumvent the English Navigation laws and simultaneously avoid the prospects of a union with England, something so politically unpopular in 1670. The logic of Scottish cavaliers in this respect is contained in an anonymous Jacobite advice to a Catholic king penned after the union of 1707: '[Scots] are so loyally affected that they want but an occasion to declare for the King & against the Union'. Unfortunately, in spite of James's promotion of an imperial solution to Scotland's economic woes, the old problems of the regal union remained. A compliant English Parliament was required, but it was a pipedream. Without military muscle and control of foreign policy, Scottish colonial adventures could only succeed if grafted to the wealthier resources of a partner, most likely England, as was the case in New Jersey. James returned to the topic of trade from time to time, a default position. When he issued his two Scottish indulgences in February and June 1687 granting toleration to Catholics and dissenters, he declared that one of his motives was to halt the 'decay of trade'. He made a link between religious toleration and free trade in Holland leading to Dutch economic prosperity. Opponents such as the exiled Gilbert Burnet, who produced various tracts that rejected toleration and the repeal of the Test Acts, claimed Protestantism rather than free trade explained Dutch economic successes. With hindsight, both were wrong. Regardless of the efforts of James's council of trade convened in Edinburgh in 1681, and the consensus that action was required, Scotland was left using economic bows and arrows against the heavy guns of European mercantilism. It is fair to say, however, that the forging of these meagre weapons was made possible by the support of James between 1679 and 1685. His detractors might be better to focus on his Scottish policies where, in a variety of guises, he was more a prince of Scotland than any Stuart since James VI.[117]

CHAPTER 4

Duke and King of Scots, 1679–1688

THE 'ANCIENT KINGDOM'

In the heat of the Exclusion Crisis and facing the prospect of a newly elected English House of Commons now dominated by Shaftesbury's Whigs – 'a Presbyterian one' as the earl of Moray described it – Charles wrote to James on 28 February 1679 explaining the necessity that he go into exile. Vain efforts the week before by William Sancroft, archbishop of Canterbury, and George Morley, bishop of Winchester, to persuade James to return to Protestantism left the king with no choice but to reassure the new parliament that he was avoiding Catholic counsel, even that of his brother. James was bitterly disappointed and became convinced that his brother was going the way of their father and needed to respond more vigorously to any threats to monarchy and the succession. James's departure into exile was a sign of Charles's weakness.[1]

The decision was made, on Danby's suggestion, to send James to the Low Countries and he and Mary Beatrice set sail for Holland on 3 March. Charles's agreement to simultaneously declare in the English Privy Council that Monmouth was illegitimate and he had never married his mother was scant consolation. In another snub that James could not comprehend, Charles would not allow them to take their daughter Anne who, only fourteen years old, was to continue her Protestant education in London. James taking refuge in the court of his seventeen-year-old daughter Mary and her husband the Prince of Orange, married just sixteen months previously, made perfect sense to Charles.[2] It was a practical solution to the political difficulties he faced. As for Danby, his supposed links to the Popish Plot, the uncovering of his more certain activity in secret negotiations with France, and the wild allegations of Titus Oates, the deluded plot informer who in 1678 and 1679 gave evidence that saw the execution of more than thirty accused, made his own position untenable, and in May he was placed in the Tower. The same month the House of Commons produced an address to Charles demanding the removal of Lauderdale from all councils, English and Scottish, for his 'arbitrarie and destructive counsells tending to the subversione of rights, liberties and propertie', though fortunately for the Secretary, Charles stood by him.[3]

Although James went first to The Hague to see Mary, and returned from time to time when she was ill, for most of the following six months he resided at Brussels in the Spanish Netherlands. From there he produced an effusion of letters to his old army and navy confidant Colonel George Legge, later Lord Dartmouth, to Prince William and to Charles himself. Most, as we would expect, concerned the securing of royal authority and the succession. He was greeted with extended silences. His correspondence with a non-committal William between May and August is full of doom-laden sentiment: he declared 'nothing will satisfy the Presbyterians but the destroying of the monarchy and the setting up of a commonwealth'; the 1650s were back.[4] In late July, by which time Shaftesbury had joined the government, Charles's proposals about limitations for a Catholic successor were revealed, the exclusion bill passed the Commons and, in spite of the dissolution of parliament, Charles still refused to let him home, James showed his despair at the turn of events:

> I wish in England some considered the good of our family so much as I do, and then things would go better than they do; and to speak freely to you, I have but a very dismal prospect of our affairs in general, and I do not see without a miracle how they can be mended, for his Majesty has so given up himself into the hands of his new counsellors, that I can see nothing but the ruin of the monarchy and that which I think is a very bad sign, is that his Majesty is not so sensible as he should be of the ill condition he is in.[5]

The duke even began to contemplate the permanency of exile. On his arrival he asked Legge, his master of horse, to ready his hounds and horses for sending over, but a few weeks later he instructed him immediately to ship over a range of coaches, horses and hunting dogs from Dover to Antwerp. Indeed, during his exile he busied himself with the distraction of as much hunting as possible, generally twice each day. He even came to a discreet accommodation with his circumstances. He confided to Ormonde that he had 'descid[ed] to be incognito, to avoyd all inconvenient cermonys', and that with the Jesuits, English priests, and those named in the Plot staying away 'for feare of doing [him] harme', his devotions would be performed privately. But there were other moments when James recommended more aggressive solutions to the threat to monarchy.[6] In late May he enclosed with a letter to Legge a series of 'Heads' to be discussed with his brother, who had been slow to reply to numerous desperate letters. These 'heads' reflected on the military solutions available to Charles:

> That his Majesty . . . is strong enough to deele with and punish his euemys if he will but be resolut, and stick to himself and countenance his friends.

The fleett is yett his, urge the concequence and advantage of that, the gards and garrisons are also his, except Hull, which might easily be made so, Scotland and Ireland yet his if he continu Lauderdail and Ormond in them, them two kingdoms will make men of estats consider well before they engage against the King.

At other times, however, James felt peevishly sorry for himself. When informed by Ossory, Ormonde's son, that some of the fleet had expressed their loyalty, James was relieved that 'any body' should 'want' him.[7] But on religion, when yet again his friends suggested that he convert to Protestantism and so solve all the difficulties *they* faced, he was made of stronger stuff – 'I never shall, and if occation were I hope God would give me his grace to suffer death for the true Catholike religion, as well as Banishment'.[8]

In these circumstances we might wonder as to the impressions from Scotland of a duke of Albany in exile. Lauderdale's position, in relation to a House of Commons baying for his blood, was badly weakened by the fall of his ally Danby. The deployment of the Highland Host the previous year had not gone well and was live ammunition to be used against him by the Hamilton and Shaftesbury axis. The exclusionists made simplistic but politically powerful links between the Popish Plot, pro-French policies, the religion of James and the arbitrary government of Scotland by Lauderdale. When some mobilisation of James's Episcopalian and cavalier support in Scotland could have been attempted to offer support in 1679, the murder of Archbishop Sharp plunged the administration into an emergency policing operation which culminated in Monmouth's victory over the Covenanters at Bothwell Brig in June. Hamilton and his party were also shocked at these events and for a period there was unanimous support for Monmouth, who introduced a new indulgence allowing nonconformists to worship in their homes, which saw many captured Covenanters return home and a minority of 300 sent off to the West Indies, only to perish on the way in a shipwreck. Meanwhile, James looked on horrified at the enhanced reputation of his rival. In Scotland the issue of a now elderly Lauderdale was temporarily set aside when, after Lauderdale and the Hamiltonians made their submissions to Charles at a conference in early July, both sides claimed victory, yet neither had won. The same tendency of the king in London to say 'yes' to everyone, which had by the mixed messages of a crackdown and toleration helped cause the rebellion in the first place, was now visited on the political factions in Edinburgh. This left the new post-Danby English ministers, a 'triumvirate' of anti-exclusionists who balanced the alliance of Shaftesbury and Monmouth – Arthur Capel, earl of Essex, George Savile, marquis of Halifax, and Robert Spencer, earl of Sunderland, astonished that Charles still refused to dismiss Lauderdale.[9]

Then an event happened to change everything. In late August 1679 James received a panicky letter from the triumvirate. Charles had been taken seriously ill of a fever on 21 August and was soon at risk of losing his life. His senior ministers and the duchess of Portsmouth needed James to return for fear Shaftesbury and Monmouth would seek revenge if they came to power. This invitation came as a complete surprise to James, who had just seen his daughters Anne and the three-year-old Isabella arrive in Brussels, but on 2 September he appeared at Charles's bedside and there was a tearful fraternal reunion. The trouble was that over the coming weeks Charles recovered. While no rebellion arose from James's return as some had predicted, and he quickly began to gather some semblance of a party of cavaliers and bishops, most agreed he had to go into exile again. James was more difficult to shift now that he could claim support, but Charles persuaded him to go into exile, this time to Scotland. Charles agreed that James's rival Monmouth would be sent to the Netherlands and the troublesome son departed the day before James returned to Brussels to bring his wife and daughters back. James was accompanied to his ship by a number of peers, proving more 'wanted' him now. After his return to London, James and Mary Beatrice set out on the three-week journey by coach to Edinburgh while Anne and her half-sister Isabella were again held back at St James's on the insistence of Charles himself.[10]

While James was briefly back in Brussels, Lauderdale wrote to his nephew the earl of Moray, treasury commissioner and the man who would succeed him as Scottish Secretary:

> by the King's good liking Their Royall Highnesses . . . are coming to dwell in Scotland . . . His Highness thought it not fitt that he should be in the power of any forrane king or state. Therefor his Majestie was willing he should reside in Scotland, his dwelling wilbe at Holyroodhous which wilbe prepared for him. This I was not free to tell you before. But the news broke out at London some days agoe, and last night the King owned it herr and comanded me to write this. Be pleased to communicate it to my Lord Chancellor, Archbishop of St Andrews and to all our friends civill and ecclesiastick, for I am not able to write to all. It is to be no secret and I am sure no honest man will repent it [at] the King's pleasure . . . Now you will not reprove at my pressing your stay in Edinburgh.[11]

While others like the English Secretary Henry Coventry and Sunderland had some part in supporting the Scottish solution, there is little doubt that Lauderdale suggested it – we might ponder why. There is a tradition of extrapolating from the eclipse of Lauderdale and rise of James in the Scottish theatre that the former was discomfited by the very idea of the duke's locating to Edinburgh – as one historian has put it, the 'move did not meet with Lauderdale's favour'. This was far from the case. The success of Monmouth was as much a concern to Lauderdale as to James, and the royal duke was Lauderdale's best chance to secure his own authority. In addition, the two had supported each other and in Scottish terms, even more than in English, were close partners in the Episcopalian interest. Lauderdale also realised he was on borrowed time. He had only just survived the conference in July where Charles had, unusually, allowed criticism of his Secretary to be openly expressed, and with his health beginning to fail him, and the king already noting the occasional lapse of his renowned memory for detail, it was time to prepare for an honourable withdrawal. We can go further – in the year to Lauderdale's resignation in September 1680, and certainly to then from his stroke in March 1680, he and Charles had worked out between them how best to ensure a gradual transition to a new regime. The great Secretary was allowed to choose his own successor and, with James's approval, Moray was appointed. It was a measure of the royal brothers' regard for Lauderdale that even when in spring 1680 a number of Scottish privy counsellors gathered in London to plan future policy, Charles still insisted that Lauderdale depart in his own time.[12]

After a somewhat mixed journey through England, where some avoided the royal party and others greeted it with enthusiasm, polite or ecstatic, James neared the Scottish Border in the certain knowledge that he was now the most divisive personality in English politics since his father. If he thought it was to be the same in Scotland he need not have worried. On reaching the Border on 21 November they were greeted by many scores of Scottish nobles and gentry, including more than thirty privy councillors led by the Chancellor, the earl of Rothes. An official report claimed that two thousand horses gathered. The Council had written to the sheriffs of the shires of Edinburgh, Haddington, Linlithgow and Berwick demanding attendance and many local elites assembled. After stopping to be entertained at Lethington, Lauderdale's East Lothian home, this welcoming party made formal procession with James and Mary into Edinburgh which they entered three days later to cheering crowds. The young Mary Beatrice was exhausted, having shortly before given in to her propensity to be sick at sea, where she vomited blood, and contracting a cold as a deepening and snowy northern winter delivered its frosty welcome. Nevertheless, Edinburgh busied itself with well-planned but warm festivities in what James himself described as 'as hansom a reception . . . as [he] could desire'. As wine flowed and bonfires burnt, the largest party took place since the Restoration itself.[13] Nevertheless, as the London press recorded further developments in the Exclusion Crisis, the juxtaposition with reports of Edinburgh's celebrations made it patently clear that down the road of exclusion lay Anglo-Scottish conflict. Thus during this visit to Scotland (November 1679 to February 1680), and the subsequent longer period (October 1680 to March 1682), English observers became increasingly exasperated at the differing reports emanating from the north on James's political reception. Speculation was rife. As the Presbyterian diarist Roger Morrice indicated in November 1680, 'we are not agreed whether his reception was very magnificent, or but indifferent and cool'. This has echoes of his comment in 1679 where he could not establish if Presbyterian unrest in Scotland had increased or declined, the letters from the north being 'inconsistent and irreconcilable'.[14] It made a change for Englishmen to be as bemused by news from Scotland as Scots were ever over that from England. This was a measure of how critical Scottish affairs now were to the fate of the three kingdoms.

Immediately, high politics aside, James, Mary and an entourage of more than a hundred servants had to be accommodated at Holyrood and in buildings round about. There was considerable confusion, in spite of the best efforts of the council and Hamilton, the hereditary Keeper of the palace. The complex, if we could call it that, was better prepared when the royal couple returned in autumn 1680. By 1679, however, Holyrood Palace had been both renovated and rebuilt according to a design rendered by Sir William Bruce and carried through by Robert Mylne, the royal master mason. The Cromwellian occupation saw the ravages of fire and billeted troops. Encouraged by Lauderdale, who was also Bruce's patron, Charles instructed the treasury commissioners in early 1671 to release funds for the work. But James and Mary were now to bring their religion to the palace as first in 1679 the Queen's Presence Chamber was refitted as a Catholic chapel for Mary, and later in 1686 King James ordered that the palace Council Chamber be converted to a royal chapel. In addition, James made his mark in a different manner and in a remarkable statement of dynastic pride and traditionalism. He was the driving force behind the commissioning of 111 portraits of the kings of Scots by the Dutch painter Jacob de Wet II. These were painted between 1684 and 1686 and hung at Holyrood. While this collection is of dubious artistic and historical merit, going back as it does to the mythical king Fergus from 300BC, it represents an extraordinary example of royalist iconography, a theme dear to James's heart.[15]

James's court also became a centre for cultural diversion, something of a surprise given his impatience with intellectualism. Through good chance and a quick realisation that being a cultural patron offered an opportunity to make a mark and build an extended cavalier party in Scotland, James gave his imprimatur to various institutional schemes. While costing the Crown little, they boosted prestige in Edinburgh when it was in short supply in London. A typical example is the Royal College of Physicals of Edinburgh founded in 1681. Proposals for such a college had been made in the 1620s and 1630s but floundered on the rocks of the self-interest of Edinburgh's college, town and guild of surgeons, who themselves were established in 1505. However, in 1680 a group of medical doctors and virtuosi, who had begun meeting informally, agreed the need to free the medical profession from the stranglehold of the surgeon-apothecaries. This mostly Episcopalian group was led by Robert Sibbald who, with the support of his intellectual and personal friend James Drummond, fourth earl of Perth, was in 1682 knighted and appointed geographer-royal and physician-in-ordinary to Charles II and later James in 1685. Perth, on the Privy Council and by 1684 Chancellor, bent James's ear to the college scheme. Sibbald confirms James was impressed when he was shown the 1621 warrant to the Privy Council authorising a college of physicians. James delighted at the document recognising his grandfather's hand.[16] From that moment on, the duke ensured the desired outcome in spite of the opposition of vested interests.

The aristocratic, royal and neo-Jacobean qualities of this affair were enthusiastically embraced by James but, in a period when the courts of Paris and London were also institutionally innovative, it was a fashionable example of royal patronage and princely preoccupation, such as Charles's for the Royal Society in London. Therefore James also lent his support to the foundation of the library of the Faculty of Advocates, established in 1680. In 1682 the Lord Advocate, Sir George Mackenzie of Rosehaugh, was elected dean, in part for his efforts to enhance the collection. Mackenzie was a high Episcopalian royalist as seen in his legal justification of royal authority *Jus regium* (1684). King Fergus was dusted down again as the progenitor of royal prerogative as Mackenzie repeated James VI's own estimation that 'Fergus made himself King and Lord as well of the whole Lands, as of the whole Inhabitants [not at] the consent of the People'. This new culture of aristocratic royalism and learning needed only an antiquarian element to complement James's sense of dynastic historicism. Princes, learned and landed, joined in an obsession with genealogy. This antiquarianism was provided by James's 'restoration' in May 1687 of the Most Ancient and Most Noble Order of the Thistle, the highest order of chivalry in Scotland. Whether or not this owed its creation to an earlier medieval manifestation, James wholeheartedly supported the idea.[17] It had been brought to him by Perth and his brother John Drummond, earl of Melfort, by then James's Secretary of State, and the siblings were among the eight founding knights. Politically, these cultural initiatives were part of the Tory reaction to exclusion in England and the suppression of extremist nonconformity in Scotland.

While in Scotland from 1679 to 1682, James and his wife and daughter entertained themselves with both outdoor and indoor activities. To James's frustration the hunting was poor, stag hunting near impossible because of the terrain, and hare hunting and shooting grouse and partridge on foot a meagre alternative. Nonetheless, he, Mary and Anne, after she came north in July 1681, seemed to go riding almost every day. In echoes of Newmarket, the duke and duchess watched as spectators at a horse race at Leith in February 1680, just before they returned to London. James played golf regularly on Leith Links, especially on clear winter days, and developed considerable ability. At one point he took as his partner a shoemaker called Paterson who was something of a sensation at the game. When James and he won their pairs, James let him keep the prize money. James also learnt to play curling in the local frozen lochs. Indoors, the main recreations were the card game basset and regular plays, often twice per week, performed at the palace by visiting players, in which Anne sometimes had a part. The palace tennis court was converted into a theatre. In November 1681 Anne and her ladies in waiting, including Catherine Sedley, put on a performance of Nathaniel's Lee's tragedy *Mithridates, King of Pontus* before her parents. A troope of Irish players resorted to Edinburgh during James's visit as did part of his own company of

London. In spite of this, his letters to his niece Charlotte Fitzroy, Countess of Litchfield, confirm how much he missed the diversions of London, his palaces and particularly his friends. It was a given that he regretted the lack of hunting, but at least in Catherine he had a new mistress.[18]

Mary Beatrice, meanwhile, a young duchess in her early twenties, showed that stoicism for which she became renowned. After arriving in Scotland unwell, she settled into the life of the northern court. However, a fall from her horse in December 1681 while newly pregnant left her badly bruised. Also in March that year she received the distressing news of the death of her four-year-old daughter Isabella at St James's Palace, and was consoled by the ladies of the Scottish court including, by intimate letters from an unlikely correspondent, Anne, duchess of Hamilton. To lift her spirits Anne sent simple gifts to Mary such as a consignment of cherries in the summer of 1681, shortly before Edinburgh filled up for the new session of parliament. Indeed, one reason why Charles allowed his brother and sister-in-law to return to London in May 1682 was so Mary could be delivered of her new child at home at St James's. In spite of rumours it was a son, a daughter Charlotte Maria was born in August but then died seven weeks later. It is remarkable that such a fertile woman was to be childless when she became queen in 1685. Casting back from then to her marriage in 1673, Mary had five miscarriages and four children who died in infancy. These included one son, Charles, duke of Cambridge (the fourth of James's sons to be given the title) who lived for only five weeks.[19] Born on 7 November 1677, ironically three days after the marriage took place between William Prince of Orange and Mary's stepdaughter Princess Mary, this infant duke represented the flimsy prospects of an alternative succession trajectory; but it was not to be.

As well as riding in and around the capital, during his second visit to Scotland James went on progress. In early February 1681 he rode with an entourage of nobles and servants to Linlithgow and then to Stirling Castle. At the latter he was entertained warmly by the earl of Argyll at his lodge below the castle. There was no public warning yet of the trouble ahead between these men, although if we believe the commander of guards that waited on James at the castle, William, twelfth Lord Ross, it was when their conversation turned to religion, and James suggested Argyll change his, that a mutual frostiness took hold. Eight months later, and after the summer session of parliament, James went on his travels again, this time to Glasgow and Dumbarton, yet another combination of royal burgh and fortress. Arthur Rose, archbishop of Glasgow, and the masters of the university hosted various receptions in Glasgow in his honour. These were lowland progresses. Given James's later sympathy for Highlanders and North East loyalists, it is curious how little time he spent meeting such individuals and certainly none in their own territories. He also never went near the Covenanting south west, no doubt for security reasons.[20]

The only hiccup when James arrived in Scotland in November 1679 was the question of his taking a seat on the Scottish Privy Council without taking the oath of allegiance. The coalition of those who advised Charles that it must be taken, which included Mackenzie of Rosehaugh and Lauderdale providing respectively legal and political advice, as well as the whole council, may seem strange and certainly briefly perplexed the duke. As James travelled north Lauderdale advised him that not to take the oath would be a gift to his exclusionist enemies – the duke held firm. What is does reveal is the innate conservatism of the Scottish cavaliers and that should have been a warning for James when later he would press on matters of religion. The Council thought it wise to suspend their deliberations until Charles issued clear instructions for his brother's dispensation.[21] They must have recognised the unlikelihood of persuading James to comply though a point had been made. Existing laws should be respected and while dispensing with the oath for the royal duke was one thing, to do so for others was quite another.

On 4 December 1679 James took his seat on the Council and shortly after wrote to Legge:

> I live here as cautiously as I can, and am very carfull to give offence to none, and to have no partialitys and preach to them laying aside all privat animositys and securing the King his owne way. None shall have reason to complaine of me, and tho some of either party here might have hoped I should have shewd my partiality for them, and some of my freinds have been of opinion it had been best for me to have done so, and by it have secured one side to me, yett I am convinced it was not fitt for me to do it, it being no way good for his Majesty's.[22]

This very much sums up James's attitude to the political scene he inherited from Lauderdale. Such accommodation was a throwback to James VI's *via media* of the 1590s with the succession as the familiar backdrop. Therefore, in order to cast a wide net to bring in support, James cooperated with Lauderdale associates Argyll, Moray and Charles Maitland, Lauderdale's brother and Treasurer Depute, whose group loyalty the aging Secretary had guaranteed, but also many who had gone in and out of opposition in the previous two decades, like Queensberry and, when reinstated to the Council in 1682, Tweeddale, as well as others alienated by the Highland Host initiative including Perth and John Murray, marquis of Atholl, and Crown servants like Rothes, the Chancellor, and Mackenzie of Rosehaugh, the Lord Advocate. This inclusive government the jurist Fountainhall labelled James's 'mongrel party'. Most, however, were united by Episcopalianism and all were willing to join James in suppressing radical Presbyterianism in the south west. The duke's objective was to carry out the will of the king, but more effectively than his older brother. As he put it on his return to England in March 1682 when the job was well in hand, 'Scotland [had] been too long governed by two kings [Charles and Lauderdale] and he would 'endeavour to have it so no mor'. Hamilton meanwhile remained detached and, although he could be inconsistent and even feckless in his political machinations, not finding a way to include him in the long run weakened support for James by 1688. As for policy to tackle religious dissent, James had to listen to bishops' complaints about concessions being made to Presbyterians, yet at the same time was forced to recognise that Monmouth's indulgence had been popular. The prevailing mood did not favour oppression. James was reluctant but a realist:

> I find the generallity of the best men here much troubled at the indulgence the Duke of Monmouth gott for the Phanatiks here after they had been beaten, and say it will encourage them to another rebellion. I am of that opinion, tho I do not thinke it proper to take it from them till they forfitt it againe, which they will certainly do if great care be not taken to prevent their rising in to arms.[23]

Unfortunately for the Covenanters, moderation was abandoned after James's return to London in February 1680. Bishops in Scotland and England pressed successfully for more aggressive measures to be taken and the Privy Council in Edinburgh responded accordingly.

'RESTORING' AUTHORITY:
COERCION OR COMPROMISE

One individual who was on the majority of Privy Council committees established from December 1679 to the following February was Argyll. His membership of the Committee Anent the Militia and the Committee Anent the Peace of the Highlands confirms his preoccupations but also James's. Before James went north, Charles stripped Monmouth of his commission as Captain General in Scotland and returned command to Lieutenant General Tam Dalzell. James was to have no competition from his wayward nephew. Charles had also made clear that the one policy he looked to for action during his brother's stay in Edinburgh was the reconstitution of the militia into a leaner standing army. The fact of Bothwell Brig that summer gave some urgency given that Charles's initial instructions on this subject, given in October 1678, had not yet been put into action. Now the communications between James and Lauderdale on this question and responsive letters from the king via his Secretary confirm that James was the driving force behind these discussions. One giveaway is Charles's directive that 'one method' should be adopted for drilling forces 'in all dominions', a uniformity favoured by James's military philosophy. The 20,000 foot and 2,000 horse first offered by the estates in 1663 were now to be 5000 foot and 500 horse with the king assisting the Scottish treasury with the financial burden. An expanded committee for the militia agreed that such a force should rendezvous on thirty-two days each year, rather than the eight originally proposed for the larger force. If this was a standing army it would stand intermittently, but it would be better prepared for disturbances in the west and also, being mustered equally from each shire, would not repeat the geographical asymmetry of the Highland Host. English Whigs enjoyed spreading alarm at James's 'success' in remodelling the militia although as always, other than the remarkable 1640s, Scottish military preparedness was mostly illusory. By the time James returned to Scotland in the winter of 1680/1 the Privy Council had admitted they had inadequate funds to pay the officers for the new 'model', and in March 1681 they and James agreed to fall back mostly on traditional rendezvous methods.[24]

Restoration Highland policy had been a somewhat haphazard affair before 1679 as long-held government fears of inveterate lawlessness persisted.[25] At the core of these difficulties was the forfeiture and then restoration of the Campbell earldom of Argyll in 1663. The fate of the lands had been awkwardly contrived and left other clans and creditors jostling for position. Since the reign of James IV, the Campbells had acted as royal lieutenants in the western Highlands with considerable autonomy, and by the 1670s it was Argyll himself and his kinsman John Campbell of Glenorchy who policed the western Highlands through two independent Highland companies raised mostly from Campbell retainers. Argyll was in heavy dispute with the Macdonalds of Glengarry and, more especially, debtors such as the Macleans, a clan who he was by force seeking to remove from Mull. Meanwhile, Glenorchy had, as a major creditor of the late earl of Caithness, acquired in 1672 the land and in 1677 the title. However, that earl's young successor George Sinclair began to press the Privy Council and ministers for relief from Glenorchy's 'oppression', attempted an unsuccessful process of treason in 1681, and then petitioned to have the style 'earl of Caithness' returned to his family, which as a compromise was granted, with Glenorchy compensated with the new earldom of Breadalbane. Finally, in spring 1683 Sinclair successfully concocted a libel for treason against Breadalbane that looked by the summer as if it would come to trial. In an outcome revealing of James's motivations in such affairs, he had the process halted on Breadalbane's full and personal submission to him in July 1683.[26] It was all so astonishing given that in June 1680 Charles expressed his strong support for the rights of Glenorchy.

The alteration in Argyll's fortunes is even more striking. Just as protests at his arbitrary behaviour were gathering momentum in the late 1670s, the crisis of 1678–9 saw the government turn in some desperation to the Campbell companies under Argyll and Glenorchy to improve security. In spring 1679 the king commended Argyll's 'prudent deportment' over Highland affairs. Argyll even cemented his strong position by slandering his enemies as Papists when the timely Popish Plot emerged.[27] However, in December 1679 James sought compromise not confrontation, and invited Highland chiefs and nobles to a conference in Edinburgh in late January. Unfortunately a number did not arrive and no meaningful discussion took place before the duke left for London, though James did begin to make hints about a grand vision for the Highlands, while also saving 'these poor [MacDonalds and Macleans] with the satisfaction of Lord Argyle'. After James's return to Scotland, Argyll's star was still in the ascendency. At the parliament of 1681 his possession of the barony of Duart was ratified, one of the key bones of contention with the Macleans. Also, even when at the same time petitions appeared before the Lords of the Articles concerning his creditors and more significantly from the Lord Advocate regarding his jurisdictions and the siphoning of various royal revenues, James stopped the proceedings, as he did in late autumn 1681 when it was suggested that a commission be set up to investigate Argyll's heritable rights.[28] This equilibrium was, however, shattered by reactions to the manner in which Argyll took the Test and Oath in November 1681.

The circumstances surrounding the fall of Argyll are remarkable.[29] The Test Act was widely seen as contradictory by contemporaries when it was drafted for the parliament of 1681. It was intended to secure Protestantism, the royal supremacy and the succession, but with its declaration of the Confession of Faith of 1567, which acknowledged lawful resistance, it was patently illogical, especially if the monarch was Catholic. The insertion of the Confession, at the instigation of James Dalrymple, Viscount Stair and President of the Court of Session, who himself could not take the oath and soon went into exile, was clearly an attempt to strangle the threat of Catholicism with a legalistic anomaly. Argyll took a leading role in opposition to the Test claiming it was unnecessary, and in particular that all members of the royal family should take the Test save the king, James and his future sons. John Hamilton, Lord Belhaven, found himself briefly imprisoned for declaring that the act secured their religion but not that religion 'against a Popish or phanticall successor to the Crown'. In the end, after much opposition, with perhaps up to seventy rejecting the act, the legislation was carried by a court majority of thirty to forty votes. Certainly, this was no invitation to oppress those who could not take the Test. Nevertheless, Argyll's taking of the oath on two occasions with an accompanying explanation was taken as an opportunity by his political enemies, and mostly those erstwhile opponents of Lauderdale, to accuse him of treason and leasing-making (the ancient crime of fomenting discord between the monarch and the people) or as one loyalist pamphlet put it, for making 'the oath no oath'. Mackenzie, in his prosecution of the case, warned of political and moral chaos if the meaning of oaths were at the behest of the individual.[30] It would have been better to have refused than take it with qualification.

James, present on the second occasion when Argyll made his qualified oath, went along with the sense of outrage, but why? James had three overriding priorities as his brother's viceroy in Scotland: to ensure a level of political harmony that broadened royal support; to engineer circumstances where individuals declared personal allegiance to his brother and himself, with a view to the succession, and lastly to underpin security from the threats of nonconformist rebels or over-mighty subjects. Over each aspect Argyll began to be seen as a liability. It appeared that he was unwilling to compromise with his Highland opponents and that his heredi- tary privileges made him too immune from royal obligations. There can be little doubt also that James's sympathy for Argyll had been eroded as Mackenzie provided more evidence of unscrupulous financial and jurisdictional activities of the earl, and other opportunistic lawyers, George Mackenzie of Tarbat and George Gordon of Haddo, pressed the treason charge. Argyll's role in the debate in Parliament clearly went against him. Yet while the political vultures circled to gain scraps from the land and income of the earldom and the offices and commissions he held, the royal brothers were merely making an example of him, but to the point of allowing him to be found guilty of treason and sentenced to execution. It was never their intention to have the sentence carried out, although Argyll, not appreciating this, escaped from his cell and went into exile to be condemned in his absence. It was a case of political misadventure though also a marked failure of policy by James and Charles. In England, even loyal ministers like Lauderdale and Halifax found the whole episode distasteful. Nonetheless, Burnet's claim that Argyll's power and position as a potential leader of opposition Protestantism made it necessary for James to 'either gain him or ruin him' is the nub of it.[31] One of the great ironies of James's political career was that this reliance on the Test, a device so efficient in delivering loyal support in the Estates and in Council, was incom- patible with his later policy to free Catholics from the civil penalties of their faith. In that sense Stair had the last laugh.

James also fostered a more general policy for the Highlands and not one that depended solely on the Campbells. As an alternative to the Highland companies, in January 1680 James announced his plan for the policing of the Highlands to be delegated to five administrative zones headed by a regional magnate with judicial authority; the earls of Argyll, Atholl, Huntly, Moray and Seaforth. Commencement was delayed, however, until the summer of 1681 as the companies were not disbanded until April as Lauderdale had convinced Charles that a delay was neces- sary. The fall of Argyll required a rethink, and in August 1682 James came up with the Commission for Securing the Peace, a scheme where four divisions, in north- ern, central, eastern and southern areas, each with a number of named commissioners, were to police the Highland shires with biannual courts bringing justice over a range of serious and minor cases of disorder and criminality. The southern division, incorporated Argyll, Dumbarton, Perth and Stirling, was the most active and was still meeting in November 1688, just before the Revolution. On top of this, in 1684 Atholl took over the lieutenancy of Argyllshire with all the confusion of parallel jurisdictions. That year he led a punitive expedition into Argyll and it was he who had the honour of defeating the great Campbell earl when he landed in 1685 to carry out his futile rebellion. Contemporaries seem to have seen the commission system as an effective means of control and in 1685 it was renewed for the new king. Even the self-righteous Atholl began to use less strident methods, taking bonds of caution, amnesties and a range of punishments, from brief spells in prison to transportation, though also the occasional public execution as a deterrent.[32] In an age of increasingly personal monarchy, one of James's major successes was his remodelling, after returning to London, of the means of policing a major part of the Scottish population. Of course, in this respect he and his brother's ministers were helped by the eclipse of Argyll.

If the reforging of the Scottish militia and the trial of Argyll were grist to the mill of English Whig pamphleteers and scaremongers, what can be said about conventicles and Presbyterianism? When James and Mary set off by sea from Leith to London on 17 February – Charles making good on his promise in late January to recall his brother as soon as possible – the policy of moderation underpinned by the indulgence was still intact. Meanwhile, James's reputation in England was enhanced at court and in Anglican circles, if not in the Swan Tavern in Fleet Street where the Whigs met to plan strategy. His twelve weeks in Scotland had been a great success. In March Sunderland had to admit 'we apprehended [the duke] would have disordered [Scottish affairs] but we find quite the contrary'. On the eighth of that month the mayor and aldermen of the City of London entertained James and Charles to a banquet of celebration.[33]

While James was in Edinburgh, Charles had had to balance his support for his brother with delaying tactics to prevent further attacks from the Westminster Parliament, while also appealing to populism through anti-Catholic measures and a pro-Dutch and anti-French policy. The first exclusion parliament, which in the Commons had passed an exclusion bill, had been dissolved in July 1679, and Charles had called a new parliament for October. By the time James returned, the elections had taken place and, unfortunately for the king, Whig domination continued, and Charles prorogued the session. Indeed, when in December 1679 he extended the prorogation for a further eleven months, there was uproar in the English Privy Council. In the winter of 1679/80, Shaftesbury – dismissed as Lord President of the Council before James left for Scotland because of the failure of Charles's policy of seeking to cool his ardour by including him in government – had become more dangerous. He coordinated an extensive petitioning campaign to press the king to meet Parliament over exclusion. Also, the continued proroga-tion had led some councillors, such as Halifax and Essex, to retire temporarily from the Council in frustration. Charles now turned to a new triumvirate of ministers: Sunderland, along with Laurence Hyde, soon to be earl of Rochester, who became First Lord of the Treasury in November 1679, and the brilliant Sidney Godolphin. This new generation became a more intimate council for Charles who, as a result of the Exclusion Crisis, developed a preference for small committees less likely to challenge him. Hyde, James's brother-in-law, was a natural ally and James sought mutual support when in Brussels and Edinburgh. Meanwhile, Sunderland and Godolphin were to James slippery and intellectually impenetrable respectively. This was, nevertheless, the group tasked with building up royal support and advising Charles on how to handle the conundrum that was his brother. That difficult task appeared to be mitigated by James's submission – unwilling, of course – to his brother's convoluted anti-Catholic political games, and his rival Monmouth showing up uninvited and further irritating his father by regularly associating with Shaftesbury and his terriers.[34]

No sooner had James returned but Shaftesbury and Essex, himself formerly viceroy in Ireland, placed evidence of an 'Irish Plot' before the council on 24 March 1680. Thus far the Exclusion Crisis had had a minimal impact on Ireland, although Ormonde, reappointed Lord Lieutenant in 1677, had initiated a clampdown on Catholics from early 1679 which included the arrest of some priests, such as Peter Talbot, titular bishop of Dublin, who died in prison. Further measures were deployed against Catholics who were not able to carry firearms, and Jesuits and the regular Catholic clergy were instructed to leave the country. However, the English first exclusion parliament expressed fears that not enough was being done and to the Whigs, looking to add Ormonde to their list of Catholic-inspired despots which also included James and Lauderdale, the fate of all three were intertwined. During the exclusion debates in the Commons in October 1680, Sir Henry Capel, Essex's brother, outlined a conspiracy where the majority Catholics in Ireland would benefit from Protestant division between England and Scotland, caused by the arbitrary and absolute behaviour of the administration in Scotland and the threat of a large Scottish army. Memories of the Irish Catholic rebellion of 1641 reminded Protestants of how their brethren could be slaughtered by a papist majority. Therefore the plot that Shaftesbury revealed in 1680, which confirmed a French-supported Catholic rising and massacre of Protestants, could be planted in fertile soil. Although many were unconvinced, Charles was forced to allow a government enquiry to take place which concluded there were grounds for concern. Though innocent of plots if not maladministration, Oliver Plunket, titular archbishop of Armagh, was brought to London, tried for treason, found guilty and executed on the first day of July 1681, his consolation being beatification in 1920.[35] The day after his demise Shaftesbury himself was arrested – the wind was changing. However, in 1680, when the Popish Plot was running out of steam, Ireland as well as Scotland served to concentrate Protestant minds on what a future might hold for the three kingdoms under a Catholic King James.

Although Charles's decisions over the prorogation of the English Parliament were the beginnings of a loyalist backlash, by spring 1680 James's position remained precarious. This was underscored in late June when Shaftesbury engaged the new tactic of having James and the duchess of Portsmouth indicted before the grand jury of Middlesex, he as a Catholic recusant and she as a prostitute or common nuisance. In fear Portsmouth joined the exclusionists, even though the justice of the court used delaying tactics and dismissed the jury before any serious harm could be done. The impeachment of James by the new Commons seemed more likely than ever, however, and the duke's apparent popularity when he returned to

London had clearly dissipated. On Charles's instructions yet another attempt was made to make him reconvert. Just before James returned 'great hopes [were] conceived' of this final solution. But Barrillon, the French ambassador, reported to King Louis James's reaction: he could 'see nothing but ruin' in such a change and there was 'no reason to believe [he] would comply', in any case. That being to no avail, after taking advice from his council, Charles instructed his brother to take ship for Scotland before the next parliament opened on 21 October 1680. When there, he was to have clear objectives: to complete the remodelling of the militia and ensure 'the general settlement of the peace of that our ancient kingdom'. James was crestfallen and quite baffled by it all. Two months before he confirmed to Barrillon a soldier's frustration at the endless negotiation and wrangling:

> The Duke of York's design is that things should be brought to extremities, and come to an open rupture. He is persuaded that the royal authority can be established in England only by a civil war.

Louis, the 'Sun King', marvelled at the prospect of seeing England so discomfited and instructed his ambassador to offer his full support. So it was that when the duke relocated to London, the political atmosphere had not changed after all, and by degrees it dawned on Charles that James had to go back to Edinburgh. Charles also understood his brother's instinctive and peevish petulance.[36] James's unpopularity was not merely on account of his religion.

Only days before James departed, Lauderdale finally resigned as Scottish Secretary. Essentially, however, his influence gradually waned in the course of 1680 and especially once James was back in London. For the first time in approaching two decades, the political vacuum in Scotland was not caused by Lauderdale's absence. Some privy councillors continued to give him reports, however, including Rosehaugh, General Dalzell and Hatton, his brother. His last two significant political acts were both destined to alienate James, though the notion of James's 'hatred', as suggested by some, is not borne out by their correspondence in 1681. Before then, on 6 April 1680, a few weeks after returning to London, James visited a sickly Lauderdale at his English home of Ham House in Surrey, in what Lauderdale's wife described as a warm gesture of 'kindness'. Almost contemporaneously, one Scottish bishop noted how the Secretary was still 'in very high regard at court by both king and duke'. And yet firstly, in the House of Lords in late 1680, Lauderdale voted for the execution of the Catholic William Howard, Viscount Stafford, a decision much resented by James. Another victim of the Popish Plot, Stafford was a surrogate target when the royal duke was out of range. Also, a year later Lauderdale's support for Argyll created tensions but must have been expected given their family ties and long association. The Secretary's reduced significance, however, appears to have dawned on Scottish privy councillors the moment James left as can be seen by the rush to follow him to London in April. The Edinburgh

PLATE 1. James, duke of York, with his father Charles I in late summer/autumn 1647. Both were then in the custody of the English Parliament. James, almost fourteen years of age, had his last intimate meetings with his father at Hampton Court, Charles's prison from August to November.

PLATE 2. James, duke of York and Albany, and Anne, duchess of York, with their daughters Mary and Anne (c.1673–5), a happy ensemble with no sign of the family troubles ahead.

PLATE 3. John Maitland, duke of Lauderdale, Secretary of State and chief Scottish minister for Charles II, c.1665. The greatest Scot of his age.

PLATE 4. William Douglas, third duke of Hamilton,
1682. The opposition leader who galvanised
parliamentary opposition to Lauderdale from 1669 and
headed the revolution party in Scotland in 1688/9.

PLATE 5. James, duke of Albany, as printed after an
engraving by Richard White, itself after a portrait by
Sir Godfrey Kneller, 1682. This image was bound in
with volumes of the Acts of the Scottish Parliament of
1681, at which session James presided as High
Commissioner for his brother Charles II.

PLATE 6. John Drummond, earl of Melfort (formerly of Lundin), James's leading Scottish minister and hate-figure for many contemporaries, 1688.

PLATE 7. William of Orange (William II of Scotland and III of England), 1690, James's nephew and son-in-law who, for reasons of religion, continental strategy and personal ambition, delivered the Revolution of 1688/9.

PLATE 8. Canongate Kirk, Edinburgh, the parish church which was built from 1688 to 1691 using a fund mortified by Thomas Moodie. Opportunistically King James used the endowment to re-house the congregation of the Abbey Church at Holyrood, so the church could be converted into a Catholic chapel and accommodation for the Order of the Thistle. The Italianate gable, seen here, is very unusual and has the arms of Moodie above an inscribed tablet with the words: 'In 1688 King James VII ordained that the Mortification of Thos. Moodie, granted in 1649 to build a Church, should be applied to the erection of this structure'; and atop, as if to emphasise the Revolution, are the ornately carved arms of King William.

PLATE 9. The Château Vieux de Saint-Germain-en-Laye, the palace in which James and the exiled court resided from 1689. This was part of a palace complex, with the nearby Château Neuf and extensive ornamental gardens and parks. The palace Château Vieux was larger at the time with additional pavilions extending each wing (the two seen here are from the north side) of an unusual, irregular pentagon shape.

PLATE 10. The royal chapel at the Château Vieux de Saint-Germain-en-Laye, venue of many religious, musical and ceremonial events of the exiled court, as well as the place where some of James's last illnesses became evident.

PLATE 11. The courtyard of the Château Vieux de Saint-Germain-en-Laye. One awkward aspect of the building was the inconvenience of circulation which required not merely going up and down stairs but often out of doors as the court and servants moved from apartment to apartment. The clock tower can be seen on the right (north-west corner), and the larger turrets have the salamander symbol of King Francis I, who built the oldest parts of the surviving palace.

PLATE 12. James and Queen Mary
(of Modena) and their children James
Francis Edward, Prince of Wales, and
Louisa-Maria Theresa in 1694. The
royal family in exile were painted
numerous times to sustain the cult of
Jacobite legitimacy. In this picture the
boy prince, now five to six years of
age, points to the royal crown.

PLATE 13. Queen St Margaret, the
medieval queen of Scots who was also
a saint. The painting was at the
symbolic centre of the art collection
at Saint-Germain.

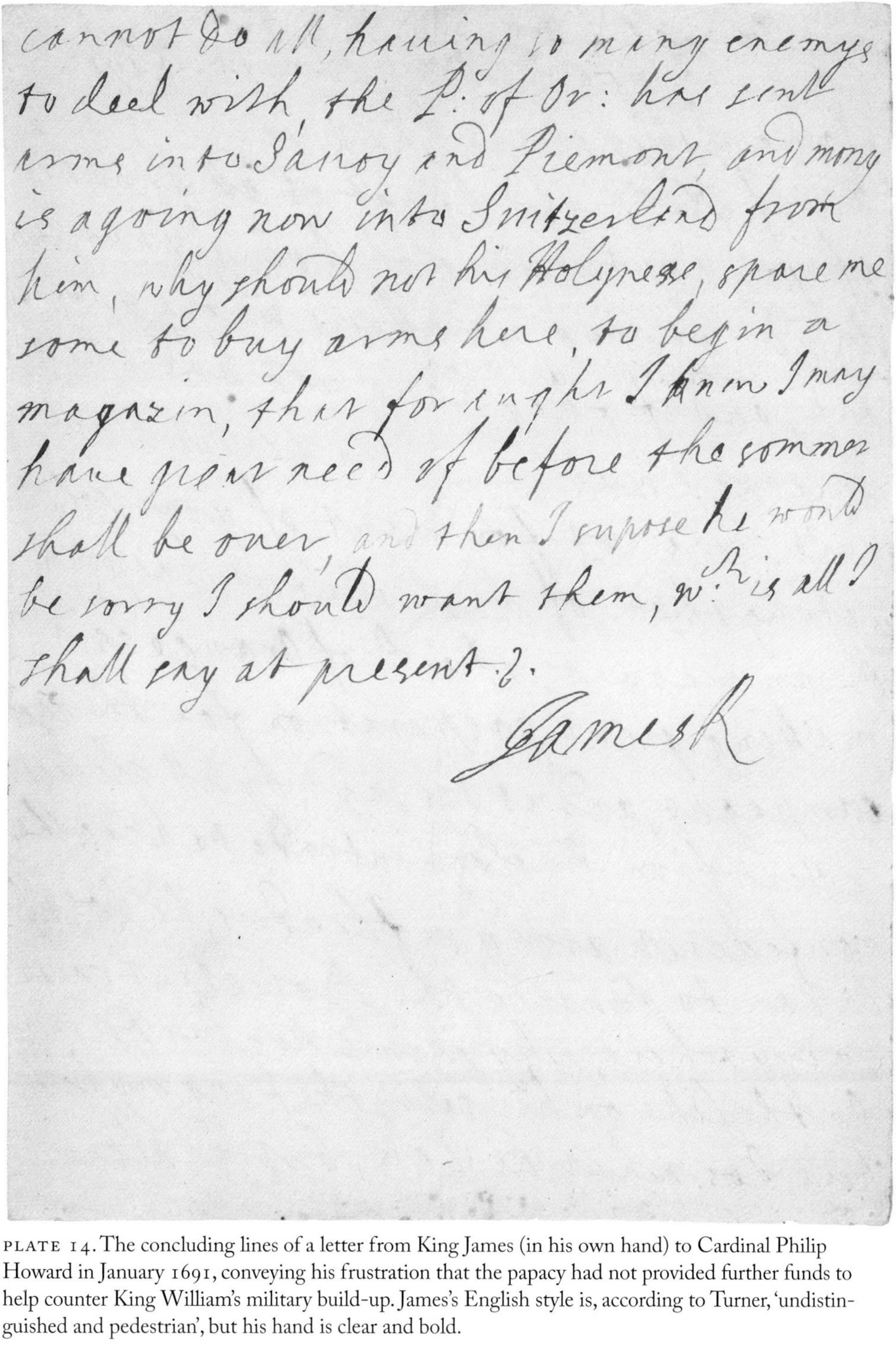

cannot do all, having so many enemys to deel with, the P: of Or: has sent arms into Savoy and Piemont, and mony is a going now into Switzerland from him, why should not his Holynesse, spare me some to buy arms here, to begin a magazin, that for ought I know I may have great need of before the sommer shall be over, and then I supose he wou'd be sorry I should want them, w:ᶜʰ is all I shall say at present ?.

James R

PLATE 14. The concluding lines of a letter from King James (in his own hand) to Cardinal Philip Howard in January 1691, conveying his frustration that the papacy had not provided further funds to help counter King William's military build-up. James's English style is, according to Turner, 'undistinguished and pedestrian', but his hand is clear and bold.

PLATE 15. The Scots College in Paris in the Rue du Cardinal Lemoine (formerly the Rue des Fosses Saint Victor) which today houses the Association Franco-Ecossaise, and in which monuments exist to James, Mary Beatrice and James Drummond, duke of Perth, and other Jacobites.

PLATE 16. The tomb of King James in the parish church of Saint-Germain-en-Laye situated to the west of the palace. The church was commissioned by Louise XIV in 1683 but re-built in the 1760s. Later in the 1820s, when new foundations were being dug, lead boxes containing the praecordia of King James and probably those of Queen Mary Beatrice and Princess Louisa were found and these remains were re-interred and the white marble monument erected at the spot in 1855 by the family of Saxe-Coburg and Gotha. The Latin inscriptions read: 'What good is a throne or noble birth? Death wears away all things. But the glory of his faith and character remain forever.'

PLATE 17. The ceiling painting above the tomb in the parish church of Saint-Germain-en-Laye with the depiction of James as St George fighting the dragon.

PLATE 18. The plaques placed on the outer wall of the parish church of Saint-Germain-en-Laye erected by Queen Victoria and the Association Franco-Ecossaise.

PLATE 19. King James's final words as printed (in Paris, 1702) on silk for Elizabeth, duchess of Gordon, a remarkable keep-sake for a pious Catholic duchess who entered a convent in Flanders in 1697.

Privy Council suspended its meetings from 15 March to 8 April to allow some to travel south. Rothes, Moray, William Douglas, earl of Queensberry, and others went to the court to resolve the question of who was to be in overall authority after James. The orthographically challenged Rothes, Chancellor since 1664, was selected, though he would not be back to preside over the Council until July.[37] By then a new phase in the campaign against nonconformity had begun.

Accompanying the group of privy councillors travelling south in 1680 was John Paterson, bishop of Edinburgh. Now undoubtedly the major political ecclesiastic, he was despatched to London by the Scottish bishops to appeal to Charles, James and Archbishop Sancroft to abandon the policy of indulgence which weakened their position. They claimed that field conventicles were on the increase. This persuaded Charles to add restrictions to Monmouth's concessions, to limit house conventicles and to recall some licences for such meetings. In particular, no house meeting could now take place within twelve miles of the capital.[38] This merely provoked a dramatic response from the Cameronians, the radical wing of the Covenanting Presbyterians led by Richard Cameron, an exiled minister who had returned in October 1679. Two revolutionary statements of the Covenant then emerged in June 1680, the Queensferry Paper and the Sanquhar Declaration, reprising the Rutherglen Declaration produced between the murder of Sharp and the Covenanter's victory against Claverhouse at Drumclog in June 1679. The first of these new documents, discovered north of Edinburgh, declared the objective to free the Church from 'the thraldom, tryranny, incroachment, and corruption of Prelacy ... and Erastianism'. The paper publicly owned at Sanquhar in Dumfriesshire also cried 'tryanny' and specifically rejected the succession of James 'a professt papist'. This was followed in September by the formal excommunication by the field preacher Donald Cargill of Charles and James at a gathering at the Torwood near Stirling. These were stark personal attacks on the royal brothers as they boldly condoned their 'preventive murder'. By then, a crackdown – including the censorship of 'false and seditious' printings and echoing such measures in England – had been ordered and in July Cameron had been killed by royal dragoons at Airds Moss in Ayrshire. Cargill also met such a fate, being captured and executed in 1681.[39] Therefore a new phase of brutal oppression and judicial torture had now arrived. James more than went along with this regime of rigour when he returned in October 1680, and to begin with, few disagreed with the need to defeat such extremism. Events in 1680 merely confirmed to Charles and James that Paterson and the bishops were correct. The royal brothers shared, we should remember, an intense hatred of 'presbyterian republicanism'.

Although quite able to show responses ranging from indifference to mercy when viewing the suffering of others, it is too simplistic to claim that James delighted at the torture of prisoners. Burnet's slur that he watched torture when in Scotland 'as a man that had no bowels nor humanity in him', and George Lockhart of Carnwath's sense of outrage that this did not correspond to the duke's 'naturall temper' as known by most contemporaries, both fail to put events into context. A number of the most notorious occasions of torture took place when James was not actually in Scotland, such as in the immediate aftermath of Airds Moss in the summer of 1680, or the interrogation in October 1683 of the likes of Argyll's secretary William Spence to glean details of the Rye House Plot. Also, in early October 1681, James, present on this occasion, offered clemency to six accused if they 'acknowledged the king to be their true and lawful sovereign', and one was pardoned as a result. The day after the five were executed, another four were brought to the Council for interrogation and the duke, the moderate Presbyterian Fountainhall informs us, 'caused hastily to remove them, that they might not also hang themselves with their owne tongue[s]'. They were sentenced to transportation. Claims by Wodrow that James had a plot invented in late 1680 so that he could have an excuse to 'sharpen the persecution' of Presbyterians, ignore the extreme nature of Cameronian manifestoes with their justification of regicide.[40] Admittedly under torture and with James in attendance, after five of Cargill's followers were interrogated in November 1680, a plot to blow up Holyrood and the duke himself soon emerged. Three of the five – James Skein, John Potter and Archibald Stuart – were executed as they were unwilling to recant their views. On being pressed on whether it was lawful to kill the king they declared they would 'nather call it lawful or unlawfull' for their creed allowed, as expressed in the 1660s, for the removal of 'persons abusing sacred authority'. In spite of some effort by the duke to get Skein to retract, he met his fate. For James loyalty to the sovereign could not be qualified and, we should not forget, only just over a year before, Sharp had been brutally killed. Furthermore, James's opinions on the value of torture were legally accepted. Both officers of state and the legal profession viewed the procedure as an entirely legitimate means of gathering information in the most serious cases, such as treason. It was also Charles, not just James, who, before a special meeting of a Scots council in Whitehall with them both present, sanctioned that the Scots Rye House plotters should be returned to Edinburgh for torture by the 'boot', a device not introduced by James but used in Scotland for many years and found commonly throughout Europe. Execution was, moreover, not the fate of all those interrogated with Skein in November 1680. Fountainhall spoke to Skein the night before his execution and suggested passive resistance could be entertained with conscience – 'private persons war not to answer for the faults of governors, but only to pray and mourn for them'. Skein could not accept this. However, John Spruel, Glasgow merchant and apothecary, who the authorities were convinced was behind the financing of the Covenanter's press and military activity, was imprisoned on the Bass Rock for six years. No doubt his vigorous interrogation promised, James and his advisors realised, more information in the future. And yet, under the amnesty and relief to Presbyterians resulting from James's second indulgence proclamation of June 1687, Spreul was freed. In short, Whig slanders, as perpetuated by the likes of Macaulay, seem especially futile when there are many other justified criticisms to be made of our subject.[41]

The impact on the conforming Scottish clergy as a result of the Test was great indeed and Burnet and Wodrow estimate that perhaps eighty ministers, acting out of conscience, refused to take the oath and were deposed in the winter of 1681/2, some of them qualitatively irreplaceable. As one anonymous and fearful observer reflected, the Test was seen as 'a wedge of divisione . . . laying a trap for solid sincere Protestants'. Nevertheless, the government campaign against Protestant nonconformity could be seen as successful from 1680 to 1682, although yet another phase was entered into in 1683. Since the arrests and trails of 1680/1, a Cameronian remnant continued to meet in quarterly gatherings from December 1681. While they issued a statement, an 'Apological Declaratione of the trew Presbyterians of the Church of Scotland' which recapped earlier accusations of Crown tyranny, their impact and numbers were slight. Only a handful suffered hanging, and a small number were subjected to punitive fines and transportation to Carolina or New Jersey. However, in September 1683 James Renwick, an exiled minister, returned to Scotland and galvanised the Society People, as the Covenanters were also called, and field conventicles began to reappear.[42] Under James's guidance Charles instructed the Privy Council to respond.

But another factor increased anxiety over law and order when the details of the Rye House Plot emerged in June 1683. As a threat to the royal brothers this was more credible than the convoluted and at times absurd Popish Plot. In addition, it was a chance to attack exclusionists and leading Whigs. For Scotland, alarmingly, intelligence suggested that not only was a rising to be led in Scotland by the exiled Argyll, with various other exiles involved, such as Stair and George, Lord Melville, and James Campbell, earl of Loudoun, who had recently taken flight to Holland, but it was believed that thousands of Covenanters in scattered cells in England were waiting to spring into action. Some of this was fanciful, yet it was used as both excuse and reason for a clampdown in England and Scotland. When in October the key Scots suspects, Sir Hugh Campbell of Cessnock, William Spence, William Carstares and Robert Baillie of Jerviswood, were transferred to Edinburgh for interrogation and trial, the coincidence of a new wave of field meetings left the Privy Council linking the two aspects and looking to increase the policing presence in the offending shires.[43] What had now developed was the period known as the 'Killing Times'. Between late 1683 and the summer of 1685 some hundred or more Covenanters of middle and insignificant rank were, with or without due process, shot or executed by those with Crown commissions.

The extent to which this notorious period was James's responsibility leads us to speculation. No parliament met from 1681 to 1685 so the Privy Council was left to deliver its own ordinances to tackle nonconformity based on previous legislation. From May 1682 it put new measures in place by requiring local officials and sheriffs to take immediate action in their own locations. Nevertheless, in the next twelve months we see a gradual reliance placed not on local authorities but on military men. In late May Lieutenant General Dalzell and Captain Adam Urquhart of Meldrum were given a watching brief over the shires of Lanark and Ayr, and Roxburgh, Selkirk and Berwick respectively. In August a Major Andrew White was given commission for Ayr, and Meldrum revised commissions for Berwick, Haddington, Peebles and Selkirk. Then in March 1683, White, Meldrum and James's favourite, now Colonel, John Graham of Claverhouse were given authority to inspect the records of local courts to ensure that Covenanters were being swiftly processed. Heritors could not be processed summarily through these commissions, but the statutes demanding attendance at Episcopalian services were imposed on all. As Tarbat, the Clerk Register, put it in October 1682 in relation to Edinburgh and Leith, the Council carried out a 'vogerous executione of the law against withdrawers from the church'. Indeed, Claverhouse's success in Galloway, including the shires of Wigtown and Kirkcudbright and part of Dumfries, where many ordinary Presbyterians had taken the Test out of fear and recalcitrant heritors were rounded up to be taken to Edinburgh to take the Test or oath and face death if they did not, made the government feel this level of intervention was paying dividends. The caricature by Presbyterian contemporaries and historiography of 'Bluidy Clavers' as a relentlessly brutal individual rests on a small number of well recorded, callous, summary executions. Others were more guilty than he, but his statement that he 'rifled so their houses, ruined their goods . . . that their wyfes and schildring were broght to sterving' confirms a bleak regime of oppression to enforce compliance, compounded by the reputation of Claverhouse and the other military officers. Church attendance boomed as the majority Presbyterian population feared they would be seen as fanatics if they did not conform. Charles then authorised six circuit courts, under military protection, to be set up to take the law to shires where the Society People still practised their activities, yet also against any nonconforming Presbyterians refusing the Test Act and an agreed oath of indemnity. Measures continued to escalate as Council and commissioned officers became more frantic over a problem which, being a conflict of conscience, seemed never to be finally resolved. Some cases of small detachments of troops being attacked and prisoners forcibly released confirmed more effort was required as force begot force.[44]

The first of the new circuit courts met at Stirling in June 1683 with the Justice General, James Drummond, earl of Perth, presiding and Rosehaugh prosecuting, with a small number of privy councillors offering support and legal credibility. Charles Middleton, earl of Middleton, joint Scottish Secretary with Moray since 1682, was of the view that 'all honest men [were] mightily pleased with the happy success of the Justice Aires'. Not all were convinced, and Hamilton, having taken the Test himself at the last minute in March 1682 after being told by King Charles that he must, observed the circuit court in Glasgow in 1683 and confessed to Queensberry he '[could] not find out the advantage of this circuite court, either to king or countrey'. His uncompromising Presbyterian wife insisted he do everything possible to protect their own retainers. Nonetheless, by the winter of 1683/4 these courts, along with an increasingly vigorous High Court of Justiciary in Edinburgh, delivered the submission of many and the execution of perhaps a score of ex-Both-well Brig soldiers, Sharp murderers, unrepentant conventiclers, and some others where the evidence was doubtful but an example was required. Rumours that Argyll was purchasing arms in Holland drove on the Crown officers. It was there-fore in some desperation that the Society People remnant, led by Renwick, at last retaliated on 8 November 1684. On this day they published their *Apologetical Declaration and the Adminatory Vindication of the True Presbyterians of the Church of Scotland* which was affixed to market crosses and churches throughout the south west. This was not only a restatement of previous manifestos but, in effect, a decla-ration of war against their oppressors. Several fatal attacks on individual soldiers and even the murder of an Episcopalian minister showed a desire to take the fight to the authorities. Faced with 'war' the expected response of the Crown thereafter took policing activity to another level. Charles demanded the 'utter extirpation of the . . . bloody and irreclaimable rebels'.[45]

In the previous November James and Charles issued a commission for a new 'secret committee' of the Privy Council, one that excluded all bishops including Paterson who, like many a political bishop before him, had temporarily fallen out of favour. The wider standing Committee for Public Affairs still included the two archbishops but this was to be a military campaign. This inner group consisted of the earl of Aberdeen, Chancellor; Queensberry, Treasurer Principal; John Murray, marquis of Atholl, Keeper of the Privy Seal and the man who policed the Argyll and the west Highlands; the earl of Perth, Justice General; Lundin, Treasurer Depute; Sir George Mackenzie of Tarbat, Lord Register, and Rosehaugh, the Lord Advocate. There was a slight reshuffle in June 1684 when Aberdeen was replaced by Perth, with George Livingstone, earl of Linlithgow, former commander-in-chief in Scotland, becoming Justice General, and John Keith, earl of Kintore, a commander of militia, Treasurer Depute, with Lundin now one of the secretaries in London. Essentially, the Episcopalian and military ethos of this committee remained constant and, with much enthusiasm, they tackled nonconformity with or without James's direction. Meanwhile, from late 1683 James issued various instructions for garrisons to be strengthened, and further orders were given in November 1684 to Lieutenant General Drummond, master-general of the king's ordnance, and new commissions were despatched for two new troops of horse to assist Claverhouse, one each to Queensberry's two sons James, earl of Drumlanrig and Lord William Douglas. These military instructions from the duke developed from a range of commissions and policy directives he issued since his return to England in May 1682. Much of this was based on regular briefings from mili-tary-minded privy councillors, such as Dalzell, Drummond, Queensberry, but also Claverhouse, who visited James in London in the summer of 1683.[46] The deploy-ment of scattered military detachments with experienced officers supported by local militia was James's tactical solution, given that his preferred option for a larger standing army was too costly and impractical. However, more of the same was not sufficient. Therefore on 22 November, the Council agreed, after taking legal opinion, to impose an abjuration oath such that anyone refusing to disown the *Apologetical Declaration,* a 'treasonous declaratione', could 'be immediatly put to death'. Then on 27 November 1684 it finally removed the remaining accommodation for indulged ministers and began their wholesale dismissal. Those who would not promise to abandon their calling were imprisoned. Then in January 1685 the Council instructed commissioners not to interrogate women 'but such as hes been active in these courses in a signall manner, and these are to be drowned', a license infamously acted upon two unfortunate women, the so called 'Wigtown martyrs', by Robert Grierson of Lag at that burgh three months later. Unprecedented fines and transportation overseas were also now commonly imposed, the latter to relieve grimly overcrowded prisons. More than ever before, Presbyterianism was now the target. This persecution, indeed, continued unabated after the death of Charles II with new commissions granted to the likes of General Drummond. Thus when the Argyll Rebellion took place in May and June 1685 James and his ministers in Edinburgh assumed that the Cameronians would throw in their lot with Argyll – it was not to be. They had always been an isolated sect. As it was, once the arrests and trials from the Argyll affair had taken their course, very few executions of extreme Covenanters occurred thereafter. Subsequently, in James's drive as king to remove the penal laws against his co-religionists, he went on to introduce two indulgences by proclamation. The first of these in February 1687 was little comfort to Presbyterians who, for example, could not, like Catholics and Quakers, build meeting houses, and also could only be ministered to by clergy who accepted the indulgence and took an oath of non-resistance. However, the second indulgence in the following June lifted all significant penalties other than meetings in fields. As a result of this amnesty many exiled Presbyterian clergy returned from their Dutch exile and, gathering in Edinburgh in July with those released from prison, they penned an address to their Catholic monarch thanking him for their new freedoms. Only Renwick and his few followers persisted without compromise and with field meetings, and it was after one of these that he was captured and finally in February 1688 met his end by execution.[47] To the Episcopalian militarists of the 1680s this was all astonishing, while on the ground, congregations in the south and west migrated from their parish churches. North of the Tay, however, there were less Presbyterian meeting houses and episcopacy remained strong. The religious divisions of Scotland were as marked as ever.

James, as the prime manager of Scottish affairs from 1681 to 1688, must certainly take much responsibility for an infamous period of Crown violence. During these years he was, indeed, duke and king of Scots. The agreement with his brother for his return in May 1682 was to step back from public affairs in England yet be given a free hand in Scotland, and so for the most part he did. When he left

Scotland for the last time, however, he had not as is claimed, left behind 'the complete ruin of the policies of comprehension and toleration and yet more savage persecution of dissenters', for it was after his departure that this savagery intensified.[48] As a royal prince he was able when in Scotland to pardon individuals in a way not so readily available to officers of state and of the army dealing with immediate circumstances. Nevertheless, James encouraged this reaction from a Privy Council of loyal Episcopalians and vitally created the military and security infrastructure to allow them to be so uncompromising. Also, by his direction to the Privy Council and his invitation to bend traditional and established legal codes, he encouraged the approach whereby the end justified the means. The ruling by the Court of Session that it was legal to impose the charge of treason against someone who failed to disown the content of a treasonable paper is sign enough of that. Add to this the fact that James, other than over his Catholicism, was ever influenced by bishops north and south of the border who whispered alarm at nonconformity, and we get some idea of the dynamics of this policy of austerity. Nevertheless, the toleration dispensed to Presbyterians in 1687 confirms that for James Presbyterianism was a political not a religious threat. If only Presbyterians could be depoliticised, they represented yet another group of Christian brethren who in time, like his old mentor Turenne, would see their error and turn to Rome.

THE ALBANY GOVERNMENT

In October 1685 George Mackenzie, Viscount Tarbat, recently maligned by the confessions of Sir John Cochrane that he was somehow linked to the Argyll Rebellion, expressed nostalgia for the old days of Lauderdale:

> the state of the king's servants was happy in those days, that only rebels opposed them, happy in Lauderdale's tyme, when albeit they divided in parties, yet each was just to ther colleagues [while now] these who should defend are more suspicious foes then those who prefess to offend.[49]

This was not how the political elite of Scotland saw things when James returned for his second visit in autumn 1680. The duke, his duchess and their households arrived by ship off Kirkcaldy in Fife late in the evening of Monday 25 October, coming ashore the following morning and spending a few days at Leslie being entertained by Chancellor Rothes, now the major Crown servant in Scotland and basking in the glory of his new dukedom. Yet again Edinburgh put on a spectacular welcome when the prince crossed the Forth and entered the capital the following Friday. The official account of the festivities, printed simultaneously for propaganda purposes in London and Dublin as well as Edinburgh, as the second exclusion parliament deliberated at Westminster, describes a cacophony of 'cannon, trumpets, [and] drums' with church bells ringing and 'great bonfires' lighting up the sky. When the royal party reached Holyrood they were greeted by the archbishops and bishops, delighting more than most at the return of a great protector of episcopacy, and James was presented with the keys to Edinburgh Castle. Charles's instructions to the Privy Council that the welcome be appropriately choreographed to indicate a 'publick demonstration of joy' proved unnecessary. There were, however, a few small imperfections in this carnival atmosphere. The great medieval gun Mons Meg was 'riven' when it was fired from the Castle and a popular idea spread that this was a bad omen, especially as the gunner was English. Not many weeks later on Christmas Day 1680 a group of students from the College of Edinburgh, supported by town apprentices, burnt an effigy of the Pope in the High Street, after evading troops deployed by the authorities who came to hear of the plan. This 'inhospitall affront' to the duke, as even Fountainhall decribed it, was compounded when the house of the provost, Sir James Dick of Priestfield, was torched in early January, he being the first to alert the Council to the anti-Catholic protest. Although there was no firm evidence of student involvement in the firing of the building, the Council took firm action and closed the college for a month and issued severe warnings to students and parents about future conduct. Consequently we can see that popular anxiety over popery lay just below the surface, and yet the well of goodwill for James was as deep in 1680 and 1681 as on his first arrival in autumn 1679. This was intended to spill over to benefit Charles, and it did. The most obvious sign of this was the public celebration of the king's birthday on 30 May 1681, delayed by a day as it fell on a Sunday. James gave his support to the festivities and for good reason. After church services of thanks the day before, a huge party ensued with a 'noble banquet' preceded by street merriment, yet another cacophony of noise of bell, drum and gun, and, most telling of all, a giant bonfire at the palace gate at which laird and noble pledged on their knees support for the royal family.[50] This gave a powerful royalist signal from the north only weeks after Charles had dissolved the third exclusion parliament at Oxford, and just before a purging of Whigs began in England at local level, in county commissions of the peace and of lieutenancy. Yet again, Scotland would be an example to England. In fact, later in the year on 14 October Edinburgh also gave the duke his own elaborate birthday celebration followed on 15 November by one for the Queen. James and Mary's departures from Scotland in February 1680 and May 1682 were also send-offs marked by ceremonial and thanksgiving.[51] These ritualised events were a deliberate extension of the royalist reaction in England as well as a consolidation of Stuart prestige as kings of Scots.

When the festivities subsided in late 1680 James turned to governing Scotland. Although this would involve additional measures to clampdown on Protestant nonconformity and deliver some of his reforms for the militia, it also turned on the formation of his administration in Edinburgh. James has been accused of narrowing the base of government to a point where it produced additional risk for his own reign, but to what extent is this true? The Presbyterian and Williamite jurist Fountainhall had religious, constitutional and party reasons for condemning James's style of government and, in particular, his use of a small 'juncto' or secret committee. Responding to the new commission for such a committee in 1683 he declared:

> The Juncto and Committee of Safety ware words invented in the rebellious tymes; and therefor they shuned these terms, and called themselves the Secret Committee. They are as the Articles to the Parliament, so to be a preparatory Committee to the Privy Cousell, to mould, form, and prepare matters; so that the rest of the counsellors will have little more to doe save to ratify ther conclusions . . . There is nothing to be transmitted to the King, but by them.

This comparison with the management committee of the Scottish Parliament may be instructive. Lundin delighted at the introduction of 'our juncto', as he termed it, when it was confirmed at a meeting with the royal brothers at Whitehall in November 1683. Charles, Lundin reported to Queensberry, was 'so well pleased with [it] that ye never saw the lyke, and when we had given our reasons, he said no man wold doe business by himself . . . [and] . . . if any one man did . . . it wold doe ill with Scotts hearts'. Convinced of the merits, when James read out the proposed list of committee members, Charles promptly agreed.[52] Was this then an innovative procedural development and did it have wide-ranging political implications?

The history of Scottish council membership for the first two decades of the Restoration period is one of continuity. From Charles II's first commission of 1661 to James coming north in 1679, only two new commissions were granted, in June 1674, when the duke was first listed, and July 1676, with James given the title Lord Admiral of Scotland. Both reaffirmed membership for many existing councillors from the noble, clerical, military, legal and commercial elite. Since 1661 new members were introduced to compensate for natural wastage and occasional political casualties, like the duke of Hamilton in 1676, removed on the insistence of Lauderdale for his political opposition but reinstated by James in 1682. Others such as George Mackenzie of Tarbat and John Hay, Earl of Tweeddale, were deprived of their seats but were also reinstated, and some who lost high office remained councillors.[53] James therefore took over from Lauderdale a coherent body little affected, in its totality at least, by factional imbalance. From 1681, however, this continuity began to weaken with the departure of a few actual and some potential councillors. Firstly, as we have seen, the Test Act affair led to the removal of the likes of James Dalrymple of Stair and Argyll. By early 1682 various nobles who were not council members became sidelined from political life by their refusal to take the Test, such as the earls of Callendar, Cassillis, Findlater, Galloway,

Haddington and Nithsdale, although this process certainly freed up promotion prospects for others, though not those such as Melville and Loudoun who the following year fled overseas because of the Rye House Plot. Therefore the new commission that James initiated in July 1684 tidied up the depredations of physical and political mortality over the past decade. And yet nearly half of the Council of 1676 was reappointed. James's first commission as king, of May 1685, was almost identical to that of the previous year with a few new faces, including his son-in-law George, Prince of Denmark, while his favourite Claverhouse was temporarily struck off for behaviour unbecoming, having at council delivered a jealous rant in Queensberry's face over the military seniority of his sons. However, the commission of May 1687 was another matter altogether. With the flagship policy of securing a statute-based Catholic toleration in tatters, Lundin (now earl of Melfort) made clear James's wishes, 'to clear the Council of all who opposed' and to compose a council 'firmly concurred in His Majesty's service'. No less than nine of the Council of 1685 were set aside for their unwillingness to support James's Declaration of Indulgence of the previous February which suspended the penal laws against Catholics. This group included the earls of Mar, Glencairn, Dumfries and Panmure; William, Lord Ross, who had served under Claverhouse; Mackenzie of Rosehaugh and the shire commissioner John Wedderburn of Gosford, who also lost his commission as a lieutenant colonel of dragoons. James and Melfort attempted to compensate for this by building an admixture of Catholics and loyal Protestants. In the former category were added George, duke of Gordon, a new entrant to politics who like James served under Turenne, and George Douglas, earl of Dumbarton, soldier and brother of Hamilton, who became James's commander-in-chief in Scotland, as well as more recent converts like Kenneth Mackenzie, earl of Seaforth, nephew of Tarbat, and Andrew Wauchope of Niddrie-Marischal, who replaced his octogenarian father Sir John who had been a councillor for over twenty years. In the other category were the lawyers Sir John Dalrymple of Stair, son of the exiled jurist, who replaced Rosehaugh as Lord Advocate, and Sir George Lockhart of Carnwath, President of the Court of Session, or royalist Episcopalian military men like Claverhouse himself and the ultimately Williamite John Gordon, Lord Strathnaver, who would succeed to the earldom of Sutherland.[54] Not all of these councillors attended regularly and commission was no guarantee of political interest or influence. Nevertheless, the discarding of so many individuals and the arrival of thirteen new men was the greatest personnel upheaval in the ruling elite since 1660. As many left the stage in alienation as entered to disappointment and disillusion, and, whatever policies were entertained, this was dangerous. James saw it differently – the Council was a key mechanism for inclusive patronage and since 1676, leaving aside the now traditional addition of four Englishmen, it had expanded from thirty-eight to forty-eight members. In 1687 preparations were being made to govern by Council instead of Parliament if that was to prove necessary in the long term.

In late 1680, while the earl of Moray had now replaced Lauderdale as Secretary in London, on his return James made no major changes to the Council in Edinburgh – the 'mongrel party' or 'policy of accommodation' continued. The campaign against the Cameronians had been led since August by a secret committee consisting of Rothes, Argyll, Queensberry and the bishop of Edinburgh.[55] The existence of such a committee is problematic for the student of Restoration government. In an unhelpful manner the official record and correspondence intermingle the terms 'privy' and 'secret'. From the reign of James VI, it was understood by the Crown that a large Council was well and good but a small number of key decision makers was the most effective way to manage policy. This had caused limited tension between Parliament and Council or political elite and the Crown as the membership of such committees, though small, was selected by the Council itself, and their remit was for a specific purpose. This included, for example, questioning an accused or coordinating a response to a particular security threat, such as investigating Sharp's murder or, as in this case, organising the campaign against Covenanters. Indeed, a 'committee of conventicles' was established in 1676, a large Committee for Public Affairs designed to tackle religious dissent emerged in 1677, and, in parallel, a ten-man Committee Anent the Peace of the Kingdom was formed in September 1681 to enforce the Test and to report on the consequences for office-holding.[56] Ad hoc committees were therefore common. Moreover, all councillors took an oath of secrecy as seen in the commission of 1661 which, it must have been felt, equipped each for membership of such committees if required. Equally, both John, earl of Middleton, and Lauderdale had governed through small coteries of advisors and, whatever the limitations of the official record, it is impossible to imagine Council business being carried out regardless of these intimate groupings. In due course James's ministers would be no different, and in this he was at one with his brother. Once Charles had removed Shaftesbury from his English Council in late 1679, and then finally dissolved the third exclusion parliament in March 1681, he too increasingly favoured a small team of advisors where there was less debate and more agreement. While this chimed with Charles's natural lethargy over business, it suited James's desire for authoritarian control.

The control asserted from November 1684 was, however, of another level. In the wake of the Rye House Plot, with the transfer of prisoners to Scotland in October and the intensification of an English Tory reaction, which was appalled at the plot and either sympathetic or indifferent to Crown authoritarianism, James got Charles's agreement to a new 'secret committee' of the Scottish Privy Council. The suggestion that James was passive or simply carried out the will of the Scottish ministry does not convince and takes little account of his preferences in style of government. Too much reliance has been placed on his polite and apparently yielding style of letter-writing, which gives the impression all things are possible and yet was generally followed by firm decisions by the royal brothers. This was, moreover, the first time the committee had been commissioned and its membership directed by the Crown. In the first instance it consisted of the earl of Aberdeen, Chancellor; Queensberry, Treasurer; the marquis of Atholl, Privy Seal; Perth, Justice General; Lundin, Treasurer Depute; Tarbat, Lord Register, and Mackenzie of Rosehaugh, the Lord Advocate. This might appear a sensible group given their respective offices although others felt excluded. Hamilton derided the committee as a 'Side-bar Counsell' though he was also added in November 1685, at a time when James wished to persuade him to cooperate over future religious plans, as was Dumbarton, James's commander-in-chief, the previous May, and the Catholic duke of Gordon in February 1687. Others such as Aberdeen and Queensberry were removed as they fell from the Council. Critically, James began to direct policy to this committee, not to the Chancellor or the whole Council. Its remit was to vet all political and security business before the whole Council considered action, but it ranged widely over all matters. When James was king, Melfort became the main information conduit for sending instructions from London directly to the committee, bringing his own interpretive and censorious style to proceedings, though being a demented letter-writer he wasted no time in penning notes to individuals as well. This committee, though, also made it easier for the further contraction of the management of Scottish affairs placing it into even fewer hands than the original seven members. By October 1688 it had become Perth, Atholl, Colin Lindsay, earl of Balcarres, Tarbat and a rehabilitated John Paterson, now archbishop of Glasgow, although by then almost all policy was mediated through the conduit of Perth and his brother Melfort in London.[57] It seemed and was a closed club, and those new privy councillors added since 1685 had yet more reason to be disenchanted.

In the seventeen months that James resided in Scotland, from October 1680 to early March 1682, he employed the existing officers of state to carry out the prime task of exerting more pressure on Presbyterian nonconformity. Preparing and managing the parliament of 1681 and securing the succession and the Test Act and oath, with James's personal insistence that they be applied as universally as possible, were his main preoccupations. It has been argued, though, that during this time 'more than half of James's attention was devoted to the English political scene'. This may be true, and certainly he and the duchess were desperate to get back to St James's, but the Scottish agenda was a full one and there was still the overriding purpose of winning the succession battle in Scotland and so the war in England. James felt out of touch, and no wonder, as Charles kept him out of the loop over his negotiations with Barrillon for a new, secret Anglo-French treaty. These talks began in November 1680 and concluded successfully in the middle of the following March – three years of pension was agreed in exchange for Charles not calling the English Parliament for the same period and abandoning an alliance with Spain only concluded the previous summer. But in spite of this foreign policy activity, which would in time relieve Charles of the necessity to summon the Westminster Parliament for taxation, exclusion was still a credible threat and so he despatched Laurence Hyde to Edinburgh in January, before the Oxford parliament, to try again to convince James to return to the Church of England. James having stuck to his faith, Hyde was sent north for a second time in September with additional coercive threats from Charles. He could no longer support his brother and allow him home without some compromise, such as his agreeing to attend Anglican services publicly while remaining Catholic in private. The timing of this mission to Holyrood seems odd, Charles having the exclusionists on the run after March 1681, but it was not yet so obvious to contemporaries that the Whigs were in retreat. Also, news that James had defended episcopacy and Protestantism so well at the Edinburgh Parliament that summer – as confirmed by communications from Scottish bishops to their English brethren and a stream of English Tory pamphlets commending his '[overcoming] the Scottish nation; not with arms, but with love and wisdom' – encouraged Charles to try one more time to cure his brother's obstinacy. There were rumours that James's behaviour in Scotland indicated a change of heart over his faith. As it was, he stood as firm to Rome as when the Exclusion Crisis began. Depressed at what seemed the snatching of English defeat from the jaws of Scottish victory, he informed Colonel Legge he had no allies at the side of his brother other than the high Anglicans Hyde and Sir Leoline Jenkins, the latter having in 1680 replaced Henry Coventry as one of the two English secretaries of state.[58] Yet five months later Charles agreed that James could return, at least on a trial basis. Once more it was Portsmouth who instigated contact. She sought James's help with her shortage of income and the duke went along with this while stressing it would require his presence to London, which invited the royal mistress to ensure just that. Charles came to his own conclusions. Shaftesbury had been arrested and charged with treason in July 1681 and the king and his advisors thought to wait until the earl was convicted before welcoming James back. However, in February the case against Shaftesbury collapsed and on considering James's fate anew, Charles's leading ministers split on the issue. Portsmouth's intervention tipped the balance in favour of Hyde's faction who favoured calling James back and, out of exasperation, bringing the political crisis to a head. Many appeared ready to welcome him. The Scots community in London offered James and Charles their support against those who would 'deprive any of our Royall successors of their respective Rights in due course of succession', as confirmed in the loyal address of the Scots Corporation in the Cities of London and Westminster made by over thirty of their number on St Andrews day, 30 November 1681.[59]

Charles despatched to Edinburgh William Legge, brother to James's faithful friend, to bring the good news. James set sail from Leith on 6 March 1682, without his family but accompanied by many of his Scottish privy councillors, making landfall at Great Yarmouth four days later. At the port, and thereafter at Norwich, Newmarket, where he was instructed to meet his brother, and then back in London after their warm reunion, James was greeted with 'all imaginable demonstrations of joy'. Typically on 20 April, passing through the streets of the City of London on the way to a great banquet hosted by the Honourable Artillery Company, for whom James was Captain General, he was roundly cheered by the people of London. It all seemed a remarkable turn round compared to those furtive movements around the south of England when he returned from Brussels, but it was their prince of the royal blood and military hero, not his Catholicism, that they were pleased to welcome. James could be a poor analyst of the nuances of his own popularity.[60]

If Charles had doubts about the permanency of James's return, two quite distinct considerations clinched it. Firstly, James presented himself in a grateful and sombre manner making clear he would not become involved in English affairs; he would live privately. Secondly, Charles was relieved over a foreign policy matter which had vexed him for the previous nine months. The Prince of Orange visited Charles in July 1681 for secret discussion about continental affairs. James heard of the meeting and fretted about William's motives, remembering that he had refused to come to England in 1679 to help stem the initial exclusion hysteria, and had shown too much an even hand over Whig and Tory divisions. Exclusion put the prince in a dilemma. It might on the one hand bring the crown nearer to him through his wife Mary, but on the other, not necessarily help combat French military strength. Essentially William pressed Charles to come to terms with the Westminster Parliament as it controlled the purse strings for future military activity while Charles wished to avoid holding parliaments given the Commons desire to narrow the royal prerogative. The talks between William and Charles were, therefore, bad tempered and inconclusive.[61] Then in October 1681 King Louis began a siege of Spanish-owned Luxemburg, and Dutch and Spanish pressure intensified for Charles to protest and call Parliament to finance an anti-French campaign. All of this could put the new secret treaty at risk. However, in February Charles, then at Newmarket, heard that Louis had withdrawn and was taking up Charles's earlier suggestion to use himself to arbitrate between the parties.[62] Charles could relax and briefly bask in the glow of a minor diplomatic success and, of course, would not call the English Parliament for the remainder of his reign. Had it met in early 1682 then James could still have been subjected to impeachment.

After discussions in London on the make-up of the Scottish administration, in the first week of May James left by ship for Edinburgh to return briefly to order his affairs and bring back Mary Beatrice and Anne. What then ensued is one of those events of James's life over which Whig historians and detractors have delighted in embellishment. On the morning of 6 May, owing to a navigational error compounded by James's intervention, his own frigate *The Gloucester* ran aground on the sandbanks off Great Yarmouth and was sunk. Being reluctant to leave the ship and hoping that it could be saved, James lingered so long that the deployment of the long boat was delayed. This situation was not helped by his insistence that his strong box, containing his papers, was given priority. Therefore, even though the tragedy happened in daylight, and small yachts criss-crossed picking up survivors, about a hundred and thirty seamen, servants and a small number of men of quality were drowned, including the Scots Robert Ker, earl of Roxburghe, and Lord Hopetoun. Amongst those who survived were Charles, second earl of Middleton, Perth, Haddo and George Legge. Burnet's slander that James saved his dogs and priests before others can be dismissed, but Legge's own account confirms his poor judgment if not a disregard for human life. Nevertheless, Callow is probably correct when he judges that James's reaction to the incident shows his tendency to 'self-obsession'. His reflections in his own writings confirm understandable relief at his own deliverance and of most 'people of quality', some effort to blame the pilot, who was arrested and suffered a short prison sentence, yet almost no mention of those who died or the part he played in the debacle.[63] This may lead us to question his ability to command at the time. Others have also seen in the sinking some early sign of a physical or mental 'degeneration' which intensified later, but it is not proven that he ever entered such a phase. The affair, at the least, presented Tory propagandists with a miraculous survival narrative with which to work.

His party regrouping, taking advantage of a strong southerly wind, James arrived at Edinburgh the next day. Between 8 and 15 May, the day of his final departure from Scotland, he went to five Council meetings during which he announced some personnel changes. It was to prove an Episcopalian triumph. The duke of Rothes died in July 1681, the result of years of heavy drinking, just two days before the formal opening of Parliament that year, and Lord Privy Seal Atholl, a safe pair of hands, was James's choice to be President of the Session. There had been no need to replace Rothes as Chancellor while James could be present in person at Scottish Council meetings but, to Atholl's 'great disappointment' and the surprise of many, James now appointed Haddo, a mere judge, as Chancellor. This was certainly James's choice and was the first sign of the duke's wish to plant his own men. Charles knew little of the laird, though his handling of the prosecution against Argyll had brought plaudits. But Haddo had been a close advisor of James's during the 1681 session and brought administrative skill to his new position. Yet even though he was raised to the earldom of Aberdeen in November 1682, he never had sufficient noble support to withstand a concerted attack. Meanwhile, other beneficiaries of James's largess were Queensberry, newly created a marquis, who became High Treasurer in place of a treasury commission, whose membership may have altered over time but had existed since 1667, and Perth who was given Queensberry's old post as Justice General. By the autumn Lundin, another favourite of James's whose political career was an inextricable part of his master's nemesis, was the new Treasurer Depute. As the squeeze was put on Lauderdale's remaining interest, his brother Hatton was the next casualty and in the summer he was stripped of this post, a position he had held since 1671, and, after a complex investigation, convicted of embezzlement and maladministration of the mint which saw him heavily fined. Being well liked by the royal brothers, however, he was saved from more serious penalty and was allowed to succeed to the title of fourth earl, if not duke, of Lauderdale when the great Secretary died in August 1682, and went through a period of political rehabilitation. His own son Richard Maitland of Gogar lost his post of Justice Clerk in early 1684, falling foul of spurious suspicions that he was a supporter of his father-in-law Argyll. That rehabilitation process was a strange mixture for the Maitlands. While Richard was back in favour by 1687, being appointed Treasurer Depute that year, and went into French exile with James at the Revolution, his own brother John, who became the fifth earl after Richard died in Paris in 1695, was an active pro-Revolution man.[64]

Once James settled back at St James's, and rediscovered his taste for hunting, he did not abandon interest in Scottish affairs. Indeed, he had a greater involvement in matters Scottish than any Stuart prince since his grandfather James VI – he took advice but did not function 'as a puppet for others'. He saw his main task in ensuring a loyal administration north of the Border that would be no hindrance to Charles's opportunistic English campaign, the period of Tory or 'royalist reaction', as it was played out from 1681 to 1685. In this, step by step, Crown authority was reasserted. This was more ad hoc than coordinated, but Laurence Hyde helped it along as did especially Sunderland, who returned to favour and became reconciled to James. Numerous English borough charters were reissued giving Charles or local Tory interests power to remove or reduce numbers of Whig office-holders, control local government and, if and when required, deliver a firm grip of Westminster elections. This 'reversionary interest' gathered in reaction to the Rye House affair and the final flight of Monmouth, and saw the increasing persecution of English nonconformity. English Quakers suffered imprisonment for their religion while Catholic recusants were, as a reflection of James's influence, dealt with more leniently with a range of fines. English prisons could be a grim as those that housed Scottish Covenanters in the 'Killing Times'. Moreover, by the end of 1684 James was fully re-engaged in English affairs, forgetting his promise in 1682, and was regularly at meetings of the Committee for Foreign Affairs, was reinstated on the Privy Council in May 1684 and was once more virtually English Lord High Admiral with Charles signing his papers. Increasingly James was listening to less moderate counsel such as Sunderland and the judge Sir George Jeffreys who, in a repeat of the Haddo business, became James's English Chancellor in September 1685.[65] Nevertheless, Scotland was not forgotten. If by the end of Charles's reign he was an equal partner in English affairs, he remained from 1682 onwards indisputably duke of Scotland.

For long it has been argued that the fundamental weakness of the Scottish Restoration government was the 'factional infighting' of ministers. This was the political culture of the age, however, and was the inevitable backdrop to 'protoparty' politics. It affected England as well as Scotland, and was a feature before and after the Revolution of 1688/9. Nonetheless, James became exasperated with his Scottish ministers, once pleading with them in 1685 to 'avoid piques and animositys that may be amongst you', and he had regularly reflected on this problem since 1681. Handling Hamilton outside the inner circle was one thing, but he expected his core ministerial team to cooperate with each other. He hoped that harmony would break out, and, for example, dealt sensitively and successfully with a new arrangement for there being two Scottish secretaries. James wished to promote the earl of Middleton to the post but he and Charles came up with the compromise in September 1682 where Moray and Middleton would alternate responsibility, and when required, as with Parliament, one would go to Edinburgh. That the two worked well together says as much about their qualities as James's diplomatic skills. But the first major victim of James's new team of 1682 was the Chancellor Aberdeen. From the summer of 1683 a campaign had been waged against him by some of the secret committee, Queensberry, Perth and Lundin, the latter of whom, when in London from August to November, did his best to undermine Aberdeen in the eyes of James and Charles. Although Rosehaugh and Moray offered support, Aberdeen was accused of being too weak in pursuing conventicles. The new opportunity to undermine him came when he balked at the legality of a new proposal; to add the fining of husbands if their wives failed to attend the established church to that for attending conventicles, the 'black bond' as it was called by opponents. Rosehaugh will have agreed that existing law did not extend to this. As the accusations mounted the Chancellor went to London to clear his reputation but to no avail – in June he was replaced by Perth. His fate was sealed when a large bribe was paid to the duchess of Portsmouth to convince the king, while James's renowned loyalty to servants was posted missing. Before long, Perth's brother Lundin also benefitted as, with the resignation due to illness of Jenkins, one of the English secretaries of state, Middleton, was moved over and Lundin, not Moray's preferred partner, was appointed. Lundin now became a firm favourite of Mary Beatrice which would have profound implications for James's years in exile. Nevertheless, for now there was to be yet more disputation within the secret committee.[66]

Despite making a proclamation to the contrary, when James succeeded his brother in February 1685 he proceeded to reshuffle his own administration in England, making, for example, Laurence Hyde, earl of Rochester, Treasurer once more, replacing Sidney, Lord Godolphin, now Lord Chamberlain; Henry Hyde, earl of Clarendon (Rochester's older brother) Lord Privy Seal and Halifax, replaced by Clarendon, President of the Council. Some of these individuals would be dismissed over the next two years including both Hyde brothers. In Scotland, however, there was no immediate change because James had already forged his own Scottish ministry, confirming he was master of Scottish politics in the last years of Charles's reign.[67] From the decision to appoint Queensberry High Commissioner for the parliamentary session of 1685, a post Melfort coveted, relations between the two men deteriorated. Perth was also jealous that Queensberry, as mere Treasurer, appeared the chief minister in Scotland when the position of Chancellor should have given him seniority. In due course the secret committee split between Queensberry, Moray and Middleton on the one hand, and the Drummond brothers and Hamilton on the other, the latter of whom was brought into the government in the course of 1685. Before Parliament convened Moray warned that Melfort was spreading slanders that Queensberry was now 'more asbsolut then [Lauderdale] ever was'. Questions were being asked about maladministration of the treasury and payments to clients in echoes of the Hatton investigation. Hamilton joined the fray as he was in dispute with Queensberry over his liberal use of accommodation at Holyrood, which came under the duke's remit as Keeper of the Palace. To stop the bickering two conferences were held at Whitehall instigated by James. Firstly, in autumn 1685 James invited Perth and Queensberry to court but before long dozens of Scots nobles descended, much to his annoyance. The result was inconclusive though Queensberry was given strong support by James and a formal exoneration. However, somewhat like Aberdeen, the slander stuck, and Hamilton began to claim Queensberry was behind his family's lack of commissions. Another meeting in December produced an unconvincing reconciliation. Atholl and Breadalbane seemed to be allying with the Treasurer though Middleton now decided to keep out of Scottish business. In the end, however, Queensberry was fatally undermined and though the auditing of the treasury could prove no malpractice, he was removed from power in two stages; firstly, when the treasury was put back into commission in March 1686 and then, after the next season of parliament, when he was removed from all offices. Only Hamilton now had the authority to challenge the Drummond brothers. Queensberry's fall, the last great reversal of fortune of James's Scottish managerial phase, reveals a weakness in the king's treatment of personnel. Although Queensberry could indeed be 'haughty' and 'imperious', as described by Burnet, he had the potential to be the new Lauderdale with the personal authority to manage business. But when pressed enough, James listened to his favourites, like Melfort and Perth, before the counsel of the capable. This explains why Middleton and Moray, looking to their own futures, took a step back before Queensberry's fall. Nevertheless, James's appointment of Moray and not Melfort as commissioner for the 1686 session of parliament suggests he realised the need to placate both the 'sides' that emerged from the extraordinary squabble of 1685/6.[68]

If James struggled to control the Scottish elite at times, his great managerial success was the Scottish Parliament itself.[69] In 1681 James was able to convince his brother to summon the Scottish Estates for five related purposes: to secure the succession, to protect and build on the royal prerogative, to obtain additional supply to finance the continued battle against the conventicles, to sustain the Episcopal church and, in consolidation of these, to 'serve as a good example' to the Parliament of England. During the Exclusion Crisis the English parliaments of 1680 to 1681 had, of course, withheld supply in order to increase pressure on Charles. In June 1681, therefore, Charles appointed his brother as his High Commissioner for the coming Scottish session. At last James had official status and would henceforth be addressed with this title. In fact he was unique in Scottish parliamentary terms as the only prince to serve as High Commissioner and head of state. Being that he felt himself procedurally experienced there were later implications for his handling of the sessions of 1685 and 1686. But in the early months of 1681 James consulted widely with privy councillors on the correct agenda and exchanged correspondence with Lauderdale on how to manage Parliament. The Secretary knew how to work elections. Also, James saw how effectively he had delivered for the Crown in the past, including his success in getting the Act of Supremacy through the Scottish Parliament in 1669, in spite of opposition from the bishops. The act was perhaps the most absolutist piece of Scottish legislation in the seventeenth century, giving the king 'supreme authority and supremacy over all persons and in all causes'. Rothes being unwell, Lauderdale was the only former High Commissioner who could offer advice and, although it was eight years since the last full parliament, his experience was as recent as a convention of estates in 1678. He was consulted over the now regular mechanism of separate public and private commissioner's instructions, and while the former listed items under the five heads already mentioned, the latter advised James on the management of the Estates: James was told to avoid 'unparliamentarily methode' and observe 'the ancient laudable methods and order of proceeding'; to preserve 'the ancient power and rights of the articles'; to clampdown on all 'unusual and extraordinary meetings . . . during this session', and to report to Charles those who 'oppose [his] service'.[70]

The session of 1681 was actually more easily managed that the convention of 1678.[71] While at the latter Hamilton's party fought a hard election and aired grievances, the elections of shire commissioners in 1680 (at Michaelmas in late September) and of burgh commissioners in early 1681 were less closely contested. If elected, the 'opposition' members were unwilling to challenge James in the way they had Lauderdale. This is confirmed in the amount as well as the nature of legislation: thirty-five public and fifty-two private acts in all, a greater volume than at any session since 1661. The plethora of private acts was a sign of James's dissemination of patronage, and the public measures satisfied the priorities of the Crown, though also other matters such as encouraging trade. A more important piece of legislation for James was the 'Act acknowledging and asserting the right of succession to the imperial crown of Scotland' which assured the succession for James, regardless of religion or other act of parliament. We would have expected controversy but it passed with a large majority. Hamilton prepared a draft which was rejected and the final wording tightened with the phrase 'no difference in religion, nor no law nor act of parliament made or to be made, can alter or divert the right of succession'. Importantly, it also made starkly clear to the English Parliament that if it wished to exclude the rightful succession then it may suffer 'the fatall and dreadfull consequences of a Civil warr'; to focus minds the act was widely printed in England. Various measures were also designed to sustain the church and increase the persecution of nonconformity, and an act was approved confirming five years of supply using the cess, extending that agreed in 1678, to pay for the armed forces, although only after an amendment was pressed by Hamilton to give some relief to landed heritors. Other pieces of legislation were more problematic for the government. The passing of the Test Act, as we have seen, produced a number of dissenting voices and votes. In addition, when the drafting of an act for securing the Protestant religion was given to a sub-committee of the Lords of the Articles, the 'committee of religion', awkward proposals seemed to strengthen existing laws against Catholics, and James dismissed the committee and approved a short and generalised 'Act ratifying all former laws for the security of the Protestant religion'. This was the first act passed by the session and needed to be handled before any progress could be made on other matters.[72] James had, nevertheless, secured his legislative programme still riding high on a wave of popularity. His attitude to it all was triumphant and peevish, as seen in a letter to Ormonde written a few day before he adjourned the parliament: 'I hope what is done here will encourage people there [in England], and lett his Ma[jesty] see that resolution and sticking to his old friends will secure him against all his enemys'.[73]

Once Parliament was adjourned James and his Council could get on with imposing the Test Act. It was perhaps a time for him to pause and reflect on what might in the future be possible without the strictures of a Test Act. Subsequently, Charles was to violate the English Triennial Act in March 1684 by failing to call the Westminster Parliament after a three-year interval. Plans were nevertheless made for a Scottish session – the 1681 parliament was adjourned, not dissolved. Initially a session was planned for the summer of 1682, Charles instructing the Scottish Council to remain in Edinburgh to wait on James's arrival; and in January 1685 a warrant was issued to the duke of Hamilton to prepare Holyrood for a visit of James for a parliament in February or March 1685. Indeed, a total of eight adjournments and postponements, and a final confirmed dissolution in August 1683, requiring new elections for any new parliament, were after all related to Charles's dissolving in 1681 of the last English exclusion parliament at Oxford.[74] While Charles's and James's dislike of calling unnecessary parliaments seems less evident in a Scottish context, they nevertheless had sufficient income to avoid calling the parliaments in England, Scotland and Ireland (which had not met since 1666). In part this was down to the purgative powers available to them. Charles's use of these, and the courts when necessary, allowed him to build up a firm Tory hold on English local politics. So when new elections took place for the English parliament called by James in May 1685, a landslide ensued where the Tories took nine out of ten seats in the Commons. In Scotland the 'Act asserting his majesties' prerogative in point of jurisdiction', also passed in 1681, said it all. This measure, intended to limit noble jurisdictions in the Highlands, could and would be widely applied: 'notwithstanding of these jurisdictions and offices, his sacred majesty may by himself or any commissionated by him, take cognizance and decision of any cases or causes he pleases'.[75] Essentially then, finances secured, in all other business the Crown was supreme. On 28 July 1681 the traditional state opening, the 'riding of parliament' where the estates processed from Holyrood to Parliament Hall, gave this supremacy symbolic resonance. Even the cynical Fountainhall reported it was 'riden with great pomp and magnificence' though, all too typically, James's fiddling with the running order produced a series of noble protests over precedency.[76]

LONG LIVE THE KING

Charles enjoyed the final years of his reign. His bouts of illness in 1679, 1680 and 1682 had temporarily caused panic among his ministers and family, but other than gout, brought on by his diet and immoderate drinking over the years, he was considered healthy and still enjoyed long and brisk walks twice each day. However, on 2 February 1685 he collapsed in a 'fit of Apoplexy' and it soon became clear he was mortally ill. After four days of invasive prodding, in line with the grim medical knowledge of the day, he passed away. Before this James arranged for Father Huddleston, the Catholic priest who helped Charles escape from England thirty-three years before, to be smuggled into the room through a side door, and he received Charles into the Catholic Church and administered the last rites. He was fifty-four years old. Although the precise details of Charles's death-bed conversion are shrouded in mystery, as we have seen, the fact of it is not doubted. Thereafter James, like other Catholics, took the opportunity to make capital out of the conversion, publishing printings of two tracts, supposedly written by Charles, explicating his preference for Rome. But now, on the day of his brother's death, with tears of genuine emotion still in his eyes, James made an impromptu speech to the councillors present, and made reassuring promises to 'preserve this government in Church and State as it is now by law established'. James, himself fifty-one years old, was proclaimed king in London, Dublin and the colonies. In Edinburgh on 10 February he was proclaimed James VII at the 'mercat cross' by Chancellor Perth before the Council, burgh magistrates and population of the capital. They celebrated to the sound of bells and cannon and the setting of bonfires, though also, as Fountainhall qualified, mourned 'ther dearly beloved king'. Ten days later the impending session of the Scottish Parliament, then due on 10 March and with James presiding, was recognised as dissolved by the death of the late king. With a new reign, a new parliament with fresh elections was required, and it was summoned for 9 April, and then adjourned to 23 April, St George's Day, the day of James's English coronation. There would be no such Scottish ceremony and he would be the only Stuart never to take the Scottish coronation oath, for even William and Mary and Queen Anne were administered the oath, not in Edinburgh but at Whitehall. In fact no Scots are listed in the official form of proceeding for the English coronation. In London James announced after a few days his intention to hold a parliament there in May and, realising his rashness, explained to Barrillon, the French ambassador, that there was nothing for King Louis to fear. He would immediately dissolve the Westminster Parliament if it began to talk about foreign matters that interfered with their special relationship. In the meantime, a coronation service was devised that, as Turner remarks, 'gave complete satisfaction to neither Protestant nor Catholic', and James was installed at Westminster Abbey by Sancroft without taking Anglican Communion. Celebrations were certainly lively but James, perhaps sensibly, avoided some aspects of public procession unsure how the crowd would react. Only two days after he succeeded he began to openly attend Catholic services. That the crown slipped from his head during the coronation ceremony was seen by some as a bad omen. Soon, in spite of his religion, he did much to affirm the mysteries of divinely ordained monarchy and he followed his brother's marking of medieval tradition when in early March he began in elaborate ceremonies to touch for the king's evil to 'cure' scrofula. This 'medievalism' continued for weeks until Easter when he washed the feet of over fifty poor in the Banqueting House at Whitehall before they were fed, clothed and sent away with money.[77]

That James imposed such a tight schedule shows he was energised but also apprehensive, even though he must have mused over the possibilities of these events for many years. Oddly, he explained the urgency of the coronation as 'absolutely necessary for the establishment of the royal authority, for after it has taken place everything done or said against the King is high treason'. Assuming he was drawing a distinction between a *de facto* and *de jure* sovereign, this was not something that troubled his father or brother in 1625 and 1660. It was agreed then that the Scottish Parliament would meet before the English, in part so the former could yet again act as model for the latter, but also because preparations were more advanced. Michaelmas shire elections had already taken place the previous September and burgh elections could be joined quickly. Crucially, of course, this was the first election to take place according to the Test and as such, a parliament more cavalier than 1681 assembled on 23 April. Although according to the veteran burgh commissioner for Cullen the riding 'had not that splendour' of 1681 or before, it must have been a strange affair being also blended with a less sober coronation party.[78]

Queensberry, still supported by James, was appointed the king's High Commissioner and, even though planning had gone on in the secret committee for some months, before the Estates convened he went to London with the earl of Perth to consult with the new king. The overall outcome was unprecedented. John Lauder of Fountainhall, who only entered parliament in 1685 but came into view as one of Argyll's legal defence team in 1681, had some insight into the personalities of the old and new kings:

in the last king's tyme mirth, playes, buffoonerie, &c. domineered, and was incouraged; now, ther is little to be seen but seriousnesse and businesse, for *Regis ad exemplum totus componitur orbis*: [James] is grave, and of much application in public affairs; and the same imitation also holds in religion.[79]

This last preoccupation would become significant from the next session but in 1685 'much application' saw James obsessed with fine detail. On 28 March Queensberry received a remarkable forty-one separate instructions and thereafter, from 15 April to 10 June, another eleven sets on individual or grouped matters. This was not Charles II. The effusion produced no less than forty-eight specific acts, an unusually large amount of public legislation and a 50 per cent increase on the session of 1669. Some of it represented a meddling in the lives of the population and this spilled into the next session. For example, in a particular farming act parents were made liable for the fines made against children trespassing in fields, and if the child was over fourteen years, they could alternatively be turned over for public beating. Such authoritarianism cropped up at various moments during the Parliament's history, though it was key government measures that mattered now. The first legislation passed was the 'Act for security of the Protestant religion', the drafting of which was viewed by James as especially significant in relation to England. No doubt he recalled his own difficulties with the committee of religion in 1681. He told Queensberry: 'that only the words and all acts against Popery should be left out, and let them be left out, for tho they signify but little in themselves where you are, it might do a great deele of harme here'. Therefore the reassuring act of 1681 was sanitised with not merely the words 'all acts made against poperie' removed but also specific reference to the legislation of James VI and I and Charles I which sustained the anti-Catholic code.[80] Even at this stage James was deluded about the level of anti-Catholic feeling in Scotland.

Later the 'Act obliging husbands to be lyable for their wives' fynes' gave a legal basis to the very policy that helped bring down the earl of Aberdeen. Acts on the policing of the oaths, the use of the Test, on extending supply, on the militia, on protecting the Episcopal clergy from attack and against conventicles passed easily enough. James told Queensberry to secure an act 'continuing the excise during our life', as had been voted for Charles II, but in loyal mood the Estates agreed to annex the excise to the Crown forever. In its extraordinary words, later amplified and 'vindicated' by Rosehaugh, the act extols 'the great blessings we owe in the first place to divine mercy, and in dependance on that, to the sacred race of our glorious kings, and to the solid, absolute authority wherewith they were invested by the first and fundamentall law of our monarchy'. In fact, of the original forty-one instructions, all but five were passed, though many were subjected to amendment by the house and the Articles. A sub-committee of the Articles also rejected James's suggestion to set up an interval committee of parliament, with parliamentary power, to process cases against rebels as it was 'inconsistent with law, justice and the king's service'.[81] Nevertheless, contemporary Presbyterians viewed the legislative mix of the 1685 parliament as an unprecedented attack. The session saw a number of Test Act and Rye House deviants processed for treason, and a list of twenty-two such accused was drawn up by James, Lundin and Rosehaugh in early March to make sure that none was missed. Most Scottish parliamentarians were as anxious as they over Presbyterian extremism, but some were not sure this label described everyone listed, such as Sir James Dalrymple of Stair and Andrew Fletcher of Saltoun. The case of Baillie of Jerviswood, one of the conspirators executed 1684, demonstrates that James reaped what he sowed. He was treated with appalling cruelty by the Council with James's and Charles's approval: finding Baillie very ill in prison and likely to die, they decided to take the opportunity to find him guilty of treason and execute him swiftly as an example. Subsequently, he had his estates forfeited and transferred to the duke of Gordon at the 1686 parliament, yet this was one of those cases where James showed compassion. The next month he gifted to the widow Rachel Johnston and her nine children Baillie's escheat, his property and goods though not the land, and also her juncture. The fact that she was a daughter of the great Covenanter Archibald Johnston of Wariston made no difference. Baillie had other familial nonconformist connections being brother-in-law to James Kirkton, the field preacher, and a cousin of Gilbert Burnet, who would himself rush into exile in 1685 for fear of being associated with the Monmouth and Argyll rebellions. Burnet, of course, became chaplain to Prince William and a close confidant of his wife Mary, and came over with the invasion force at the Revolution. With them was Baillie's son George, a committed Revolution man. To some James was merciful. In the same week in September 1685 that 700 English rebels were transported to the West Indies, he pardoned Argyll's two sons who had been charged with treason in Scotland.[82]

James is sometimes judged one of the monarchs who most abused the position of the Lords of the Articles for close management of parliamentary business. We need to be cautious, however; by the Restoration the committee was large, consisting of forty members, and so in many ways a parliament within a parliament. Lauderdale was certainly no less 'managerial' than James and his ministers. As was the norm, in 1685 most Privy Council members were also selected for the committee and so no constitutional innovation took place. However, dating back to 1681 the committee had changed in structure. In that year and 1685, respectively, twelve and eleven sub-committees were formed when in 1669 there had been only eight. In part, of course, this was because more business was being conducted. In addition, whereas Lauderdale in 1669 employed bishops sparingly in sub-committees, Queensberry, prompted by James, made sure that they were represented on every committee, regardless of the topic at hand. In this respect it can be argued that scrutiny was maintained under James though with more of his clients present, but balanced by the creation of the secret committee of the Privy Council which managed the preparation for Parliament in a narrow manner that excluded the wider Council.[83] A recent proliferation of sub-committees, rather than long-standing disillusionment, may well account for the committee being such a grievance at the Revolution.

The traditional loyalty expressed at the start of a new reign and the fresh cavalier input from a general election was not the only reason for a loyal Scottish Parliament in 1685. Like the Westminster Parliament which met from 19 May to 2 July, it did so in the context of the futile rebellions of the duke of Monmouth in south west England and Argyll in western Scotland. The plan was for a coordinated rebellion although from the onset it fell apart. After setting sail from Holland, departing separately, Argyll landed on 11 May and Monmouth on 11 June, but soon both were defeated and executed. The English Parliament had agreed to finance James to grow the English standing army to 20,000 to deal with the threat, while Scotland was able to handle Argyll with existing forces under Dumbarton and Atholl. When the crisis broke, James asked Prince William if he could send over the brigade of English and Scottish regiments in Dutch service, three of which were Scottish and commanded by Hugh MacKay, to which he and the States General agreed, in his case to salve strained relations with his father-in-law. In the end, however, Mackay's regiments were not required and he and they returned to Holland although, after James reviewed them in person at Blackheath and admired their discipline when watching them exercise in Hyde Park, he added Mackay to the Scottish Privy Council having already promoted him to major general.[84] Later their relations would be transformed. By then, in silent moments, even James must have marvelled at the inexplicable ways of God when so many men of talent became his enemies.

Although James authorised Queensberry to adjourn the 1685 session of parliament if the needs of security required it, in the end the Argyll Rebellion petered out. He never had a force of more than 2,500 or so men, and soon most of that simply melted away. Neither Cameronians nor moderate Presbyterians rallied to his banner as he had hoped. At least Monmouth's cause came to a military denouement at the Battle of Sedgemoor on 5 July, whereas that of the great chief of clan Campbell ended ignominiously as his final supporters scattered and he was captured crossing the Clyde trying to make it back to his Highland heartland. In fact the king showed great confidence in the entire defensive operation, long before the size of the 'rebellious crue' was known. He wrote regularly to Perth giving encouragement and a week after Argyll was apprehended, in typical soldierly raillery, he expressed his hope that 'Argil's business be not doine for him before the three Scots reg[iments]' get a chance to deal with his supporters.[85]

The period between the close of the first session of the Edinburgh parliament on 16 June 1685 and the opening of the second on 29 April 1686 saw dramatic changes in the intensity of James's religious policy. He also temporarily abandoned the strategy of summoning the Scottish Estates first, although the initial adjournment to late October 1685 suggests this was originally planned, as the next English session met in November. What had changed was James's new sense of confidence. The Westminster parliament of 19 May to 2 July 1685 had been a financial success for James and it went better than he might have expected. The Commons, too, had its committee for religion which pressed an awkward Anglican agenda yet stepped back from a full confrontation. However, over religion it had become abundantly clear that the Anglican-Tory dominated Commons would support him loyally only as long as he defended the Established Church.[86] Did that mean that a level of toleration for Catholics was possible?

Some punishment of Protestant rebels was necessary first. The infamous 'Bloody Assizes' of the south west followed the month after the parliament. Judge Jeffreys and his colleagues delivered the prosecution of thousands and execution of dozens, many insignificant victims, and the level of judicial violence alarmed some Anglicans. Jeffreys's reward on return to London was the chancellorship. In addition, the king used the security emergency as an excuse to appoint a hundred or so Catholic officers to his newly expanded standing army; an army whose quartered regiments in scattered parts of England created considerable resentment amongst local populations. James demanded their better behaviour although, nevertheless, felt that the victory they had achieved against the rebels confirmed not merely God's approval but his encouragement to do more to promote Catholicism, including the retention of the Catholic officers. His conviction was fortified by the endorsement of two prominent co-religionists. Firstly, just as Parliament gathered, came the arrival at court of the papal envoy Ferdinando, Count d'Adda. This followed the despatching of James's own ambassador to Rome the previous September. Secondly, the English Jesuit Sir Edward Petre, who had suffered imprisonment in the 1670s and 1680s because of his faith, had been appointed by James as dean of the new Chapel Royal in St James's Palace and was increasingly looked to for advice. James added him to the English Council in November. Indeed, from autumn 1685 he attempted to procure Petre a bishopric or a cardinal's hat but Rome was unimpressed. Finally, in October, to make an example, James dismissed Halifax from the Council for objecting to the commissioning of Catholics. It was the beginning of the catholicising of his inner circle; a process completed fourteen months later with the dismissal of Rochester and Clarendon, both to be replaced by Catholics. Then, and the year before, James's view was consistent: 'he found it absolutely necessary for the good of his affairs that no man must be at the head of his affairs that was not of his own opinion [in religion]'. In 1685 Halifax refused to agree to the repeal of the English Test Act of 1673 and of *habeas corpus,* and in 1686, even as James pleaded in tears for Charles's 'conversion' papers to be read by him once more, Rochester refused to covert to Rome. This was no surprise given the consistent high Anglicanism of his family, and his brother Clarendon concurred. It was then, with this devotion to his primary objective, that James made his opening speech to the Westminster Parliament in November. On his confident request for more money for a standing army, it having proved itself more effective than a weak militia, and his full expectation that no one would challenge the continuation of Catholic commissions in the military or his employment of others in the future, the Commons reacted in uproar. Even the house of peers was shrill, debating the speech in detail and insisting upon the retention of the Test to secure their religion. Therefore after only just over a week, in which a declaration by the predominantly Tory Commons told James flatly he could not employ Catholic officers, a disgusted James prorogued the parliament – it would never meet again.[87] James even failed to get his additional supply, though not all factors were under James's direct control. Just before he brought forward his proposals on the Test, Louis rescinded the Edict of Nantes which ended the toleration of Huguenots in France. There were many stories of atrocities thereafter, some invented and many true, and they reached London as the Parliament sat. National and international concerns conflated for a Catholic king and a Protestant parliament.

James then turned to his other kingdoms to look for points of least resistance. In Ireland a process of catholicising had begun which made both Irish and mainland Protestants uneasy. The old reassuring presence of a Protestant Ormonde, who for all his faults understood Ireland and kept it quiet when others could not, was to end, and in September 1685 he was replaced as Lord Lieutenant by Rochester's brother Clarendon. Energetic and politically acceptable to the Old English in Ireland and Anglicans on the mainland, Clarendon had comparatively limited understanding of Irish affairs. He took up his post in January 1686 but his authority was already being undermined. James took advice on Irish affairs from his old friend Richard Talbot, now earl of Tyrconnell, not the wise Ormonde. Out of his old English Catholic background, Tyrconnell ferociously drove on at criticism of Clarendon and promoting a more forceful Catholic programme. James gave him responsibility for military appointments which produced remarkable results: from a position in 1685 where almost all officers and men were Protestant, by autumn 1686 two-thirds of men and two-fifths of officers were Catholic. Such a transformation would be impossible in the other kingdoms yet stories brought over by returning Protestant officers intensified sectarian fears that had been relatively muted since the Popish Plot. In early 1687 Clarendon was recalled for dragging his feet and Tyrconnell made Lord Lieutenant. His co-religionists were now being appointed to all civil positions in Ireland and the thorny question of the Restoration land settlement was being reconsidered.[88] But Scotland, not Ireland, was the favoured laboratory for testing James's British policies.

In Scotland catholicising was slow to build though no less controversial. James, nonetheless, took great encouragement from even small alterations. Essentially, it was from the summer of 1685 that the Scottish political temperature, as taken by James himself, his supporters and Jacobites, became overheated by exaggeration and delusion. There were, however, a few key conversions to Rome. Remarkably, during the 1685 parliamentary session, Perth converted having been mesmerised by the details of Charles's deathbed experience. Over the next few months he persuaded both his wife and brother Melfort to follow suit. Moray converted in the summer of 1686 but only made this public in early 1687. These three have been criticised for undergoing political rather than spiritual conversion although the manner of their subsequent lives makes plain their sincerity. Not for them the cynicism or intellectual peculiarism associated with the conversions of Sunderland and Sibbald. Nevertheless, James made Moray his High Commissioner to the 1686 session of parliament on account of his managerial skills and his support for Catholic toleration, and Moray's secret declared intention to convert strengthened the logic of this. During the previous session James had not made it especially obvious to Queensberry that he wished the removal the penal laws against Catholics but he was disappointed that foundations conducive to toleration had not been laid. For this 'failure', as well as the combined efforts of secret committee members to unseat him, Queensberry was sidelined and finally dismissed after the adjournment in June 1686. However, another reason lay at the heart of this, stemming from a discussion similar to James's with Argyll in 1681. If Burnet is to be believed, when Queensberry was in London in 1685 planning for the impending parliament in Edinburgh, he told the king flatly 'that if he had thoughts of changing the established religion he could not make any step in that matter', and also subsequently refused all efforts by James and others to convert.[89] Therefore, as preparations were made for the session of 1686, the Episcopalian interest of the previous session was under threat.

Popular discontent with increased levels of Catholic activity had been evident in Scotland in the winter of 1685/6. James had used his prerogative to dispense with the Test Act and so Catholics began to be appointed to positions closed to them for many decades, never mind since the Test Act itself. For example, James utilised his dispensing power to allow some twenty-six Catholic commissioners of supply to be appointed in November 1685. Catholic tax collectors seemed a strange concept for many Protestants. Alarming news of Catholic military commissions in England, though they never rose above one in ten, and yet more sweeping changes in Ireland, were added to with the fact of Dumbarton, brother-in-law to Perth, as commander-in-chief and James's placing of Catholic officers (William Oliphant and Captain Douglas) in command of two new Scottish companies of troops in January 1686. Soon the duke of Gordon would be made Master of Edinburgh Castle, the store for most of Scotland's armaments. In January Perth began to worship publicly. Popular disgust was dramatically shown in the riots that took place in Edinburgh in January 1686 which, after a particularly ugly riot on the last day of the month, saw troops fire on the crowd and some Catholics, including Sibbald, leave the capital in fear of their lives. James insisted on the severest penalties for those found guilty of the riot but also advised Perth, in a typical aside, that he had also discussed this business with his English bishops 'that they may now see the effects of indiscretion in pulpits'.[90]

In the context of this popular discontent, in February Hamilton advised the king to delay parliament to October because of the 'strange malitious temper got into the heads of the people against the papists seeing their worship so publicke'. The duke also wanted to allow more time to consider the wisdom of repealing the penal laws and the Test; Protestantism had to be protected and perhaps the dispensing power was sufficient. He, nevertheless, expressed some optimism in early March that 'if matters of religion [were] not pressed at the next parliament the king's affairs should go very well'. However, two days later James wrote to the secret committee, bolstered by Tarbat's view that enough of the Estates would support the king, confirming his desire to completely remove the 'sanguinary laws against Papists', to 'the taking away of the Test' to be replaced by a simple oath of allegiance, and to retain the 'laws against [Presbyterian] phanaticisme'.[91] Shortly afterwards Melfort informed James that some members of the secret committee were unhappy that toleration should be offered to Catholics yet not Presbyterians, and the king summoned to London Hamilton, Major General William Drummond, and Sir George Lockhart, President of the Session, all Protestants, to discuss their concerns. They were accompanied by the earl of Dundonald, Hamilton's son-in-law and a Presbyterian. James no doubt thought that if the four could be convinced of the rightness of his policy then they could in turn persuade noble, military, legal and moderate Presbyterian opinion. What then ensued was one of the most extraordinary conferences in the politics of the period. If the sincerity of all parties is to be believed, the four Scots and James and Melfort left the conference with completely different impressions of what had been agreed. James, however, did have his brother's habit of telling people what they wanted to hear. While the king said he was unable to promise to do nothing to prejudice the Protestant religion, which the four felt the Parliament might demand in order to agree to repeal the Test, he gave them the impression that moderate Presbyterians would be accommodated in a draft toleration act. In fact, as Melfort indicated to Moray a week before the Parliament opened, he and James had agreed to 'hav the test taken off and pay nothing for it [for] all art must be used that it may be a great example to England' and, as for the toleration of moderate Presbyterians, 'this must be consulted with the S[ecret] comitty as to the forme but the King will hav it [by] his own act and not an act of parlia-ment . . . that the people hold it of him that it may sho his inclinations and terminate with his pleasure'. Thus Catholicism was to be secured by statute and Presbyterianism by dispensation, something only workable if the political community had complete trust in the king's intentions. When the session began Hamilton expressed shock at the confusion and took the blame himself while expressing loyalty to James. But the duke's position in all this is central. As the four left by coach for London, Perth wrote to Moray reminding him that 'much may depend on the managing of [Hamilton]'.[92] James, as duke and king, included Hamilton in the government in a way not evident before 1681, but there was also an appreciation that he could not be coerced, intimidated or handled in the manner of a Queensberry or an Argyll. Hamilton's opposition to aspects of the Toleration Act as it was being drafted, and his proposal that Catholics should only worship privately, emboldened others and did much to ensure its rejection.

On 12 April 1686 Moray was passed a fifteen-point list of formal instructions; most were economic in nature though no supply was requested, but the first was for a toleration act. He was told that no public acts were to be touched with the sceptre, indicating royal assent, until 'the act concerning Roman Catholicks be past'. Moray was given his instructions on moderate Presbyterians as well, and told to say nothing in his commissioner's speech about protecting the Protestant religion; breaking long tradition, there was no opening act passed confirming just that. Before the session began on 29 April it had been established that both Atholl and Rosehaugh were unhappy with a toleration act and Melfort sent north letters from James to dismiss the Lord Advocate if he failed to vote in favour.[93] Even before the session opened coercive tactics were being considered.

When James's letter was read out on the opening day – explicating his desire to protect 'those of the Roman Catholic religion' and offering free trade with England as an unstated but obvious bargaining position – it was what was omitted that shocked the chamber. James's political mistake was to fail to issue a protection for the Protestant religion and to give Presbyterians the same assurances as Catholics. Hamilton was surprised at both these points as he felt they were agreed. On 6 May, in an atmosphere of intense opposition to James's proposals, the house debated for many hours on merely the appropriate wording for a letter of reply. It became so heated that Hamilton barely managed to prevent a move to have the Chancellor expelled from the chamber on account of his religion.[94] The Toleration Act itself was clearly in trouble. When the Lords of the Articles began formulating a draft act, opposition was such that, before the committee even took a vote, Moray moved to dismiss Rosehaugh. Having been provided with letters to dismiss the errant bishops of Galloway, Ross and Dunkeld, but told to use only one at this stage, he also removed Andrew Bruce, bishop of Dunkeld. By mid May the carnage was extensive as pensions, military commissions and places on the Privy Council were ended and other posts threatened. Hamilton believed these tactics were counterproductive as they merely entrenched opposition. Certainly, the atmosphere of intimidation failed to deter opposition in the committee and when on 27 May a full draft was put to the vote, it just passed by eighteen votes to fourteen. Good to their promise to James, even though they had argued for amendments, Hamilton, Lockhart and Drummond voted for the draft, but four of the six clergy voted against, including Alexander Cairncross, archbishop of Glasgow, who would be turned out six months later. In spite of threats made to bishops, this confirms a major breach between the episcopacy and the Crown as well as division in the episcopate. In spite of an impassioned speech from Moray pleading for the Estates to 'obediently complye with the just & resonable demands of so excellent a prince;

who will ever protect you and never forget thos that are dutifull & affectionat to him, & will as certinly show his displeasur against sutch as doe otheruayes', the act was roundly rejected when submitted before the house. In early June the sub-committee of the Articles came up with a second draft which added back some of the legal restrictions on public worship and although this was approved by James with only minimal changes, he and Moray took Hamilton's advice and withdrew the act before a second vote. James may have wished to avoid another humiliation but Hamilton no doubt calculated that even more fellow Protestants would lose their positions if the Crown were to suffer another reversal. Therefore, with no toleration act agreed, on 15 June Moray prorogued the parliament to August before it was dissolved on 8 October, like the English Parliament, never to meet again during James's reign.[95]

The management of the 1686 session was a disaster for James and his closest Scottish ministers. James's British policy was in tatters and, if Scotland was to yet again be a testing ground for English policy, non-parliamentary ways had now to be found. The Melfort and Moray correspondence while parliament sat reveals a charged atmosphere of arrogance followed by panic, and of irresolution followed by vengeance. One minute Moray is told to pass nothing but a toleration act and to delay other business, and the next to pass other matters without delay, taking the chance to end the session as swiftly as possible. In fact the enactments were similar in volume to the 1681 session, though private legislation predominated as Moray and Perth planned for the big prize. Melfort was bitter that it eluded them and that 'the king's own servant [were] resolved to oppose him' and declared that the Council and secret committee would need to be reforged in the royal interest. 'They who are not for the king are against him', he declared. However, the first thing was to 'secure the castles and the army which are the first steps and must be so done as not to allarme at all, till . . . the King take such measures as may be lasting and secure for half acting will not doe ouer business'.[96] Melfort's nature was to react to setbacks with fearful petulance.

More importantly, James's attitude to all this must be understood. If Melfort is to be believed, when parliamentary opposition strengthened in May, James was relaxed. Although he told Moray he expected obedience to his will, by 20 May he was confident of success 'go things as they may [for] what the parliament will not doe his prerogative will'. Or, as he explained to Barrillon in July, as 'the factious cabal had hindered the well intentioned from doing what was reasonable . . . by the authority which the laws give him, he could establish in Scotland that liberty in favour of the Catholics which the parliament refused to grant'.[97] And yet certainly his wish was to achieve a statute-based toleration for his Catholic subjects and, essentially, turn the clock back to before the Reformation. Two parallel strategies would now be employed; firstly, a medium term plan to use the royal prerogative to relieve his co-religionists and to create some permanent foundations given the inevitable succession of his Protestant daughter Mary and her husband

(Queen Mary had miscarried yet again in May); and secondly, if time permitted a longer term effort, to seek the 'holy grail' of placing enough Catholics and cavaliers in county and town, sheriffs and provosts in the Scottish context, to enable the management of new elections and calling of new parliaments in Scotland and England. They could then deliver the required legislation. It was as regressive as it was revolutionary. Scotland also presented some unique difficulties for James. Government could not operate without the involvement of the Protestant and mostly Episcopalian nobility and it was impossible to govern through Catholics only, notwithstanding the Drummond axis. Also, put simply, if a Father Petre had been added to the Scottish Council he would have feared for his safety without a security effort beyond the finance and military capabilities of Scotland. A toleration act allowing only private worship was the most sensible option were it not for James's idealism for his faith.

REVOLUTION, BETRAYAL AND FLIGHT

In May 1686, while stirring Moray to greater efforts to secure a toleration act, Melfort declared dramatically 'the affair [is] the greatest consequence of any in Europ for the generall peace'. These were prophetic words and chimed with the views of his most bitter enemies. This was seen most obviously when Prince William landed his 15,000 strong army at Torbay on 5 November 1688 and the 'Glorious Revolution' was begun. William had been invited in June 1688 by the 'immortal seven', as they came to be called, the earls of Danby, Devonshire and Shrewsbury, Lord Lumley, Edward Russell, Henry Sidney and Henry Compton, bishop of London; two Tories and five Whigs, all Englishmen. William insisted on an invitation to emphasise his was an army of liberation and his most trusted confidant and diplomat Hans Willem Bentinck used his agents to negotiate such a welcoming as well as protection for the Dutch Republic by forces of the German Princes. Therefore, during October William made several vain attempts to set sail but an easterly 'Protestant wind' enabled him to do so on 1 November and at the same time kept James's navy in port.[98] William was a lucky general and so it was that the metaphorical insistence of the Revolution myth was founded.

James had since the summer made preparations for a potential invasion, though too half-heartedly, Louis and his ministers believed. At the reported growth of the Dutch fleet he ordered in May the fitting out of twenty new ships, and then spent his usual summer season exercising troops on Hounslow Heath. The Revolution was a family affair, though, and all the more remarkable for that. James had never been close to his nephew William, who in turn resented the domineering way in which he had been treated by his uncles, and contact had been strained since 1685 when bones of contention, such as James's wish to appoint Catholic officers to the Dutch brigade, soured relations. This episode ended with James's failure when he demanded to get the Dutch brigade sent back to England in January 1688. More contentious were his efforts to get William and Mary to support his Scottish and English indulgences of 1687, not merely in terms of a general toleration but the removal of the Test Acts. This William could not agree to. Meanwhile, in international affairs James was on the horns of a dilemma and in little control of events. Because of Louis's aggressive foreign policy (as seen in his annexing of Luxembourg in 1684), the States General concluded by 1688 that William needed the funds he requested to build up the Dutch army and navy. This view intensified with the commercial war waged by the French as they attacked Dutch merchant shipping. Also, every time Louis appeared to offer James military or diplomatic support, whether real or imagined, this further convinced the States General that war was inevitable, had to be prepared for and James was part of the problem. He meanwhile still could not quite believe that his own family would attack him, or that the States General's attitude or the season of the year would make it likely. Nevertheless, when Louis decided in mid September to assault Philippsburgh in the Rhenish Palatinate, convinced that it was now too late for the Dutch to make a sea crossing to England, William saw his opportunity. James despaired at his cousin's decision: 'I no longer know what can be done. What help or diversion can I expect from them?' The timing of the invasion, therefore, owed much to military and diplomatic considerations in Paris and The Hague. Once James was signalled by his ambassador to The Hague, Ignatius White, marquis d'Albeville, that the invasion was imminent, he set about forming new regiments.[99] But in any case James had numerical superiority and by October his army was at least double William's expeditionary force. The king's position was by no means hopeless.[100]

Most in the three kingdoms were, however, astonished at the developments of the next two months, though the seeds were planted long before. We would expect James could always rely on the English Anglican hierarchy, yet since the summer of 1686 a series of confrontations alienated these natural upholders of monarchy. In September that year his new Commission for Ecclesiastical Causes, formed to police clerical conduct and the impact of James's dispensing power and given legal standing by the test case *Godden* v *Hales* in June, controversially suspended Bishop Compton of London. He refused to dismiss clergy who could not guarantee avoiding sermons touching on Rome. The Commission harked back to grievances in the reign of his father but James was growing weary of Anglican intransigence. Following the English Declaration of Indigence in April 1687, which suspended the Test and penal laws, James switched to appointing Protestant nonconformists as well as Catholics as commissioners of the peace and depute lieutenants. Then in July this Commission deprived the fellows of Magdalen College Oxford for their refusal to appoint James's favoured candidates as their president, even after a browbeating by the king in person. In March 1688 he placed a Catholic vicar apostolic in the position, and Cambridge also suffered from such unwanted interference. When in May James instructed the clergy to read the reissued Declaration of

Indulgence from their pulpits, most promptly refused. Sancroft and six bishops published a petition explaining their actions, and in a fury, James prosecuted them for seditious libel only for the jury to acquit all seven to much public rejoicing.[101] This was a disaster for James's religious policy, nothing being so demeaning for a bully than a public failure. But now in late September and October 1688, after James had crisis meetings with his bishops and allowed them to submit demands, he fell back on the old Tory hierarchy; he restored all burgh charters, including London's, shut down his hated Commission, and began to remove Catholics from local positions. Torne between the Catholic and Anglican factions at court, one minute procrastinating and then being decisive, James sacked Sunderland and replaced him with Middleton as senior Secretary of State.[102]

Once William had landed, James busied himself with further military plans to keep the enemy pinned down in the west. After preparing his will he set off to join the rendezvous of his forces at Salisbury on 19 November. Exhausted with over-work, suffering insomnia and beginning to panic, James had to take to his bed for two days with bad nosebleeds, no doubt brought on by stress-related high blood pressure. Taking too much upon himself he became disorientated by indecisive-ness. Advance or retreat back to London; every decision presented competing options that were equally unattractive. After a Council meeting he left to return to London on 24 November. Before he did so, the entire Scottish standing army joined. It consisted of some 3,000 men under the command of Queensberry's brother Lieutenant General James Douglas, including the regiments of Claverhouse and Colonel Thomas Buchan. In late September it marched to the south of England, and the troops now found themselves part of the debacle that was Salisbury. In particular, as an element of James's own crisis of confidence, a muddled order to disband was conveyed via his commander in the field, the earl of Feversham. Defections to William depleted his officers and created chaos and a collapse in morale. Moreover, James was to hear that on 24 November Lord John Churchill, the duke of Grafton (Charles II's natural son); the new duke of Ormonde (grandson of the great duke who died in the summer), Prince George of Denmark, his son-in-law, and Lord Drumlanrig, eldest son of Queensberry, had all gone over to William. Prince George explained by posing a question in words James would understand: 'were not religion the most justifiable cause?'. The high profile nature of these defections more than their number made the impact all the greater. It became clear that a military conspiracy had been long in the planning. Then the following day James's daughter Anne joined her husband.[103] James took especially badly the betrayal of his daughter and of Churchill, his former mistress's brother, who he had raised from nothing. Anne like her sister Mary was brought up a strict Anglican. She made her views clear when she wrote to Mary 'I am wholly of your mind that in taking away the Test and Penal Laws they take away our religion'. From 1686 Mary undertook a regular correspondence with her father on religious belief as he tried in vain to shake her trust in the Church of England

and cure her Catholic phobia, citing the conversion of her own mother, and placing the blame for her attitudes at the door of the exiled Gilbert Burnet. The
correspondence ends in early October 1688 with his appeals to her as a dutiful
daughter to stop William's 'unjust designs', and the Queen also penned such letters
in a tone of disbelief. Both sisters were, however, suspicious of the last piece of the
revolution jigsaw that accounted for the removal of James; Mary's delivering of a
son, James Francis Edward, Prince of Wales, on 10 June 1688. To James the birth
of a male heir after all this time was miraculous; a sign of divine providence. Once
the Queen's being with child became known, doubts were aired over the reality of
the pregnancy, and when she gave birth the 'warming pan' myth circulated widely,
with the slander that James and his Jesuit advisors had smuggled a child into the
room. There is no evidence for this but it was what many wished to believe. Anne
expressed to Mary her own doubts as the Queen seemed too healthy and showed
too much too soon, with a 'false belly' as she put it, although later admitted 'it may
be it is our brother but God only knows'. The Queen wrote to Mary in July 1688
distressed at her step-daughter's lack of recognition of the newborn child: 'you
have never once in your letters to me taken the least notice of my son, no more
than if he had never been born', she complained.[104] On 22 October, as all waited
for William to land, James summoned an emergency council meeting at which the
'supposed child' slander was countered by recording detailed depositions of
witnesses attesting to the authenticity of the birth. As he prepared to risk death in
the expected conflict ahead, it was his duty to cure 'the poisoned minds of [his]
subjects'. Unfortunately, James failed to realise that doubts over the birth were not
a cause of the revolution about to engulf him but one of numerous factors, as
made abundantly clear in William's declaration or manifestos for England and
Scotland which appeared in September. While both emphasised 'arbitrary government', the Scottish text highlighted the attack on Scotland's 'ancient constitution'.
Justifications over the birth were counterproductive yet James would 'rather die a
thousand deaths than do the least wrong to any of [his] children'.[105] To Anne and
Mary, however, their brother was a necessary victim of a revolution about religion,
though fundamentally it was also a family affair.[106]

The birth of a male heir ended the wait and see strategy favoured by Anglican
and Scottish Episcopalian moderates. James himself was uncertain how the fact of
a son would impact on his levels of support in the country, although it meant that
in the course of 1688 he became increasingly rash and at times even unconcerned
at the outcome of events that were in any case the will of God. This character trait
would bring both political weakness and personal consolation for the remainder of
his life. But from the beginning of the invasion, and especially when William's
army was preparing to move into London, James felt an acute sense of responsibility to send his wife and son to safety, probably to France. After some hesitation he
had them leave Whitehall and board ship for France early in the morning of 10
December.[107] By then many others had also fled, including Petre, Melfort,

Sunderland and D'Adda. James himself vacillated. On agreeing at a gathering of available nobles in late November to summon an English parliament for January, he began issuing warrants for elections, and commissioned Halifax, Nottingham and Godolphin to enter negotiations with William over the details. Yet these were delaying tactics. Meeting William's terms was hard to swallow and meeting him in person not something to be entertained. Therefore, almost exactly twenty-four hours after Queen Mary, he slipped away in darkness to take ship to France; tossed the Great Seal into the Thames and destroyed the writs to hamper the elections, and ordered Feversham to stand down his remaining troops. Unfortunately, James was apprehended by seamen off the coast of Kent. After being 'rescued' by Middleton and some few of the remaining loyal lords, he returned to Whitehall on 16 December, more at their instigation than his own. Perversely, he was greeted with wild enthusiasm as he re-entered the city.[108] Some Catholics and Tories hoped he would reimpose public order which had collapsed further, and James had a month before been forced to close all London's Catholic chapels for fear of attacks. Meanwhile, for William the tidiest solution was for James to go overseas with minimal violence and without a long and awkward period of house arrest.

As negotiations recommenced – where it was agreed on William's insistence that James withdraw from London to Rochester before the prince entered the city and summoned a free parliament – for a few days the king slipped back into an illusion of authority and called a Council meeting. At this twelve attended, all Protestants, headed by none other than the duke of Hamilton. The re-establishing of law and order was the priority. Like many Scottish nobles Hamilton had come hotfoot to London once the invasion started, although given his particular plans, he would have been as surprised as anyone that James was back in town. Continuing the pervasiveness of Scottish counsel closer to the king, on 17 December James was accompanied on his regular morning walk by Claverhouse and the earl of Balcarres; moments of paradoxical and becalmed normality. Both, as the earl Aislebury had done before, made a final appeal to James to stand and fight and rally loyalist elements in the army, but the king had lost all hope. The fact that William imposed Dutch guards for his protection was meekly accepted. In the last two months he had experienced some form of mental breakdown and this made him both fearful and passive. In this frame of mind, accompanied by his party and guards, James arrived at Rochester on 19 December to linger for a few days while he made good his escape. For James and William the location near the Kent coast made this an ideal staging post. There, at a final dinner, a small gathering begged him one last time to stay, but to no avail. This group included the earl of Arran, Hamilton's son, Middleton and Dumbarton, and also James's son Berwick. Not for the last time would the number of Scots who were his close advisors be dispro-portionate. Therefore to William's great relief, early on the morning of 23 December James departed, arriving on French soil on Christmas Day, never to return to England or Scotland. He left a paper with his reasons for leaving and instructed Middleton to ensure it was published.[109] With its defeatist and resigned tone, however, Williamites argued that this desertion of his kingdoms was indeed abdication. It was certainly an abdication of authority by a commander-in-chief. Nonetheless, the events of the last quarter of 1688 prove that James's failings were less of military command than of political leadership.

Following the disbanding of the royal army there was the question of what to do with the Scottish contingent. Some of the senior Scottish officers had dispersed to political discussions with William and other Scottish nobles in and around London, or in Claverhouse's case, to the final days with the king. The core of his troop stayed with him and returned in February but rather than disband the remaining forces in confusion, William agreed that the Scots army, now under the command of George Livingstone, later third earl of Linlithgow, could march in good order back to Scotland which they did in January.[110] Law and order was re-established, although the Scottish political classes paused nervously, pondering what would happen next. They had seen a revolution ignited in England – were they unprepared or even reluctant to participate? While the specific circumstances of the Scottish Revolution differed to that of England that did not make Scots more or less 'reluctant'. The fact that the revolution against Charles I began in Scotland obviously did not weaken England's willingness to join the fray in that case. The historiography of 'reluctance' is, though, quite extensive, and seems to read backwards from Scotland's popular Jacobitism in subsequent decades, especially after 1702.[111] The causes of these two 'events' are distinct. It is helpful to generalise that while the Scottish revolution was motivated by widespread religious anxiety and political dysfunction amongst the elite, Jacobitism was mostly concerned with the economic and political failures of the Union of the Crowns and that of 1707, with grievances of the Episcopalian minority and social and political nationalism adding to the mix. But the history of Scotland for two centuries had been about religious change, consolidation, diversity and retrenchment. Having sacrificed so much in these decades a coalition of Protestantism might take the opportunity to secure the reformed faith against a feared papist threat. Scotland and England had their own reasons for engaging in the upheaval, yet how extensive was the provocation?

From the autumn of 1686 the catholicising of England became geographically widespread as James's dispensing power was used to place Catholics in local government, the universities and military commissions. Many of James's appointments were, in fact, loyal Tories and some nonconformists in 1688, and the frequency of Catholic appointments was not as great as it appeared, although the alarm was very real. In fact, in local offices the number increased markedly by the summer of 1688 when one third of deputy lieutenants and a fifth of justices of the peace were Catholic, astonishing levels considering the relatively small Catholic population of England and Wales. Importantly, many of those Anglicans who monopolised such positions were removed and three quarters of the Justices of the Peace in post in 1685 were discarded during James's reign. Chapels also opened in most large English cities and provincial towns. In London by autumn 1688 no less than eighteen chapels were active, including three royal chapels, five existing ambassadorial chapels, and ten new creations, as well as two Jesuit colleges and five communities of Benedictines, Franciscans and Carmelites.[112] Catholics had decisively moved from private and often secretive devotion to more public demonstrations of worship. In Scotland, however, there was less public activity, even though James's great mission was to make his 'ancient kingdom' more Catholic.

In August 1686, after the failed parliament that year and coinciding with the beginning of his political purges, the king informed his Privy Council in Edinburgh that he was giving Catholics the right to worship in private and that rooms in Holyrood Palace would be converted into a Catholic chapel. Three months later the chapel was consecrated and endowed by James. Then in 1687 he announced that the Abbey Church was to be given to the new Order of the Thistle which he had established the month before. Six of the eight original founder members of the order were Catholic, the exceptions being Atholl and Hamilton. The difficulty was that this was the parish church for the burgh of Canongate. James opportunistically endorsed plans to use the remaining funds mortified by Thomas Moodie of Dalry in 1649, intended for a church in Edinburgh's Grassmarket, to build a replacement parish church on the Canongate near Holyrood (see Plate 8). James sanctioned the project in May 1688 and in August work began. By the end of the year the interior of the Abbey Church was finished in all its magnificence, just in time to be ransacked at the Revolution. While converting existing churches was uncommon in England there was one further example in Scotland where St Nicholas Chapel (or Trinity Chapel) in New Aberdeen was given over to Catholics. The tradesmen of the burgh, whose chapel this was, opposed the arrangement but a letter from James in May 1688 insisted. In August 1687 the Chancellor's apartments at the Palace were converted into a Jesuit college, and a Catholic press set up in the complex printed the regulations of the college the following March. Therefore, while most Catholics still worshiped in relative privacy, and in a small number of private chapels in Edinburgh and in the homes of the Catholic nobility, there was no comparison to the physical evidence for Catholic worship found in England. Perth, however, wrote in February 1688 to Philip Howard, Cardinal Norfolk, expressing in desperation the need to make more progress in Scotland.[113]

James also offered financial support to the general Catholic mission. Out of the yearly pensions for Scotland from 1685 he provided £200 sterling each for the Jesuit mission, the mission of secular clergy, the Highland mission and the Benedictine monks in Edinburgh, as well as smaller amounts to various individual priests and Jesuits. The monastery of Ratisbon (Regensburg) in Bavaria received £100 each year and it supplied many of the Benedictine monks. Similarly he gave £100 to the Scots Colleges at Paris, Rome and Douai. Later, in his 'Advice to his

Son', he would recommend the education of young Scots 'to be fittly qualified for the Highland mission' at the Scots College in Paris, to remove reliance on Irish (Gaelic) priests.[114] But how many of these priests were there? In June 1688 at Gordon Castle a conference of ten secular priests took place and wrote to Perth thanking him for his continuing efforts on their behalf. This was an annual gathering insisted upon by the Propaganda Fide of Rome to justify annual subsidies to priests. Lewis (Louis) Innes, principal of the Scots College in Paris, travelled to Britain in the summer months and convened three such Scottish meetings in 1684 (also at Gordon Castle), 1686 and 1687. During the visit in 1684 Innes met James for the first time and they developed a close relationship which in the 1690s would see Innes become an advisor at the exiled court. At the next visit, matters turned to appointing a Scottish Catholic bishop or vicar apostolic, and Innes found himself trying to convince James to reject a Jesuit appointment as unacceptable to Rome. The opinion of Scottish episcopacy at this idea is not hard to imagine but the Revolution intervened. James found the disunity of the Catholic Church as bemusing as that in the secular political sphere. By then the quantity of missioners had increased to perhaps twenty secular priests, a similar number of Jesuits and ten or more Benedictines. This large group of fifty returned to more secretive practices after 1688.[115] As for the overall Catholic population in Scotland, there is considerable debate with estimates ranging from a mere 1,000 to 50,000. It seems likely that by 1688/9 the lower figure represents Lowland recusants and that the total may have been ten to fifteen thousand including Highland Catholics, many of whom were converted through the zeal of these missioners. It is true that the number of Catholics rose considerably during James's reign but their proportion of the total population remained very small, much less than 5 per cent. One of the legacies of the years 1685 to 1688 was, nevertheless, the effective mission to the Highlands which would help to underpin Jacobitism in the future.[116]

As a convert James naturally hoped that others would follow his example. In his papers of devotion he declared that 'converts have a special duty to explain' their faith and Anglicans should be their particular target. However, the success rate in Scotland was very low other than in a few high profile cases. No Scottish bishop converted to Rome, not even the most politic like John Paterson. They realised that their futures lay more in cooperation with English bishops than with the king, though perhaps had they known the rout they faced in 1690, some might have thought again. Equally those Catholics in the government and Council were mostly already of Rome but dispensations from the Test allowed them to take the stage as never before. Those, like Perth, who did convert suffered more from the threatened violence of sectarian mobs, and the mockery of sermon and printed pamphlet. In view of this the secret committee sought to both censor the press and produce propaganda in support of James's policies and some Catholic works. The Council took measures to ban works critical of popery and in August 1687 interrogated, fined and briefly imprisoned some printers and booksellers for circulating seditious material imported from England. Also in 1688, a final list of twelve forbidden titles was drawn up, many emanating from the exiled press in Rotterdam. Catholic works that broke the existing legal code went unmolested. For the purpose of producing official propaganda a printing press was required and James Watson, the elder, himself a Catholic, was set up at Holyrood in 1685 in the anomalous post of Household Printer to James VII in breach of the legitimate rights of the King's Printer Agnes Campbell who was a moderate Presbyterian. When Watson died in 1687 the German Catholic Peter Bruce (Breusch) replaced him and continued to print explication of royal policy. To assist with this campaign, the English royal censor and pamphleteer Roger L'Estrange took on the management of the Edinburgh press between 1686 and 1688, mostly from London but also visiting the press from time to time. Views from the likes of Burnet were refuted by counterblasts or clarifications such as *Reasons for abrogating the penal statutes* (1686).[117]

James and his ministers also wished to shape opinion in the exiled community. The king, convinced he was in the right, only had to explain his intent to get broad agreement. With this in mind in May 1686, as the Scottish Parliament was in session, he despatched the Quaker William Penn to discover Prince William's view on the repeal of the penal laws and the English Test, a precursor to a possible new English parliament. This mission having failed, in autumn 1687 James engaged the exiled Presbyterian James Stewart of Goodtress in a similar task in a Scottish context. Penn made this possible by acting as an intermediary and securing a royal pardon for Stewart. He was certainly a strange choice, he having been condemned for treason for his association with Rye House and the rebellions of 1685, and as the author of various controversial pamphlets. James oiled the process by also issuing pardons to Stair and Melville and some other exiles. Stewart, meanwhile, had gone over to explain the Scottish second indulgence which allowed Presbyterians to worship, and was seen as a useful go-between because of his close relationship with William Carstares, Prince William's chaplain. Indeed, a pamphlet debate ensued between Stewart and Gaspar Fagal, the grand pensionary of Holland, where the latter made a strong case on William's behalf that the Test was the only sure way to protect the reformed religion in Scotland, and his repost to Stewart was printed in numerous languages and widely circulated. Stewart, embarrassed over what he thought was a private correspondence, retired from public life before the Revolution. Another of James's plans had failed. However, the fact that Stewart became a prosecutor and Lord Advocate for William suggests he may have played the double agent.[118]

While a number of Presbyterian ministers returned home to take advantage of James's second indulgence, with the exception of Stewart and a few others the majority of the secular exiles remained around The Hague to engage in the Revolution conspiracy. As well as Gilbert Burnet, who attended as much to English affairs, Robert Ferguson, the arch-conspirator, and Carstares brought their pens to the Williamite cause. In addition, Archibald, tenth earl of Argyll; Melville; his son, the earl of Leven; Stair; Fletcher of Saltoun; the Lords Ross and Cardross and Sir Patrick Hume, later earl of Marchmont, were some of the most significant players who came over with the prince and shaped the Scottish Revolution settlement in 1689/90. Carstares provided reports on Scottish affairs to William, including the dangers to the prince of the key religious argument of James's court:

> That the great argument made use of by the court partie to draw off presbiterians of Scotland from their Highnesses was that his Highness would be oblidged in gratitued to support prelacie in England the episcopall partie there being so fixt to him, and that if he were thus engadged to favour episcopacie in England it was not to be ecspected that he would stand out against the solicitatins that the English bishops would haunt him with for continuing episcopacie in Scotland.

William's Dutch-style toleration was the key to counter this criticism. Carstares did more than pen occasional memorials. While he and Stair handled intelligence and communications with Scottish conspirators, all offered advice to William, who Hume addressed as 'the great wheel which under God must give life and motion to any good project'.[119] These were not unwilling revolutionaries.

James's failure to change opinion by his indulgences, dispensing power or diplomacy, was also highlighted through those he brought into the government. The Episcopalian lawyer Sir John Dalrymple of Stair was favoured by James and after a personal meeting in London was pardoned for suspicions over his father's activity and appointed Lord Advocate in January 1687. Following James's dispensation he took up his post without taking the Test. Although Rosehaugh was brought back to this post twelve months later, Dalrymple was made Justice Clerk on the death of the incumbent and was seen as a talented administrator. Another younger man in favour was Queensberry's son Drumlanrig, a soldier. Having delighted James with his military activities in the south west of Scotland in 1684, as the crisis unfolded in 1688, he was issued in September with a new commission as lieutenant colonel along with orders to march south. Unbeknownst to James, Dalrymple and Drumlanrig had become the key intriguers with domestically based revolutionaries. Their strategic positions in London and Edinburgh were crucial to the success of the scheme. Indeed, the circumstances of the army conspiracy that afflicted James in November and December 1688 make it certain that many Scottish officers were, like Drumlanrig, willing revolutionaries.[120] While some of them hoped for a regency of William and Mary rather than overthrow, few having predicted that James would desert his cause, they were no less committed to change than their English counterparts.

The institutions of Scotland all seemed to foster their own grievances. Most of the Scottish army silently concurred with the population that the appointment of

Catholic officers was wrong in principle, even though Dumbarton was respected enough. Making the duke of Gordon Master of Edinburgh Castle caused popular alarm. The Established Church was in crisis. Episcopalian clergy had seen freedoms granted to Presbyterians empty their churches as the well-established Presbyterianism of the majority was able to reassert itself. The courts of law were manned by Protestant lawyers who found the dispensing power legally anomalous and contradictory, even with the reputed flexibility of the Scottish legal system, and many of them were Episcopalians or moderate Presbyterians. James's 'absolute' power as conveyed in the 1669 Act of Supremacy and in 1685 did not mean to legal opinion that he could dispense with every inconvenient piece of legislation, even though the former meant he could sack Scottish bishops with relative ease. Municipal government was also undermined. After the parliamentary debacle of 1686 James made an assault on the composition of the councils of royal burghs aiming to control their electoral make-up for a future parliament. As Fountainhall put it 'the burrows ware the brazen wall the Papists found hardest' though they were also easier to control than shires with their larger electorates. Burgh elections were suspended by James in autumn 1686, 1687 and 1688 and he proceeded to nominate his own men as provosts, magistrates, deans and ordinary councillors without due elections and in contravention of the burghs' ancient representative privileges. In this way a compliant third estate could be positioned for a future parliament. The imposition of Claverhouse as provost of Dundee was just the most well-known example of this level of coercion. In fact, from 1686 and 1687 thirty-five royal burghs were subjected to such interference, though given that there were sixty-six represented in parliament, this was unfinished business. Sir Patrick Hume warned William in February 1687 of the dangers of waiting for intervention given James's pre-election strategy: 'if he get such Parliaments, though they may have litle more than these Courts in them but the name, he wil so act as that he shall need no more of them to finish his whole [grand] designe'.[121] Like provosts, sheriffs responsible for administrating the election of parliamentary shire commissioners were also appointed according to royal whim, firstly with the Test and then by the imposition of 'loyal' men. That did not mean that all the 'disloyal' could be easily removed given the wider franchise in shire elections. Indeed, in these constituencies something remarkable was underway. Annual shire elections had not been activated without royal warrant since the Restoration, but under an act of 1681 such elections were permitted, the previous parliament being dissolved in October 1686. In early October 1688 Linlithgowshire (West Lothian) held a Michaelmas election and two very committed Revolution men were elected, Thomas Drummond of Riccarton and Patrick Murray of Livingstone. Both took the Test as they were commissioners in 1686, yet showed their willingness to suppress political beliefs until the time was right.[122]

As for the summoning of the Scottish Parliament by James, there were rumours in 1687 and in April 1688 that Perth and Gordon were in London for discussions over a possible docile, 'favourable' parliament in the summer. James wished to reconvene one in due course to achieve his objectives over toleration and the Test. In February 1688 he began consulting again as to attitudes on removing the Test, entering into yet another tortuous correspondence with Hamilton who stalled, first to consult with legal and clerical advice, but then to state frankly: 'I have been ever . . . of the opinion that none should suffer for conscience sake . . . but how this is to be done with security to the protestant religion . . . will disearve serious consideration & is above what I [can] presently determine myself in'. As the Presbyterian James Johnston once said of Hamilton, 'he grasps at favour with one hand and throws it away with another'.[123] James failed in one fundamental way, though with his understanding of his faith he was unlikely ever to succeed. By autumn 1688 he had made almost no progress in convincing the majority of the political men of England and Scotland that there were adequate safeguards for Protestantism. In addition, he not only, as we have seen above, created the conditions for revolution, but had done much to dictate the timetable for the Dutch intervention. Many Scots were committed to this intervention, yet as in England, the majority did not so much embrace a Dutch prince as not support a Stuart king.

While James was making good his escape, Scotland had suffered a security collapse. The standing army being in England, the local militias could no longer be trusted to be loyal and hold back anti-Catholic protest, especially in Edinburgh where Presbyterians took the initiative. Chancellor Perth was at first forced to resign by the remaining privy councillors before attempting to flee the capital and then on 20 December being discovered and arrested at the mouth of the Forth in the act of setting sail for the Continent. He was imprisoned at Stirling Castle for over three years before going into exile. After he left Edinburgh, a mob attacked the palace and abbey at Holyrood on 10 October and initially the remaining guard held them back, firing and killing a dozen or so rioters. Then a second crowd of several thousands, grown larger by widespread support from all levels of society including Drummond of Riccarton and Murray of Livingstone, stormed the complex to take revenge on the guards and ransacked the chapel, abbey and Catholic press. The printer Bruce joined Perth in prison. This event in itself captures the essence of intermittent crowd activity and protest in this period of crisis. Since the abbey and chapel were consecrated, mass could only take place under the protection of Dumbarton's troops. One priest recorded increasing difficulties in early November as their post was intercepted and plans were made on the last day of that month for 'the musik of our chappell to be discharged [tomorrow and] apprehending the totall shutting of it up'. The Jesuit college had ceased teaching two days before. Also, from time to time from early 1686, the print workshops of James Watson, the elder, and Peter Bruce had been attacked by rioters, and their Dutch printers beaten up. These assaults took place with burgh soldiers and Presbyterian printers joining the fray.[124] Deep-rooted sectarianism of Scotland's urban population was also an indication that the Scots were not reluctant revolutionaries. The extent to which James alienated this Scottish subjects is all the more remarkable for their instinctive loyalism to the Stewart line.

On the very day that James arrived in France, a meeting took place at St James's Palace between Prince William and a group of Scottish nobles, including Hamilton, Lord Ross, Lords Murray and Yester, respectively the sons of Atholl and Tweeddale, and the earls of Crawford and Dundonlald. At this meeting they thanked the prince, offered their service and agreed to reconvene, some of them – Ross and Crawford, for example – having just travelled from Scotland and with others on the way. On 7 January William convened a more formal meeting of those lords and lairds then in London, some hundred and twenty or so, and he asked them to advise on 'how their religion and liberties might be saved'. Having chosen Hamilton as president, over the next three days they rejected his son's idea that James be recalled before a free Scottish parliament met to resolve all differences. Arran was the only noble present who openly held on to the regency idea, though his father had mentioned this as a possibility previously at the first meeting on Christmas Day. William agreed to the suggestion of calling a convention of estates in Edinburgh on 14 March. He had already called an English convention which opened on 22 January. There, after some wrangling and William making it clear behind the scenes that he would accept nothing less than sharing the monarchy, but not the power, with Mary, it was declared that James had 'abdicated' and left the throne 'vacant'. Therefore on 14 February William and Mary of Orange were declared King and Queen of England. James's habit of summoning a Scottish parliament before an English one was now reversed and eyes turned to Edinburgh. What Jacobites feared was that his exile would be like that of Mary, Queen of Scots: his desertion not only a disaster for his party but placing trust in Louis who, like Elizabeth, was another crown head of Europe with a specific agenda.[125]

CHAPTER 5

The First Jacobite and the Final Exile

THE IRISH ADVENTURE

His reign in ruins, James was relieved to make landfall at Ambleteuse near Calais after a stormy crossing from Sheerness. In his now familiar manner, he fell to his knees to thank God for a merciful deliverance. Two days later, on 27 December/7 January (NS) he arrived by coach at the Château Vieux de Saint-Germain-en-Laye, just west of Paris, where a multitude of French courtiers and his cousin King Louis had gathered in welcome (see Plates 9–11). He was then reunited with Mary and his baby son. In fact, Louis had agreed to make the palace available to James and his exiled court; it was where he himself was born and lived until 1682 before moving to Versailles, conveniently only a short journey to the south. Louis handled the occasion with sensitivity and as a meeting of equals, although, as Whig's jibed and Jacobite's feared, James was now a slave to French interests. Unsurprisingly, given the events of past weeks, in contrast to the healthy fifty-year-old French king, James was a pale, gaunt and crumpled figure of fifty-five years. In this new company he became admired more for his fortitude and religiosity than his charm, wit or political acumen. This was not the young man who four decades before set out from the same palace to fight with Turenne. Negative impressions were quickly drawn. As Gaspard Rizzini, the Modenese envoy, described James some weeks later:

> He lives always surrounded by friars and talks of misfortunes with indifference, as if he did not feel them or had never been a king; in this way he has entirely lost the respect of the French and those who knew him in Flanders as Duke of York say that he was quite another man then, so great is the change in his Majesty, who, however, is as affable and courteous to everyone as could be desired.

Rizzini had had to escape London himself and so first hand observed some of James's 'transformations'. Nevertheless, James and Mary were treated with sibling-like affection by Louis and his pious, morganatic second wife Françoise d'Aubigné, marquise de Maintenon. Whereas some visitors with more secular tastes considered James 'infatuated with religion and abandoned in an extraordinary manner to the Jesuits', Madame de Maintenon found this admirable. Furthermore, her friendship with Mary as it grew was one of the strongest cards that Jacobites could play at Versailles. James's queen, only thirty years old and with a lively personality, was very popular.[1] Also, as if to compensate for the fatalism of her damaged husband, she became more assertive in court politics than ever before.

A small band of exiles reached Paris ahead of James and some of these were Scots, including the irrepressible Melfort (see Plate 6). James, and to begin with Louis and his French ministers, saw him as the only available candidate with the skills and experience to be James's senior minister, and so he was appointed principal Secretary of State. Whereas Mary's close relations with Madame de Maintenon aided the Jacobite cause, those of James and Mary with Melfort held it back. Also the earl of Seaforth, Tarbat's nephew, appeared at this time having journeyed over to France with his family. In the early 1680s James had encouraged him to marry into the wealthy Catholic family of the English marquis of Powis and he promptly converted. In their different ways, Melfort and Seaforth would undermine the prospects for James's counter-revolutionary strategy for Scotland. Yet at James's direction, and with King Louis's approval in the most serious of initiatives, such Scottish loyalists served in the military, constitutional and diplomatic campaigns aimed at achieving a restoration. In addition, and in a manner extraordinary considering the small numbers compared to the English contingent in and around Saint-Germain, a few Scots became the leading figures at the Jacobite court.[2]

James's fortunes in Ireland contrasted with the lamentable collapse in the other two kingdoms, and that meant there was a credible military option. Over the last few months Tyrconnell had raised a large army of over 40,000 men, almost exclusively Catholic, yet he was short of arms, supplies and money. James was initially reluctant to leave the secure comfort of Saint-Germain but he was embarrassed into decisive action by Tyrconnell's urgent pleas and by Louis's insistence. The French king took a strategic and Continental view of the possibilities in the Irish theatre. The Revolution in Britain was part of the new European conflict, the Nine Years War (1689–97), which got into full swing after Louis's fateful decision to attack the Palatinate and occupy the Rhineland in September 1688, only to unite the German Princes and be forced back the following year. A full-scale war was now in prospect, with France and the Turks pitted against a Grand Alliance, consisting of the Princes, the Holy Roman Empire centred on Vienna, Sweden and Spain (the League of Augsburg), joined by the Dutch Republic and England. In February 1689 the States General declared war against France and thereafter the Spanish Netherlands became the main theatre of war. So while friendship, honour and religion ensured that Louis genuinely wished to see James restored to his thrones, more importantly, an Irish, Catholic revolution would occupy William's forces, opening up a new front in the expanding conflict. Therefore, on 15 February 1689 James left Saint-Germain to travel to Brest to embark with a flotilla of ten ships loaded with supplies, arms and French livres; enough to sustain 20,000 troops. They landed at Kinsale on the southern coast of Munster on 12 March to, if James's memoirs are to be believed, a 'joyful reception'.[3] The French contingent was small, however, consisting of only a hundred or so French officers, commanded by the experienced General Conrad de Rosen, and James was disappointed with the scale of this commitment, although he could hardly complain too openly to his host. A senior French diplomat Jean-Antoine de Mesnes, comte d'Avaux, accompanied him as ambassador extraordinary and Louis's representative. Melfort, along with Seaforth and Powis, also travelled with James, and his council was composed of Tyrconnell, d'Avaux and Melfort, with distant communications with King Louis and his own chief secretary, the marquis de Louvois.

Within days it became clear to this group that the Irish military and political situation was extraordinarily complex and, in spite of the recriminations of contemporaries and modern historiography, the disease was probably beyond cure. Firstly the generals found Tyrconnell's forces disorganised, ill-disciplined and too inclined to accept command from only their own feudal superior, a mixed blessing visited upon many a Scottish Highland force. Unpaid troops preyed on available forage in a chaotic manner, especially plundering Protestant livestock. This in itself pointed to another problem. Although over the winter large numbers of Irish Protestants fled to England in panic, others gathering in the north and in Ulster, organised themselves into an effective resistance force and declared for William. When he arrived James hoped for a swift elimination of rebels in the north while granting pardons to those Irish Protestants who would declare their loyalty. Yet the sectarian nature of this civil war made such amnesties impossible to deliver on the ground and extended the conflict until William could send more troops. Derry in particular became the focus of a grim four-month siege from early April. In the midst of this siege James held a Dublin parliament, the 'patriot parliament', which he had summoned to meet on 7 May. Although poorly timed, this seemed politically wise in order to counter claims that James had behaved arbitrarily in his governing of England and Scotland. However, whereas for the majority Catholic parliamentary membership (who constituted over 95 per cent) the most urgent need was to remove the Act of Settlement which had restricted their land ownership since 1662, for James it was to make reassuring signals about the toleration of Protestantism and to get taxes agreed for the war effort. James got the latter but was overwhelmed by the politics of necessity when he accepted the effective end to the land settlement. Various other laws granted considerable independence for Ireland in relation to England and diminished the royal prerogative. This was directly contrary to his concept of monarchy and his imperial vision of government. By ending Anglo-Protestant domination, he in effect unravelled the Restoration settlement in Ireland and facilitated a Catholic revolution by accident. This pushed Irish Protestants into the arms of William and alarmed waverers in England and Scotland. Therefore, James's opening speech declaring 'liberty of conscience and against invading a man's property' was seen as empty rhetoric, and in any case was incomprehensible to Catholics and even the likes of d'Avaux. Tyrconnell understood the strategy while judging it impossible. Unfortunately, when the parliament dissolved on 18 July 1689, the Catholic members who dispersed were left feeling they had stood by a king who had delivered a decisive blow against Protestantism. His last institutional setpiece of his reign therefore did nothing to further the prospects of an English or Scottish restoration and much to hinder it. British monarchs have unwisely used English solutions to Scottish problems; this was a rare case of Irish solutions to Anglo-Scottish problems and it was always destined to fail. Indeed, ten days later a Williamite force led by Major General Percy Kirke relieved the siege of Derry.[4] Kirke was one of those English officers who defected to William in November 1688.

The whole Irish campaign was a patchwork of conflicting objectives. For James, the exercise was to create a bridgehead to land an army in Scotland or England. In other words Ireland was a minor concern. Consequently, at almost every opportunity James pressed Louis for French troops to support a landing in Scotland or England and Melfort was fully behind this approach, waxing lyrically and unrealistically about the enthusiastic welcome James would get on the mainland. Tyrconnell's main aim was to make Ireland a fortress, and that did not involve England or Scotland at this stage. The French, on the other hand, after the reports they had got from d'Avaux of James's indecisive leadership and the condition of his troops, were strongly opposed to any attack on England or Scotland or exposure of French troops to such a risk. If James could not take control of Ireland, how could he hope to do so in the other kingdoms? As d'Avaux described it, 'If the King of England does not take steps to settle Ireland and make it safe for himself before crossing to England he is lost'. Also, Louis and Louvois observed that intelligence-gathering by James and his senior advisors was poor and was chronically prone to overestimations of support. The inability to better predict William's invasion was a case in point. Meanwhile, James was convinced that the French ministers and king just did not understand reports from the British mainland. Overall, therefore, d'Avaux tended to sympathise with Tyrconnell, but all were united in their disregard for Melfort. His sycophantic behaviour in agreeing with all of the king's ideas and his ability to seed disharmony in the Council was infuriating. The French commander General Rosen declared that 'it was impossible to work with a man who said not a word of truth'. Eventually, even James concurred with their criticism of Melfort's competence and the Secretary was sidelined in early July and left Ireland in late August to return to Saint-Germain in October, slipping away as there were rumours of a plot to have him murdered. Once there, he used his closeness with Mary to press Louis one more time for an invasion of either Scotland or

England, but with no success. Having alienated Louvois and much of the French court, Louis and Mary cleared him away to be ambassador to Rome where he took up residence in December.[5]

Back in Ireland a reconstituted council emerged with Henry Jermyn, Lord Dover, James's old companion during his first exile in France, representing English interests and Seaforth replacing the administrative, but not political, role of Melfort. Immediately, James's capacity for not believing bad reports caught him out again when in early August Marshal Schomberg, the veteran commander who had fought for and against James in the 1650s, landed a Williamite force of 10,000 at Carrickfergus and made his headquarters at Dundalk. Irish Protestant resistance was more formidable than ever. But over the next two months, judging by d'Avaux's despatches, James was reinvigorated at the prospect of being pitted against the renowned marshal. He deployed his army in battle order in front of Schomberg's lines and spent many hours in the saddle like a man half his age. It evoked memories of the glory days of his youth.[6] Even though battle was not joined – because of Schomberg's caution, deteriorating weather conditions and the marshal's error in camping on marshy ground – the incident was seen as a morale-boosting 'victory' for James and his forces. Both sides suffered thousands of casualties from dysentery and fever.

As a stalemate set in for the winter, D'Avaux and Rosen were recalled to France in November, Rosen in particular at James's request owing to the dishonourable ferocity of his approach to the siege of Derry. In effect, both Frenchman were replaced by the Comte de Lauzun, a man unpopular at the French court but favoured by Mary for helping her escape from London, though with limited military experience. It was with this individual that Louis made good his promises to Mary to send French troops, and by the end of 1689, progress in the Continental campaign made this possible. In mid May 1690 Lauzun landed with a force of 8,000 yet the lift this gave the Jacobites quickly evaporated. Schomberg's deployment reflected William's realisation that the Jacobite threat in Ireland had to be defeated expeditiously so he could concentrate on the Continental war. The arrival of William himself on 14 June with another 15,000 well-trained troops to deliver the final blow simply confirmed Tyrconnell and Lauzun's estimation that defeat was inevitable.[7] Frustrated with the scale of French support and growing Irish hatred for the French officers, Dover retired to Flanders. But as preparations were made for what proved a Jacobite defeat at the Battle of the Boyne, not far from Dublin, on 1 July 1690 James engaged in more vigorous horsemanship. He showed no sign of such negativity. Fate almost delivered an extraordinary intervention when William was wounded by stray shot the day before the battle, and on the same day the French defeated the Anglo-Dutch fleet off the coast of Beachy Head in the English Channel. The new queen presided over an anxious council meeting in London. As it was, the Boyne was not a brilliant tactical victory by William so much as a battlefield miscalculation by James, who must take some of the blame for the defeat. Essentially, the more numerous and better-trained troops in William's army were more able to respond to James's exaggerated defensive deployments than James's forces were to make the required readjustments. The battle resulted in fewer than two thousand casualties in total, but it was the nature of the defeat that was so debilitating for Jacobite morale. Seeing so many of his Irish army flee in disorder, James promptly left the field, and two days later, after a panicky ride from Dublin to Kinsale, took ship to Brest. He arrived back at Saint-Germain on 16/26 July and, now remarkably unperturbed, began a process of justification and recrimination. He also doggedly appealed to Louis to attack England by land. In some irritation Louis asserted his precondition for any future French landing on the British mainland: it had to follow a domestic rising.[8] This would prove the intractable dilemma of Jacobitism for over half a century. The Irish affair also drew questions from Jacobites, let alone French courtiers, about James's leadership qualities given the ignominious nature of his second flight. James's only recourse was his faith and he began more than ever to embrace the regularity of his devotions.

The Irish conflict did not conclude as soon as William had hoped, and a number of Scots officers joined in the remaining campaign to eliminate opposition, including Hugh Mackay, who William removed from Scottish duties to serve as lieutenant general under the Dutch General Ginckel. The end would come with the Treaty of Limerick on 3 October 1691. This treaty also allowed for about sixteen thousand Irish Catholic troops to go abroad, some with their families, the so-called 'Wild Geese', in a Williamite plan to reduce guerrilla warfare which became a new Jacobite opportunity. They landed in France in the winter of 1691/2 under the command of Major General Patrick Sarsfield who negotiated their departure. It was this treaty rather than the Boyne that marked the return to Anglo-Protestant domination that would persist for more than two hundred years and shape the sectarian history of the island. And while Whig notions of the immaculate and peaceful English 'Glorious Revolution' in England are now rightly dismissed – the level of sectarian violence was widespread and sometimes brutal – there was nothing on the mainland to compare with the bloodshed in Ireland.[9] In a devastated landscape, those that stayed behind generally fared worse than the 'Wild Geese'.

MILITARY COUNTER-REVOLUTION

Although not numerically great, a band of Scottish officers served in the Irish conflict on the Jacobite side. One, Major General Thomas Buchan, with experience in French service, participated in the siege of Derry. Buchan and others travelled over with James from Saint-Germain, including Brigadier General Alexander Cannon, Brigadier General Robert Ramsay, and less senior officers such as William Erskine, earl of Buchan; Lewis Crichton, Viscount Frendraught; Sir

William Wallace and Sir George Barclay. These were the officers James intended to use for his descent on Scotland. In the Scottish theatre, two factors delayed a counter-revolution: firstly, the outcome of the convention of estates was awaited, and secondly, the winter of 1688/9 was one of worst in living memory with snow falling in May. Any reliance on Highland forces in a rebellion would be subject to weather conditions. When in mid March 1689 the convention went against James, Claverhouse (now Viscount Dundee) left Edinburgh and, after touring Perthshire, Fife and Angus consulting on the best course of action, raised James's royal standard on 13 April on the slopes of Dundee Law above Dundee. He then toured the Highlands to garner support. On his way from Edinburgh, the viscount consulted with the Duke of Gordon, who still held the Castle for James, and in the process caused a brief panic at the convention as some feared a bombardment from the Castle; none came. In one of a series of letters to encourage Scottish loyalists, Queen Mary wrote to Gordon two months later thanking him for his 'courage keeping for your Master what he left in your care', and to begin with, Gordon resolved to stay put but gave Dundee authority to raise the Gordons.[10] Also, since William had arrived in England, some Highland chiefs, in particular Sir Ewen Cameron of Lochiel, had been forming an association with clans adhering to James. He and the likes of the Macleans and Macdonald of Keppoch, one of the Lochaber chiefs, faced ruin from a successful Argyll restoration with the return of Archibald, the tenth earl. The traditional Campbell versus Macdonald feud would be relived yet again. It was natural, though, for Dundee to look for armed support from these clans. James had reports of how unfavourable things appeared after the withdrawal of loyalists from the convention and how an alternative Jacobite convention needed military protection. He issued commands from Dublin to Dundee and Balcarres, also a Jacobite sympathiser, and enclosed a proclamation in which, in typical Melfort speak, loyalists were to be welcomed with open arms and Williamites treated as heretics. However, James's own phraseology is in the words of reassurance:

> Assure yourselves, we will stand by you, and, if it shall please God to give success to our just cause, well let the ancient cavalier party know that they are the only true basis the monarchy can rest upon in Scotland; and we have found such effects of our mercy in times past, as will make us now raise our friends, upon the ruine of our enemys.[11]

Unfortunately, James also promised to send 5,000 troops over from Ireland, a decision that required French ships and agreement which he did not have. Instead, on 10 July three French frigates sailed from Carrickfergus with probably fewer than six hundred men, mainly consisting of an Irish infantry regiment, Lords Buchan and Frendraught, along with more than seventy junior officers, all under the command of Cannon. Some of the supplies and men were captured as they took landfall in and around Mull. Dundee, for his part, was on the one hand in despair over James's meagre reinforcements, yet also conscious that he needed to engage the enemy soon before his Highlanders dispersed. He, Argyll's forces and those of Scotland's new commander-in-chief and Dutch brigade veteran General Hugh Mackay, had led a merry dance checking each other's movements but avoiding a full-scale battle. In fact, Mackay was as anxious as Dundee to join battle soon for fear that Highland Jacobite strength would increase over time.[12]

Not all the potential followers gathered. In vain, Dundee wrote a pleading letter to Lord Murray to raise the men of Atholl, although many joined anyway. Cameron of Lochiel was typical of many Highland Jacobites in that he meandered a convoluted path between rebellion and submission to the government, and one of his oldest friends was in fact Colonel John Hill, Williamite commander of Inverlochy, soon to be renamed Fort William, and the garrison was vital to the economy of Lochiel's clansmen. Nevertheless, he joined with some of his clan at the Battle of Killiecrankie on 27 July 1689, at the pass of that name near Pitlochry in Perthshire, in which action the Highland charge of just over two thousand Jacobites overcame almost four thousand exhausted troops under Mackay. Dundee himself was killed and, of course, became one of the most celebrated heroes of Jacobitism. As for James's 'ancient cavaliers', they were represented by James Seton, earl of Dunfermline, who with Cannon took the victors from the field and commanded instead of 'Bonnie Dundee'.[13] James enjoyed the victory, but his cause would have been better served if Dundee had survived, he being the most effective Scottish Jacobite commander, given the long illness that Dumbarton had suffered from since his arrival at Saint-Germain in early 1689, and which had seemingly prevented him from going to Ireland.[14]

James made two further efforts to bring relief to Cannon's troops who, in spite of capturing hundreds of Mackay's men, were hard pressed after their victory. Cannon was no Dundee and was badly mauled on 21 August at Dunkeld by a newly formed Cameronian regiment, the commander falling like Dundee in his hour of victory.[15] Effective leadership of such disparate forces was required. Buchan, who was initially James's choice to command Cannon's group but was kept back to help with the siege of Derry, was sent over from Ireland in January 1690 to fill the leadership vacuum, bringing with him a few officers. He was instructed to give the usual assurances from James that further relief would be forthcoming, this time 8,000 men under James's son the duke of Berwick, then in Ireland with his father. Yet with so few accompanying Buchan, some clansmen began suggesting they submit to the government rather than continue. Many disaffected lowland lords might seek commissions and declare for James, although only if Berwick arrived with a large force. In April, out of necessity, Buchan, Dunfermline and Cannon began raiding in Inverness-shire seeking forage, but then at Cromdale in Strathspey on 1 May, Buchan was convincingly defeated by government forces under Sir Thomas Livingstone. While the senior officers made their escape, an effective Highland rising would never again be possible in the 1690s. Nonetheless, James made one more effort to relieve the clans in Lochaber who were holding out. He despatched Seaforth from Dublin in May, promoting him to marquis and to major general before he departed, but his performance resembled Argyll's in 1685, moving from place to place, seeking support and achieving very little in the process. On meeting Buchan and hearing of the defeat at Cromdale, Seaforth became dispirited and began to look for means to surrender on terms, acting through his kinsman Tarbat. After reneging on negotiations, he was captured by Mackay and spent most of the next seven years in prison or close confinement.[16] James's last Highland commission was even less successful than those of Cannon and Buchan.

While the Seaforth debacle ended James's Highland initiatives, this was not an end to Jacobite skirmishing and the general precariousness of the security situation. For the Williamite regime it had, however, become more a policing exercise than suppression of rebellion. Government oppressive measures under Mackay in 1690 now turned to discussion about indemnities in 1691. Tarbat and Colonel Hill had been suggesting since the previous summer that rebellious clans could be bought off. Now Breadalbane's negotiations with Jacobite leaders for an armistice, leading to the Achallader agreement in June 1691, coupled with William's agreement to issue a proclamation on 27 August such that pardons would be granted to those who took the oath of allegiance before 1 January 1692, offered an opportunity for the Highland clans to recover from two years of disturbance. As Breadalbane argued to Jacobite intriguers, this was an opportune truce whether or not a Jacobite invasion force was ever to appear. Most Jacobites, however, required James to grant permission to take an oath to William and Mary. Initially, in September James refused permission, but Breadalbane sent an envoy back to make it clear there was no other choice. Late in the day in December, his permission arrived. Some clan chiefs quickly sought competent officers who could tender the oath. It was in these circumstances that the infamous Glencoe Massacre occurred, where on 13 February 1692 government forces slaughtered forty or so Macdonalds of Glencoe, as their chief Alasdair MacIain had been too slow to take the oath. This was a shocking example of 'murder under trust' as the Macdonalds had acted as hosts for the soldiers the day before. It was a deliberate attempt by John Dalyrmple, master of Stair, now William's joint Secretary of State, and other members of the Privy Council to make an example of a lawless clan. The subsequent political scandal was a significant recruiting sergeant for Jacobitism, but also for government opposition in the Scottish Parliament. For his part, James's initial callous response to the indemnity would seem to have all the hallmarks of Melfort, yet at that time he was still in Rome and James's secretary was the Englishmen Henry Browne, later Viscount Montagu. The king's delayed second response seemed justified on the basis that the French were considering a fresh invasion plan in 1691, though this was little comfort to the Macdonalds of Glencoe.[17] James no doubt regarded

Highland clansmen somewhat like the Irish, a means to an end. In Scotland these were rarely the 'ancient cavaliers', the core adherents of monarchy.

Invasion plans came and went until 1697, but in 1692 a firm plan evolved. This was encouraged by the return of Melfort to Saint-Germain in late 1691, and the simultaneous arrival of the 'Wild Geese' from Ireland. Louis now had a total of about thirty thousand Irish soldiers and, whereas some of these were fighting in other theatres, the existence of such a force was an obvious signal that an invasion of England or Scotland was credible. In December and January James took time to travel to Brittany to review the troops and to discuss training methods with the officers, and felt a new sense of purpose. In the spring it was agreed by Louis that a force of 30,000 troops would be gathered as an invasion force including 13,000 Irish. Coupled with this, a number of Scottish officers landed at Le Havre in April, having been granted passes by the Edinburgh Privy Council either to remain or go into exile. Among these were Buchan and Cannon, and as soon as they appeared, James ordered them to join the Irish forces with other Scottish officers including Dunfermline and Barclay. All seemed ripe as in Scotland the Glencoe Massacre had badly weakened the government and in England secret communications had been undertaken through Jacobite agents with some of William's most senior current or former ministers. Re-energised, James was very optimistic and prior to departing for the coast, he held a ceremony at the chapel at Saint-Germain where he awarded the Order of the Garter to Powis, Melfort, and his four-year-old son. He also composed his 'Advice to his Son' in case he lost his life in the coming adventure, a work produced in the tradition of princely and fatherly guidance. As it was, the enterprise was bungled for two reasons. Firstly, Melfort drafted an ill-judged declaration which was counterproductive at a time when Tories and Scots cavaliers were needed on side. Melfort's text showed the more vindictive possibilities of a restoration under James's Catholic party. Drawing attention to the corruption or hypocrisy of William's government was fine, but it also stated that those who still opposed James after his invasion would 'fall unpitied under the severity of our justice', a tenor that discouraged potential supporters. James approved the text and encouraged its wide circulation in Scotland and England. This certainly confirms that Melfort plugged into James's natural authoritarianism and aversion to disloyalty. He knew his master too well and was too often a medium, not an advisor. The second failing was blind trust in the latent loyalism of the English establishment which, James believed, just needed an opportunity to return to the fold. Initially the fleet under the French admiral Tourville was damaged by storms which delayed their departure for several weeks. They knew that the combined English and Dutch fleet was positioned off the coast and yet the French Mediterranean fleet was due to arrive imminently. Tourville asked for a delay but this Louis rejected on the basis of James's assertions, backed up by Melfort, that half the English fleet would desert to his cause. James had been told months before that tentative contact had been made by agents with Admiral

Edward Russell, who commanded the Anglo-Dutch fleet, and they were convinced that Russell would turn. Unfortunately, the difference between gripes and real grievance was not understood and Russell did his duty. The French fleet was destroyed at the Battle of La Hogue over five days (19–24 May) in what was one of the greatest military defeats to befall the French during the reign of Louis XIV. James watched from the shore and irritated his French hosts by commending the skill and bravery of the English seaman. King Louis, who at the time was besieging the fortress of Namur in the Spanish Netherlands, took the bad news calmly enough, while James made a fulsome apology, reflected on 'la providence divine', and entered into a deeper depression about his prospects.[18] All now turned on a restoration in favour of his son, not himself. Back in London, with William in Flanders, James's daughter Queen Mary took firm action, imprisoning suspected and real Jacobites, such as John Churchill, duke of Marlborough. Middleton and Atholl's son Charles Murray, earl of Dunmore, two Scots then in London who had plotted a possible rising, were also apprehended. Some marvelled at how Englishmen would have reacted to a force composed of their greatest traditional enemies, the French and the Irish.

James's Scottish end of the 1692 affair was characterised by vagueness and more blind faith. The plan was to send the Scottish officers, about a hundred in total including those who had only just returned from there, back to Scotland to lead a new rebellion. They were to land at the coastal fortresses of Dunnottar or Slains in the North East, and James wrote letters to various lords of Aberdeenshire expecting their willing support. Queensberry and Arran were also written to but they did not stir to further the cause, although the Scottish commander-in-chief Sir Thomas Livingstone and the Privy Council were on alert. Lists of loyal Highland supporters were drawn up. Melfort also penned a declaration for Scotland in April and in this, as in the English equivalent, a number were excluded from indemnity, such as Tweeddale, Melville and Sir John Dalyrmple. Glencoe was rounded upon as an event showing 'what the usurper will do when he is free of restraint' but disloyalty would be subject to the gravest penalties and those sentenced in 1688 would get no pardon.[19]

The question of the declarations of 1692 highlighted another divisive issue at Saint-Germain and amongst Jacobites in England and Scotland. Since James returned after the Boyne, and emphatically since Melfort's reappearance, the exiled court had split into two competing factions. For Melfort, James's confessors and other zealots determined on a Catholic restoration, all was secondary to these religious objectives. In opposition were the 'compounders' who judged the only hope for a restoration was to reach out to English Anglicans and Scottish Episcopalian and Presbyterian moderates. This was a re-enactment of the divisions in the councils of London and Edinburgh from 1686 to 1688 where Rochester opposed Petre and Queensberry opposed Perth, although the efforts to involve Hamilton showed that Perth was not able on the ground to deliver the confessional domination his brother favoured for Scotland. The difference in the 1690s was that the French court, led especially by Charles Colbert, marquis de Croissy, Louis's foreign minister, distinguished religion from political reality and saw it as imperative to reach out to moderate Protestants. In English terms, this was about promises to protect the Church of England. Therefore in the aftermath of the discredited 1692 declarations, Croissy pressed for a new declaration, reminiscent perhaps of Charles II's statement at Breda, and the Frenchman drafted the words 'to agree to any laws, that shall, be desired at our hands to secure the Protestant religion, as now established by law in the church of England' and 'to secure liberty and property . . . against any invasion [that] may be designed by our posterity'. James rejected these notions for their limitations on the Catholic mission and the royal prerogative and Croissy even began to suspect that Melfort was deliberately sabotaging James's chances of regaining his kingdoms. Croissy's next move was to suggest an agent approach the Jacobite 'compounder', the earl of Middleton, to establish if he would offer his services to the Jacobite court and help draft a revised declaration. Middleton secretly made his way to Saint-Germain in April 1693.[20] After the veiled threat of withdrawing all support, Louis forced James to accept a list of eight articles drawn up by Middleton, including the wording 'protect and defend the Church of England' which James's confessors found so offensive. The declaration was published, though to little impact, but within weeks Middleton was in post as senior Secretary of State over Melfort. Whereas the moderate party won out, two aspects emerged from the dispute: firstly, James continued to put faith before practical politics which made him a liability during delicate negotiations, and secondly, even his closest appointments were now under French control. One further step was required to push home this party victory. After repeated complaints from visiting Jacobites that no English and Scottish followers could stomach Melfort anymore, Louis insisted he was dismissed and, after a brief campaign offered up by James and Mary to keep him, he resigned and was sent from the court in June 1694.[21]

James did what he could to offer moral support to those followers in Scotland who held out for as long as possible. Gordon eventually capitulated and handed back Edinburgh Castle in July 1689, although he was a prisoner himself in the castle cells until the following January. For his pains, he was not to be trusted at the exiled court and retired to his estates. The Bass Rock on the Forth estuary, for long a prison, was another celebrated case, though of more minor military significance. In June 1691 Jacobite prisoners seized control and held out, being supplied occasionally and eating what they could. In 1693 the island was to be supplied from Norway, the ex-prisoners becoming desperate. Melfort and James wrote encouraging letters to Captain Michael Middleton who held the rock, and belatedly sent his father Major Middleton to relieve him along with a priest, one James Nicol. This last initiative was in March 1694 and it seems to have galvanised the Edinburgh authorities into action. James asked Middleton to '[keep] the garison in Union & discipline & [encourage] all Our faithfull subjects under your command to stand firm to their duty [promising] due reward of their services & sufferings'.[22] Manifesting Jacobitism was strange mixture of small detail and grand strategy.

The final military intervention in the 1690s which had James's tacit involvement was an invasion plan for 1696 linked to an assassination plot against King William. There were hopes that on Queen Mary's death at Kensington Palace in December 1694 a favourable opportunity might present itself, but attempts to cause friction between a grieving William and Princess Anne, in spite of their difficult relationship, conspicuously failed.[23] Yet this new invasion had no Scottish dimension. As in February 1696 a French fleet and army assembled on the coast, Berwick crossed to London to lead an uprising. He found a disappointingly small conspiracy unwilling to act before a French landing. Also, it had been intertwined with a desperate plan to assassinate William while at hunting. Unimpressed, Berwick returned to France. Louis and James were informed about the assassination plot and, though not involved, would no doubt have welcomed the advantages that might accrue from the death of their adversary. A forlorn figure, James spent several months on the coast awaiting news (at Calais, Dunkirk and Boulogne), although the fleet never sailed. When news came, it was of arrests and the failure of the conspiracy, while association with such an asassination scheme proved damaging to Jacobitism, as some moderates in England gave up in horror, and tarnished the reputations of James and Louis. In the aftermath James wrote to his confessor Armand-Jean de Rance, abbé of the Cistercian monastery of La Trappe, Normandy, that 'God did not wish to restore me. May his will be done always'. These revelations, and an exhausted French war effort, made Louis seek a peace treaty with William in early 1697. Before this, a possible solution to Louis's Jacobite problems presented itself. The death of King John of Poland created a vacancy and Louis suggested James could be nominated as a replacement. But James rejected this out of hand as accepting the Polish throne would be to deny his son's birthright. Earlier in 1694, in a year when the French suffered military reverses, he pondered whether Louis 'would leave him in the lurch . . . excluding him in [any] peace' and recognise King William. Now, as the peace talks began, James felt betrayed and entered into a futile propaganda effort to assert his rights, whatever the outcome of a treaty. Drawing from Melfort's manual of politics, he feared 'secret court intrigues'. He sent envoys to Vienna, and manifestos were published to rally Catholic Europe in defence of religion and monarchical rule and railed against his 'unjust treatment', while in any case the agreement, the treaty of Ryswick, was signed in October 1697. Louis, however, refused William's demand that James leave Paris and go beyond the Alps.[24] And yet the option of a Jacobite military restoration in the name of King James was now gone.

Diplomacy was obviously one of the main weapons deployed by the exiled court and two Scots played significant roles in this respect, Melfort and his brother, the Earl of Perth. Melfort himself was in Rome from December 1689 to October 1691. His mission was twofold: to secure papal backing and so wider Catholic support in Europe for James's cause, and to press for a subsidy from the Holy See. The death of Pope Innocent XI, rabidly anti-French and frosty when James sought support as a martyr to his faith in 1689, offered new possibilities with the election of Alexander VIII, but the same problem remained. Rome had sided with the Empire in the Nine Years War and so James found himself on the wrong side, if the only side that could offer a military solution to his woes. Melfort obtained 30,000 crowns for those of Irish, Scots and English who had suffered through the Revolution, though no general support. Before Melfort returned Pope Alexander died, yet while the new pontiff Innocent XII wished to mend relations with France, he would only provide funds in time of peace. James's diplomacy with Rome was not helped by the divisions in his own English mission as a result of his replacing in 1687 the competent Cardinal Norfolk as cardinal protector with Mary Beatrice's uncle Rinaldo, Cardinal d'Este. Later in 1694, when d'Este resigned his cardinal's hat to inherit the title of Duke of Modena, most help from Rome finally dried up. Melfort penned a stream of letters detailing the difficulties he faced, especially to Mary, while working diligently for her uncle to get permission through her to return to Saint-Germain. His pain at getting so few letters was 'unexpressible' and as for his progress 'I do all that's possible but to no returne at all but faire words'.[25] Perth's ambassadorship to Rome then ran from May 1695 to March 1696. He had negotiated his release from prison in Scotland in 1693 and, after a year in Antwerp, travelled to Venice and Rome on a cultural tour when he was conveniently commissioned by James. His mission had the same objective but he was no more successful and frustratedly declared to James – 'Religion is gone and a wicked policy set up in its place'. Or, as James wrote angrily to Cardinal Howard in January 1691, as William was reported distributing arms to the Protestant princes and to Savoy and Piedmont (see Plate 14):

> why should not his Holynesse spare me some to buy arms here to begin a
> magazine, that for aught I knew I may have great need of before the
> sommer shall be over, or then I supose he would be sorry I should want
> them.

While James was in exile he could not comprehend the divisions in Catholicism that prevented a full focus on his restoration and the great mission. When in Dublin in November 1689, he emphasised how vital it was that the Pope press for peace amongst the Catholic princes to grasp the common cause.[26] It was a policy which fell on deaf ears, fortunately for King William as well as the ambitions of King Louis.

CONSTITUTIONAL COUNTER-REVOLUTION

The constitutional campaign of Scottish Jacobitism focused, in the first instance, on the convention of estates which met in Edinburgh on 14 March 1689. While Catholics by necessity kept a low profile, loyalist as much as revolutionary Protestants had reason to attend given that the nature of the constitutional and religious settlement was far from certain. There was much to play for with a range of objectives for individuals and groupings, and although there has been some historiographical cynicism about motivations, the first six months of 1689 saw more political and ideological debate in Scotland than at any time since the 1640s. This was evidenced in a range of distributed memorials and petitions, some submitted to William in January and February, including a signed address favouring the end of bishops from the Presbyterian clergy and nobility, the earls of Argyll and Crawford, as well as Lord Cardross and James Dalrymple of Stair; the Episcopalian, *A Memorial . . . to the Affairs of Scotland* drawn up by the lawyers Tarbat and Rosehaugh, arguing the case for maintaining episcopacy as a Prince committed to Scotland's laws must be 'honour bound to support' it being so necessary for monarchy; and unionist ideas conveyed in the 'Haddington address', sponsored by Tweeddale, where 'a more strict and inseparable union' was proposed between England and Scotland which would guarantee 'religion and liberty' and a more moderate settlement of the church. William himself favoured union, as he indicated in his address to the Convention – with the two kingdoms, 'liveing in the same island, haveing the same langwage, and the same comone interest of religion and liberty' – although it is fortunate that this idea dissipated in April and May, the English Parliament uninterested and the Scottish Estates, while willing to send commissioners for discussions, not especially keen either.[27] Rejecting Anglo-Scottish union became a rallying cry for Jacobitism from 1703 onwards, and had it been attempted in 1689 when swords were drawn, it would have brought a new dimension to James's cause and left the likes of Hamilton in a dilemma.

James signalled his approval that loyalists should attend the Convention, though the delay gave the revolution party a head start in the electoral process. Moreover, the agreement in London in January that elections should proceed without taking the Test and that the electorate 'be Protestant, without any other Exception, or limitation whatever' extended the franchise to the advantage of the Williamites. In royal burghs this meant abandoning the limitation to council members only and, as the summons instructed, gave the vote to 'the whole burgesses', many of them Presbyterians. In the west and central royal burghs especially, it brought Society People into an aggressive canvassing operation. Shire elections, meanwhile, were held regardless of any Michaelmas elections held in October, though as we have seen, some of these were already cast in the Revolution interest. No attempt was made to alter the franchise and existing property qualifications still applied, although again the elimination of the Test brought in new electors and candidates to the system of electing two commissioners for each shire.[28] Nevertheless, in January and February Dundee, Balcarres and Atholl organised a considerable loyalist effort in the shire and burgh elections, and this was augmented by Episcopalian candidates supported by Tweeddale, Queensberry and Tarbat. Jacobite candidates produced a close result in Edinburgh, victories in the likes of Stirling, Perth and Brechin and in Border and northern shires. The Presbyterian radical Sir James Montgomery of Skelmorlie claimed that Episcopalians 'bestirr[ed] themselves more vigorously about Elections' than ever before, although some refused to participate in what they viewed as an illegal process. In fact Montgomery won his Ayrshire commission with ease but there were indeed frantic levels of contest in elections right across Scotland. Unfortunately for James's adherents, once the Estates convened, a Presbyterian dominated committee of controverted (disputed) elections ensured that where there was dubiety the revolution candidates were approved. Other dynamics, such as noble family networks in certain areas and existing town councils aiming to preserve their status, brought additional complexities to energetic politicking. Tarbat was convinced that it was success in the burghs that secured Presbyterianism as most shire and noble members were 'not for presbitery', yet subsequent parliamentary attendance shows many Episcopalian gentlemen became reconciled to the new regime. Nonetheless, the fact that 70 per cent of the elected members were new to Parliament also made the house more unpredictable in the long term.[29]

Although in the western shires the Society People and their Presbyterian followers initiated some attacks of Episcopal clergy, or 'rabblings' as they became known, the bishops nurtured some hope of compromise when they travelled to the Convention. However, the atmosphere in Edinburgh was one of intimidation. Two thousand Cameronians and Argyll adherents had been brought into Edinburgh to provide security and at moments were seen to overawe the Estates, though given the chance it is just as likely that Dundee and his impressive troopers would have done the same. For the time being, this ad hoc force was put under the command of David Melville, earl of Leven, Lord Melville's son, and remained in the capital until the end of March and the arrival of Hugh Mackay's disciplined Scottish regiments. Melville would become William's chief advisor on Scottish affairs in London and was appointed Secretary of State in May, while Leven, a soldier who landed at Torbay and did military and diplomatic service for William, was his official envoy at the Convention. Leven and Hamilton viewed the ad hoc security force as a counter to the guns of Edinburgh Castle under the control of the Duke of Gordon. Fear encouraged tension and partisanship. Expressing Jacobitism openly invited attack from the hostile Cameronians, and bishops sought protection as they came and went from the chamber. When Alexander Rose, bishop of Edinburgh, was heard to pray for King James's restoration on the first day, it did not go down well with the crowd.[30]

From the first day of the Convention, it was obvious things would not go well for James, as Hamilton was elected President of the Convention defeating Atholl, the 'compromise' Episcopalian candidate.[31] Two days later James's infamous letter, stating his terms, was read to the chamber. This was considered after a similar letter from William. The prince's was more conciliatory and, noting that he made reassurances about 'securing the Protestant religion, the ancient laws and liberties of that kingdom', the Estates swiftly passed the 'Act declaring this to be a free and lawfull meeting of the estates'. James's letter was drafted by Melfort and was a shock to Dundee and Balcarres. They had sent a draft to James along with a request that Melfort be dismissed as his involvement was hampering recruitment to the cause. Unfortunately, by then Melfort was back in the saddle of his master's affairs and also his mail. When James's letter was read out it was seen as hectoring and full of threats. So, they having met on the 'usurped authority of the prince of Orange', James demanded they 'condemn the base example of disloyal men'. He declared he would 'pardon all such as will return to their duty before the last day of this month [but] punish with the rigour of our laws all such as shall stand out in rebellion against us and our authority'.[32] The tone was not so much a shock to Williamites, who expected nothing less, as a crushing disappointment to loyalists. It was also, given the electoral arithmetic, relatively inconsequential but demoralising nonetheless for Jacobites.

Dundee withdrew after this disappointing day to take an alternative constitutional initiative. Other Jacobites withdrew before the end of March with James's deadline in mind, thirty-five or so doing so, some feigning illness and others returning later. In their absence the Estates carried out a constitutional revolution. While security measures were handled, arms sent to Glasgow for fear that James would land from Ireland, and negotiations continued with Gordon, long debates were held on formulating a declaration equivalent to the English Parliament's declaration of James's abdication. A Committee for Settling the Government was formed on 26 March consisting of twenty-four members, eight of each estate, the bishops being excluded, and including Hume of Polwarth, Skelmorlie and Tarbat, all of whom had penned memorials on government. The influence of the first two Presbyterians seems strongest even though Tarbat was now considered a Williamite. The final 'Vote declaring the throne vacant and the reasones therof' was taken on 4 April. James had been deemed to have 'forfaulted' the throne on account of a list of misdemeanours, and 'the seclusion of King James, the pretended Prince of Wales and the children of their bodies', so allowing Mary and Anne to succeed. The act concludes:

The estates of the kingdom of Scotland find and declare that King James VII, being a professed papist, did assume the regal power and acted as king without ever taking the oath required by law, and has by the advice of evil and wicked counsellors invaded the fundamental constitution of this kingdom and altered it from a legal limited monarchy to an arbitrary despotic power and has exercised the same to the subversion of the Protestant religion and the violation of the laws and liberties of the nation, inverting all the ends of government, whereby he has forfeited the right to the crown and therefore the throne has become vacant.[33]

A week later, on 11 April 'The declaration of the estates containing the Claim of Right and the offer of the crown to the king and queen of England' was voted upon which relisted the same series of accusations, including arbitrary government, imposing Catholicism contrary to law, keeping a standing army 'in time of peace without consent of parliament' and of 'using inhumane tortures'. But the second part of this document itemised conditions for offering the throne, in effect by insisting that certain activities are no longer acceptable, including arbitrary behaviour since 1660. The Convention was harking back to the settlement imposed on Charles I at the Covenanting parliament of 1640 and 1641, where the executive and judiciary came under the control of the Estates. In 1689 this involved a theoretical reduction in the royal prerogative and the restriction on certain of the Crown's 'legitimate' legal powers: for example, 'that the imposing of oaths without authority of parliament is contrary to law' would mean that many such royal or council proclamations for oaths, going back to the 1570s, would have been illegal; or 'that the imprisoning of persons without expressing the reason thereof and delaying to put them to trial is contrary to law', when Scotland had no act of *habeas corpus*, not until 1701. Two days later, the Estates produced their third constitutional declaration consisting of fifteen Articles of Grievance designed to limit crown authority in specific areas. The 1669 Act of Supremacy 'aught to be abrogated' and the 'committee of parliament called the articles . . . a great grievance to the nation' should be abolished. Given the electoral shenanigans before the Convention, we can wonder at the fourteenth, 'that all grievances relating to the manner and measure of the lieges their representation in parliament be considered and redressed in the first parliament'. These, then, were the documents read to William before he took the Scottish coronation oath in May. Argyll, Skelmorlie and Sir John Dalrymple, as representatives of the three estates, had been commissioned by the Convention to go to London and witness the ceremony and deliver their terms. The words, based on the existing form, would, the Covenant notwithstanding, have been familiar to Charles II who took the oath at Scone in January 1651. James could never take such an oath because of his religion and could never have accepted such limitations on his royal authority. William also agreed to turn the Convention into a parliament and thereafter there would be no general election until 1702.[34] Jacobites were therefore starved of parliamentary campaigning for the rest of James's life.

On hearing of the initial decisions of the Convention in Edinburgh, in late March James wrote from Ireland to Dundee and Balcarres confirming his instinctive trust in the 'antient cavallier pairty', and that an alternative Jacobite convention should be summoned so they could express their constitutional opposition to the Edinburgh meeting. Unfortunately his correspondence was intercepted. Ten days later, however, he wrote again to Dundee authorising him to summon a convention of estates of those gathered with him in common cause. He was to inform the convention of James's intention 'to secure the protestant religion established by law in parliament' and the 'laws, liberties, properties and rights of our subjects'. Therefore, to encourage cavaliers and clan members to rally to James's standard, Dundee dispersed letters highlighting James's moderation and constitutional promises. King James had 'given us power to meet in a Convention . . . to counteract the mock Convention at Edinburgh, whom he hath declared traitours'. Dundee and Balcarres planned an assembly to meet at Stirling, but it depended on the participation of Atholl, who got cold feet and changed his mind; William Johnstone, earl of Annandale, a Presbyterian noble who decided to stick with that religious agenda, and George Livingstone, earl of Linlithgow, Dundee's army friend who refused to join. Another key player was Charles Erskine, earl of Mar, who as Keeper of Stirling Castle could provide security. However, Hamilton adjourned the Convention and Mackay sent Linlithgow to billet at Stirling to ensure Mar was kept in line. Even Balcarres decided that it was too soon and Dundee was isolated.[35] An alternative, parallel meeting of estates, as occurred in 1544 and 1570/1 during periods of civil war, did not happen.[36] Other outside factors reduced the chances of a Stirling parliament. Exaggerated news of the violence of a Catholic resurgence in Ireland and the uncompromising spectre of Melfort made many question if a moderate constitutional restoration was possible. Dundee had written to Melfort gently pleading with him to resign, yet to no avail.[37]

Two of the matters not concluded in the Convention of March to May 1689, and the parliamentary session from June to August thereafter, were the fate of the Lords of the Articles and the legal establishment of Presbyterianism. The abolition of episcopacy, as per the Claim of Right, was agreed by the Estates in July 1689. On both issues, however, William was committed to compromise. He wished to preserve the management committee and got Melville and Hamilton, now High Commissioner, to submit various draft proposals that were all rejected by the Estates. In religion, he also hoped that Episcopalians could be saved from extinction and that some comprehension or toleration could be achieved. Stalling on these matters was seen as a betrayal by the more extreme Presbyterians in the Estates. Partially on account of such disillusionment, an opposition grouping of allied Jacobites, Episcopalians and rogue Presbyterians formed a parliamentary group known as the 'club', and came under the leadership of Skelmorlie, the ambitious Presbyterian. In spite of religious differences, the 'club' could unite in pressing for a constitutional revolution in the summer parliament of 1689, especially over the committee of the Articles. Hamilton, however, found the Estates unmanageable and was forced to adjourn the session – he could not deliver the 'near' *status quo* that William desired.[38]

After the session was adjourned, Skelmorlie and key 'club' members Annandale and Lord Ross went to London in a vain attempt to persuade William to pass the reforming measures tabled in Edinburgh. What then followed was one of those strange twists in political history – exasperated at the slow rate of reform over civil grievances, and the limited access to the new conduit of patronage, they gravitated back to King James. From December 1689 Skelmorlie led the others into secret contact with James in a plot to 'ruin [William's] intrest in Scotland in a parliamentary way', as it is described in James's *Life*. Their plan was to restore James on condition he accepted the full reform agenda. This would be achieved by persuading enough Jacobites to attend parliament, swallow pride and take the oath of allegiance to William and Mary, and then insist on excessive concessions. This would lead to a failure to agree taxation, a fiscal crisis and eventual military collapse in Scotland; a far-fetched plan indeed. Nonetheless, preparations were made and in the first quarter of 1690 draft parliamentary instructions were despatched to James. A declaration by the 'noblemen, chieftains of clans, [and] gentleman' was produced claiming the Privy Council was now more arbitrary than ever. In return James issued commissions for a subsequent restoration parliament with Annandale High Commissioner and Skelmorlie Secretary of State, a position he much craved in 1689 when it was given to Melville. Instructions were provided for a general act for liberty of conscience, a typical staple for James. It was even envisaged that military support would be provided by James's sudden move to England while William switched to Ireland, a simultaneous Highland and Cameronian rising and additional French support.[39]

This grand plan came to naught being contradictory and misconceived, as many of Skelmorlie's conspiraces proved to be. More importantly, when the second session of the Revolution parliament met between April and July 1690, with Melville taking over from Hamilton as High Commissioner, the Estates remained loyal to William while he in turn delivered the required concessions. The Act of Supremacy of 1669 was rescinded, the Lords of the Articles were abolished and Presbyterianism became yet again the established church form. The Presbyterian clergy ousted in 1661 were even reinstated, the church legislation being drafted by none other than James Stewart of Goodtress. Between June and August the Montgomery plot began to unravel as Ross and Annandale confessed. The role of the English Jacobite agent Henry Payne came to light and he was tortured in Scotland, an interesting case given the aversion to such methods by the Convention parliament. Running scared, Skelmorlie himself made a partial confession to Queen Mary in London but, posing as a double agent, was released.[40] His subsequent career as a Jacobite conspirator and pamphleteer was paradoxical and inconsistent. James to begin with revered him as 'a man he esteem[ed] as one of his best friends', yet between 1692 and 1694 he was held at arm's length due to his inveterate intriguing. In one respect his impact on Jacobitism was significant, however, as he supported the moderate 'compounders' who championed cooperation with Protestant Jacobites. He also promoted the Prince of Wales's conversion to Protestantism as a means to a restoration. This, of course, James would never accept, and nor would the 'no-surrender' Catholic party of Melfort. The issue raised itself again in late 1701 after James's death and that of Anne's only surviving son, the eleven-year-old Duke of Gloucester, which began an Anglo-Scottish succession crisis. John Hamilton, Lord Belhaven, visited Saint-Germain to ask if James VIII would convert to Protestantism and come in person to Scotland to lead a revolution to preserve an independent Scottish nation and Parliament. He represented disenchanted Scottish parliamentarians, including his kinsman James, fourth duke of Hamilton, who succeeded his father in 1694 but continued sporadic contact with Saint-Germain, though not as recklessly as when he was Earl of Arran. A new political crisis had engulfed Scotland with the collapse of the Darien Scheme to set up a national trading colony at Panama. Mary Beatrice said no on behalf of her young son, although the very fact that a patriot like Belhaven was at the exiled court confirms that patriotism was increasingly the new opportunity for Jacobitism. As for Skelmorlie, as a 'compounder' he helped facilitate Middleton's switch to Saint-Germain. Thereafter though, Skelmorlie was dropped and was never given a position at court. He craved Melfort's post when, yet again, the earl was sent away for irregularities, including some believed involvement in Skelmorlie's brief arrest in London. The position under Middleton went to the Irish Catholic John Caryll; unambitious but competent. Skelmorlie's diplomatic efforts with The Netherlands and Sweden to explore international Jacobite allies were nonetheless groundbreaking and would influence a new generation of Jacobites, and suggest that he may have been an effective secretary for William or James. He therefore continued to provide Saint-Germain with reports on the business of the English Parliament and encouraged Jacobites in London, yet had to flee to France in early 1694, dying near Paris later that year.[41] In the end Skelmorlie and James made strange bedfellows when it came to constitutional Jacobitism. James concurred with his brother's opinion that parliaments should be called infrequently, and, in a Scottish context, that the committee of the articles was an essential Crown mechanism for parliamentary management. In a manner all too typical for Jacobites, both were deluded over the help each could offer the other in progressing mutually exclusive political objectives.

THE LAST HOUSEHOLD

Much of the negativity associated with the exiled court, from its apparently intolerant attitude to Protestants to the demeaning and inadequate accommodation afforded by the Château, has been passed down to us by the politically motivated.

Slanderous and plainly inaccurate accounts from the likes of John Macky, an obscure Scottish and Williamite spy, spread disinformation and exaggeration. Macky's pamphlet, *A View of the Court of St. Germain from the Year 1690–1695, with an Account of the Entertainment Protestants meet with there* (1696), with the backdrop of another invasion scare, was a deliberate attempt to inject religious fear into the minds of those Englishmen and Scots disaffected with William's government and the endless war against France. Less overtly distorted but no less critical were the reports of the English poet and secretary Matthew Prior. He was secretary to the ambassador to Paris from June 1698 to August 1699, initially for William Bentinck, now first earl of Portland, who after the treaty of Ryswick, arrived in magnificent style with a huge entourage to negotiate with Louis over the problematic Spanish succession. Prior was relentlessly disparaging of the intelligence and prejudice of James and his court. It is necessary to set this aside when assessing the qualities of the exiled Jacobite court.[42]

Excluding the sixteen months that James spent in Ireland, he was to live in and around Paris for almost the entire period of his second exile. His home for over eleven years was the Château Vieux de Saint-Germain-en-Laye. In some respects this stability was unusual given his enforced peripatetic life. He had, after all, resided in a greater number of cities than any other Stuart monarch before him – the capitals Brussels, The Hague, London, Edinburgh, Dublin and Paris being just the main selection. His last court, indeed, became a home; a place for his new family to set down roots, in a Francophile yet international domesticity. His son James Francis was barely six months old when they arrived, his wife Mary Beatrice, England and Scotland's only Italian Queen, merely thirty years. In the summer of 1692 Louise-Maria Theresa, the last of her six children to survive childbirth, was born to Mary and this delicate, essentially French princess was destined to spend her whole life at the Château and would die of smallpox before she reached her twentieth birthday. In the 1690s, though, beyond the conspiracies and invasion plans aimed at rejuvenating the Jacobite cause and the claustrophobic party politics and faction of the court, infants played in the corridors, governors and governesses were chosen, and children were educated and taught the skills of life. The great source we have for these domestic details is the remarkable journal of David Nairne, James's Scottish under-secretary who worked under Melfort, Caryll and Middleton from 1689 to 1701 and then carried out the same function for James VIII and III. Most important of all, he and James became very close and Nairne was given various private duties, handling intimate papers and correspondence and being present at many of the king's devotions, including in April 1698 joining James's own Co-fraternity for a Happy Death (*Bona Morte*) in the Royal Chapel at Saint-Germain. Nairne recorded family events with disarming simplicity: in June 1692 'the queen is brought to bed of the princess' and in May 1696 'the prince began to ride'.[43]

That another Scot should make such a prominent contribution to our understanding of the court reminds us again not to exaggerate the numerical strength of Scots at the court. In 1696 a mere 4 per cent of those employed at the court were Scottish with almost 70 per cent Englishmen and women, with more Irish, French and Italians than Scots. The three households of James, Mary and the Prince of Wales combined totalled about 225, a similar size to that which straddled St James's Palace and Whitehall when they were duke and duchess of York, but diminutive compared to the royal courts at Whitehall and Versailles with their sprawling complexes. Given that many senior royal appointees had themselves servants, there were probably up to a thousand individuals in the entire Jacobite court, all vying for space and pensions.[44] Finance was certainly a factor in the reduction of the scale of the court, even though Louis was generous enough. However, although compromises had to be made, James and Mary established and retained a court of such organisation, etiquette and magnificence as to be no embarrassment to visiting French courtiers or foreign ambassadors.

The court was not merely a magnate for foreign envoys but also foreign artists. In spite of James's disapproval of plays and decision to leave idle the fine theatre at Saint-Germain – stemming from his own youthful experiences of the vulgar theatre of Restoration London – musical entertainment and dance was not frowned upon. At the children's birthdays, both of which were in June, musical events were the norm each year with 'musique' on 10/20 June on the Prince James's birthday and, eight days later, a ball on that of the princess. In 1698 a supper with the prince was entertained by a Welsh harpist. Concerts were common in the rooms of Mary and the prince and leading courtiers, some of whom were themselves talented amateur musicians like Caryll, who played the viol, and Nairne who played the violin, bass viol and flute. A court musician and composer, or Master of Music, the Italian Innocenzo Fede, delivered musical performances in the chapel and secular apartments. Professional French musicians were recruited but Italian styles were the most common, such as the Italian sonata. Beyond the Château, music also featured at Versailles, and James and Mary attended various balls and operas, the latter of which would become common again at Saint-Germain, with the theatre recommissioned, after James's death. Spiritual music was also regularly heard by James and Mary in the local churches, in particular at the parish church of Saint-Germain where James regularly worshiped, and the Chapel Royal at the Château.[45] The sounds in and around the court were not always those of soldiers marching, even when so many Irish officers lingered looking for pensions and duties to perform.

While poetry and literature were also evident in the intellectual environment of the Jacobite court, the commissioning of artists and the hanging of paintings were frequent and dynamic activities. In specific years the artists Benedetto Gennari (1689–91), Nicolas de Largillière (1691–2, 1694–5), Pierre Mignard (1694), Françios de Troy (1698–1701) and Alexis-Simon Belle (1698–1714) (all Frenchmen other than the Italian Gennari) contributed canvasses in an effusion of

Jacobite image-making. Miniatures and engravings were made based on major compositions to disseminate the iconography of Jacobitism to the British Isles and to Rome. In particular, images of the prince were sent over, generally via Flanders, to confirm the health and Stuart appearance of the rightful heir to the throne. In the summer of 1694, for example, two batches of paintings were despatched to England in June and July, probably copies and miniatures of Largillière's portrait of the six-year-old prince finished that year. One batch was sent to Robert Ferguson, the Scottish pamphleteer and conspirator recently switched to the Jacobite cause, and he distributed these to help satisfy and build an 'underground' demand in Britain. This was the same year the octogenarian Mignard, principle painter of Louis XIV, produced his great portrait of James, Mary and the two children, the only painting of the full family in exile (see Plate 12). In the foreground a crown and a sword symbolise the righteous fight for the three kingdoms. This large canvas was given pride of place at Saint-Germain, taking up a whole wall in James's antechamber and deliberately placed in full view of visitors. As far as sittings were concerned, James became unwilling to sit for martial portraits from 1691, especially after, in the wake of the Battle of the Boyne, Louis would not allow him to attend the siege of Mons in the spring of that year. James took this decision badly, describing it 'a great mortification which had descended upon me which touches me where I am most sensitive'. His military reputation was now seriously damaged when for all his days it had been a source of encouragement and self-confidence. But as a connoisseur of art James might have some credibility, although faith and family image mattered more than patronage of art or accumulating items for their intrinsic beauty, and it was Mary who commissioned many of the works, gifting them to others and festooning the palace with sculptures and busts. Two of James's Scottish servants, Melfort and Perth, were enthusiastic collectors of art and could engage him in debate on the subject. Melfort gathered a very large collection in London which was confiscated and sold at auction in 1693, but when in exile, he accumulated a new collection from his time in Rome and Paris. Eventually, long after his political role at Saint-Germain had ended, in 1705 he opened up his collection to the Paris public who marvelled at his Italian pictures. Perth meanwhile had a more modest yet still remarkable collection in Scotland, and in March 1689, after his arrest, entrusted seventy paintings to his sister Anne, countess of Erroll, at Slains Castle in Aberdeenshire, and in 1707 had them shipped over to join those acquired in exile.[46] Therefore, when resident at Saint-Germain, Melfort and Perth hung their collections in their respective apartments adding lustre and depth to an already impressive spectacle that complimented in miniature the grander scale of Versailles.

Interaction between the courts of Versailles and Saint-Germain was frequent and Louis proved particularly attentive to Mary when James was in Ireland. James and Mary made regular visits to have supper with Louis at the nearby Château de Marly, a more modest country retreat near forests equidistant from the royal courts, and occasionally at the Trainon Palace near Versailles, another less formal environment for intimate gatherings of the royal families. Also, every September and October they joined Louis for several weeks at the old Palace of Fontainebleau south of Paris. James's passion for hunting could be given full rein in the nearby forests and not infrequently he rode out in the company of his French cousin. Relations between the families remained warm and, excluding 1689, on average Louis was entertained at Saint-Germain on nine occasions each year. However, during phases when the condition of James's affairs was more awkward, as after the debacle of La Hogue and the treaty of Ryswick was signed, the visits of the 'Sun King' tailed off. A more natural reduction in interaction arose from James's declining months of ill health.[47]

In spite of the Mons affair, part of the interaction between the two princes was their shared involvement in military ceremonial and training. Usually in the spring and early summer, James attended a review of troops with Louis on the plain of Poissy west of Paris and cast a critical and experienced eye over their discipline and order. It took his mind back to the optimistic days on Hounslow Heath with his beloved standing army. At each review, Irish troops that were attached to or integrated into the French army took his salute. The grandest occasion was, though, in September 1698 when a large exercise took place on the plain of Compiègne, north of Paris, half way between it and the border with the Spanish Netherlands. James marvelled at the sight of 60,000 'well clad and so well mounted' men in mock battle and declared 'never was any thing of that kind better worth seeing'. This was to impress visiting dignitaries and ambassadors that the military might of France was still intact regardless of the current peace, but also was a reminder to James of the military power he no longer wielded. Other reminders came in more emotional forms. After La Hogue in 1692, James summoned his 150 Scottish officers for a final review at Saint-Germain before they departed in French service to Catalonia to fight against Spain. James was tearful as he thanked these veterans of Killiecrankie, Dunkeld and Cromdale, including Buchan, Cannon and Barclay, for their loyalty and sacrifice. The treaty of Ryswick produced a more dramatic integration and disbanding of the Irish 'Wild Geese' in the spring of 1698, as Louis insisted it was no longer possible to sustain their numbers, although he wished to preserve their best fighting men because of their effectiveness. James and his son, the Duke of Berwick, won the argument that a core of 6,000 should be retained as a distinct force, and did so a year later when the issue arose again. But they were indisputably under French command. James and his court were then faced with scores of demobilised Irish troops roaming the towns and countryside in search of food and shelter, and it took some months for them to dissipate. James did what he could, as did Louis and the Catholic Church, to provide funds for the poor Irish. The entire episode was a humiliation for a prince of war.[48]

As diplomatic and military business shrank during the 1690s, a structured daily regime was ever more predictable for the exiled king. His life had become increasingly one of strictly timetabled activities and routine. As he grew older these habitual patterns of behaviour turned a methodical younger man into a compulsive-obsessive older one. Hours for sleeping, rising, prayers, bathing, meals, brisk walks and attending to business all had specific times and regimented durations. He visited these attitudes on his family, motivated by a sense of responsibility that it was his duty as a parent. Just before James Francis Edward reached his seventh birthday James penned a list of 'rules of the family', approving set patterns of behaviour for a prince and how he should be monitored by a governor. These were written down by Caryll to be handed to the prince's new governor. From his arrival as a baby to May 1695, the prince had been under the watchful eye of female governesses in children's accommodation and now, in June that year, he was 'put into mens hands', and allocated his own apartments. To begin with, no suitable candidate as governor was found but after writing to the Pope for permission, Perth was called to Saint-Germain and in July 1696 appointed governor. He promptly received his own copy of the governor's instructions. This twenty-eight point manifesto set out how to bring up the royal boy, including point fourteen which states: 'none must be permitted to whisper or run into corners with the Prince' and other rules about the correct behaviour of his friends, guests and daily routines. Perth noticed that the prince turned from a spirited into a somewhat sullen boy and contrasted the natural 'affability' of his younger sister. Prohibition implemented by an authoritarian Catholic convert, the ideal governor in James's eyes, did not make for a happy childhood. But this fatherly control was no more than we would expect from the king who bombarded his parliamentary commissioner with instructions in 1685, and the same year produced directives for his servants of the bedchamber – precedence, supervisory duties, dispute resolution and who should carry a candle before him were all meticulously itemised. This fastidiousness is also found in one of James's last acts of paternal advice. In 1700, in signs of weakening health, James thought to give his son the benefit of his many years of military experience. He wrote out in twelve folios a series of 'Rules for General Officers', directing his son about how officers of foot or horse and a general of forces should conduct themselves. Details are indicated on drill periods, scouting out the enemy, the best location of camps and the best times for troops to rise and to retire, and such wisdom as 'If the Ground will permitt one Camps in Order of Battle . . . to be covered from any Sudden attempt of an ennemy'. The only surprise is that it took him until 1700 to compose such a document, though it is brief and apparently incomplete. It may have been prompted by James's last appearance at a military review in April 1700. On James's death, Berwick would be left to continue his half brother's military education.[49]

There was one aspect in James's life which, more than any other, defined his obsession with routine; his devotions. His unmistakable commitment to the Roman Catholic faith as repeatedly expressed since the 1670s should never be forgotten. James's confessor for most of his years at Saint-Germain, since 1692, was Father Francis Saunders, an English Jesuit who provided a constant reminder of the perilous condition of the human soul. However, James's whole outlook on his faith altered when in November 1690 he met Armand-Jean de Rancé, abbé of the Cistercian monastery of La Trappe in Normandy. He was introduced to La Trappe and Rancé by the French commander Marshal Bernardin Gigault de Bellefonds and was quickly impressed by the simple declarations of faith and the warmth of the welcome offered to him. There he was consoled with the notion that his fall had been a wonderful sacrifice to his faith. James made annual pilgrimage each summer to La Trappe and to de Rancé, who was until his death in October 1700 James's chief confessor through correspondence and private meetings. Bellefonds had made pilgrimages to La Trappe since the early 1670s and could commend the abbey convincingly as a soldier of reputation and honour. This gave James supporting motivation to embrace this new part of his religious life. Nevertheless, Louis and even Father Saunders became worried over James's close association with La Trappe as it bred in him a fatalism and reconciliation with death, as witnessed in his devotional writings and his 'Advice to his Son', that did not sit well with a king who needed by aggressive means to win back his kingdoms. It was, of course, de Rancé and the monastery of La Trappe which brought to Catholic Europe the strict observance of the Trappist monk and the many thousands of pilgrims that gathered there to admire such piety. Mary, meanwhile, was patron of the Convent of Chaillot near Paris, the Convent of the Visitation which James's mother Henrietta Maria founded in the 1650s. Mary visited the nuns several times each year.[50] Therefore, James and Mary built up independent institutional support for their faith and, of course, Mary's personal confessors were her Italian priests, some of whom had come with her from London.

The religious life in and around Saint-Germain embraced James and his family. Not only did they worship at the parish church but also their approbation was sought for clerical appointments. After Abbé Benoit had been appointed to the cure of Saint-Germain in May 1698 he was presented to James by the archbishop of Paris. James also took particular interest in the annual meetings of the Assembly of the French Clergy. These were convened in a hall in the nearby Château Neuf, a separate, smaller and less monumental palace complex, east of the Château Vieux and equidistant between it and the River Seine, backed onto a ridged 800 metre drop to the river basin below. James discussed faith with the assembled bishops each year and in June 1700, during the assembly, he and Mary gave audience to the bishops of Montauban and Troyes who 'harangued [them] in the name of the assemblie'.[51] Since 1697 and a treaty that ended James's personal hopes, his reputation as a devoted Catholic had become widely recognised by both ordered and secular clergy. As he grew frail and talked increasingly of welcoming death, he inspired an admiring group of local and national clergy who came into contact with him, as well as those of the French court susceptible to such spiritualism, like Madame de Maintenon. Through her, even King Louis became entranced by it all.

Yet another aspect of James's religious assimilation was his regular contact with the Scots College in Paris. His under-secretary Nairne was an intimate of Lewis Innes, principal of the college from 1692 to 1713, who James had also befriended in the 1680s when Innes passed though London to and from the Catholic mission in Scotland. From James's return from Ireland, Innes became a close advisor as well as occasional court secretary and almoner to Mary, distributing her alms to the poor. From 1695 James made more frequent visits to the college, sometimes staying for several days, taking great interest in news of the Scottish mission, and the extensive historical archive and scholarly exploits of Lewis and his brother Thomas. Indeed, in 1698/9 James gifted 1,000 livres to support the needs of the college. There was, though, a further reason for the endowment. James instructed Nairne and Caryll to begin copying out his 'memoirs' based on his own original papers and correspondence, which they commenced in January 1699. He had gone to great lengths to preserve these papers, not only infamously at the sinking of *The Gloucester,* but also at the Revolution, having them spirited from London to Saint-Germain with Francesco Terriesi, envoy of the Grand Duke of Tuscany. Before James's death, the 'memoirs' had been completed to the year 1677, and in March and August 1701, various tomes were deposited by Nairne with the Scots College for safe keeping, and other volumes, making in total ten of memoirs and four of letters, were assembled after James's death. Starting in 1707, William Dicconson, a clerk at Saint-Germain, spliced all this material together to create the 'Life' we know today.[52] With the archival expertise of the Scots College we can see why James would wish to deposit his papers in their safe hands to secure them for posterity. Fortunately copies were taken of Dicconson's text before the archives were destroyed in 1793 at the French Revolution.

James was, however, more obviously a man of action than a scholar and one of James's enduring pleasures was hunting. A frustrated man in Scotland for the modesty of such sport, in the forests of Saint-Germain or Fontainebleau the possibilities were boundless. Deer, foxes, wolves and even bears could be hunted, along with the shooting of numerous types of fowl. Most of these activities involved pursuit on horseback and James was a very fine horseman. Indeed, one of the reasons for Turenne's favour for the young duke in the 1650s was his ability to ride swiftly and not a little fearlessly under fire. At Saint-Germain James hunted regularly, sometimes on days when Mary was at Chaillot but essentially, when it took his fancy. Louis knew his man and provided a Master of the Hunt and replacements for all the dogs and horses that James was unable to ship over from England. If Nairne's journal is to be believed, James last went hunting in August 1700, almost sixty-seven years old, though his last burst of activity was in the late summer of 1699, and at the end of that same year he was so incapacitated that he had to be carried to the dining table on a chair. James was renowned for bounding from his horse and despatching the helpless creature with his own blade, yet it is doubtful that he could still maintain this level of athletic aggression from the mid 1690s. He was, though, remarkably fit. We might question those historians who marvel at his fitness in old age while contrasting the mental deterioration from the Revolution, but there is no doubt that his physical energy was always superior to his mental agility. The hinge of 1688 must, though, be challenged as a medical watershed. As one modern historian has put it, 'it was not as a psychologically sick man, limping towards syphilis-filled degeneration and a premature state of senility that James arrived in France'. There is no evidence for syphilis, and James's weaknesses were psychological, not medical. As for his private life of mistresses, other than the two Irish women who, when in Dublin, satisfied his rather aggressive taste for sexual activity and briefly scandalised Paris, he abandoned such liaisons when he returned to St German; more correctly, they abandoned him.[53]

Remarkably, James had no serious illness in his life, other than an attack of smallpox in 1667, the disease that would afflict both of his children in 1712, leading to Louisa-Maria's death but, fortunately for Jacobitism, his son's recovery. Therefore, although aging and increasingly gaunt – and in January 1699 he had Nairne complete his will afresh on vellum on the same month that the copying of his memoirs began – it surprised everyone when on 21 February/4 March 1701 (NS), while hearing mass at the Chapel Royal of Saint-Germain, he suddenly bled from his nose and had 'a fainting fit'. After being carried to bed he seemed to recover and was able to walk, but a week later collapsed with a stroke and was paralysed down one side of his body. Louis sent his doctors to assist and James was subjected to hot irons and 'blistering plasters' to a paralysed arm and leg. By the end of the month he had recovered enough to travel and, under advice of these doctors and his own physician Sir William Waldegrave, James and Mary took coach to the waters of Bourbon, a spa south of Paris and Orleans renowned for the healing properties of its water. Before he left, James had a private meeting with Nairne and passed to him 'his memoirs to his son' for the secretary to copy out: 'he would trust them to no other body, there being secret advices in them of great concern'. This was an unexpurgated version of the 'Advice to his Son' with all the worldly advice on mistresses and the dangers of sin. Yet when James returned in late May he was much better and could walk freely, even though he had another fainting fit a month later. In fact, his last illness began on 22 August/2 September (NS) when, again taking mass in the Chapel Royal, he had a second stroke and began to vomit blood, probably the result of stomach ulcers. Taken to his bed, he knew he was dying and was administered the sacraments by Father Saunders. His health then improved and then worsened in waves for the next two weeks, sometimes fevered and then becalmed. Nairne reprepared his will and it was read out to James by Middleton, who signed on James's behalf before witnesses, including Perth and Nairne. The Duke of Berwick had rushed from Flanders to be at his father's side and Louis and the Dauphin also attended. The scene as they assembled on 2/13 September (NS) captured a mixture of emotions. James, after taking the sacrament for the second time:

charmed wth his sensibility & devotion [said] – I forgive the Prince of Orange, the Princess of Denmark and all that have wronged me, & remember F Sanders (said he) that I forgive the Emperor also. In the afternoon the K of France came & told him, if it please God to dispose of him, he would own the Prince of Wales K of England which gave great satisfaction to the K & comfort to the Q & to all their subjects and servants who weapd for joy & grief mingled together.

Louis wept for a fellow king and royal 'brother' as he declared he would recognise the Prince of Wales as James VIII and III. And so the following day, the prince and Mary were brought to James for the last time, and the young boy was told the wonderful news about his succession and a debt owed to the king of France. Then at three o'clock in the afternoon on 5/16 September (NS), after losing speech but kissing a crucifix whenever it was offered, James slipped away having 'rendered his last breath with a sort of smile'. Perth then went to the next room and presented the new King James.[54]

Conclusion: For God, the King and St Andrew

After James's death he was subjected to processes of dissection and presentational rebirth. The biographer seeks to do no less. Twenty-four hours after his death his body was opened and embalmed and his internal organs removed and distributed around the religious houses of Paris. For keepsakes and, as we shall see, vehicles through which to seek the intercession of a pious prince, lengths of linen were dipped in his blood, cuttings were taken of his hair along with the flesh from his right arm. His heart was placed in a silver-gilt locket and given to the nuns of Chaillott; his brain in a lead casket to the Scots College in Paris (in the Rue des Fosses Saint Victor, now the Rue du Cardinal Lemoine); his entrails placed in two gilt urns and split between the parish church of Saint-Germain (see Plates 16–18) and the English Jesuit College of St Omer in Calais, and the flesh from his arm to the English Augustinian nuns of Paris. Remarkably, many of these 'mementos' still survive and can be found in various colleges and stately homes throughout England. The ritual scission complete, James's embalmed body was carried in a procession of three coaches and '40 gards with flambeaux' to the English Benedictines at St Edmonds Priory in the Rue St Jacques, Paris. There in the chapel, having first had a death mask made, the monks placed the body in a triple coffin, and raised it above ground on a high, black and covered tomb, a temporary resting place. James's request was that his body be buried humbly at the church of St Germain but King Louis thought differently and the embalming and temporary location was to make James ready for his eventual burial at Westminster Abbey. During this elaborate process, Mary went to seek comfort from the nuns of Chaillot.[1]

James's faithful secretary David Nairne describes writing to many with the news of the king's 'good death and his exemplary piety', and from this day, the cult of King James was born. His shrine became a place of pilgrimage for his servants and family, for Jacobite followers, but also for French worshippers in general. Within three years this cult had spread, encouraged by the nuns of Chaillot, the English Benedictines and Mary herself, on the basis of both reputed cures and the tone taken in the writing of several histories of James's final years. Of the latter, with the help of Father Saunders, two brief histories of James's life appeared in 1701/2 and were printed in London, and work begun under Joseph Johnston, Prior of the English Benedictines, to compile with Benet Weldon a 'History of England's late most Holy and most glorious Royal Confessor & Defender of the true Faith, King James II, most evidently shewing mortals that in vaine some wretches have delivered, *Quod sit utilitas in scelere* (the benefit of crime)', the usurpation of James's kingdoms being in vain compared to the kingdom of God. In addition, the Jacobite taste for artefactual reassurance was animated by printed versions of James's final words, including for example, the text printed on silk for Elizabeth, duchess of Gordon, who had taken to a convent in Flanders in 1697 to escape her adulterous husband, the castellan duke (see Plate 19). Appropriately, another printing released by the propagandists of Saint-Germain was an expurgated version of James's 'Advice to his Son'. This appeared in London in 1703 under the title *The Late King James, His Advice to His Son*, but with references to James's immorality and mistresses struck out, which, of course, were awkward revelations for an aspiring saint. The original 'Advice' was private and circulated only in manuscript, but in this edited text, a king's need to prosecute war 'with the help of his parliament' was replaced with 'the assistance of the people', and all mentions of the Parliament of Scotland and the promotion of Catholicism were removed. This 'English edition' appealed to Anglican Jacobite sensibilities and the prospects of the succession of James VIII and III.[2]

The other and most astonishing driving force behind of the cult of King James was the many miracles associated with his interventions, mostly after the application of the detritus of his body parts, such as blooded linen, or desperate prayers at his shrine. Mary wrote to Rome supporting the case for her late husband's beatification and canonisation. Johnston was given the role of 'Pronotary apostolic' to verify and collate testimony for the miracles attributed to James and the details of over forty cases have survived. Craftsmen, artisans, officials, aristocrats, nuns and priests were all cured, it was believed, by James's intercession over various maladies, most commonly paralysis, fevers, blindness, facial growths and psychological illness, such as suicidal tendencies. Normally the sufferer or his or her close relatives would visit the tomb and offer up a novena of prayers, a nine-day vigil in the hope of obtaining special intercessory graces from the 'St. Roy d'Angleterre'. The case in October 1701 of one Gilbert Marest, young brother of the vicar of the town of Saint Pourcain, is typical. Marest was suffering from a 'lethargic apoplexy' where his limbs went cold, paralysed and during which he suffered convulsions, which went on for six weeks. His surgeon Lucron tried many treatments including bleeding and the waters of the spa at Nery, but to no avail. His two legs began to atrophy, until one day the young man came to the surgeon on his own two feet, thanking him for his services. Lucron was surprised and told Marest that such a sudden cure could only be a miracle. At this, Marest told the surgeon that he had been cured by the intercession of King James:

that as soon as he had made the wish to go on foot to his tomb if it pleased God to cure him by his intercession, that he immediately felt relief in his head and his stomach, which had caused him considerable suffering, and that now he walks without difficulty and almost as he did before his illness.

In another case a woman's breast cancer was cured 'not caused by [doctor's] remedy but by a higher power', yet this proved no help to Queen Mary herself who had operations for breast cancer in 1703 and 1705 and finally died in 1718 from complications associated with her condition. In the end her campaign was unsuccessful in persuading Rome of James's case for beatification, and her son and the then bishop of Paris got no further when a fresh attempt was begun in the 1730s. It is tempting to picture Charles II laughing at these antics visited on his brother's memory, although we should remember that Charles was very keen on the tradition of touching for the King's evil. To some Jacobites, this was one power wielded only by a divinely ordained *de jure* monarch.[3]

James's own religious beliefs may not justify the sainthood his wife and followers wished to bestow upon him, though he was undoubtedly sincere. His conversion in the late 1660s was real and wholehearted. Given his psychological need for routine and order in his life, the certainties he perceived in the Catholic faith and papal continuity over centuries, unjustly and diabolically broken at the Reformation, had enormous appeal: Luther and Calvin 'cut the banks of infallibility and let in those waters which at last drowne', he wrote. His emphasis on the evidence of his first wife's conversion and the embracing of Rome by his brother at his deathbed was regularly cited by him, not only to justify the general mission to others but to confirm his decision was 'correct'. His devotional writings, surviving from 1694, confirm his straightforward rationalisation of the events of his life in relation to his faith. In the Civil War of the 1640s and 1650s 't'was devine providence that drove [him] early out of [his] native country [to pass] most of twelve years . . . in Catholike Kingdomes' so he could experience their faith at first hand. This fatalism extended to everything he did in public and private life once king, a characteristic that could be awkward for ministers and generals in the conduct of state affairs. The same God that saved him from smallpox, horses shot from under his body and cannon fire on sea and land, also made him succeed his brother and at the eleventh hour provided, miraculously, a son and heir. Conversely, when so many turned against him in 1688 it was God's judgement on a sinful life. That 'perpetual course of sin' is the constant theme in his 'Advice to his Son' and his devotional papers. His son must reject 'pride and ambition', 'the sins of Lucifer', take drink in moderation, forsake anger as it damages judgement, and put no trust in 'riches and honours'. Yet the most perilous danger, especially to princes, is 'forbidden love', for which he 'paid dear'. All those years of debauchery in London which Charles took to be good clean fun, James came to believe put his very soul in danger. Converts and potential converts, the intended audience of his devotional writings, must also respond to his obsession with sin, and especially those of the flesh whose 'voluptuous pleasures never satisfy', but also that idleness, theatre, operas, reading romances (though 'History is usefull') merely encourage 'foolish thoughts' when people elsewhere are sick or dying. As for himself, he attests that his conversion to Rome in effect saved him and he can thank God for losing his kingdoms, a righteous punishment that brings him nearer to God's grace.[4] With this attitude, manifested or solicited by his contact with the monks of La Trappe, we can perhaps understand why the French clergy considered him a martyr to his faith. Equally, this predilection made it more difficult for James to show the necessary drive to hold and then to retake his kingdoms. Private religion was one thing, and certainly of political significance in the person of the monarch, but public religion was the great untouchable in England and, in spite of confessional disunity, also in Scotland.

James's personal faith was oddly and inadvertently controversial to those who cared to scrutinise. Contemporary Protestant critics believed he had been manipulated by Jesuits at court in London, particularly just before the Revolution. However, his closeness to Armand-Jean de Rancé and La Trappe's views of original sin, predestination, the necessity of divine grace and the denial of free will, left James associating with Jansenism; that is the beliefs of those who endorsed the ideas of Cornelius Jansen, the Dutch theologian of the early seventeenth century. Jesuits condemned Jansenism as heresy, linking it to Protestantism, and its tenets would, in fact, be forbidden by a papal bull issued by Pope Clement XI in 1713. James, though, never commented on the controversy in any of his writings. On the one hand he took a Bourbon view of a monarch's relations to the papacy where he considered he had much autonomy over appointments to cures and diocesan vacancies as demonstrated by Louis XIV. Also, if a Jesuit, as in the case of Father Petre, seemed the best candidate for a particular position, then James expected his recommendation to be respected by the Vatican. He seemed blind to the fact that Jesuits were not employed as secular clergy. This strange cocktail of approaches and confusions confirms that while James was a devoted Catholic, he had a pick-and-mix engagement with the institutions of Catholicism, reflective of a 'head of the church', like the king of England. Politically, James was never completely convinced that kings were answerable to popes.

Macky's caricature of the exiled court depicts a humiliating environment for Protestants but is misleading. James welcomed the likes of Middleton and other Protestant servants, offering protection as reward for loyalty and service. Louis was sometimes unhappy with this, although his ministers understood the need to reach out to Protestants in England and Scotland, and to build on the 'compounder' agenda.[5] Generally, James's view of toleration depended on circumstances. Quakers were tolerated, and James offered amnesty to the Aberdeen Quakers led by Robert Barclay and George Keith. Associated with William Penn, a close friend of James, their nonconformity could be accepted based on their philosophy of non-violence.

They were no challenge, other than a moral one, to royal authority. Presbyterians were another matter. No more or less than Charles II, for practical reasons, James had to take Presbyterian allies in England and Scotland when circumstances dictated. Charles's taking of the National Covenant in 1650 was more hypocritical. At a personal level, James found he could come to terms with Presbyterians who were most obviously loyalist in their sympathies, such as Skelmorlie or Stewart of Goodtress. Nevertheless, James and Charles maintained a profound hatred of political Presbyterianism, as it advocated resistance to Crown authority and brought with it a system of church government that denied Crown control in church matters. These were republicans by another name. The memories of the 1640s and 1650s ran deep and the manner of James's life confirms he never understood the dynastic royalism of the majority of Presbyterians. The proclaiming of Charles II as king of Scots after the execution of his father was an obvious indication of such beliefs. That alone might have promoted an alternative outcome to Scotland's Restoration crisis as it developed from 1660. But James's reliance on Anglicans and Scottish Episcopalians was logical, mobilising Tory and cavalier interests that favoured order and the repression of nonconformity, as Charles had done before him. James's alienation of Scottish and English bishops in 1686 and 1688 respectively was therefore a grave political error, and one Charles would not have made. Scottish Episcopalians proved too weakly rooted in Scottish soil to withstand a major political crisis or revolutionary storm. That storm, we are used to being told, came when a king decided to impose Catholicism on his people. Toleration was just a feint to achieve the objective of the Catholic mission. The problem is that James's belief that those exposed to Catholicism would eventually, like him, gravitate to the Church of Rome, proves that catholicising was not seen as an aggressive act by James. In these terms, granting toleration for Catholics was a logical extension of a wider freedom of worship as long as his own authority and royal prerogative were maintained. Therefore, although James may have lost his throne on account of his faith, he also weakened his hold on power from a genuine belief in a wide but authoritarian religious toleration. In Scotland, meanwhile, popular and urban attitudes to popery made prospects for the mission bleak indeed, even if we set aside the rabid sectarianism of Society People in the south west. If James had been more successful in catholicising England there would have been yet another excuse for an Anglo-Scottish war with Dutch involvement. Meanwhile, catholicising in Scotland made minimal progress before the Revolution. In short, his religious policy was impractical in a Scottish context.

James's military experience and phobia for disloyalty had him govern his kingdoms in a defined manner. This was a high Anglican and Tory philosophical approach where the royal prerogative had to be preserved from any encroachments by interest groups, be they mercantile, ecclesiastic or parliamentary. However, James was concerned with a little more than retrenchment or the *status quo*. He wished to build on his position, a progressive absolutism, looking by stages to advance and extend the royal prerogative into areas where religious policies could be advanced and political loyalty enhanced. This is the reason why, with Melfort's encouragement, he happily adopted royal proclamations to grant toleration in England and Scotland. His lack of concern that his parliaments failed to deliver legislative toleration, even in Scotland where mistakenly he had higher hopes, comes from his appreciation that he could make a virtue of political failure. So those granted liberty of conscience would owe their new status to their king who, of course, if necessary could withdraw that right. This was revolutionary in two ways. Firstly, it underscored that James wished to summon parliaments as infrequently as practicable, and secondly, it signalled a diminishing significance of ancient legal safeguards enshrined in the parliamentary cultures of England and Scotland. In the Scottish model, regardless of legislation in 1669, 1681 and 1685, no profound changes in established religious policy were acceptable without recourse to the Estates of the Scottish Parliament. This was seen graphically in the political reaction to the imposition by proclamation of the Prayer Book into Scotland in 1637. In this respect James failed to learn from his father. Miller's argument that James 'did not set out to undermine the English constitution' does not absolve him from being a monarchical opportunist.[6] In addition, the difference between James's interference in England and Scotland in local government and the outcome of future elections was but a matter of scale, not intent. Moreover, he believed that a successful Scottish Parliament could be called, imminently in late 1688 in fact, as it was the burghs that were the only stronghold of resistance to his plans, or so he thought. Those he had appointed as provosts or deacons may not have been Catholics yet they were, like Claverhouse, deeply committed to supporting their master.

English Whigs, some disaffected Tories and similarly aggrieved Scottish cavaliers could therefore argue that James was a constitutional absolutist in England and Scotland, and perhaps a religious absolutist in England, but what of the question of law and order and the policing of dissent? As far as more radical Scottish nonconformity was concerned, there was continuity from the previous reign as Claverhouse and his troopers delivered severe justice to the Covenanting shires. This gave the impression, or provided pamphlet headlines at least, of unbridled military activity which alarmed Whigs in England and some of the exiled Anglo-Scottish community in The Netherlands. But the scale was small, even though the suffering was real enough. It recalled imaginary fears in the 1670s that Lauderdale would descend on England with an army of 20,000 Scots. When in Scotland, James was not unusually vicious in demanding summary justice and was no more vengeful than other princes of the age. Also, he had made almost no progress in Scotland over expanding the standing army from the few thousand which had existed since the 1660s. There was no Hounslow Heath in the northern kingdom. As we have seen, when resident in Scotland he attempted to reform the militia but the project stalled due to the familiar shortage of funds, even to meet the cost of foot soldiers wearing red coats. There were, as ever, more Scottish soldiers serving abroad than at home, some of whom, of course, came over with Mackay at the Revolution. The standing army issue had limited impact as a political grievance in Scotland although individuals, such as Queensberry and Sir John Dalrymple, were concerned at the behaviour of such troops in their localities. There were, of course, those hoping to benefit financially from James's militia plans and any officer commissions that could arise.

Foremost, James was a soldier and, as king, commander-in-chief. His personal bravery in the field or at sea is not in doubt. What he feared, both in 1688 and 1690, was not death but capture; capture in the way of his father Charles I, a lingering wait in the Tower of London followed by a slow walk to the cold embrace of the executioner's axe. As he said in his last words to Lord Ailesbury before he set out for France: 'if I do not retire I shall certainly be sent to the Tower and no king ever went out of that place but to his grave'.[7] The idea, out of Whig machismo, that it was a king's duty to face death, is not a very common thought in the minds of the crown heads of early modern Europe. Louis XIV, after all, never plunged himself into personal danger and never 'played' the brave young soldier as did James, duke of Albany and York.

James engendered fierce loyalty from some of his servants and this must surely testify to his loyalty to them. His own behaviour during his brother's reign shows studied loyalty and he expected the same in return when he took the throne. However, a politician is only as effective as his staff. In England the exclusion of Anglicans like Rochester and Clarendon narrowed and badly weakened James's administration, as was the case in Scotland when Queensberry was sidelined. In Ireland the adoption of Tyrconnell as viceroy was popular there, though not in London. In Scotland, however, it is William Douglas, third duke of Hamilton, who is of most interest. Although apparently rehabilitated and placed on the Privy Council and the secret committee, James was unable to daunt this man in the way of Argyll. James knew that if the duke could be convinced of his policies then he would bring many waverers with him, but it was not to be. Hamilton's necessary evasiveness over the Test Act and his covert contacts with exiles, suggest that Duchess Anne might be a better judge of his political skill than posterity has been. After his death she wrote:' everything I see is marks of his industry. I fear his son will not leave such behind him' and the fourth duke, who opposed the union of 1707, was no match for his father. Hamilton was the great prize that eluded James.

During the crisis at the end of 1688, the narrowing of James's administration was perceived by outsiders and commented upon by ambassadors. Middleton seemed the only servant offering sound advice. His arrival at Saint-Germain greatly improved administration as well as relations with French ministers. However, James's dogged refusal to dismiss Melfort was such a spectacular political error that poor judgement and misplaced loyalty are the only explanations. Even if Melfort proved to be a competent secretary, he had so alienated the English, Scottish, Irish and French political communities that he had to go. Equally, that he was the only candidate to become secretary in exile confirms that the government in London had become too narrow, and that many others, like Sunderland, were taking their chances elsewhere. Melfort is one of those historical characters who challenge one to find redeeming features, in spite of exercising analytical self-control. He was a fine connoisseur of art.

The appearance of a 'secret committee' in the Scottish Privy Council can also be seen as reflecting James's style of government. Charles put his affairs into fewer and fewer hands, especially after he defeated the exclusionists in England, but never to the extent of enforcing a 'political coup' and dismissing large numbers of councillors who did not bend to Crown policy. With Charles change was gradually achieved and, even when John, earl of Middleton, was dismissed, many of his supporters lingered and remained involved. James's more unforgiving response to hesitant acquiescence is an example of a vengeful side to his nature learnt from his father and, if it was Perth and Melfort and not he who sought these changes, he was guilty of facilitating the culling of council members. Charles, under James's direction, selected the secret committee in November 1684 and, by doing so, removed the right of the Edinburgh Council to form its own central grouping. This was to destabilise the Council as seen when the final crisis broke in late 1688. James would have been better to continue with his broad-church 'mongrel party' which he 'adopted' in 1679.

Using contemporary evidence to assess James's approach to kingship throws up puzzling contradictions. One of our better sources is the French envoy d'Avaux who travelled with James to Ireland. In Dublin James was trapped by the conflicting policy demands of a king of England and Scotland and a king of Ireland. As James struggled under this dilemma a frustrated d'Avaux charged him incapable of decisive leadership: 'he believes that he does not govern if he does not meddle in everything but he meddles in matters only to spoil them', and as he listens to everyone d'Avaux had to 'spend as much time destroying the impressions left on him by bad advice as instilling good'. Yet by the estimation of Sir James Hay of Linplum, writing to his cousin John Hay, earl of Tweeddale, in the heady Jacobite summer of 1688: 'in truth the King is not governed by any body'.[8] James's private demeanour in controlling his household, before or after exile, and his manner of engaging with public duties, such as the navy office in London when Lord High Admiral, shows him a man obsessed with detail who was blind to the bigger picture. He believed that if minutia were well deployed then strategic outcomes would be achieved. If he expressed his preference, he was too easily comforted by those, like Petre or Melfort, who congratulated him on his reasoning and appeared to dare others to contradict the royal will. This was often an adequate or relatively harmless set of characteristics for an officer under the Vicomte de Turenne or as a royal duke under a fraternal king, but not best suited to a head of state or commander-in-chief.

James was essentially a medieval king, not a Catholic moderniser. He was not a clone of Louis XIV who sought to create an extensive Catholic and revolutionary bureaucracy but a traditionalist. His hope was to re-catholicise England and Scotland in a new counter-reformation using the authority he felt he already possessed, sustained as it was by English jurist argument and the royalist interpretations of Scots law, as seen in Mackenzie of Rosehaugh's *Jus Regium* and *Vindication*. It was a mission set in conservative Tudor and Stuart foundations. Kings holding sway over parliaments and also over churches was the familiar ground trod by James VI and I and also by Catholic monarchs like James V of Scotland and Mary I of England. In two respects, however, James admired the French way. Firstly, he wished to be spared papal domestic interference other than over spiritual guidance, although the monarchs of the Empire and Spain felt no differently. Secondly, he favoured a large standing army if it could be afforded, yet he was from middle age a defensive military man. Such a force was not a vehicle for oppression but for stability, security and order. In a telling, even 'liberal', extract from his 'Advice to his Son', he confirms his approach to law and order. England's *habeas corpus* legislation of 1679 was a misfortune to the people as well as the Crown, 'since it obliges the crown to keep a greater force on foot than it needed otherwise to preserve the government'. The act therefore encouraged dissent and then oppression, although, as we have seen, no such act formally appeared in Scotland until 1701. James seemed to wish to be a liberal although his drive for Catholic emancipation in the teeth of opposition made this less and less credible. Thus is was that the clash between these philosophical beliefs, as rendered in the mind of a Catholic king, and English and Scottish political communities with a 'reflexive distrust of popery', doomed James's religious policies. To these distrusting Protestants the enemy was not so much a new absolutism – for after 1681 what was Charles II if not an absolutist – but the threat of Catholic absolutism.[9]

This study has sought to explore James as duke and king of Scots, but how Scots was this Stewart prince and how engaged was he in the affairs of Scotland?[10] David Nairne reports in his journal that early one morning in April 1697 James sat with him and 'spoke of several places in Scotland', reminiscing of his two years in his northern kingdom, the circumstances of his Scottish exile quite forgotten. There is no doubt that he felt a closer affinity with Scotland than Ireland. There is, of course, much evidence of his pride as an Englishman, in what was an instinctive nationalism. When fighting for Spain and the Prince de Condé in the 1650s, he marvelled at the bravery of Cromwell's English forces, suggesting it was their very nationality that prepared them for the rigours and order of warfare, and we have already noted his admiration for English seamanship at La Hogue. Also, when in Scotland he occasionally let slip a 'that is not how we do things in England' comment. Nevertheless, he was acutely aware that his hereditary legitimacy depended on the ancient Stewart line. This was a divinely ordained line of succession. In his 'Advice' he states that Henry VIII used 'unchristian ways' to annul his marriages and place the succession away from Mary, Queen of Scots, but God judged these proceedings and gave his daughters no children and so delivered the crown 'back' to James VI, Mary's son. This dynastic purity was expressed in other ways. One of the symbolic centrepieces of the 'gallery' that was Saint-Germain was Nicolas de Largillière's 1692 rococo portrait of St Margaret, the medieval queen of Scotland (see Plate 13). What better way to emphasise the divinity of his right to rule and closeness to God than Margaret, both as a prince and a royal saint. James could also show some latent antiquarianism when it came to things Scottish as seen in his dealings with the secular priests at the Scots College in Paris (see Plate 15). In 1692 Thomas Innes began cataloguing the charters of the college archive and in 1694 he discovered in the nearby Carthusian priory a charter of Robert II. In this is confirmed the king's founding of a chaplaincy at Glasgow in exchange for a dispensation from consanguinity and affinity for his marriage to Elizabeth Mure, thus confirming the legitimacy of Robert III's succession and the Stewart line thereafter. Thomas's brother Lewis showed the charter to King James and there was much excitement but also caution. In May a committee of scholars and lawyers, witnessed by twenty or so Scottish nobles at court, proceeded to establish the authenticity of the document. A sceptical Montgomery of Skelmorlie, who was present, was duly impressed. Moreover, in May 1696 a copy of the 1326 Treaty of Corbeil between Robert I of Scotland and Charles IV of France, a restatement of the Auld Alliance first entered into in 1295, was made from the original, held in the Colbertine Library in Paris, and lodged with the Scots College. The reaffirmation of the 'ancient alliance' with France was yet another apt symbolic gesture to James's host and to his Scottish ancestors.[11] Small wonder, with these activities, that James endowed the college. He also promised in May 1697 a further 100 pounds sterling 'after his majesties restoration' and in this promise commended the work on the Robert II charter. To James, of course, all of this underpinned the loyalty of the Scottish cavaliers, the 'antient loyal familys that have had no taint of presbytery or accustum'd to Rebell . . . being a great support to [monarchy]'. This was entirely logical and more than Henry V's sentimental 'I am a Welshman' in Shakespeare's unionist drama. As an anonymous 'Treatise of advice to a Catholic King of Great Britain' put it: 'The Royal family is originally of [the Scots] nation; t'is therefore very natural to expect they should be more zealous and affectionat to the King's interest than any of his other subjects'.[12]

As a duke and king of Scots, James had more credibility than his father and brother. Not since James VI had a monarch been so willing to engage with Scottish affairs, be they economic, military, cultural or religious. Unlike Charles I and II, he established a significant party in his personal interest, yet by unwise distillation weakened it in the course of the 1680s. Even then, those remaining 'few' were enough to make Scotland the most credible vehicle for counter-revolution, as it would be for his son and grandson. Nevertheless, following the natural political priorities of James VI, the main orientation for James's policy had to be England. His reign in England started with much promise and he was after all the most mature English monarch to date to ascend to the throne, with many years of experience as the prominent subject during his brother's reign. Such a long apprenticeship should have equipped him well for the challenges ahead. As it was, his political failings in England delivered the outcome his brother once predicted; 'long[ing] impatiently for a crown [James] would lose it within three years', and so it proved.[13] In Ireland his reign was welcomed as a gift for Irish nationalists and their religion but, as was feared by the second Duke of Ormonde, the great duke's grandson, the three kingdoms might fly apart. Meanwhile, as a King of Scots James was the oldest to succeed since Robert III in 1390, not an especially promising comparison, yet his experiences between 1679 and 1682 should have found him able to handle the key imperative of Scottish politics – keeping the nobility loyal. In this sense James's failure in Scotland was his most dramatic reverse, one disguised by later Jacobitism. In the north enthusiastic expressions of loyalism in 1679–81 and 1685 gradually evaporated from late 1686. It was an extraordinary outcome for a Scottish prince of the blood and resembled the disharmony and division of the reigns of James III and James V. James's natural ancestor was the more martial James IV. Well might he and that renaissance prince have discussed military tactics and shared an obsession with heraldry and knightly valour. James was no more 'modern' that this fellow prince, other than as expressed in his military and economic objectives. James IV, however, was a victim of the Anglo-Scottish problem, just as the kings and queens of the Union of the Crowns were of the enigma that was the three kingdoms, and whatever can be said of our King James, he was not a solution to that conundrum. He failed there where others would struggle before and after.

Father Saunders, James's confessor who witnessed his master's death, wrote the following words in a short history of King James:

> That which seems to me most extraordinary and most to be admired in the conduct of Divine Providence towards him, is, that in the height of world prosperity his heart should be toucht, and that he should then take a resolution so contrary to his interest in this world of becoming a Roman Catholick

James's religious policies were incapable of a practical resolution in England and Scotland – his faith was the gravest setback – but he died contented and not in torment or disappointment. He was certainly profoundly disturbed at the nature of the Revolution, not foreseeing the extent of his predicament. 'God help me, even my children have forsaken me', he declared emotionally, and the sense of betrayal was so deep that in 1690 he sought some solace from the Duchess of Orleans, asking her if his daughter Mary had 'truly written to [her] that she was glad he had not lost his life in Ireland'. Over the remaining years of that life, resignation grew as the family betrayal merged with his acceptance of political failure and a building sense of religious fatalism. In his twilight years he became obsessed with explaining his fate, and religion was the answer. He was not a poor king, merely a sinful one. His journey from dashing young cavalry commander to pious prince in exile appears oddly incongruous given the many political and personal trials that we have explored along the way. That journey was much more of Scotland than previous studies have suggested – indeed, he was in many ways the last King of Scots. Let us leave it to his memoirs to provide one of the most pertinent epitaphs: Scotland '[gave] a king to England' in 1685. Some grew to wish it otherwise.[14]

Notes

Other than where indicated, all dates in this work are Old Style with New Year commencing on 1 January, not 25 March as was the English manner at the time.

ABBREVIATIONS

AUL	Aberdeen University Library
BL	British Library (Blair Letters in context of AUL, SCA, BL references)
Bod. Lib.	Bodleian Library
Burnet, *History*	Gilbert Burnet, *History of His Own Time, The Reign of Charles the Second*, 2 vols (Oxford, 1897)
CCSP	W.D. Macray, O. Ogle, W.H. Bliss, and F.J. Routledge (eds), *Calendar of Clarendon State Papers preserved in the Bodleian Library*, 4 vols (Oxford, 1872–1932)
Clarendon, *History*	W.H. Macray (ed.), Earl of Clarendon, *The History of the Rebellion and Civil Wars in England, Begun in the Year 1641*, 6 vols (Oxford, 1888)
CLC	S.W. Singer (ed.), *The Correspondence of Henry Hyde, Earl of Clarendon and His Brother Laurence Hyde, Earl of Rochester; with the Diary of Lord Clarendon from 1687 to 1690, Containing Minute Particulars of the Events Attending to the Revolution*, 2 vols (London, 1828)
CSPC	*Calendar of State Papers, Colonial Series, America and the West Indies*
CSPD	*Calendar of State Papers Domestic*
CSPV	*Calendar of State Papers Venetian*
Dalrymple, *Memoirs*	J. Dalrymple, *Memoirs of Great Britain and Ireland*, 2 vols (London, 1790)
EHR	*English Historical Review*
Fountainhall,	D. Laing (ed.), Sir John Lauder of Fountainhall, *Historical Notices of Scotish [sic] Affairs*, 2 vols (Edinburgh, 1848)
HMC	*Historical Manuscripts Commission*
Life	J.S. Clarke (ed.), *The Life of James the Second, King of England, Memoirs Collected out of the Writ of his own Hand, together with the King's Advice to his Son, and His Majesty's Will*, 2 vols (London, 1816) and available as an E-book through TannerRitchie Publishing (Burlington, 2004).

LP	Osmund Airy (ed.), *The Lauderdale Papers*, 3 vols (London, 1884–5)
Morrice	Dr Williams' Library, Roger Morrice Entring Books, 3 vols
NA	National Archives (formerly Public Records Office)
NLS	National Library of Scotland
NRAS	National Register of Archives (Scotland)
NRS	National Records of Scotland (formerly National Archives of Scotland)
NUL	Nottingham University Libary
ODNB	*Oxford Dictionary of National Biography*
RA	Royal Archives Windsor
RCGA	A.F. Mitchell and J. Christie (eds), *The Records of the Commissioners of the General Assemblies of the Church of Scotland . . . 1646 and 1647, 1648 and 1649, 1650, 1651 and 1652*, 3 vols (Scottish History Society, Edinburgh, 1892–1909)
RPCS	P.H. Brown et al. (eds) *The Register of the Privy Council of Scotland, 1661–1691*, third series, 16 vols (Edinburgh, 1908–1970)
RPS	K. Brown et al. (eds), *Records of the Parliaments of Scotland to 1707*, at http://rps.ac.uk/
SCA	Scottish Catholic Archive, University of Aberdeen (formerly Edinburgh)
SHR	*Scottish Historical Review*
SHS	Scottish History Society
SPCC	R. Scrope and T. Monkhouse (eds), *State Papers Collected by Edward Earl of Clarendon*, 3 vols (Oxford, 1767-86)
SR	A. Lauders et al. (eds), *Statutes of the Realm*, 12 vols (London, 1810–25)
ST	T.B. Howell (ed.), *State Trials*, 33 vols (London, 1810–26)
TRHS	*Transactions of the Royal Historical Society*
Wodrow, *Sufferings*	R. Burns (ed.), Robert Wodrow, *The History of the Sufferings of the Church of Scotland from the Restoration to the Revolution*, 4 vols (Glasgow, 1830)

Notes

INTRODUCTION

1   *Life*, ii, 585.

2   For the 'contested reputations' of historical characters see G. A. Fine, *Difficult Reputations: Collective Memories of the Evil, Inept and Controversial* (Chicago, 2001), 1–31.

3   Burnet, *History*; Gilbert Burnet, *Bishop Burnet's History of the Reign of King James the Second* (Oxford, 1852); G.M.Trevelyan, *The English Revolution* (London, 1936); Macaulay, *The History of England* (1848–61, Harmondsworth, 1979), 358–432, and helped by C.H. Firth's 'Macaulay's Treatment of Scottish History', *SHR*, 15 (1918), 273–91; Edmund Burke, *Reflections on the Revolution in France* (1790, Harmondsworth, 1968), 98–102; J. Lingard, *History of England* (London, 1855) and H. Belloc, *James The Second* (London, 1928). For a summary of Whig and Tory views of the revolution and James VII see J. Callow, *The Making of King James: The Formative Years of a Fallen King* (Stroud, 2000), 8–16.

4   S. Pincus, *1688: The First Modern Revolution* (Yale, 2009), 21–9; Wodrow, *Sufferings*; D. Hay Fleming, *Scottish History and Life,* 3 vols (Edinburgh, 1902); P.W.J. Riley, *King William and the Scottish Politicians* (Edinburgh, 1979).

5   F.C. Turner, *James II* (London, 1948), 456–9; M. Ashley, *James II* (London, 1977), 9–14; W.A. Speck, *Reluctant Revolutionaries* (Oxford, 1988), 119–20; Callow, *Making of King James*, 16–21.

6   J. Miller, *James II: A Study in Kingship* (1679, reissued 1989 and 2000); W.A. Speck's *James II: Profiles in Power* (London, 2002); E.E. Testa, *James II – Bigot or Saint?* (Lewis, 1987); M. Mullett, *James II and English Politics 1678–1688* (London, 1994); Callow, *Making of King James* and Callow, *King in Exile, James II: Warrior, King and Saint, 1689–1701* (Stroud, 2004).

7   J. Miller, *The Glorious Revolution* (London, 1997) and *Popery and Politics in England, 1660–1688* (Cambridge, 1973, reprinted 2008); P. Seaward, *The Restoration, 1669–1688* (Basingstoke, 1991); R. Hutton, *The Restoration: A Political and Religious History of England and Wales, 1658–1667* (Oxford, 1986, reprinted 2001); T. Harris, *Restoration, Charles II and his Kingdoms, 1660–1685* (London, 2005) and *Revolution, The Great Crisis of the British Monarchy, 1685–1720* (London, 2006); K. Sharpe *Rebuilding Rule 1660–1714: The Restoration and Revolution Monarchy* (London, 2013).

8 R. Hutton and S. Pincus (eds), *A Nation Transformed: England after the Restoration* (Cambridge, 2001, reprinted 2011); T. Harris and S. Taylor (eds), *The Final Crisis of the Stuart Monarchy: The Revolutions of 1688–91 in the British, American and European Context* (Woodbridge, 2013); L.K.J Glassey (ed.), *The Reigns of Charles II and James VII & II* (Basingstoke, 1997); C. A. Dennehy (ed.), *Restoration Ireland* (Farnham, 2008).

9 R. Hutton, *Charles II: King of England, Scotland and Ireland* (Oxford, 1989); A. Fraser, *King Charles II* (London, 1979, 1993, reprinted 2002); B. Lenman, *The Jacobite Risings in Britain 1689–1746* (London, 1980), 11–78; D. Szechi, *The Jacobites: Britain and Europe 1688–1788* (Manchester, 1994), 41–65. The best volume on the court in exile is E. Corp (ed.) (with contributions from E. Gregg, H. Erskine-Hill and G. Scott), *A Court in Exile: The Stuarts in France, 1689–1718* (Cambridge, 2004).

10 G. Donaldson, *James V–James VII* (Edinburgh, 1978); W. Ferguson, *Scotland 1689 to the Present* (Edinburgh, 1978) and *Scotland's Relations with England: A Survey to 1707* (Edinburgh, 1977 reprinted 1994), 142–79; K.M. Brown, *Kingdom or Province? Scotland and the Regal Union, 1603–1715* (Basingstoke, 1993); D. Stevenson, *The Scottish Revolution, 1637–44: The Triumph of the Covenanters* (Edinburgh, 1973 reprinted 2003) and *Revolution and Counter Revolution in Scotland, 1644–51* (Edinburgh, 1977 reprinted 2003); J.R. Young, *The Scottish Parliament 1639–1661: A Political and Constitutional Analysis* (Edinburgh, 1996); A.I. Macinnes, *Union and Empire: The Making of the United Kingdom in 1707* (Cambridge, 2007).

11 R.A. Lee, 'Government and Politics in Scotland, 1661–1681' (University of Glasgow, unpublished PhD thesis, 1995); D.J. Patrick, 'People and Parliament in Scotland 1689–1702' (University of St Andrews, unpublished PhD thesis, 2002); K.F. McAlister, 'James VII and the Conduct of Scottish Politics, c.1679–c.1686' (University of Strathclyde, unpublished PhD thesis, 2003). R.W. Lennox, 'Lauderdale and Scotland: A Study in Restoration Politics and Administration' (University of Columbia, PhD thesis, 1977) and K.M. Colquhoun, '"Issue of the late civill wars"': James, Duke of York and the Government of Scotland, 1679–1689' (University of Illinois at Urbana-Champaign, PhD thesis, 1993) provide some useful sources.

12 G.H. MacIntosh, *The Scottish Parliament under Charles II, 1660–1685* (Edinburgh, 2007); K.M. Brown and A.J. Mann (eds), *The History of the Scottish Parliament, volume 2: Parliament and Politics in Scotland, 1567–1707* (Edinburgh, 2005), including G.H. MacIntosh, 'Arise King John: Commissioner Lauderdale and Parliament in the Restoration Era', 163–83, A.J. Mann, '"James VII, King of the Articles": Political Management and Parliamentary Failure', 184–207 and D.J. Patrick, 'Unconventional Procedure: Scottish Electoral Politics after the Revolution', 208–44; A.J. Mann, 'James VII as Unionist and Nationalist: A Monarch's View of the Scottish Parliament Through his Writings' in *Parliaments Estates and Representation*, 33/2 (November 2013), 101–19; C. Jackson, *Restoration Scotland, 1660–1690: Royalist Politics, Religion and Ideas* (Woodbridge, 2003); A.D. Kennedy, *Governing Gaeldom: The Scottish Highlands and the Restoration State, 1660–1688* (Leiden, 2014).

CHAPTER I

1 C. Carlton, *Charles I: the Personal Monarchy* (London, 1995), 1–2.

2 J. Haig (ed.), *Sir James Balfour, The Historical Works of Sir James Balfour of Denmilne and Kinnaird*, 4 vols (Edinburgh, 1825), i, 409; M. Lynch, 'Court Ceremony and Ritual

during the Personal Reign of James VI' in J. Goodare and M. Lynch (eds), *The Reign of James VI* (East Linton, 2000), 91, fn. 5.

3   *CSPD, 1633–34*, 251; *CSPV, 1632–36*, 157; C. Oman, *Henrietta Maria* (London, 1951), 16 and 70.

4   M. Wood (ed.), *Extracts from the Records of the Burgh of Edinburgh, 1626 to 1641* (Edinburgh, 1927), 133.

5   *CSPD, 1633–34*, 297; *CSPV, 1632–36*, 165–6, 172.

6   BL Edgerton MSS, 2542; *Registrum Magni Sigilli Regum Scotorum: Register of the Great Seal of Scotland*, xi (1660–68), 11.

7   *CSPD, 1633–4*, 297; Callow, *Making of King James*, 31–2.

8   Ashley, *James II*, 17; *CSPV, 1632–36*, 159–61.

9   Callow, *Making of King James*, 32; Burnet, *James the Second*, 3.

10   Anon, *A Short View of the Life and Actions of the Most Illustrious James Duke of York* (London, 1660), 2–3; *CSPD, 1635*, 43, 70, 138; *CSPD, 1635–6*, 191; Turner, *James II*, 10.

11   Ashley, *James II*, 16–17.

12   Anon, *Some Historical Memoirs of the Life and Actions of His Royal Highness, the Renowned and most illustrious Prince, James Duke of York* (London, 1683), 10; Turner, *James II*, 13.

13   *Memoirs of Mademoiselle de Montpensier*, 3 vols (London, 1848), i, 123, 93; T. Lonqueville, *The Adventures of King James II of England* (London, 1904), 4; G. H. Selly (trans.), *The Memoirs of La Grande Mademoiselle* (New York, 1928), 69–78.

14   Burnet, *James the Second*, 3; Callow, *Making of James II*, 34; *CSPD, 1636–7*, 474; *1637*, 63; *1638–9*, 426 and 485; *1641–3*, 493.

15   A.I. Macinnes, *Charles I and the Making of the Covenanting Movement 1625–1641* (Edinburgh, 1991), 26–48; Brown, *Kingdom or Province*, 98–110; Ashley, *James II*, 16.

16   M. Lee Jr. 'Charles I and the End of Conciliar Government in Scotland' in *The 'Inevitable' Union and other Essays on Early Modern Scotland* (East Linton, 2003), 169–88; Brown, *Kingdom or Province*, 100–3; Macinnes, *Charles I*, 50–2.

17   Macinnes, *Charles I*, 82–6.

18   Macinnes, *Charles I*, 54–72; Brown, *Kingdom or Province*, 101.

19   A.I. Macinnes, *The British Revolution, 1629–1660* (Basingstoke, 2005), 86–93.

20   J.R. Young, 'Charles I and the 1633 Parliament' in Brown and Mann (eds), *Parliament and Politics in Scotland, 1567–1707* (Edinburgh, 2005), 103–14.

21   Young, '1633 Parliament', 114–37; Macinnes, *Charles I*, 135–41.

22   Macinnes, *Charles I*, 89–92.

23   Macinnes, *British Revolution*, 101–4.

24   Macinnes, *Charles I*, 45, 97, 144–49; A.J. Mann, *The Scottish Book Trade 1500 to 1720 : Print Commerce and Print Control in Early Modern Scotland* (East Linton, 2000), 39–40; Mann, 'The Anatomy of the Printed Book in Early Modern Scotland', *SHR*, 80 (2001), 192.

25   Macinnes, *Charles I*, 157–61; Brown, *Kingdom or Province*, 108–14.

26   J.J. Scally, 'The Rise and Fall of Covenanter Parliaments, 1639–51' in Brown and Mann (eds), *Parliament and Politics in Scotland, 1567–1707*, 142; Brown, *Kingdom or Province?*, 111–22.

27   C.V. Wedgewood, *The King's Peace 1637–1641* (London, 1983), 246–82, 328–61; Macinnes, *British Revolution*, 74–110; Stevenson, *The Scottish Revolution, 1637–44*, 127–61 and 183–233.

28   *CSPD 1641–3*, 308, 312; *1640*, 495; Clarendon, *History*, i, 482–5; C.H. Firth (ed.),

Edmond Ludlow, *Memoirs*, 2 vols (Oxford, 1894), i, 24–7; Hutton, *Charles II*, 4–6; Ashley, *James II*, 19; Wedgewood, *The King's Peace*, 340; C.V. Wedgewood, *The King's War 1641–1647* (London, 1983), 17–18.

29 Clarendon, *History*, ii, 45–50; *CSPD 1641–3*, 315–17; *Life*, i, 3–6 and ii, 649–53 (where the tone of vengeance is developed); J.R. Powell and E.K. Timings (eds), *Documents Relating to the Civil War, 1642–1648* (London, 1963), 2 and 10–11; John Spalding, *Memorialls of the Trubles in Scotland and in England, 1624–1645*, 2 vols (Spalding Club, Aberdeen, 1850–1), ii, 133; Callow, *Making of King James*, 36–8; Ashley, *James II*, 19–20.

30 *Life*, i, 6–10; Ashley, *James II*, 20; Callow, *Making of King James*, 38; S. Murdoch, 'James VI and the Formation of a Scottish-British Military Identity' in S. Murdoch and A. Mackillop (eds), *Fighting for Identity: Scottish military Experience c.1550–1900* (Leiden, 2002), 26–7. Rupert fled to England following the defeat of Frederick, the Elector Palatine, his father and Charles I's brother-in-law, who as king of Bohemia had been defeated at the start of the Thirty Years War (1618–48).

31 *Life*, i, 12–18; Clarendon, *History*, ii, 50; P. Young, *Edgehill, 1642. The Campaign and the Battle* (Kineton, 1967) *passim* but especially 50–5, 73–9; Callow, *Making of King James*, 38–9.

32 G.F. Warner (ed.), *The Nicholas Papers*, 4 vols (London, 1886–1920), i, 76; Anon, *A Short View of the Life of James Duke of York* , 3; *Life*, i, 20–1; S.R. Gardiner, *History of the Great Civil War, 1642–1649*, 5 vols (London, 1893), i, 198–9, 206; Hutton, *Charles II*, 7–13; Callow, *Making of King James*, 39–42.

33 For the 1643 Scottish Convention of Estates see *RPS*, 1643/6/1–96 and esp. at 1643/6/30, 75, 84, 86 and 90; Gardiner, *Civil War*, i, 232–5; D. Stevenson, *The Scottish Revolution*, 276–98, 258–61; Wedgewood, *The King's War*, 193–255; D.L. Smith, *A History of the Modern British Isles, 1603–1707: The Double Crown* (Oxford, 1998), 140–2; *Life*, ii, 638.

34 *Life*, i, 22–7, ii, 634–5; NRS, Montrose Muniments, GD220, 3/137 (letter James to Montrose, 11 September, 1648, The Hague), 3/138 (same to same, 23 July, 1649, Saint-Germain), 3/139 (same to same, 26 January 1650, Jersey); John Nicoll, *A Diary of Public Transactions and other Occurrences Chiefly in Scotland, from January 1650 to June 1667* (Edinburgh, 1836), 330–3; Stevenson, *Revolution and Counter Revolution*, 1–10; Smith, *History of the Modern British Isles*, 142–7; Wedgewood, *The King's War*, 334–42, 378–81, 450–5;. E.J. Cowan, *Montrose: for Covenant and King* (Edinburgh, 1995), 152–251, 252–75, 282–3, 299–300; M.D. Young (ed.), *The Parliament of Scotland: Burgh and Shire Commissioners*, 2 vols (Edinburgh, 1993), i, 203. For Wishart's editions see, for example, George Wishart, *The history of the Kings Majesties affaires in Scotland under the conduct of the most Honourable James, Marques of Montrose, Earl of Kincardin, &c., and generall governour of the kingdome, in the years 1644, 1645, & 1646.* (Amsterdam, 1649).

35 *Life*, i, 27.

36 *CSPD 1644–5*, 429, 449 and 470; *CSPD 1645–7*, 433; Callow, *Making of King James*, 43–4; *Life* i, 29.

37 *CSPD 1637–8*, 321, 351 and 445; Callow, *Making of King James*, 33–4; *Life*, i, 29.

38 *Life*, i, 29–30; *ODNB*, G. A. Drake, 'Algernon Percy (1602–1668)': doi: 10.1093/ref:odnb/21923.

39 *CSPV, 1643–47*, 279; Turner, *James II*, 15; Callow, *Making of King James*, 48–9.

40 *Life*, i, 30–3; *CSPV, 1643–47*, 298; Clarendon, *History*, v, 27; *CSPD, 1648–9*, 38–9; S.R. Gardiner (ed.), *The Hamilton Papers* (Camden Society, London, 1880), 156, 160; Callow, *Making of King James*, 48; Turner, *James II*, 16.

41 *RPS*, 1646/11/1–636 and esp. 1646/11/154; H.W. Meikle (ed.), *The Correspondence of the Scots Commissioners in London* (Edinburgh, 1917), 104–5, 148–52, 173–7, 181–2, 186–216; Anon, *Papers from the Scottish Quarters, containing the substance of two votes made by the Estates at Edinburgh at their general meeting this present Septemb. 1646* (London, 1646); J. G. Fotheringham (ed.), *The Diplomatic Correspondence of Jean De Montereul and the Brothers De Bellievre, French Ambassadors in England and Scotland, 1645–48*, 2 vols (SHS, Edinburgh, 1898), i, 238–367; ii, 583–94; G. Burnet, *The Memoirs of the Lives of James and William, Dukes of Hamilton* [Burnet, *Memoirs of Dukes of Hamilton*] (London, 1677, Oxford, 1852), 285–6, 294–5, 306; *Life*, i, 30; Stevenson, *Revolution and Counter Revolution*, 60–7; Macinnes, *British Revolution*, 170–3; Scally, 'The Rise and Fall of the Covenanter Parliaments, 1639–51',151–3; J.R. Young, 'The Scottish Parliament and the Covenanting Revolution: The Emergence of a Scottish Commons', in Young (ed.), *Celtic Dimensions of the British Civil Wars* (Edinburgh, 1997), 164–84; Wedgewood, *The King's War*, 608–12.

42 Clarendon, *History*, iv, 236–8; [David Jones], *The Life of King James II, Late King of England – Containing Accounts of His Birth, Education, Religion and Enterprises both at home and abroad* (London, 1702), 3; Smith, *History of Modern British Isles*, 154–6; Macinnes, *British Revolution*, 184.

43 Clarendon, *History*, iv, 249–53; Callow, *Making of King James*, 46–7; Turner, *James II*, 15–16.

44 Callow, *Making of King James*, 49.

45 For example, *A Short View of the Life [of] James Duke of York*, 9–10; [Jones], *Life of King James II*, 3. The most lively account of Charles II's adventure is R. Ollard, *The Escape of Charles II after the Battle of Worcester* (London, 1986).

46 *Life*, i, 33–9; Turner, *James II*, 17–18; J Loftis (ed.), *The Memoirs of Anne, Lady Halkett and Ann, Lady Fanshawe* (Oxford, 1979), 23–6; J. Loftis and P.H. Hardacre (eds), John Bampfield, *Colonel Joseph Bampfield's Apology* (London, 1993), 69–70; Gardiner, *Civil War*, iv, 99–101; Ashley, *James II*, 23–4.

CHAPTER 2

1 Turner, *James II*, 15; Callow, *Making of King James*, 46.

2 The best account remains Stevenson, *Revolution and Counter Revolution, 1644–51*, 68–102.

3 Miller, *James II*, 9–10; *SPCC*, ii, 242–329 *passim*; Hutton, *Charles II*, 17–19.

4 Clarendon, *History*, iv, 338–42; *Life*, i, 43–4; *Hamilton Papers*, 222–3 (letter Sir William Bellenden to Earl of Lanark, 25 June 1648); Powell and Timings (eds), *Documents Relating to the Civil War*, 353–4; Hutton, *Charles II*, 24–5. The numbers of ships in this fleet varied in reality and estimation. In August, the Earl of Lauderdale reported eighteen ships. See *Hamilton Papers*, 238.

5 *Hamilton Papers*, 236 and 237–8 (letter Lauderdale to earl of Lanark, 10 August 1648); Hutton, *Charles II*, 27–8.

6 *Hamilton Papers*, 'Instruction from the Committee of Estates to the earl of Lauderdale', 232–4; *CCSP*, i, 433–4; NRS, Papers of the Dukes of Hamilton, GD406/1/2479 (letter Lauderdale to duke of Hamilton, 20 August 1648); R.C. Paterson, *King Lauderdale, The Corruption of Power* (Edinburgh, 2003), 94.

7 Bod. Lib., Clarendon MSS, 31, ff. 233, 241–3, 246; Sir William Batten, *A true relation of what past betweene the fleet his Highness the Prince of Wales, and that under the command of*

the Earle of Warwick (1649); Bod. Lib., Clarendon MSS, 31, f. 282; *Life,* i, 44–5; Hutton, *Charles II*, 29–30; Stevenson, *Revolution and Counter-revolution*, 94–9.

8   *Hamilton Papers*, 222 (letter Sir William Bellenden to the earl of Lanark, 25 June 1648); Clarendon, *History*, v, 18, 22; Paterson, *Lauderdale*, 64, 100–3.

9   *Life*, i, 44–5; Clarendon, *History*, iv, 415–6; *Documents Relating to the Civil War*, 392–3; H. Cary (ed.), *Memorials of the Great Civil War, 1646–52: Edited from the Original Letters in the Bodleian Library,* 2 vols (London, 1842), i, 60; Hutton, *Charles II*, 30; Callow, *Making of King James*, 54.

10 Turner, *James II*, 22; Callow, *Making of King James*, 54; Ashley, *James II*, 26; Smith, *History of the Modern British Isles*, 174.

11 *Life*, i, 43–4; Clarendon, *History*, iv, 407, 417; A.L. Sells (ed.), *The Memoirs of James II: His Campaigns as Duke of York, 1652–1660* (Bloomington, 1962), 292; *Hamilton Papers*, 230 and NRS, Hamilton Papers GD406/1/2418 (letter Sir William Bellenden to the Earl of Lanark, 9 July 1648); Clarendon, *History*, iv, 328, 338–9.

12 Clarendon, *History*, iv, 338–9; Miller, *James II*, 10; Turner, *James II*, 30–1.

13 T. Carte (ed.), *A Collection of Original Letters Concerning the Affairs of England from the year 1641 to 1660 found among the duke of Ormonde's Papers*, 2 vols (London, 1739), i, 222.

14 Paterson, *Lauderdale*, 97–100; Miller, *James II*, 9; T. Carte, *The Life of James Duke of Ormonde,* 6 vols (Oxford, 1851), iii, 601.

15 *Life* i, 45–6; *CSPV, 1647–52*, 84 (Report with Sir Edward Nicholas letter); J. Nalson, *A True Copy of the Journal of the High Court of Justice for the Trial of King Charles I* (London, 1684), 29–32; C.V. Wedgewood, *The Trial of Charles I* (London, 1964), 130, 199–200; Smith, *History of the Modern British Isles*, 161–2. These dates are presented Old Style even though James in his memoirs, like Nicholas, reports them in New Style. See Miller, *James II*, 11 and Ashley, *James II*, 26 for differing approaches to this. For a general account of the Fronde see O. Ranum, *The Fronde. A French Revolution* (London, 1993) or, in summary, D.J. Sturdy, *Louis XIV* (Basingstoke, 1998), 25–34.

16 Burnet, *History*, i, 86–88. For pressure on James see for example 'Philanax Verax', *A Letter to His Royal Highness the Duke of York touching his Revolt from, or Return to the Protestant Religion* (London, 1681), 3. Callow, *Making of King James*, 153; E. Almack (ed.), *Eikon Basilike, Or, The King's Book* (London, 1903), from edition of 1649 at http://anglicanhistory.org/charles/eikon; J.P Kenyon, *The Stuarts* (Glasgow, 1958), 144; Mann, 'James VII as Unionist and Nationalist', 104–5.

17 T. Birch (ed.), *The State Papers of John Thurloe*, 7 vols (London, 1742), i, 666; Turner, *James II*, 45–6; Callow, *Making of King James*, 69–70. For the 1696 plot to assassinate King William, first mooted in late 1695, see *Memoires du Marechal de Berwick* 2 vols (Paris, 1778), i, 133–4; Burnet, *History*, iv (book vi), 165–7; *Life*, ii, 544–52; C.T. Wilson, *James the Second and the Duke of Berwick* (London, 1876), 397–404.

18 Clarendon, *History*, v, 32–6, 44–5, 59; Hutton, *Charles II*, 34–6, and 35, fn. 3; Turner, *James II*, 22–3.

19 *RPS*, 1649/1/71.

20 Carte, *Original Letters*, i, 263–4; D. Laing (ed.), *The Letters and Journals of Robert Baillie*, 3 vols (Bannatyne Club, Edinburgh, 1841–2), iii, 84–5.

21 Stevenson, *Revolution and Counter Revolution*, 121–4.

22 *RPS*, 1649/1/361; P. Gordon of Ruthven, *A Abridegment of Britane's Distemper* (Spalding Club, 1844), 223–6; Burnet, *Memoirs of Dukes of Hamilton*, 384–405; *ST*, iv, 1155–94.

23 Baillie, *Letters*, iii, 71–90, 512–20; Carte, *Original Letters*, i, 271, 300; *CCSP*, ii, 12;

M. Napier (ed.), *Memorials of Montrose and his Times*, 2 vols (Maitland Club, 1848–50), ii, 376–83; Clarendon, *History*, v, 13–23.

24 Clarendon, *History*, v, 50, 64–5; Ashley, *James II*, 26.

25 Ormonde, *Letters*, ii, 306–7; Turner, *James II*, 23; Hutton, *Charles II*, 398–40.

26 *Life*, i, 47; S.E Hoskins, *Charles II in the Channel Islands*, 2 vols (London, 1854), ii, 314–18, 320–1; Turner, *James II*, 24–6.

27 V. Balfour, *Henry Bennet, earl of Arlington, Secretary of State to Charles II* (Oxford, 1914), 15–16; Turner, *James II*, 24.

28 Balfour, *Historical Works*, iii, 417; Baillie, *Letters*, iii, 99–103; NRS, Committee of Estates PA. 11/8, ff. 118v, 146–8v; *RPS*, 1649/5/383 and A1649/5/47; Young (ed.), *Burgh and Shire Commissioners*, ii, 736; *Life*, i, 48.

29 Carte, *Original Letters*, i, 337–9, 355–8; *Nicholas Papers*, i, 160–1; *RCGA*, ii, 354–5.

30 Clarendon, *History*, v, 106, 160; Turner, *James II*, 25.

31 *CCSP*, ii, 50–51, 53; Turner, *James II*, 26.

32 *SPCC*, ii. app. li–lix; *RCGA*, ii, 381–5, 389–92; S.R. Gardiner (ed.), *Charles the Second and Scotland in 1650* (SHS, Edinburgh, 1894), 41 and 74–5; Clarendon, *History*, v, 107–8; Turner, *James II*, 27; Miller, *James II*, 13; Stevenson, *Revolution and Counter Revolution*, 133–35, 140–1.

33 *SPCC*, ii, app. lxiii–lxv; *RCGA*, ii, 436–8; BL, Clarendon MSS, 40, f. 80; Gardiner, *Charles the Second and Scotland*, 140–2.

34 *Miscellany of the Maitland Club* (Edinburgh, 1840), ii, pt 2, 472–81; A.G. Reid (ed.), 'Notice of an Original Letter of Instructions for Sir William Fleming', *Proceedings of the Society of Antiquaries of Scotland*, xxxiv (1899–1900), 199–202; Stevenson, *Revolution and Counter Revolution*, 138–9; Cowan, *Montrose*, 295. For discussion of the date confusion over Fleming's movements and the various letters see Cowan, *Montrose*, 235 at fn. 138 and Hutton *Charles II*, 474–5 at fn. 40.

35 Napier, *Memorials of Montrose*, ii, 400–6, 413–15; Gardiner, *Charles II and Scotland*, 49–50; R. Gordon, *A Genealogical History of the Earldom of Sutherland* (Edinburgh, 1813), 551–7; Balfour, *Historical Works*, iv, 9–16; NRS, PA 12/5, minutes of committee of estates April 1650; W.D. Macray (ed.), *The Ruthven Correspondence: letters and papers of Patrick Ruthven, Earl of Forth and Brentford, and of his family: A.D. 1615–A.D. 1662; with an appendix of papers relating to Sir John Urry* (Oxford, 1868); Cowan, *Montrose*, 276–301; Stevenson, *Revolution and Counter Revolution*, 134–7.

36 *Nicholas Papers*, i, 173–4; HMC, *Sixth Report* (London, 1877), app. 695 (letter James to Argyll, 24 August 1650); *Life*, i, 48; Stevenson, *Revolution and Counter Revolution*, 143–9; J.D. Grainger, *Cromwell Against the Scots: The Last Anglo-Scottish War, 1650–1652* (East Linton, 1997), 37–50.

37 Clarendon, *History*, v, 163–4; *Nicholas Papers*, i, 196–7.

38 Clarendon, *History*, v, 162–3 and iv, 424.

39 Edward Hyde, *The Life of Edward, earl of Clarendon*, 3 vols (Oxford, 1827), i, 286–7; Clarendon, *History*, v, 163–5; *Nicholas Papers*, i, 207–15, 242–6; Miller, *James II*, 13–14; Turner, *James II*, 31–2; Callow, *Making of King James*, 58–9.

40 Clarendon, *Life*, i, 287, 289–91; Clarendon, *History*, v, 163; *Nicholas Papers*, i, 209–12; HMC, *Thirteenth Report, Appendix, Part 1, Manuscripts of the duke of Portland* (London, 1891), 595; *CSPD, 1650*, 182; Turner, *James II*, 32–3; Callow, *Making of King James*, 59.

41 *Nicholas Papers*, i, 204, 221, 233, 247–8; *SPCC*, iii, 29; Clarendon *History*, v, 168–9; *Life*, i, 49–51; Turner, *James II*, 33–4; Callow, *Making of King James*, 60.

42 W. Bray (ed.), *The Diary and Correspondence of John Evelyn* (London, 1862–3), iv, 194–7; Balfour, *Historical Works*, iv, 109–16; Edward Walker, *Historical Discourses upon Several Occasions* (London, 1705), 188, 196–7, 199; Grainger, *Cromwell Against the Scots*, 62–3; Stevenson, *Revolution and Counter Revolution*, 153–5; Hutton, *Charles II*, 56–7.

43 Bray (ed.), *Diary of John Evelyn*, iv, 195; Clarendon, *History*, v, 171; Balfour, *Historical Works*, iv, 117–19, 123–35; NRS, PA7/24, ff. 30v–31, 32, 39–39v; D. Laing (ed.), *Correspondence of Sir Robert Kerr, first Earl of Ancrum, and his son William, third Earl of Lothian*, 2 vols (Edinburgh,1875), ii, 318–18, 501–502; *RPS*, A1651/3/24; *RCGA*, iii, 557–62; Baillie, *Letters*, iii, 115–16; D. Stevenson, 'The Western Association', *Ayrshire Collections*, 11, 1 (1982), 148–87. For the full text of the 'remonstrance' see Balfour, *Historical Works*, iv, 141–60.

44 Nicoll, *Diary*, 36–7; Baillie, *Letters*, iii, 125–6; *RCGA*, iii, 157–60, 267–71; *RPS*, M1650/11/25 (20 December); Stevenson, *Revolution and Counter Revolution*, 160–4.

45 *RPS*, M1650/11/2–35; M1650/11/33 (for Duke of York); [Anon], *Coronation of Charles the Second, King of Scotland, England, France and Ireland, as it was acted and done at Scone* (Aberdeen, 1651); P. C. Stuart, Marquis of Bute, *Scottish Coronations* (Paisley, 1912), 141–217. For a romantic account which places the coronation in the context of others see J. Cooper, 'Four Scottish Coronations' in *Transactions of the Aberdeen and Glasgow Ecclesiological Societies* (Aberdeen, 1902), 31–40.

46 *RPS*, M1651/5/11 and A1651/5/11 (2 June); A1651/5/10 (4 June); A. Peterkin (ed.), *Records of the Kirk of Scotland, Containing the Acts and Proceedings of the General Assemblies* (1838), 626–36; Stevenson, *Revolution and Counter Revolution*, 165–72.

47 Laing (ed.), *Ancram and Lothian Correspondence*, ii, 360; Balfour, *Historical Works*, iv, 313–14; Nicoll, *Diary*, 43–55; S.R Gardiner, *History of the Commonwealth and Protectorate*, 3 vols (London, 1897–1901), ii, 26–8, 44–57; Cary (ed.), *Memorials of the Great Civil War*, ii, 348–60; Bod. Lib., Clarendon MSS, 42 ff. 149–50; *SPCC*, ii, 561–3; *Mercurius Politicus* (4–11 September, 1651); Granger, *Cromwell Against the Scots*, 128–46; Ollard, *Escape of Charles II, passim.*

48 T. Carlyle (ed.), *Oliver Cromwell's Letters and Speeches*, 4 vols (Leipzig, 1861), iii, 93; Hutton, *Charles II*, 66–7; Stevenson, *Revolution and Counter Revolution*, 174; Paterson, *Lauderdale*, 114.

49 *SPCC*, iii, 80; *Life*, i, 52; *Nicholas Papers*, i, 315; Clarendon, *History*, v, 212–3, 225; Miller, *James II*, 15; Hutton, *Charles II*, 73.

50 Sells (ed.), *Memoirs of James II*, 57; *Life*, i, 54; Clarendon, *History*, v, 225–27, 230–1.

51 Sells (ed.), *Memoirs of James II*, 57–8; *Life*, i, 54–5, 63; Callow, *Making of King James*, 62. For James's praise and deep respect for Turenne see Sells (ed.), *Memoirs of James II*, 64, 67–8, 140, 166–7, 171, 222.

52 *Life* i, 55–6; Ashley, *James II*, 34.

53 Sells (ed.), *Memoirs of James II*, 60–217; *Life*, i, 64–266. The term 'Jacobite Life' is used by Harris, see his *Revolution: The Great Crisis of the British Monarchy, 1685–1720* (London, 2006), 70, 230, but his life could hardly be anything else.

54 *Life*, i, 266, 270–81; Sells (ed.), *Memoirs of James II*, 218, 222–25; Bod. Lib., Clarendon MSS, 5, ff. 147–54; *State Papers of John Thurloe*, iv, 592, 677; Hutton, *Charles II*, 98–100.

55 *Life*, i, 99, 106; Sells (ed.), *Memoirs of James II*, 94.

56 *Life*, i, 214–28, 362–5, 247, 339–40, 264, 328, 182–3, 318–9; Sells (ed.), *Memoirs of James II*, 174–85, 275–78, 202, 255–6, 216–7, 246, 148, 239; Callow, *Making of King James*, 63; *SPCC*, iii, 67; Bod. Lib., Clarendon MSS, 55, f. 54; *State Papers of John Thurloe*,

i, 590, v, 396, 422; C.H. Firth (ed.), *Clarke Papers*, 4 vols (Camden Society, London, 1891–1901), iii, 71; F.D Dow, *Cromwellian Scotland* (Edinburgh, 1979, reprinted 1999), 193.

57 *Life*, i, 97,150, 173–4, 242, 261, 304–11, 321, 336, 347, 357–8; Sells (ed.), *Memoirs of James II*, 86–8, 140–1, 198, 214, 229–34, 239, 252–3, 263, 271–2.

58 M. Glozier, *Scottish Soldiers in France in the Reign of the Sun King: Nursery of Men of Honour* (Leiden, 2004), 31–8; Glozier, 'Scots in the French and Dutch Armies in the Thirty Years War', in S. Murdoch (ed.), *Scotland and the Thirty Years' War* (Leiden, 2001), 123.

59 Glozier, *Scottish Soldiers in France*, 43, 39–40, 42, 181–203; *ODNB*, D. Parrot, James Hepburn (d.1637):doi:10.1093/ref:odnb/ 13003; A.N.L. Grosjean, John Hepburn (c.1598–1636): doi:10.1093/ref:odnb/13005; M. Glozier, George Douglas (c.1636–1692): doi:10.1093/ref:odnb/7886; Fountainhall, *Historical Notices*, ii, 644; *RPCS, third series*, xi, 230–1; *Life*, i, 102, 151; Sells (ed.), *Memoirs of James II*, 91, 123.

60 R. Latham and W. Matthews (eds) *The Diary of Samuel Pepys*, 11 vols (1970–83); repr. (1995); repr. (2000), iii, 282–3, iv, 116; R. Latham (ed.), *Samuel Pepys: The Shorter Pepys* (1987), 241. J.Balfour Paul (ed.), *The Scots Peerage*, 8 vols (Edinburgh, 1904), vii, 374–5; *RPCS, third series*, ii, 7, 247–8; Glozier, *Scottish Soldiers in France*, 43, 57–68. For Rutherford's career and death during service in Tangier see L. Addison, *A discourse of Tangier under the government of the earl of Teviot* (1685).

61 W. Forbes-Leith, *The Scots Men-at-Arms and Life Guards in France, 1458–1830*, 2 vols (Edinburgh, 1882), i, 116; *ODNB*, D. Stevenson, Andrew Gray (d. 1663): doi:10.1093/ ref:odnb/11327; *Scots Peerage*, iv, 545–6; Glozier, *Scottish Soldiers in France*, 41.

62 Glozier, *Scottish Soldiers in France*, 41; M.V. Hay (ed.), *The Blair Papers, 1603–1660* (London, 1929), 246; *ODNB*, R. Dunlop and H. Murtagh, Frederick Herman de Schomberg (1615–1690): doi:10.1093/ref:odnb/24822; Sells (ed.), *Memoirs of James II*, 74–5, 133, 151, 156–90, 191, 200–1, 206–8, 210–12; Burnet, *History*, ii, 5.

63 *Life*, i, 297–8; *Mercurius Politicus*, 16–23 April, 1657; C.H. Firth, 'Royalist and Cromwellian Armies in Flanders, 1657–1662', *TRHS*, new series, 17 (1903), 68–74. For Grace see *Life*, i, 268–9.

64 *CCSP*, iii, 203–4; T. Thomson (ed.), Sir James Turner, *Memoirs of His Own Life and Times* (Edinburgh, 1829), 120–30; Firth (ed.), *Scotland under the Protectorate*, 336–45; *State Papers of John Thurloe*, vi, 76, 90; D. Middleton, *The Life of Charles 2nd earl of Middleton* (London, 1957), 32–3; G. H. Jones, *Charles Middleton: The life and Times of a Restoration Politician* (Chicago, 1967), 4. For Cranston's regiment in the service of Sweden see A. Grosjean, 'Royalist Soldiers and Cromwellian Allies? The Cranstoun Regiment in Sweden, 1655–1658' in S. Murdoch and A. Mackillop (eds), *Fighting for Identity: Scottish Military Experience c.1550–1900* (Leiden, 2002), 61–82.

65 *RPS*, 1661/1/358; *RPCS, third series*, i, 2; *Mercurius Publicus* 21–28 March 1661; Sir George Mackenzie of Rosehaugh, *Memoirs of the Affairs of Scotland from the Restoration of King Charles II* (Edinburgh, 1821), 187; C. Dalton, *The Scots Army 1661–1688, with memoirs of the commander-in-chiefs* (London and Edinburgh, 1909), part 1, xvii, 5; part 2, 3–4; *ODNB*, J. Callow, Charles Stuart (1639–1672): doi:10.1093/ref:odnb/26696; R. Marshall, James Livingston of Kinnaird (1621/2–1670): doi:10.1093/ref:odnb/16807. Newburgh was not, as Hutton describes him, 'an aged Scottish royalist' in the mid 1650s and, by then, was only in his mid thirties, though he was dismissed, with full pension, in 1670 on account of his corpulence and gout. Hutton, *Charles II*, 79.

66 Young (ed.), *Burgh and Shire Commissioners,* ii, 436; Sells (ed.), *Memoirs of James II,* 224, 246, 263–7.

67 Sells (ed.), *Memoirs of James II,* 226–80, at 229–31, 239–43, 247; *Life,* i, 300–4, 320–24; *SPCC,* iii, 354.

68 *State Papers of John Thurloe,* vi, 345; *SPCC,* iii, 347 (Ormonde to Hyde, 21 June 1657); Sells (ed.), *Memoirs of James II,* 260–63; *Life,* i, 297, 342–47; *Clarke Papers,* iii, 154–5; Firth, 'Royalist and Cromwellian Armies', *TRHS,* new series, 17 (1903), 75, 85; Dalton, *The Scots Army,* part 2, 15–16; Macray (ed.), *The Ruthven Correspondence,* 150–5.

69 Sells (ed.), *Memoirs of James II,* 263–75; *Life,* i, 347–60; *State Papers of John Thurloe,* vii, 156, 160; *Clarke Papers,* iii, 154; Clarendon, *History,* vi, 84; Firth, 'Royalist and Cromwellian Armies', *TRHS,* new series, 17 (1903), 86; Callow, *Making of King James,* 77–8.

70 Sells (ed.), *Memoirs of James II,* 276–80; *Life,* i, 364–8.

71 Callow, *King in Exile,* 262–3.

72 Sells (ed.), *The Memoirs of James II,* 232, 239–40; *State Papers of John Thurloe,* vi. 665, 676, 680, 686, 735; *Life,* i. 308–9, 319–320, 326–29.

73 Callow, *Making of King James,* 80–1. For Turenne's memoirs see A. M. Ramsay, *The History of Henri de la Tour d'Auvergne,* 2 vols (London, 1735), ii, at 185–8, and also M. De Buisson, *La Vie du Vicomte de Turenne* (Cologne, 1687), 300; T. Lonqueville, *Marshal Turenne* (London, 1907), 265, and J. Berenger, *Turenne* (Paris, 1987), 335–6.

74 *CCSP,* iii, 11–14; *Nicholas Papers,* ii, x, 24, 162; D. Underdown, *Royalist Conspiracy in England 1649–1600* (New Haven, 1960), esp. chapter 6; Hutton, *Charles II,* 113–14, 81–2; Fraser, *Charles II,* 181–4; Smith, *History of the British Isles,* 188–9.

75 *Nicholas Papers,* iii, 314; C.H. Firth (ed.), *Scotland and the Commonwealth* (SHS, Edinburgh,1895), 47–7, 65–70, 89–93, 99–103, 144 fn., 184–5; *CCSP,* ii, 158, 166, 188; Sells (ed.), *Memoirs of James II,* 119–22; Gardiner, *Commonwealth and Protectorate,* ii, 396–7; J. Willcock, *A Scots Earl in Covenanting Times: Being the Life and Times of Archibald, 9th earl of Argyll (1629–1685)* (Edinburgh, 1907), 54–74.

76 Firth, *Scotland and the Commonwealth,* 202–3, 221–2, 227, 231, 264–7, 276, 286; *The Diary of Mr John Lamont of Newton, 1649–1671* (Maitland Club, Edinburgh, 1830), 61; Nicoll, *Diary,* 116. For the best account of the entire Glencairn Rising and its impact see Dow, *Cromwellian Scotland,* 74–142.

77 C.H. Firth (ed.), *Scotland under the Protectorate: Letters and Papers Relating to the Military Government of Scotland From January 1654 to June 1659* (SHS, Edinburgh, 1899), 25–30, 52, 56, 88–9, 91, 95; *CCSP,* ii, 310–12; *CSPD, 1653–4,* 297–8, 364–5, 382; C.H.Firth and R.S. Rait (eds), *Acts and Ordinances of the Interregnum,* 3 vols (London, 1911), ii, 813–22; Gardiner, *Commonwealth and Protectorate,* ii, 407; Dow, *Cromwellian Scotland,* 84–5, 115, 120–1.

78 Firth (ed.), *Scotland under the Protectorate,* 97, 103, 110–11, 113, 133–8, 143–53, especially the report from Monck to Cromwell headed 'Narrative of the Proceedings in the Hills from June 9 to July 1654' at 149–54; J.Y. Ackerman (ed.), *Letters of Roundhead Officers written from Scotland and chiefly addressed to captain Adam Baynes, July MDCL– June MDCLX* (Bannatyne Club, Edinburgh, 1856), 71–83; *State Papers of John Thurloe,* ii, 389, 465; Dow, *Cromwellian Scotland,* 124–29. For Dalnaspidal see *Letters of Roundhead Officers,* 83–4, 86–7 and *State Papers of John Thurloe,* ii, 483.

79 Bod. Lib., Clarendon MSS 47, f. 258; 49, ff. 39–44, 259, 264; *Miscellanea aulica: or, a collection of state-treatises, never before publish'd. Containing, Letters by K. Charles and K.*

James II. in their Exile. (London, 1702), 108–9; *State Papers of John Thurloe*, ii 502, 556, 567, 585–7; Clarendon, *History*, v, 353; *Nicholas Papers*, ii, 79–80; Turner, *Memoirs*, 114–15. For Balcarres *Nicholas Papers*, iv, 3, 8; Bod. Lib., Clarendon MSS 58, ff. 166–7; NA. SP 77/32, f. 156. For Dunnottar see D.G. Barron (ed.), *In Defence of the Regalia, 1651–2: being selections from the family papers of the Ogilvies of Barras* (London, 1910), 17, 110–12 ; *CCSP*, ii, 118, 127.

80 Clarendon, *History*, vi, 87–8, 98; *CSPD, Interregnum, 1658–9*, nos. 26, 50; Bod. Lib., Clarendon MSS 62 f. 201; *HMC, Fifteenth Report, Appendix II, Hodgkin* (London, 1897)124–5; Underdown, *Royalist Conspiracy*, 233–5; Hutton, *Charles II*, 114.

81 New Style (NS) signifies dates according to the Gregorian calendar, common in Europe from 1582, and not the Julian calendar used in England. Scotland also used the Julian calendar but from 1600 started each year at 1 January rather than at 25 March as was the English convention until 1752. In the period of James's life the Gregorian calendar was between ten and eleven days ahead.

82 Clarendon, *History*, vi, 99–107, 117, 134–5, 138–40; *SPCC*, iii, 536–8; *Life*, i, 371–9; Sells (ed.), *Memoirs of James II*, 282–9; Carte (ed.), *Original Letters*, ii, 186, 192–5; A. Bryant (ed.), *The Letters, Speeches and Declarations of King Charles II* (London, 1935), 76–8; *Nicholas Papers*, iv, 185, 188; Underdown, *Royalist Conspiracy*, 248–9; J.R. Jones, 'Booth's Rising of 1659', *Bulletin of the John Rylands Library*, no. 39 (1957), 416–43; Ashley, *James II*, 66–8.

83 Sells (ed.), *Memoirs of James II*, 291; *Life*, i, 381; Bod. Lib., Carte MSS 30, f. 532 (Bennet to Ormonde), f. 539 (Peter Talbot to Ormonde); Bod. Lib., Carte MSS 213, f. 557r–v (Talbot to Ormonde), f. 702 (Colonel Nugent to Ormonde); Callow, *Making of King James*, 85–6; Turner, *James II*, 58.

84 Clarendon, *History*, vi, 143–51, 193–4; *SPCC* , iii, 604–5; Carte, *Original Letters*, ii, 237–8; *ODNB*, V. Stater, John Grenville (1628–1701): doi:10.1093/ref:odnb/11492; Ashley, *James II*, 70. For a summary of the army crisis see Hutton, *Restoration*, 68–79 and, even more succinctly, Smith, *History of the Modern British Isles*, 193–6.

85 Clarendon, History, vi, 177–9; Bod. Lib., Clarendon, MSS 71, f. 124.

86 Bryant (ed.), *Letters of Charles II*, 83–5; Clarendon, *History*, vi, 194–200. For county declarations in support of fresh elections see B.L. Thomason, 669, *et seq.*

87 Bryant (ed.), *Letters of Charles II*, 85. The text of *King Charles II: his declaration to all his loving subjects of the kingdom of England. Dated from his Court at Breda in Holland, the 4/14 of April 1660. And read in Parliament, May, 1. 1660* (Edinburgh, 1660), was widely printed, including in Scotland by Christopher Higgins, an English printer working in Edinburgh.

88 Sells (ed.), *Memoirs of James II*, 290.

89 Ashley, *James II*, 26, 72–3; Fraser, *Charles II*, 150–1, 191–2; Callow, *Making of King James*, 85–6; Hutton, *Charles II*, 92–3; *State Papers of John Thurloe*, i, 744; F.C Routledge, 'The Negotiations Between Charles II and the Cardinal de Retz, 1658–9', *TRHS*, fifth series, 6 (1956), 49–68.

90 Clarendon, *History*, vi, 339–40, 361–4; Bod. Lib., Clarendon MSS 49 f. 149; Bryant (ed.), *Letters of Charles II*, 29–30, 31–3; Hutton, *Charles II*, 92, 117–8; Fraser, *Charles II*, 193; R. Norrington (ed.), *Dearest Minette: The Letters between Charles II and his Sister Henrietta, the Duchesse d'Orleans* (London, 1996), 25; J.R. Jones, *Charles II. Royal Politician* (London, 1987), 28. Ashley's suggestion that James was negligent in pressing his brother's wishes on account of some interest in Roman Catholic religion seems a little farfetched. Ashley, *James II*, 47–9. For the best account of the affair see N. Greenspan 'Public Scandal,

Political Controversy, and Familial Conflict in the Stuart Courts in Exile: The Struggle to Convert the Duke of Gloucester in 1654', *Albion: A Quarterly Journal Concerned with British Studies*, vol. 35, No. 3 (Autumn, 2003), 398–427, although some of the chronology is suspect and it is doubtful that Henry had his own independent plans for a military career.

91 *SPCC*, iii, 323. For summaries of this dispute see Callow, *Making of King James*, 72–3; Hutton, *Charles II*, 120, and especially Turner, *James II*, 48–53.

92 *Life*, i, 269–81 (before James entered Spanish service), 281–93 (continuing disputes over James's servants); *SPCC*, iii, 317–24; Bod. Lib., Clarendon MSS 53, ff. 160, 187, and 55, ff. 162, 299, 333; *Nicholas Papers*, iv, 1–2, 4; *CCSP*, iii, 223–4; Turner, *James II*, 54.

93 *SPCC*, iii, 360–1, 363, 369; Bod. Lib., Clarendon MS 58, ff. 158–9, 160–1; Bryant (ed.), *Letters of Charles II*, 57–8, 58–9; Hutton, *Charles II*, 121.

94 *Scots Peerage*, vi, 183–4; Clarendon, *History*, v, 240; Bod. Lib., Clarendon MSS 60, ff. 403, 509; Turner, *James II*, 56–7; *ODNB*, E.M. Furgol, John Middleton (*c*.1608–1674): doi: 10.1093/ref: odnb/18674. For Middleton's commission and instructions from Charles see *HMC, Laing Manuscripts at the University of Edinburgh*, i (London, 1914), 301–4. For Newburgh's violence see, for example, *State Papers of John Thurloe*, ii, 586 (1654), vii, 353 (1658) and for a summary, Hutton, *Charles II*, 123.

95 *SPCC*, iii, 387 (Ormonde); Bod. Lib., Clarendon MSS 54, f. 225 (Hyde). For summaries of Charles's mistresses, with occasional references to James, see B. Masters, *The Mistresses of Charles II* (London, 1997), D. Wilson, *All the King's Women: Love, sex and politics in the life of Charles II* (London, 2004) and S. Wynne, 'The Mistresses of Charles II and Restoration Court Politics' in E. Cruickshanks (ed.), *The Stuart Courts* (Stroud, 2000), 171–90.

96 *Life*, i, 492; J. MacPherson (ed.), *Original papers . . . and life of James II*, 3 vols (London, 1775), i, 76; Wilson, *All the King's Women*, 43–4, 57–60; Fraser, *Charles II*, 54.

97 BL, Add. MS 15900, 'Memorandum Book of Lady Hyde' (1653/1671).

98 Sells (ed.), *Memoirs of James II*, 219; Clarendon, *Life*, i, 375–404; *Nicholas Papers*, iii, 4; *CCSP*, iii, 45; *Life*, ii, 387; A. Fea, *James II and his Wives* (London, 1908), 27–32.

99 Clarendon, *Life*, i, 379–81, Burnet, *History* i, 294–5; R. Bell (ed.), *Memorials of the Civil War*, 2 vols (London, 1849), ii, 270–3 (depositions of James, Anne and witnesses, given 18 February 1661, and confirming contract of November 1659); Latham (ed.), *Shorter Pepys*, 84, 102, 104, 107; Latham and Mathews (eds), *The Diary of Samuel Pepys*, i, 261–2, 275; Sir Walter Scott (ed.), A. Hamilton, *Memoirs of Count Grammont* (London, 1902), 103–4, 189–95; Macpherson, *Original Papers*, i, 22–3; *HMC, Fifth Report* (London, 1878), 195; NA, 31/3, Transcripts by M. Armand Baschet of French ambassadors' despatches and other papers (1504–1714), 108–9; Bowle (ed.), *Diary of John Evelyn*, 185. For anti-Hyde rumours surrounding the affair see A. Browning (ed.), *Memoirs of Sir John Reresby* (Glasgow, 1936), 41.

100 Hamilton, *Memoirs of Count Grammont*, 195.

101 Firth (ed.), *Clarke Papers*, iv, 78–9, 113–6; 120–1, 151, 190–1; Nicoll's *Diary*, 257–60; J. Buckroyd, 'Bridging the Gap: Scotland 1659–60', *SHR*, 66 (1987), 1–25, at 8, 11–13. For the best summaries of these events see MacIntosh, *Scottish Parliament*, 2–8; and Dow, *Cromwellian Scotland*, 249–64, at 254–62.

102 Wodrow, *Sufferings*, i, 5–6, 8–25; *LP*, i, 13, 23; L.F. Browne (ed.), 'One more Lauderdale letter', *Bulletin of the John Ryland's Library* (1928), 134–6 and see also J. Powicke (ed.), 'Eleven Letters of John, second Earl (and first Duke) of Lauderdale to the Reverend

Richard Baxter', *Bulletin of the John Ryland's Library* (1922–3), 73–105; Clarendon, *Life*. i, 426–8; *Mercurius Politicus* 15–21 March 1660 and 16–23 May 1660; Nicoll's *Diary*, 277–8; Dow, *Cromwellian Scotland*, 258–63; MacIntosh, *Scottish Parliament*, 6–7; Paterson, *Lauderdale*, 117–26.

103　Clarendon, *History*, vi, 227–33; *Pepys's Diary*, i, 143–56; Latham (ed.), *Shorter Pepys*, 16, 48–49; NRS, CH/1/1/11, 'The results of the consultations of the Ministers of Edinburgh and some other Brethren of the Ministerie . . . 1659–1661', f. 155; Callow, *Making of King James*, 192–3.

104　Clarendon, *History*, vi, 233–4; *Shorter Pepys*, 49, 51; Bowle (ed.), *Diary of John Evelyn*, 182; Fraser, *Charles II*, 231–4. For a fanciful and celebratory account of the 'voyage' see the anonymous account translated from French by the poet William Lower (trans.), *A Relation in the form of journal of the voiage and residence which the most mighty Prince Charles the II King of Great Britain, &c. hath made in Holland, from the 25 of May, to the 2 of June, 1660* (The Hague, 1660). Lower's patrons included Princess Mary and the Queen of Bohemia, in other words the House of Orange.

CHAPTER 3

1　Nicoll, *Diary*, 283.

2　Nicoll, *Diary*, 292–3.

3　Anon, *A Short View of the Life of James Duke of York*, 25.

4　J.P. Kenyon (ed.), *Halifax's Complete Works* (Harmondsworth, 1969), 256.

5　Burnet, *History*, i, 295–7; H.C. Foxcroft (ed.), *A Supplement to Burnet's History of My Own Time* (Oxford, 1902), 50–1; Turner, *James II*, 64.

6　The *Life* is not an effective source with which to trace James's seasonal movements. For the best guidance, for the 1660s see Pepys's testimony from his regular meetings from July 1660, as Secretary to the Navy Board with James as Lord High Admiral of England, and for the early 1680s, Charles and James's intimate letters to their daughter and niece, Charlotte, Countess of Litchfield, Charles's daughter by Barbara, duchess of Cleveland. See Latham and Matthews (eds), *Diary of Samuel Pepys, passim* and H. Arthur (ed.), 'Some Familiar Letters of Charles II and James, Duke of York, addressed to their Daughter and Niece, the Countess of Litchfield', *Archaeologica*, second series, 58, 1 (Society of Antiquaries, 1902), 153–88.

7　A. Clark (ed.), *The Life and Times of Anthony Wood, Antiquary, of Oxford, 1632–1695, described by himself*, 5 vols (Oxford, 1894), iii, 67. For James's physical persistence and athleticism see L. Magalotti, *Lorenzo Magalotti at the Court of Charles II. His Relazione d'Inghilterra of 1668* (Waterloo, Canada, 1980), 36–7 and Latham (ed.), *Shorter Pepys*, 289 (22 June, 1663) and 650 (8 August, 1666). J.P. Hore, *The History of Newmarket and the Annals of the Turf*, 2 vols (London, 1886), ii, 220–88; Fraser, *Charles II*, 380–2; Callow, *Making of King James*, 114–5; Hutton, *Charles II*, 232.

8　Arthur (ed.), 'Some Familiar Letters', 153–8; 177 (James to Charlotte, 14 and 21 March 1683, Newmarket), 181 (James to Charlotte, 8, 13 and 21 September 1683, Winchester), 185–6 (James to Charlotte, 28 August 1684, Winchester), 186 (James to Charlotte, 8 October 1684, Newmarket). Charles's letters do not refer to outdoor sports. P. Braybooke (ed.), *The Autobiography of Sir John Bramston* (Camden Society, London, 1845), 226–7; Callow, *Making of King James*, 112–13; Miller, *James II*, 41–2.

 9 Clarendon, *Life*, i, 405; ii, 12–13; iii, 67–8.

10 Clarendon, *Life*, i, 405; ii, 12–13; iii, 67–8; BL, Add. MS, 18958, ff. 1–10 and 38863, ff. 1–10; Miller, *James II*, 42; Callow, *Making of King James*, 112.

11 *Lorenzo Magalotti*, 36; Clarendon, *Life*, iii, 64–5.

12 Latham (ed.), *Shorter Pepys*, 450, 371; *ODNB*, S. Lee and S. Kelsey, 'Sir William Coventry': doi: 10.1093/ref: odnb/6485; R. Hutton, 'Charles Berkeley, earl of Falmouth': doi: 10.1093/ref: odnb/37185; J. Miller, 'Henry Jermyn, third Baron Jermyn and Jacobite earl of Dover': doi: 10.1093/ref:odnb/14781; P. Wauchope, 'Richard Talbot': doi: 10.1093/ref: odnb/26940; P. Seaward, 'Sir Allen Apsley': doi: 10.1093/ref: odnb/600; B. C. Murison, 'Thomas Povey': doi: 10.1093/ref: odnb/22640; Miller, *James II*, 42–3; Callow, *Making of King James*, 110–13.

13 BL, Add. MS. 18958, ff. 1–10 (at 2v); 11–11v; NRAS, Dunmore Papers, RH4/195/1, no. 20 and no. 23; Archives des Affaires étrangères, La Courneuve, Correspondance Politique, Angleterre, 133 (Barrillon to Pomponne, January 1678).

14 John Rylands Library, Eng. MS. 294, 1–14 'Papers relating to the Revenues of James, Duke of York compiled by Thomas Povey, treasurer of the Duke's household' (1662–8); Bod. Lib., Clarendon, MSS. 79, ff. 103–5, and 88, ff. 143–7; Bod. Lib., Carte MSS. 47, f. 415, 'A Computation of the Duke of York's Estate and Revenue [in England and in Ireland]. Certified by Thomas Holden, Auditor', 18 August, 1664; Bod. Lib., Carte MSS 36, 125, 28 January, 1668; Latham (ed.), *Shorter Pepys*, 798 (June 1667), 953 (October 1688); Latham and Matthews (eds), *Diary of Samuel Pepys*, ix, 38 (June 1669); Miller *James II*, 42; C.D Chandaman, *The English Public Revenue, 1660–88* (Oxford, 1975), 117, 120, 132.

15 NRS, GD 406. Hamilton Papers, M9/164 (25 October 1679); *RPCS, third series*, vi, 331–4, 338, 341–3 (16 October to 13 November 1679); Hugh Ouston, '"From Thames to Tweed Departed": the Court of James, Duke of York in Scotland, 1679–82' in E. Cruickshanks (ed.), *The Stuart Courts* (Stroud, 2000), 270–1; Turner, *James II*, 173–4; Glozier, *Scottish Soldiers in France*, 100–46; *ODNB*, Cruickshanks, James Grahme (1650–1730): doi:10.1093/ref:odnb/11196.

16 [Nicholas French], *A Narrative of the Settlement and Sale of Ireland* (Louvain, 1668), 1–24; Clarendon, *Life*, i, 441–61; BL, Add. MS. 28085, f. 217; *The statutes at large passed in the parliaments held in Ireland . . . 1310 to 1800*, 21 vols (Dublin, 1786–1804), ii, 239–48; iii, 2–137; J.C. Becket, *The Making of Modern Ireland 1603–1923* (London, 2008, ex 1981 edition), 104–21; A. Clarke, *Prelude to Restoration in Ireland: The End of the Commonwealth, 1659–1660* (Cambridge, 1999), 1–10; Harris, *Restoration*, 86–94; Hutton, *Charles II*, 196–7; K.S. Bottigheimer, 'The Restoration Land Settlement in Ireland: a Structural View' in *Irish Historical Studies*, 18 (1972), 1–21; L.J. Arnold, 'The Irish Court of Claims of 1663' in *Irish Historical Studies*, 24 (1984), 417–30.

17 R.P. Mahaffy (ed.), *Calendar of State Papers Relating to Ireland, 1660–70*, 4 vols (London, 1905–10), i (1660–2) 322, 490, 668, 688; ii (1663–5) 9, 96–7, 199, 343, 370–1, 388, 562; iii (1666–9) 34, 96–7, 111, 199, 243, 257, 343–4, 494–7, 527–30; iv (1669–70) 5, 108; Bod. Lib., Carte MSS 143, ff. 13–14 (Ormonde to Clarendon, 11 October 1662), f. 40 (same to same, 19 November 1662); Carte 43, ff. 339–40 (Charles to Ormonde, 25 February 1664); Carte 144, f. 115 (same to same, 14 January 1668); Harris, *Restoration*, 94–6; Callow, *Making of King James*, 116–7.

18 Clarendon, *Life*, ii, 53–8; NA, SP 63/310/14 (1661 commission to Ormonde) and 29/239/55 (1668 commission of enquiry into Irish treasury); Carte, *Life of Ormonde*, iii, 62–9 and iv, 351, 355; Burnet, *History*, i, 480–2, 595; ii, 109–11.

19 *The Right Honourable the Earl of Arlington's Letters (1664–1674)* (London, 1701), ii, 290 (Bennet to Godolphin (ambassador to Spain), 18 January 1670); for examples of anti-Ormonde activities see Bod. Lib., Carte MSS 69, f. 137v (1667) and Carte 220, ff. 480 (1675); R.L. Greaves, *Deliver us from Evil: The Radical Underground in Britain, 1660–63* (Oxford, 1986), 140–50; C.E. Pike, 'The Intrigue to Deprive the Earl of Essex of the Lord Lieutenancy of Ireland', in *TRHS*, third series, 5 (1911), 89–103; Harris, *Restoration*, 96–7; Hutton, *Charles II*, 207–9, 339–40; Fraser, *Charles II*, 342–3, 409–10, 487. Hutton questions the extent to which the campaign against Ormonde was coordinated but Orrery certainly complained (justifiably) to Charles over the condition of the Irish treasury and by association about Ormonde, and Buckingham and his group took their opportunity. Hutton *Charles II*, 260–1.

20 M. Lee Jr, 'King James's Popish Chancellor' in I.B. Cowan and D. Shaw (eds), *The Renaissance and Reformation in Scotland* (Edinburgh, 1982), 170–82 and reprinted in Lee, *The 'Inevitable' Union and other Essays on Early Modern Scotland* (East Linton, 2003), 145–57; *ODNB*, M. Lee Jr., Alexander Seton (1556–1622): doi:10.1093/ref:odnb/25113. Ludovic Stewart, duke of Lennox and Richmond (1574–1624), a close confidant of James VI and I and who paraded as the senior noble of the three kingdoms at the English coronation of his master in 1603, was another well-regarded individual, but he was not greatly involved in the risky business of high politics.

21 *CSPV, 1661–1664* (1932), 72–90.

22 Ibid.; *Life*, i, 389–1; *CSPD (1660–1)*, 470–1; Latham (ed.), *Shorter Pepys,* 109–10 (7–10 January, 1661); Burnet, *History*, i, 278–9; J. Childs, *The Army of Charles II* (London, 1976), 15–17; Hutton, *Charles II*, 162–3; Turner, *James II*, 71; Harris, *Restoration*, 64–5.

23 Burnet, *History*, ii, 300.

24 *SR*, v, 226–34; P. Bayne (ed.), *Documents Relating to the Settlement of the Church of England* (London, 1862), 63–79; M. Sylvester (ed.), R. Baxter, *Reliquiae Baxterianae, Or Mr Richard Baxter's Narrative of the Most Memorable Passages of his Life and Times* (London, 1696), Part ii, 277, 429–30, 433–4.

25 *Life*, i, 393; Bowle (ed.), *Diary of John Evelyn*, 220; Burnet, *History*, i, 277–8, 315–7; Clarendon, *Life*, i, 321; MacPherson (ed.), *Original papers* i, 40; Miller, *James II*, 47–8; Callow, *Making of King James*, 164; Hutton, *Charles II*, 140–2; Harris, *Restoration*, 47–8.

26 NA, PRO 31/3, 'Transcripts by M Armand Baschet and others of French ambassadors' despatches', 108 (Montagu to Cardinal Mazarin, 9 December, 1660); A. Browning (ed.), *English Historical Documents 1660–1714* (London, 1953), 63–5; *SR*, v, 364–70; Clarendon, *Life*, ii, 214–19; Hutton, *Charles II*, 181–4; J. Miller, *Popery and Politics in England 1660–1688* (Cambridge, 1973), 91–101. The 'first' indulgence is sometimes described as the 'Declaration of Indulgence'. See G.R. Abernethy, 'Clarendon and the Declaration of Indulgence', *Journal of Ecclesiastical History*, 11, 1, (1960), 55–73.

27 BL, Add. MS 35125, ff. 130–130v (Sharp to Lauderdale, 5 January, 1666); NA, SP 104/177, ff. 12–18, 143–150; SP 29/294/15, 36; NA, PRO 31/3 (Baschet), 128, ff. 45–6 (Charles Colbert de Croissy, French Ambassador, to Louis XIV); BL Add. MS 29571, f. 195 ; *CSPV, 1673–75*, reports of Girolamo Alberti, Venetian Secretary in England, to the Doge and Senate, dated 17, 24 and 31 March 1673; A. Grey (ed.), *Debates in the House of Commons 1667–94*, 10 vols (London, 1763), ii, 9–69; Burnet, *History*, ii, 5–16; Miller, *Popery and Politics*, 116–20, 124–8. For the essence of the French approach to Charles's conversion see Dalrymple, *Memoirs*, i, appendix, 88–95 (letter Colbert to Louis XIV, 13 November 1669).

28 Bod. Lib., Carte MSS 46, ff. 540–41 (Arlington to Ormonde, 27 August 1667); Carte 35, f. 733 (Clarendon to Ormonde, 24 September, 1667, see quote); Carte 69, f. 137v (Orrery to Michael Boyle, archbishop of Dublin, 19 November 1667); Carte 35, f. 877 (Matthew Wren to Ormonde, 30 November 1667); *Life*, i, 427–3; Burnet, *History*, i, 451–60; Clarendon, *Life*, iii, 265–7, 281–97, 300–1, 310–33; Bowle (ed.), *Diary of John Evelyn*, 220, 222; Latham (ed.), *Shorter Pepys*, 822–5, 828, 841, 846, 852–3; Anon, *The Proceedings in the House of Commons, Touching the Impeachment of Edward, Late Earl of Clarendon, Lord High Chancellor of England* (London, 1700), *passim*; Miller, *James II*, 51–3; Callow, *Making of King James*, 162–66. Callow's suggestion that James misinterpreted Clarendon's grief at the death of his wife for general despair making him ready to retire from royal service is not supported by the evidence and is part of a questionable 'whig-psychological' tradition that sees James as emotionally inept. Callow, *Making of King James*, 163.

29 *LP*, ii, 70.

30 Miller, *Popery and Politics*, 108.

31 Bowle (ed.), *Diary of John Evelyn*, 188–90, 208–16 (for quote see 212); Latham (ed.), *Shorter Pepys*, 130–3, 659–72; Fraser, *Charles II*, 256–60; L. Madway, '"The Most Conspicuous Solemnity": The Coronation of Charles II' in Cruikshanks (ed.), *Stuart Courts*, 141–57; *CSPD, 1670*, appendix, 712 (8 September, 1665); Turner, *James II*, 86; W.G. Bell, *The Great Fire of London* (London, 1951), *passim*.

32 Bod. Lib., Clarendon, MSS 73, f. 215; 74, ff. 111, 284–8, 355–6; 75, ff. 99–103; Hutton. *Charles II*, 158–60; Fraser, *Charles II*, 262–5; G.L. Belcher, 'Spain and the Anglo-Portuguese Alliance of 1661', *Journal of British Studies*, 15 (1975), 67–88; Masters, *Mistresses of Charles II*, 45–94.

33 Clarendon, *Life*, i, 489–90; J. M. Cartwright (Ady), *Madame, A Life of Henrietta, Daughter of Charles I, and Duchess of Orleans* (London, 1900), 61–87.

34 Bryant (ed.), *Letters of Charles II*, 126–7 (Charles to Clarendon, 21 May, 1661); Clarendon, *Life*, i, 505–9; iii, 59–66; *CSVP, 1661–4*, 206; Bod. Lib., Carte MSS 46, f. 250; Latham (ed.), *Shorter Pepys*, 586.

35 Clarendon, *Life*, iii, 171–9; MacPherson (ed.), *Original papers*, i, 49–53; Burnet, *History*, i, 471–2; Latham (ed.), *Shorter Pepys*, 353, 586, 791; *Life*, i, 437–9; HMC, *Twelfth Report, Appendix, Part V, Manuscripts of His Grace the Duke of Rutland* (London, 1889), i, 14; Callow, *Making of King James*, 168–71. There is much confusion by Burnet, Clarendon and in James's 'Life' over the chronology of the lengthy divorce case. The initial private act obtained by Roos on 8 February 1667, which formally bastardised Roos's wife's illegitimate children, and which he requested in late 1666, has caused this muddle. See also *Journal of the House of Lords*, 12 (1666–75), 191 'petition to House of Lords by Dame Anne Roos pleading for financial maintenance from Roos', dated 22 February 1668.

36 Bryant (ed.), *Letters of Charles II*, 114 (Charles to Margaret, countess of Wemyss, 14 June 1661); Latham and Matthews (eds), *Diary of Samuel Pepys*, iv, 107.

37 Nicoll, *Diary*, 386; H.M. Paton (ed.), 'Letters from John Earl of Lauderdale and others, to Sir John Gilmour, President of the Session', *SHS, Miscellany, V* (Edinburgh, 1933), 139 (Charles to Gilmour, 27 September 1662), 150–5 (Gilmour to Lauderdale, [5] February 1663, with 'Notes by Sir John Gilmour on the duke of Monmouth's marriage' and 'Notes relative to the same'), and in general 144–59.

38 Paton (ed.), 'Letters from Lauderdale and others', 131 (Lauderdale to Gilmour, 25 January 1662), 132–3 (quote at 133) (Gilmour to Lauderdale, [?] February 1662); BL, Lauderdale Papers, Add. MS 23119, ff. 78, 88 (Lauderdale to Sir Robert Moray, 7 July and 14 July,

1663), ff. 101–2 (Moray to Lauderdale, 21 July, 1663); *RPS*, 1663/6/91, 1663/6/18; Latham (ed.), *Shorter Pepys*, 230 (27 October 1662) and 243 (24 December 1662), 247 (31 December). For the Act *salvo jure cuiuslibet*, which ended all sessions of the Scottish Parliament, see *RPS*, 1592/4/60 and 1605/6/97. For the final contract see NRS, Papers of the Scott Family of Harden, Lords Polwarth, Berwickshire, GD157, 3232 and W. Fraser (ed.), *The Scotts of Buccleuch*, 2 vols (Edinburgh, 1878), ii, 461–82. Also for background to the original entail (settlement of the succession of the estate) see GD157/3079 'An Information of the Condition of the Family of Buccleuch'. For detailed accounts of the affair see M. Lee Jr, 'The Buccleuch Marriage Contract: An Unknown Episode in Scottish Politics' in Lee, *The 'Inevitable' Union*, 223–45, esp. 233–45, and Lee, '*Dearest Brother*': *Lauderdale, Tweeddale and Scottish Politics 1660–1674* (Edinburgh, 2010), 45–52.

39 *Life*, ii, 626 ('Advice to his Son', 1692).

40 There is some doubt as to the parentage of Castlemaine's two daughters Anne (b.1661) and Barbara (b.1672), the former recognised by Charles but probably the daughter of Philip Stanhope, second earl of Chesterfield, and the latter not privately recognised by Charles and likely the daughter of John Churchill, first duke of Marlborough. For Charles II see Masters, *The Mistresses of Charles II, passim*; Wilson, *All the King's Women, passim*: L. Eduardo, *Mistresses: True Stories of Seduction, Power and Ambition* (London, 2005), 7–42, and Wynne, 'The Mistresses of Charles II and Restoration Court Politics', 171–90.

41 Lady Catherine Darnley may have been the daughter of James's keeper of the privy purse, James Grahme (1650–1730), but the duke was willing to recognise her as his daughter. A. Fea, *James II and His Wives* (London, 1908), 53–69, 136–42; R.K. Marshall, *The Days of Duchess Anne: Life in the Household of the Duchess of Hamilton, 1656–1716* (London, 1973), 105; Turner, *James II*, 60–68, 107–8; Miller, *James II*, 46–7; C.T. Wilson, *James The Second and the Duke of Berwick* (London, 1876), 1–2, 68.

42 Bryant (ed.), *Letters of Charles II*, 209–76. esp. 233–45; Bod. Lib., Carte MSS 198, ff. 28–30v, 'The substance of the Conference on the relations between the Crown of England and of France, and upon other public and political affairs', May 1670, translated and extracted from the memoirs of the Marquis de Louvois; *Life*, i, 451; C.H. Hartman, *Charles II and Madame* (London, 1934), 315; Hutton, *Charles II*, 263–6; Fraser, *Charles II*, 350–1, 358–60.

43 Latham (ed.), *Shorter Pepys*, 294–5 (22 July 1663, for quote), 228 (17 October 1662), 242 (23 December 1662), 823 (27 August 1667); J.J. Jusserand, *A French Ambassador at the Court of Charles II* (London, 1892), 91–5; Burnet, *History*, i, 203, 444; Wilson, *All the King's Women*, 178–9; Masters, *Mistresses of Charles II*, 79–80, 88–9; *ODNB*, S.M. Wynne, Barbara Palmer (bap.1640, d.1709): doi:10.1093/ref:odnb/28285.

44 Bowle (ed.), *Diary of John Evelyn*, 238; *CSPD, 1679–80*, 21; Burnet, *History*, i, 598–600; ii, 266–8; Morrice, i, 262 (28 June 1680), 280 (30 November, 280); Dalrymple, *Memoirs*, i, 363 (James to Barrillon, 1680, nd); Hutton, *Charles II*, 254–86 (esp. 279–80), 334–7, 392–5; Masters, *Mistresses of Charles II*, 138–9; Wilson, *All the King's Women*, 291–5, 304–6, 332–3; J. Delpech, *The Life and Times of the Duchess of Portsmouth* (London, 1953), *passim*. Fears of Catholicism had been growing and were expressed in print long before the Plot – see [A. Marvell], *An Account of the Growth of Popery and Arbitrary Government in England* (Amsterdam, 1677).

45 Quote ex Fraser, *Charles II*, 509; Dalrymple, *Memoirs*, i, 178–9 (Barrillon to Louis, 1 November 1677), 352 appendix (Barrillon to Louis, 14 October 1680), 369 (James to Barrillon, 1681, nd, received 16 March), 130 appendix, 364 appendix (Barrillon to Louis,

3 February 1681); *Life*, i, 482–3 (1672); Burnet, *History*, ii, 46–7 (1673), 280–2, 284; BL, Add. MS 32681 ff. 169–70; NA. PRO 31/3, 148 (Barrillon correspondence), ff. 80–5; Turner, *James II*, 119–20; Hutton, *Charles II*, 400–1

46 *Letters Illustrative of Public Affairs in Scotland addressed by contemporary Statesmen to George, Earl of Aberdeen, Lord Chancellor of Scotland, 1681–1684* (Spalding Club, Aberdeen, 1851), 37 (Bishop Paterson to Aberdeen, 29 July 1682),

47 Burnet, *History*, i, 203.

48 *Life*, ii, 628, 631; NA. SP 63/333/90, 120 and 176; O. Airy (ed.), *The Essex Papers* (Camden Society, London, 1890), i, 60–84, 122–3.

49 Paterson, *Lauderdale*, 226; *HMC, Eleventh Report, Part V, Manuscripts of the earl of Dartmouth,* 3 vols (London, 1887), i, 69–70 (letter James to Colonel George Legge, later Lord Dartmouth, 1 November, 1681); Burnet, *History*, i, 437; *ODNB*, R.K. Marshall, Anne Hamilton (1632–1716): doi:10.1093/ref:odnb/12046.

50 *Letters Illustrative of Public Affairs*, 48 (Bishop Paterson to Aberdeen, 17 August, 1682), Sir John Lauder, *Historical Selections from the Manuscripts of Sir John Lauder of Fountainhall, Volume first, Historical Observations, 1680–1696* (Bannatyne Club, Edinburgh, 1837), 110; *HMC, Fifteenth Report, Appendix, Part VIII, Manuscripts of the duke of Buccleuch and Queensberry (Drumlanrig), 2 vols.* (London, 1897, 1903), ii, 126 (Lundin to Queensberry, 25 August 1683), 130 (Lundin to Queensberry, 3 September 1683); Fountainhall, *Historical Notices*, ii, 470.

51 Jones, *Charles Middleton*, 36–44; A. J. Mann, 'Inglorious Revolution: Administrative Muddle and Constitutional Change in the Scottish Parliament of William and Mary', *Parliamentary History*, 22, pt 2 (2003), 134–40; *HMC, Buccleuch and Queensberry (Drumlanrig)*, ii, 18 (Earl of Moray to Queensberry, 16 and 18 November 1682); Fountainhall, *Historical Observes,* 127–8; Fountainhall, *Historical Notices*, ii, 745 (22 July, 1686); A. Lang, *Sir George Mackenzie: His Life and Times (1636 (?)–1691)* (London, 1909), 251–2, 255.

52 *HMC, Buccleuch and Queensberry (Drumlanrig)*, ii, 162 (Lundin to Queensberry, 30 October 1683); Fountainhall, *Historical Notices*, ii, 546 (payments by legal profession to duchess of Portsmouth July/August 1684 to secure various clerkships).

53 *HMC, Buccleuch and Queensberry (Drumlanrig)*, ii, 126 (Lundin to Queensberry, 3 September 1683); 158 (Lundin to Queensberry, 20 October, 1683); Fountainhall, *Historical Notices,* ii, 521, and for detailed narrative of Cessnock case see 510–22; *CSPD, 1683–4*, 65–7; Wodrow, *Sufferings,* iv, 71–94, 277–8; *ST*, x, 919–88; Willcock, *A Scots Earl*, 252–79; Harris, *Restoration*, 364–5; R.L. Greaves, *Secrets of the Kingdom: British Radicals from the Popish Plot to the Revolution of 1688–89* (Stanford, 1992), 241–6; McAlister, 'James VII and the Conduct of Scottish Politics', 113–23; Young (ed.), *Burgh and Shire Commissioners*, i, 96. For *habeas corpus* see A.J.Mann, 'The Law of the Person: Parliament and Social Control' in K.M. Brown and A.R. MacDonald (eds), *Parliament in Context, 1235–1707* (Edinburgh, 2010), 203; C. Jackson, 'Judicial Torture, the Liberties of the Subject, and Anglo-Scottish Relations, 1660–1690' in T.C. Smout (ed.), *Anglo-Scottish Relations from 1603 to 1900* (Oxford, 2005), 75–101.

54 Fountainhall, *Historical Notices,* ii, 521; Burnet, *James the Second*, 133–4, 279; Browning (ed.), *Reresby*, 409–10; Morrice, ii, 209 (19 November 1687); NA, PRO 31/3 (Baschet), 170 (4 June 1687), 171 (21 July 1687); Fea, *James II and His Wives*, 138–42; Miller, *James II*, 151; Turner, *James II*, 297–302; Callow, *King in Exile*, 166.

55 Burnet, *History*, i, 296; Ashley, *James II*, 94; Fea, *James II and His Wives*, 53; *Lorenzo*

Magalotti, 36; Hamilton, *Memoirs of Count Grammont,* 203; G. Davies (ed.), *Papers of Devotion of James II* (Oxford, 1924), 31 (dated 1694), 61–4 (dated 1696); *Life,* ii, 585; G.S. Stevenson (ed.), *The Letters of Madame. The Correspondence of Elizabeth-Charlotte of Bavaria, Princess Palatine, Duchess of Orleans,* 2 vols (London, 1924), i, 96–7; Callow, *King in Exile,* 125. The Sedley quote comes down to us in various versions.

56 John Huddleston, 'A Brief Account of Particulars occurring at the happy death of our late Sovereign Lord King Charles II, in regard to Religion' in Richard Huddleston, *A Short and Plain Way to the Faith and Church* (London, 1688), 35–8; RA, SP/M 1,14–15 (James's own account of Charles's death); NA. PRO 31/3/160, ff. 27–39 (Barrillon to Louis XIV, 18 February 1685); Dalrymple, *Memoirs,* i, appendix, 152–8; *Life,* i, 441–2; Hutton, *Charles II,* 263–4, 456.

57 Bowle (ed.), *Diary of John Evelyn,* 343 (2 October, 1685); *Copies of Two Papers Written by the late King Charles II* (London, 1686); BL, Add. MS 72887, Petty Papers, ff. 59–60, 60–61v, BL, Add. MSS 34508 Mackintosh Collections, ff. 31–2, 32–4; see also Huddleston, *A Short and Plain Way,* 31–4, and *State Tracts* (London, 1693), ii, 273–4.

58 Burnet, *History,* i, 134, 296–7; *Life,* i, 440–1; Macpherson, *Original papers,* i, 49–50; F. A. M. Mignet, *Négociations relatives à la succession d'Espagne,* 4 vols (1835–42), iii, 164; Miller, *Popery and Politics,* 109–10; Callow, *Making of King James,* 148.

59 *Papers of Devotion,* 1–2.

60 *Papers of Devotion,* 23, 26; Bod. Lib., Eng. Hist. MSS, C.44, f. 12.

61 M. Weygrand, *Turenne, Marshal of France* (London, 1930), 94–5, 126–7, 166–71; Callow, *Making of King James,* 143–4.

62 For example, see Miller, *James II,* 58–9 and Callow, *Making of King James,* 144–5.

63 Bod. Lib., Carte MSS 180, ff. 34–5, 58; Mignet, *Négociations relatives à la succession d'Espagne Sous Louis XIV,* 3 vols (Paris, 1835), iii, 164; *Life,* i, 452; Anne Hyde, *A Copy of a Paper written by the late Dutchess of York* (London, 1686), BL, Add. MS 72887, Petty Papers, ff. 63–63v and Add. 20731, 1, ff. 2–5 (dated/endorsed August 1670), see also *Papers of Devotion,* appendix 1.

64 BL, Add. MS 33573, Correspondence of the Hale Family, ii, f. 74; *CSPD, 1670,* 606 (letters from Clarendon to James and Anne dated December 1670); Callow, *Making of King James,* 147.

65 M.M. Verney (ed.), *Memoirs of the Verney Family,* 4 vols (London, 1899), iv, 202–4 (letter William Denton to Sir Ralph Verney, 6 April 1671); *HMC, Seventh Report, appendix* (London, 1879), 489; Burnet, *History,* i, 556–8.

66 H.M. Paton (ed.), 'Letters from John, Second Earl of Lauderdale, to John, Second Earl of Tweeddale, and Others', *SHS, Miscellany,* 6 (Edinburgh, 1939), 239 (Lauderdale to Tweeddale, 9 May 1672); Dalrymple, *Memoirs,* ii, appendix, 80 (letter Colbert to Louis XIV, 14 July 1671).

67 BL, Stowe MSS 191, 12 'Instructions for Sir Bernard Gascon [Gascoigne], Envoy Extraordinary to Leopold I, Emperor of Germany, for negotiating a marriage between James, duke of York and Claude Felicité' daughter of Archduke Ferdinand Charles' (16 February 1671/2); NA, PRO 31/3 (Baschet), all letters from Croissy, 126 (12 November 1671), 127 (1 March 1672); 128 (17 April 17 July, 31 July 1673), 129 (25 September 1673); Archives des Affaires étrangères, CPA, also letters from Croissy, 101 (2 November 1671), 104 (1 September 1672); *CSPV, 1671–72,* 114 (23 October 1671), 222 (3 June 1672); Bod. Lib., MSS Eng. C. 5237, letters from James to Thomas Butler, earl of Ossory, ff. 37–8 (4 July 1673), ff. 39–40 (25 July 1673), ff. 41–2 (28 August 1673); *CSPV,*

1673–75, 98 (11 August 1673), 125–6 (29 September 1673), 130–2 (6 and 11 October 1673); Bod. Lib., Carte MSS 77, f. 639 (Commons vote, 20 October 1673); Carte 198, ff. 28–30v, 'The substance of the Conference on the relations between the Crown of England and of France', May 1670. The best summary is Miller, *James II*, 71–3.

68 Bray (ed.), *Diary of John Evelyn*, ii, 86.

69 Ibid., ii, 112; Lonqueville, *Adventures of James II*, 184–5; Burnet, *History*, i, 523; 'The Declaration and Testimony of the True-Presbyterian, Anti-Prelatick and Anti-Erastian Persecuted Party in Scotland' in *A True and Exact Copy of a Treasonable and Bloody Paper [of Queensferry] . . . Together with the Execrable Declaration [of Sanquhar]* (Edinburgh, 1680), 10–11; James Kirkton, *The secret and true history of the church of Scotland from the Restoration to the year 1678* (Bannatyne Club, Edinburgh, 1817), 339.

70 James Kirkton, *The secret and true history of the church of Scotland from the Restoration to the year 1678* (Bannatyne Club, Edinburgh, 1817), 132, 269 (for quote); Wodrow, *Sufferings*, ii, 101, 228.

71 NRS, GD157/1636, Papers of the Scott Family of Harden, for example, *A Letter to Mr S, A Romish Priest, concerning the impossibility of the publick establishment of popery here in England* (London, 19 May, 1672); GD157/1641, 'Proclamation against papists' (Edinburgh, 16 December 1673); *A Congratulatory Epithalamium, or speech on the arrival of Her RH, and happy marriage to the most illustrious Prince James, duke of York* (London, 1673), 3; *Poems on Affairs of State* (London, 1703), i, 112–15 (at 115) 'On the Lord Mayor and Court Aldermen, presenting the late King and duke of York each with a copy of their Freedom', and 106–112 (at 111) 'A dialogue between two horses'; *RPCS, third series*, iv, 111, 117–23, 124–5; NRS, SP 4/2/370; R.Steele, *A Bibliography of Royal Proclamations*, 3 vols in 2 (New York, 1967), i, no. 3579; ii, no. 2367; Young (ed.), *Burgh and Shire Commissioners*, ii, 612–3.

72 *RPS*, 1673/11/4 (letter from the king to parliament); *LP*, iii, 75–6 (Leighton to Lauderdale, 17 December 1674); J. Buckroyd, *Church and State in Scotland, 1660–1681* (Edinburgh, 1980), 95–114; Buckroyd, *The Life of James Sharp, Archbishop of St Andrews, 1618–1679* (Edinburgh, 1987), 95–7; Paterson, *Lauderdale*, 204–6; Lee, *Dearest Brother*, 304–5; Harris, *Restoration*, 80–1.

73 Mackenzie, *Memoirs*, 142–72; 185–264, and for the topic of 1669/70 which 'began' opposition, the proposed Anglo-Scottish Union, see for the commission in London at 194–211, and also Terry, *The Cromwellian Union* (SHS, Edinburgh, 1902), appendix i, 187–218. For the best summary of the growth of the Hamiltonian party since 1669 see MacIntosh, *Scottish Parliament*, 83–98, 106–36; Paterson, *Lauderdale*, 191–211.

74 *RCGA*, iii, 90, 156, 172–3; Turner, *Memoirs*, 100–31; Burnet, *History*, i, 195; *Life*, ii, 634. For accounts of the Scottish Restoration settlement see in particular MacIntosh, *Scottish Parliament*, 1–35; Lee, 'Government and Politics in Scotland, 1661–1681', 11–52; Young, *The Scottish Parliament, 1639–1661*, 304–23.

75 Burnet, *History*, i, 199–201; *Mercurius Publicus*, 29 August–5 September, 1660; Wodrow, *Sufferings*, i, 49–52; MacIntosh, *Scottish Parliament*, 9–10; Dow, *Cromwellian Scotland*, 268–9.

76 Harris, *Restoration*, 47–8; Hutton, *Restoration*, 130–5.

77 *RPCS, third series*, i, i–xx, 1–4, 382–3; vi, 16–17, 174; *RPS*, 1662/5/4–5, 1662/5/9, 1662/5/15; *ODNB*, Tristram Clarke, 'John Paterson' (1632–1708): doi:10.1093/ref:odnb/21532; Jackson, *Restoration Scotland*, 104–5; G. Donaldson, *Scotland: James V-James VII* (Edinburgh, 1976), 362.

78 *Life*, ii, 635; Brown and Mann (eds), *Parliament and Politics in Scotland, 1567–1707*, 'Introduction' 40–3; Mann, 'Inglorious Revolution', 122–4.

79 BL, Add. MS 23114, f. 88; *RPS*, 1661/1/16–17; 1661/1/24; 1661/1/7 (wording of oath); 1662/5/70; (declaration). For the fall of Cassillis and a few other diehards see Baillie, *Letters*, iii, 463–4, Mackenzie, *Memoirs*, 23 and *LP*, i, 39–40 (Middleton's instructions), 62–3; Buckroyd, *Church and State*, 29.

80 Bod. Lib., Carte MSS 46, f. 583 (report in letter Arlington to Ormonde, 31 December 1667); *RPS*, 1661/1/14. This level of taxation had been previously agreed by the Committee of Estates. Mackenzie, *Memoirs*, 17–18.

81 *RPS*, 1661/1/159 'Act concerning religion and church government', 28 March, 1661.

82 *RPS*, 1661/1/32, 1661/1/67, 1661/1/74; 1661/1/158 'Act rescinding and annulling the pretendit parliaments in the yeers 1640, 1641 etc'; *RPS*, 1661/1/159.

83 Bod. Lib., Clarendon MSS 75, ff. 427–8 'Thomas Sydserf', Information for his sacred majestie'; *LP*, i, 76–7 (letter James Sharp to Patrick Drummond, 2 March 1661); Burnet, *History*, i, 213–16; Clarendon, *Life*, i, 433–41; NRS, Hamilton Papers, GD406/2/M9/148, 'Memorandum concerning the parliament of 1661'; Mackenzie, *Memoirs*, 28–9; Bod. Lib., Clarendon MSS 74, ff. 220–21 (Middleton to Clarendon, 4 March 1661); G. Davies and P. Hardcastle, 'The Restoration of Scottish Episcopacy', *Journal of British Studies*, 1/2 (1961–2), 39–40; Paterson, *Lauderdale*, 134–5; MacIntosh, *Scottish Parliament*, 23–5.

84 *RPCS, third series*, i, 1–4. For Scots in the post-1633 English Privy Council under Charles I, see John Scally, 'The Political Career of James, Third Marquis and First Duke of Hamilton (1606–1649), to 1643' (PhD thesis, Cambridge, 1992), 145–6.

85 *RPCS, third series* vi, 344–99, 567–624; vii, 1–429; Callow, *Making of King James*, 281; Turner, *James II*, 178; McAlister, 'James VII and the Conduct of Scottish Politics', 31–2.

86 *LP*, iii, 181–5, esp. 184–5 (letter James to Lauderdale, 24 November, 1679); Bod. Lib., Clarendon MSS 74, ff. 290–3. (letter Clarendon to Middleton, 26 March 1661). Clarendon advised caution and not bold measures as Mackenzie claims. Mackenzie, *Memoirs*, 27–8; *LP*, i, 59 (letter James Sharp to Lauderdale, undated, late 1660, warning him of how he was being portrayed in England as a zealous Covenanter); Hutton, *Charles II*, 161; *RPCS, third series*, i, 28–32; *RPS*, 1662/5/4–5, 1662/5/9; Brown, *Kingdom or Province?*, 147.

87 BL, Lauderdale Papers, Add. MSS 23117, f. 19; *LP*, i, 103–5, 106–119 (letters William Sharp to Lauderdale advising him of the billeting affair); Mackenzie, *Memoirs*, 65–9, 72–6, 78–89, 90–111; NRS, GD90/2/260, f. 11r; NLS, Dalrymple MS 3424, ff. 331–4, 425–31 (details of parliamentary investigation into billeting affair); Lee, 'Government and Politics in Scotland, 1661–1681', 33–6; MacIntosh, *Scottish Parliament*, 44–8; Paterson, *Lauderdale*, 151–6.

88 *LP*, i, 181–3 (Letter Sir Robert Moray to Lauderdale, 23 August 1663).

89 Paterson, *Lauderdale*, 169–234 and for a very general summary see R.A. Paterson. 'King of Scotland: Lauderdale and the Restoration North of the Border' in *History Today*, 53, 1 (London, 2003), 21–7.

90 *RPCS*, third series, iii, 38–40 (7 June 1669), 586–9 (3 September 1672); vi, 265 (29 June 1679). The best account of the indulgences is still Buckroyd, *Church and State*, 78–89, 101–6, 100–20.

91 For a discussion of this phase see Mann 'James VII as Unionist and Nationalist', 111–14.

92 *RPS*, 1663/61–146; MacIntosh, *Scottish Parliament*, 48–52.

93 G. Ornsby (ed.), *The correspondence of John Cosin, Lord Bishop of Durham, together with other papers illustrative of his life and times,* 2 vols (Durham, 1868–72), ii, 97; *Life,* i, 425, 431–2, 437–9; Bray (ed.), *Diary of John Evelyn,* ii, 29, 34; Burnet, *History,* i, 446–7, 456–60; *CSPD, 1667,* 189; Clarendon, *Life,* iii, 277–8, 292–7, 300–9; Callow, *Making of King James,* 166–70; Hutton. *Charles II,* 253; Hutton, *The Restoration,* 283.

94 For Episcopal anxiety and the response from Lauderdale and others before, up to and after the Pentland Rising, see *LP,* i 199–233 (Letters Rothes, Hamilton, Tweeddale and Bellenden to Lauderdale, dated 14 July 1664–24 October 1665); heated letters Kincardine to Sharp and reply, 6–14 November 1665); ii, appendix A. i–lxiv (letters Archbishops Sharp and Burnet to Sheldon, 27 February 1664 to 11 August 1668); Burnet, *History,* i, 379–87; NLS MS 2512 Papers of Charles Kirkpatrick Sharpe, ff. 54–76v (letters from Sharp and Burnet to Lauderdale, 22 August 1664–10 August 1667), f. 87 (Burnet to Lauderdale, 8 May 1666); NLS, MS 7023 Lauderdale Letters, ff. 1–4 and 34 (letters Lauderdale to Tweeddale, 15 October 1664 and 16 May 1667); Buckroyd, *Church and State,* 65–74; Lee, *Dearest Brother,* 78–95.

95 *LP,* ii, lxiv–ixix (Burnet's resignation); *RPS,* 1670/7/11; J.A. Lamb, 'Archbishop Alexander Burnet', *Records of the Scottish Church History Society,* X1 (1955), 133–48; J.M. Buckroyd, 'The Dismissal of Archbishop Alexander Burnet, 1669' *Records of the Scottish Church History Society,* XVII (1973), 149–55; Paterson, *Lauderdale,* 178–85.

96 NLS, MS 7025 Letters of John Hay, earl of Tweeddale, ff. 4, 17, 26; 7004, ff. 48, 57, 97, 109; NLS, Yester Box 5, folder 4 and 5; *LP,* ii, 181–3, 200; Burnet, *History,* i, 497–530; D. Butler, *The Life and Letters of Robert Leighton* (London, 1903), 403–13 (Leighton's original proposals for comprehension discussions, 1667); *CSPV,* 1673–75, 350 (reports in early 1675 of close cooperation between Lauderdale, Danby and English bishops); Buckroyd, *Church and State,* 86, 88, 95–102, 108, 110, 113–4.

97 BL, Lauderdale Papers, Add. MSS 23242 'Instructions to Lauderdale for the convention of estates (1678)', f. 64, and also ff. 75, 74, 79, 80 ; NRS, Hamilton Papers, GD 406/1/8678, 8095–6; NRS, Biel Muniments, 'The calling and proceedings of the convention of estates holden in Edinburgh, the 26 Junii 1678, by the duke of Lauderdale, his majesties commissioner', GD6/1108, ff. 1–46 and for the walkout on 9 July see GD, 1108, ff. 43–6; *RPS,* 1678/1/7, M1678/6/1–11; C1678/6/1–5; A1678/6/1–18 (for walkout see A1788/6/17); MacIntosh, *Scottish Parliament,* 155–71; G.H. MacIntosh, 'Arise King John: Commissioner Lauderdale and the Parliament in the Restoration Era' in Brown and Mann (eds), *Parliament and Politics in Scotland, 1567–1707,* 179–80.

98 For flavours of corruption, especially over Hatton (sometimes Halton), see *HMC, Eleventh Report, Appendix, Part VI, Manuscripts of the Dukes of Hamilton* (London, 1887),151–3 (letters Queensberry to Hamilton, 22 January –2 February 1676); *LP,* iii, 229–30 (Bishop of Edinburgh to duchess of Lauderdale, 22 March 1683); NLS, MS 3134, Yule Collection 'Memorial on the differences between the earl of Tweeddale and the duke of Lauderdale from 1666 to 1682', f. 119; NRAS, 1275 Manuscripts of the duke of Buccleuch and Queensberry, 113 (Bishop of Edinburgh to marquis of Queensberry, 26 August 1682). For immediate reaction to Sharp's murder see NRAS, 1275 Buccleuch and Queensberry, 1135, Letters Rothes to Queensberry (same to same, 5 May 1679); BL, Add. MS 28747 Letters of the Earl and duke of Lauderdale, Original Letters of Scotch Noblemen (Rothes to Lauderdale, 4 May 1679).

99 *HMC, Hamilton,* 197 (James to Hamilton, 9 December 1673); *LP,* ii, 240 (James to Lauderdale 11 November 1673); iii, 153 (same to same, 14 June 1678), 160 (same to

same, 24 July 1678); Bod.Lib. Eng. Misc. E, 4 ff. 11–12 (Letter Charles to Lauderdale, 14 June 1678); Paterson, *Lauderdale*, 214.

100 NRAS, 217, Moray Papers, box 7, no.312 (letter from bishops of Scotland to earl of Moray, Secretary of State, 9 March 1682); no. 405 (letter duchess of Lauderdale to earl of Moray, 4 April 1680); Letters of Bishops to earl of Moray (1681–86), esp. from Paterson, no. 585 (12 March 1680), no. 576 (21 September 1682), no. 558 (8 September 1683), no. 536 (31 December 1685), no. 537 (24 April 1686); no.700 (letter George Mackenzie of Rosehaugh to Moray, nd c.1684); NRAS, 1275, Buccleuch and Queensberry, 113, Bishops' letters to William Douglas marquis of Queensberry, esp. concerning appointment of Alexander Rose (Ross) (Arthur Rose, archbishop of Glasgow to Queensberry, 23 June 1684) (Alexander Burnet, archbishop of St Andrews to Queensberry 26 April ?1683) and (Rose and Burnet to Queensberry ?14 September 1683).

101 *RPS*, 1663/6/64, *RPCS*, third series, ii, 438–42, 547–8; *RPS*, C1669/10/4–6; 1669/10/14; *LP*, ii, 150–1 (letters Lauderdale to Sir Robert Moray, 28 and 30 October 1669); Mackenzie, *Memoirs*, 166–7; *RPS*, C1672/6/1, 1672/6/7a; *RPCS*, third series, vi, xix–xxii; Childs, *Army of Charles II*, 196–8; B. P. Lenman, 'Militia, Fencible Men and Home Defence, 1660–1797' in N. MacDougall (ed.), *Scotland and War AD79–1918* (Edinburgh, 1991), 170– 84.

102 NRAS, 217, Moray Papers, box 7, no. 429 (letter Sir Andrew Forrester to the duke of Lauderdale, 7 September 1678).

103 Glozier, *Scottish Soldiers in France*, 43, 57–68; Addison, *A discourse of Tangier under the government of the earl of Teviot, passim*; J. Ferguson (ed.), *Papers illustrating the history of the Scots brigade in the service of the United Netherlands, 1572–1782*, 3 vols (SHS, Edinburgh, 1899), i, 481, 509n; Dalton, *The Scots Army*, 67–9; *ODNB*, P. Hopkins, Thomas Buchan (c.1641–1724): doi:10.1093/ref:odnb/3827.

104 Wodrow, *Sufferings*, ii, 62–3; T. B. Macaulay, *History of England*, 4 vols (London, 1906) i, 589 (Johnston comment); Dalton, *The Scots Army*, 60–66, 70–78; Glozier, *Scottish Soldiers in France,* 82–3, 259; *ODNB*, D. Stevenson, William Drummond (c.1617–1688): doi:10.1093/ref:odnb/8086, and Thomas Dalzell of Binns (bap. 1615, d.1685): doi:10.1093/ref:odnb/7079.

105 Turner, *Memoirs*, 15–228; M. Linklater and C. Hesketh, *For King and Conscience: John Graham of Claverhouse, Viscount Dundee (1648–1689)* (London, 1989), 56–65, 127–38, 146–8. For intelligent summaries *ODNB*, M. Linklater, John Graham (1648?–1689): doi:10.1093/ref:odnb/11208 and D. Stevenson, Sir James Turner (b. c.1615, d. in or after 1689): doi:10.1093/ref:odnb/27853.

106 RA SP/MAIN/2/10 , 'Rules for Genll Officers', 1–8; Sir James Turner, *Pallas armata: Military Essayes of the Ancient Grecian, Roman, and Modern Art of War, written in the years 1670 and 1671*(London, 1683), i–iii (dedication to duke of Albany and York); Glozier, *Scottish Soldiers in France*, 90–2; A.M. Scott (ed.), 'Letters of John Graham of Claverhouse', *SHS, Miscellany, XI* (SHS, Edinburgh, 1990), 187–8 (Letter Claverhouse to Queensberry, 20 March 1683) and *HMC, Buccleuch and Queensberry (Drumlanrig)*, i , 275–6.

107 Fountainhall, *Historical Notices*, i, 169–72 (case dated 27 July 1677); BL, Lauderdale Papers, Add. MSS 3138, f. 59 (Letter James to Lauderdale, 7 September 1677); Willcock, *A Scots Earl*, 134–5.

108 *RPCS, third series*, iv, 1673–6, 69–71; NRS, Hamilton Papers, GD 406, L1/265, 1 and 2 'commissions concerning the admiralty court' (1673, 1676, 1680 and 1683); AC 7/5 in S. Mowat and E.J. Richards, *High Court of Admiralty Records, 1627–1750* (2005), CD-Rom;

RPS, 1681/7/40 (14 September 1681); BL, Carte MSS 216, f. 494 (Letter Bridgman to Arran, 13 May 1684); E.J. Graham, *A Maritime History of Scotland, 1650–1790* (East Linton, 2002), 26–36; S. Murdoch, A. Little and A.D.M. Forte 'Scottish Privateering, Swedish Neutrality and Prize Law in the Third Anglo-Dutch War, 1672–1674', *Forum Navale: Skrifter Utgivna av Sjohisnriska Samfundet*, 59 (2003), 39–40.

109 *LP*, ii, 75 (letter Sir Robert Moray to Lauderdale, 14 October 1667), 141–45 (Lauderdale to Charles II, 19 and 22 October 1669), 149–50 (Moray to Lauderdale, 28 October 1669), 154–5 (Lauderdale to Moray, 2 November 1669); 159–61, 165–6 (Moray to Lauderdale, 13 and 30 November 1669), appendix B, lxxvii (letter James to Lauderdale, 29 October 1669); *RPS*, 1669/10/9 (22 October 1669), 1670/7/5 (30 July 1670); C.S. Terry (ed.), *The Cromwellian Union: papers relating to the negotiations for an incorporating union between England and Scotland 1651–1652, with an appendix relating to the negotiations in 1670* (SHS, Edinburgh, 1902), 187–224; NLS, MS 14492, 'The proceedings of the commissioners of both kingdoms, 1667–68', ff. 26–113; NA, SP 104/176 Minutes of the Foreign Committee (of the English Privy Council) ff. 155–61; Lee, *Dearest Brother*, 153–62, 194–8; Paterson, *Lauderdale*, 187–9; MacIntosh, *Scottish Parliament*, 81–98, 105–8; M. Lee Jr, *The Cabal* (Urbana, 1965), 54–9. For the attempted assassination of Sharp see Kirkton, *History*, 160; *RPCS, third series*, ii, 486–9; Buckroyd, *Life of James Sharp*, 90–1.

110 BL, Lauderdale Papers, Add. MSS 23129, ff. 48–9; (letter Tweeddale to Lauderdale, 3 April 1668); Kirkton, *History*, 299–300; Mackenzie, *Memoirs*, 138–9; *Life*, ii, 635

111 *RPCS, third series*, ii, 175–8; vii, 45, 664–5 ('Memorial concerning the Scottish plantation'), 671–2; W.R. Scott, *The Constitutions and Finances of English, Scottish and Irish Joint Stock Companies to 1720*, 3 vols (Cambridge, 1910), ii, 128–51 (esp. 143–48), 377–8; *HMC, Buccleuch and Queensberry (Drumlanrig)*, i, 176 (letter James to Marquis of Queensberry, 2 November 1682); Callow, *Making of King James*, 238–61; B. Harris, 'Scotland's Herring Fisheries and the Posterity of the Nation, c.1660–1760', *SHR*, 79 (2000), 43–5.

112 W.L. Grant, J. Munro and A.W. Fitzroy (eds), *Acts of the Privy Council of England, Colonial Series, i, 1613–1680* (Hereford, 1908), 512, 516–17; *CSPC, 1669–1674*, 13–17, nos. 42, 43, 46, 50 and 51; A.I. Macinnes, M.D. Harper and L.G. Fryer (eds), *Scotland and the Americas, c.1650–c.1939: A Documentary Source Book* (SHS, Edinburgh, 2002), 135–6; R. Robert, *Chartered Companies: Their Role in the Development of Overseas Trade* (London, 1969), 103–8, 133–40.

113 *CSPC, 1661–68*, nos. 672–3, 679, 683, 685, 686 and 695; *1681–5*, nos. 413, 449, 1848 and 1910; G.P. Insh, *Scottish Colonial Schemes* (Glasgow, 1922), 145–211. For a summary of James and his American colonies see Callow, *Making of King James*, 264–81. His comment that James agreed to the New York Parliament out of 'weakness' seems unlikely given that he had just presided so successfully at the Edinburgh Parliament. James conceded out of financial need but also with more political confidence. Callow, *Making of King James*, 280.

114 *RPCS, third series*, viii, 437, 508, 599–600 (warrant from Charles II, 15 August 1682); *HMC, Buccleuch and Queensberry (Drumlanrig)*, i, 175 (James to marquis of Queensberry, 10 October 1682), 195–5 (James to Queensberry, 4 August, 1683); Wodrow, *Sufferings*, iv, 7–10; Burnet. *History*, ii, 332; *Letters Illustrative of Public Affairs*, 58–60 (Sir John Cochrane to Aberdeen, 16 September 1682), 68–9 (Sir George Mackenzie to Aberdeen, September, 1682); L.G. Fryer, 'Documents Relating to the Formation of the Carolina

Company of Scotland, 1682', *South Carolina Historical Magazine*, 99 (April, 1998), 110–34; Young (ed.), *Shire and Burgh Commissioners*, ii, 433; P. Karsten, 'Plotters and Proprietaries, 1682–82: The "Council of Six" and the Colonies', *Historian*, 38 (1976), 474–84; Insh, *Scottish Colonial Schemes*, 186–211; T. M. Devine, *Scotland's Empire, 1600–1815* (London, 2003), 38–9; Macinnes, *Union and Empire*, 165, 167–9.

115 W. Macleod (ed.), *Journal of the Hon. John Erskine of Carnock, 1683–1687* (SHS, Edinburgh, 1893), 26, 39, 64, 67–72; *CSPC, 1681–1685*, 295, 336; Insh, *Scottish Colonial Schemes*, 206–11. For parliamentary decreets of forfeiture against those Scots found guilty of involvement in the Rye House Plot, and who were accused of using Carolina as a front for their activity, see *RPS*, A1685/4/8, 4/9, 4/12, 4/18, 4/30, 4/33, 4/36 (all June 1685).

116 NRS, Papers of the Mackenzie Family, earls of Cromartie, GD305/1/122/515 (14 March 1682); *CSPC. 1681–1685*, 554 (23 November 1683); [Barclay], *Advertisement to all Tradesmen, Husbandmen, Servants and others who are willing to Transport themselves unto the Province of New-East-Jersy in America* (Edinburgh 1684) and *The Bannatyne Miscellany*, iii (Edinburgh, 1855), 385; *RPCS, third series*, viii. 37; x, 79 (prisoners from the Bass Rock, December 1684); xi, 94. 95, 114–19, 123, 125–31, 135–38, 145, 148–9, 153, 155, 157–9, 163–8, 173, 178, 208–10, 219–20, 233, 243, 251–4, 280, 329, 330 (July to December 1685); *HMC, Buccleuch and Queensberry (Drumlanrig)*, i, 215 (James to Queensberry, 16 July 1685); N.C. Landsman, *Scotland and its First American Colony, 1683–1765* (Princeton, NJ, 1985), 99–130; Devine, *Scotland's Empire*, 39–40; Macinness, *Union and Empire*, 165, 167–9; Macinnes, Harper, and Fryer (eds), *Scotland and the Americas*, 71; Insh, *Scottish Colonial Schemes*, 145–85; L.G. Fryer, 'Robert Barclay of Urie and East New Jersey', *Northern Scotland*, 15 (1995), 1–17.

117 Bod. Lib., MSS Eng. e. 3454, 66–76b, anonymous 'Treatise of advice to a Catholic King of Great Britain', c.1710; James VII, *By the King. A Proclamation* (Edinburgh, 1687); *RPCS, third series*, viii, 123–4; 156–8; Wodrow, *Sufferings*, iv, 417–19; 426–7; [Burnet], *Some Reflections On His Majestie's Proclamation of the 12th of February for a Toleration in Scotland* (?Amsterdam, 1687); Turner, *James II*, 82–3; Miller, *James II*, 167–8; Callow, *Making of King James*, 238–9, 262–3; Brown, *Kingdom or Province?*, 162.

CHAPTER 4

1 Different versions of this February letter exist, see Bod. Lib., Carte MSS 243, f. 358 and Bryant (ed.), *Letters of Charles II*, 304–5, ex Dalrymple, *Memoirs*, ii, appendix, 260; *Life*, i, 541–2; NRS, Papers of the Campbell Family, earl of Breadalbane [Breadalbane Muniments] , GD112/39/125/14; *The State Letters of Henry earl of Clarendon*, 2 vols (Oxford, 1763), ii, 268–76; Bod. Lib., Carte MSS 39, f. 21 and Carte 228, f. 147 (attempts by English bishops to convert James, February 1679); NRAS, 1275 Manuscripts of the Duke of Buccleuch and Queensberry, volume 105 (letter Earl of Moray to Queensberry, 27 February 1679).

2 S. Waller (ed.), *The Correspondence of Henry Hyde, Earl of Clarendon and his brother Laurence Hyde, Earl of Rochester; with the diary of Lord Clarendon from 1687 to 1690*, 2 vols (London, 1828), ii. 466–71; *Life*, i, 537–41; Morrice, i, 136 (4 March 1678/9); Turner, *James II*, 155–6; Miller, *James II*, 90–92.

3 NLS, Wodrow MSS Folio XXXI, 3 (cxiv), 'Petition by the House of Commons to his Matie against the Duke of Lauderdale, 2 May, 1679'.

4 For letters to Prince William (8 May to 10 August 1679), Dalrymple, *Memoirs,* ii, 296–310, and for Legge (28 March to 11 August 1679), *HMC, Dartmouth,* i, 30–37. Few survive of those sent to Charles. For the quote see Dalrymple, *Memoirs,* ii, 298–9 (letter from James to Prince William, 17 May 1679). See also Bod. Lib., Carte MSS 118, f. 338 and 141, f. 68 (letter James to Ormonde, 3 March 1679); 'Kincardine Papers' in J. Maudment (ed.), *The Spottiswoode Miscellany: A collection of original papers, illustrative chiefly of the civill and ecclesiastical history of Scotland* (Edinburgh, 1844), 217–9 (letters James to Alexander Bruce, earl of Kincardine, 1 May (The Hague), 16 June (Brussels) and 11 August (Brussels), 1679).

5 Dalrymple, *Memoirs,* ii, 299–300, 302–3, 304–5, 307–8. For the quote, Dalrymple, *Memoirs,* ii, 308–9 (letter James to Prince William, 30 July 1679); *Life,* i, 547–56.

6 *HMC, Dartmouth,* i, 30 (letter James to Legge, 4 April, 1679), 30–1 (same to same, 14 April 1679); Bod. Lib., Eng. Hist. MSS C.5237, Letters James to duke of Ormonde, ff. 13–14 (1 April 1679).

7 *HMC, Dartmouth,* i, 33–4 (letter James to Legge, 28 May 1679, with 'Heads you are to discourse with His Majesty upon'); Bod. Lib., Eng. Hist. MSS C.5237 Letters James to Thomas, earl of Ossory, ff. 51–2 (30 April 1679).

8 *HMC, Dartmouth,* i, 36 (letter James to Legge, 22 July 1679); *Life,* i, 560.

9 *HMC, Fourteenth Report, Manuscripts of Marquess of Ormonde, New Series, I-V* (London, 1895-1908), v, 135; *RPCS, third series,* vi, 280–1; W.D. Cooper (ed.), *Saville Correspondence* (London, 1858), 105, 109; Wodrow, *Sufferings,* iii, 169–71; Fountainhall, *Historical Notices,* i, 246 (15 November 1679); BL, Add MS 23244, ff. 20–27 (Mackenzie of Tarbat's 'complaint'); *Some further matters of fact relating to the administration of Affairs in Scotland under the Duke of Lauderdale offered to His Majesties Consideration in Obedience to his Royal Command* (?Edinburgh, 1679); Paterson, *Lauderdale,* 251–2; Hutton, *Charles II,* 372; Buckroyd, *Church and State,* 130–1; E.H. Hyman, 'A Church Militant: Scotland, 1661–1690', *Sixteenth Century Journal,* 26, 1 (1995), 68–70.

10 *Life,* i, 570–4; NRAS, 217, Moray Papers, box 7, no. 447 (Letter Lauderdale to the earl of Moray, 11 October 1679); Bod. Lib., Carte MSS 232, ff. 51–2 (Francis Aungier, earl of Longford to Richard Butler, earl of Arran; account of James's return, 6 September 1679); Ashley, *James II,* 127–9.

11 NRAS, 217, Moray Papers, box 7, no. 446 (letter Lauderdale to earl of Moray, Newmarket, 8 October 1679).

12 Fountainhall, *Historical Observes,* 74–5 (reflections at the death of Lauderdale in August 1682); *HMC, Ormonde,* iv, 552 (letter Ormonde to Sir Robert Southwell, 28 October 1679); *Life,* i, 571; NRAS, 217, Moray Papers, box 7, no.461 (letter Lauderdale to earl of Moray, Whitehall, 4 March 1680); *LP,* iii, 198 (James to Lauderdale, 24 April 1680), 210 (Letter Thomas Murray to Lauderdale, 25 September 1680); Buckroyd, *Church and State,* 132; Paterson, *Lauderdale,* 252–3; Hutton, *Charles II,* 387–8.

13 *RPCS, third series,* vi, 331–2; Wodrow, *Sufferings,* iii, 174; *Life,* i, 576–7 (the date being NS); *HMC, Dartmouth,* i, 37–8 (letter James to Legge, 28 November 1679); *London Gazette,* no. 1464 (21 November to 1 December 1679). The town council had beggars cleared off the streets before the royal party arrived, see M. Wood (ed.), *Extracts from the Records of the Burgh of Edinburgh,* x, 1665–1680 (Edinburgh, 1950), 381 (29 October 1679); M.V. Hay, *The Enigma of James II* (London, 1938), 12–13.

14 Morrice, i, f. 274 (6 November 1680), f. 196 (4 June 1679).

15 *CSPD, 1671,* 7 March 1671 (warrant to the Scottish Treasury Commissioners for £1,000

sterling), 3 June 1671 (appointment of Bruce); H. Fenwick, *Architect Royal: The Life and Works of Sir William Bruce, 1630–1710* (Kineton, 1970), 32; J. Gifford, C. McWilliam, and D. Walker, with C. Wilson, *The Buildings of Scotland: Edinburgh* (Harmondsworth, 1984), 127–8, 142–3; J. Harrison, *The History of the monastery of the Holy-Rood and of the palace of Holyrood House* (Edinburgh and London, 1919), 197–205; S.Bruce and S. Yearley, 'The Social Construction of Tradition: The Restoration Portraits and the Kings of Scotland', in D. McCrone, S. Kendrick and P. Shaw (eds), *The Making of Scotland: Nation, Culture and Social Change* (Edinburgh, 1989), 175–88. In late 1679 the Edinburgh town council gave some 117 of James's servants and companions the freedom of the capital. Wood (ed.), *Records of the Burgh of Edinburgh*, x, 388 (26 December 1679).

16   *RPS*, 1633/6/58 (28 June 1633), c1639/8/74 (22 October 1639), 1685/4/98 (16 June 1685, ratification of patent dated 29 November 1681); R. Maidment (ed.), *The Remains of Sir Robert Sibbald, containing his autobiography, memoirs of the Royal College of Physicians, a portion of his literary correspondence, and an account of his MSS* (Edinburgh, 1833–37), 15, 30; [William Eccles] *An Historical Account of the Rights and Privileges of the Royal College of Surgeons* (Edinburgh, 1707); R. P. Ritchie, *The Early Days of the Royal College of Physicians* (Edinburgh, 1899). For a summary see H. Ouston, 'York in Edinburgh: James VII and the Patronage of Learning in Scotland, 1679–1688' in J. Dwyer, R.A. Mason and A. Murdoch (eds), *New Perspectives on the Politics and Culture of Early Modern Scotland* (Edinburgh, 1982), 139–43.

17   NRS, Hamilton Papers, GD 406, M9 180/1, ' Copy letters under Great Seal of James VII and II restoring the noble and ancient order of the Thistle' (29 May 1687); M1, 222/18, 19, 'Copy of statutes of the most ancient order of the Thistle with extract of oath taken etc.' (29 and 31 May 1687); NRAS, 217, Moray Papers, box 7, no. 332 'Statutes and orders of the most ancient & noble order of the thistle (or St Andrews)', 1687; George Mackenzie, Mackenzie, *Jus Regium: or the Just and Solid Foundations of Monarchy in General; and more especially of the Monarchy of Scotland: Maintain'd against Buchannan, Naphtali, Dolman, Milton &c.* (London, 1684), 29; J. W. Cairns, 'Sir George Mackenzie, the Faculty of Advocates and the Avocates' Library', in J. Cairns and A. Cain (eds), G. Mackenzie, *Oratio inauguralis in aperienda Jurisconsultorum Bibliotheca* (Edinburgh, 1989), 18–35.

18   'Familiar Letters of Charles II and James, duke of York', 161–4 (letters dated 29 August 1681 to 19 February 1682); Wood (ed.), *Records of the Burgh of Edinburgh*, x, 390; C. Oman, *Mary of Modena* (London, 1962), 70; Fountainhall, *Historical Observes*, 51; H.Ouston, 'From Thames to Tweed Departed': The Court of James. Duke of York in Scotland, 1679–82' in Cruikshanks (ed.), *The Stuart Courts*, 271–3; Hay, *Enigma of James*, 23.

19   'Familiar Letters of Charles II and James, duke of York', 162–3; NRS, RH3/163, 'Letters to and from the duke and duchess of Hamilton, 'Red Book', ii 176 (Mary to Anne, 20 January [1682]), 177 (Anne to Mary, 22 February 1682), 178 (Mary to Anne, 4 April [1681]), 179 (Anne to Mary, 9 May [1681]), 181 (Mary to Anne, 15 June [1681], 182 (Anne to Mary, 21 June [1681]); Bod. Lib., Carte MSS. 219 (Ormonde to the earl of Arran, on Mary's qualities, 12 April 1683); NA. PRO, SP8/3, part 1, 7, Letter James to Prince of Orange, 12 January 1675; Morrice, i, 301; *Letters Illustrative of Public Affairs*, 45–7 (letters Mackenzie of Rosehaugh to Aberdeen, 15 and 17 August, 1682); 'The Gordon Letters' in *The Miscellany of the Spalding Club*, iii (Aberdeen, 1846), 221–2 (letter Mary to Elizabeth, marchioness of Huntly, 20 [?] 1682). Morrice reports that by 1684 'the

duke had already ten children buried in Westminster Abbey' from his two wives, Morrice, i, 437 (17 May 1684).

20 NRAS, 217, Moray Papers, box 7, no. 669 (Letter Richard Maitland to the earl of Moray, 22 January 1681), no. 640 (Letter Sir William Sharp to the earl of Moray, 3 February 1681); *A True and Exact Relation of his Royal Highness' Progress Upon the 3rd, 4th and 5th February Instant* (Edinburgh, 1681); Anon, *Some Historical Memories of the Life and Actions of his Royal Highness . . . James, Duke of York and Albany . . . from his birth, Anno 1633 to this Present Year, 1682* (London, 1683), 123; J. Maidment (ed.), *Argyll papers, 1640–1723* (Edinburgh,1834), 17–18; Willcock, *Life and Times of the earl of Argyll,* 248–50.

21 *LP*, iii, 181–4, esp. 182–3 (Lauderdale to James, 18 November 1679); *Life*, i, 275–6; *RPCS, third series,* vi, 334.

22 *HMC, Dartmouth,* i, 41–2 (James to Legge, 14 December 1679); *RPCS, third series,* vi, 334.

23 Fountainhall, *Historical Observes,* 75; *HMC, Dartmouth,* i, 42.

24 *RPCS, third series,* vi, 316 (letter Charles to council ,13 September 1679); vi, 349–93, committees chosen (11 December 1679 to 15 February 1680); vi, 346 (Lauderdale to Chancellor, 6 December 1679); vi, 345–6 (report of committee anent the militia, 18 December 1679); *LP*, ii, 186–7 (James to Lauderdale, 8 December 1679), 206–8 (secret council to Lauderdale, 4 September 1680); BL, Lauderdale Papers, Add. MSS 23136, f. 40 (James to Lauderdale, 23 December 1679), ff. 51–51v (James to Lauderdale, 1 January 1680), 69 (James to Lauderdale, 20 January 1680); Fountainhall, *Historical Notices,* i, 247–8; Morrice, i, 245 (3 January 1680); McAlister, 'James VII and the Conduct of Scottish Politics', 18–21; Lee, 'Government and Politics in Scotland, 1661–1681', 279, and in detail on military expenditure, 130–38.

25 For the best account of Highland policy in the Restoration period see A.D. Kennedy, 'The Civic Government of the Scottish Highlands during the Restoration, 1660–1688 (PhD thesis, Stirling, 2011).

26 *RPCS, third series,* vi, 1–2, 547, 572–3, vii, 6–7, 10–13; NRS, Breadalbane Muniments, GD112/43/13/20, 39/132/6, 39/135/3, 39/134/1, 39/135/7 and 19; Fountainhall, *Historical Notices,* i, 204–5, 447; NRS, PA7/11/80/1–3; Kennedy, 'Civil Government of the Highlands', 242–6.

27 NRS, Breadalbane Muniments, GD112/39/125/6, 39/127/6 and 14, 39/124/26 (Lauderdale's plea for help); *RPCS, third series,* vi, 169–72 (12 April 1679); *CSPD (1679–80),* 108 (24 March 1679).

28 *RPCS, third series,* vi, 371–2 (29 December 1679); BL, Lauderdale Papers, Add. MSS 23245, ff. 77–78 (James to Lauderdale, 12 February 1680); *RPS*, 1681/7/91 (6 September 1681); NRS, PA7/11/82, 4, ff. 250–1; *RPS*, C1681/7/31 (10 September 1681); *LP*, iii, 225 (letter Sir George Mackenzie to the earl of Moray, nd. (? September 1681); Fountainhall, *Historical Notices,* i, 312–13; J. Stewart, *The Case of the Earl of Argyle, or, An exact and full account of his trial, escape and sentence* (Edinburgh, 1683), 3–5; Kennedy, 'Civil Government of the Highlands', 232–3, 235–6.

29 For the most detailed accounts, reflecting both 'sides', see Stewart, *Case of the Earl of Argyle,* 6–12; George Mackenzie, *A vindication of His Majesties government, & iudicatures, in Scotland; From some Aspersions thrown on them by scandalous Pamphlets, and News-books: and especially, with Relation to the late Earl of Argiles Process* (Edinburgh, 1683), and for the most succinct modern account, McAlister, 'James VII and the Conduct of Scottish

Politics', 113–28. See also A. Lang, *Sir George Mackenzie, king's advocate, of Rosehaugh: his life and times, 1636(?)–1691* (London, 1909, 204–30, and Willock, *A Scots Earl*, 248–74.

30 NRS, Scott of Harden Papers, GD157/1860 'Explanation of the Test by Argyll' (3 November, 1681); *RPS*, A1681/7/16; Mackenzie, *Vindication*, 21(loyalist quote), 23; Burnet, *History*, ii, 313–15; Fountainhall, *Historical Notices*, i, 307–8, 313, 316, 323–4, 327; Wodrow, *Sufferings*, iii, 312–42; *ST*, viii, 957–8; A.J. Mann, '"James VII: King of the Articles": Political Management and Parliamentary Failure' in Brown and Mann (eds), *Parliament and Politics in Scotland, 1567–1707*, 196–7; MacIntosh, *Scottish Parliament*, 194–7; McAlister, 'James VII and the Conduct of Scottish Politics', 79–82, 114–17. There is considerable confusion over the majority for the act especially as the Test was subjected to a vote and also the combined 'Act anent Religion and the Test'. While Foutainhall suggests a majority of thirty or so, Burnet in his *History* records the much narrower seven (1724, 1815, 1818, 1833, 1840 and 1850 editions) or ten (1890 edition).

31 Fountainhall, *Historical Observes*, 55; *Life*, i, 707; *Letters Illustrative of Public Affairs*, 4; Anon, *The Scotch-Mist Cleared Up. To prevent Englishmen being wet to the skin. Being a true Account of the Proceedings against Archibald Earl of Argyle, for High-Treason* (?London, 1681); *RPCS*, third series, vii, 281 (14 December 1681); NRAS, 217, Moray Papers, box 7, no. 391 (Letter duchess of Lauderdale to the earl of Moray, 27 February 1680); McAlister, 'James VII and the Conduct of Scottish Politics', 124–8; P. Hopkins, *Glencoe and the End of the Highland War* (Edinburgh, 1990), 85–6; Jackson, *Restoration Scotland* , 150–1. Sir Thomas Murray of Glendoik, the Clerk Register, and James Dalrymple, Viscount Stair were also supported by Lauderdale. Murray subscribed the Test, though for hesitating lost his office to Sir George Mackenzie of Tarbat.

32 *RPCS*, third series, vi, 382 (31 January, 5 February 1680), 392–8 (15 February 1680), 429 (12 March 1680), vii, 507–15 (August 1682); ix, 81–3 (5 August 1684); xi, 103–4 (20 July, 1685, renewed Highland commission from King James); *HMC, Twelfth Report, Appendix, Part VIII, Manuscripts of the Duke of Athole* (London, 1891), 12–13; NRS, PC8/7 Register of the Commissioners for Pacifying the Highlands, 1682–6, ff. 2–25; NRS, GD112/39/144, 10; Fountainhall, *Historical Notices*, ii, 547; *Chronicles of the Atholl and Tullibardine Families*, 5 vols (Edinburgh, 1908), i, 187 (secret committee instructions to Atholl, 31 July 1684), 190–2 (ditto, 28 August and 6 September 1684), 192–3 (indulged ministers, 2 September 1684), 196–8 (report on instructions by Atholl), 203 (secret committee instructions, 21 May, 1685) 219–20 (ditto, 31 May 1685), 228–9 (ditto, 5 June 1685), 229–30 (ditto, 8 June 1685), 246–7 (instructions from the earl of Perth to Atholl on Argyll rebellion, 23 June 1685), 250–4 (Atholl report, 9 July 1685), 254–6 (report by secret committee to king and secretaries on Atholl's good conduct); Kennedy, 'Civil Government of the Highlands', 247–57; Hopkins, *Glencoe*, 92.

33 Quoted in Hay, *Enigma of James*, 26; Narcissus Luttrell, *Brief Relation of State Affairs, 1678–1714* (Oxford, 1857), i, 37–8.

34 Bod. Lib., Carte MSS 39, f. 68 (letter Thomas Cholmeley to earl of Arran); BL, Add. MS 17017 Hyde Papers, Miscellaneous Correspondence, 1631–1696, 167 (Letter James to Hyde, 4 April 1679 (Brussels)), 169–70 (James to Hyde, 9 November 1680 (Edinburgh)). For the petitioning campaign see M. Knights, *Politics and Opinion in Crisis, 1678–81* (Cambridge, 2006), 227–303; Hutton, *Charles II*, 386–7; Harris, *Restoration*, 184–6

35 MacPherson (ed.), *Original papers* i, 103; BL, Add. MS 25124, ff. 229–31 Extraordinary Correspondence 1678–80 (letters Henry Coventry to Charles, March 1680); Bod. Lib., Carte MSS 39, f. 107 (letter Reading to the earl of Arran, 2 February 1680), f. 127 (same

to same, February 1680); NRAS, 217, Moray Papers, box 7, Letters of the duchess of Lauderdale, no. 402 (letter duchess to earl of Moray, 27 March 1680), 403 (same to same, 29 March 1680); K.H.D. Haley, *The First Earl of Shaftesbury* (Oxford, 1968), 569–99; B. Fitzpatrick, *Seventeenth-Century Ireland: The War of Religions* (Basingstoke, 1988), 236–45; Harris, *Restoration*, 103 and 172–3. For Shaftesbury and Capel speeches on the Irish 'problem' see W. Cobbett (ed.), *The Parliamentary History of England for the earliest period to the Year 1803*, 7 vols (New Haven, 1963–75), iv, 1116–18 and 1166–7.

36 *Life*, i, 590–1, 666–7; Luttrell, *Brief Relation of State Affairs*, i, 49, 69; Anon, *Reasons for the Indictment of the Duke of York* (London, 1680); Morrice, i, 262 (26 June 1680); Dalrymple, *Memoirs*, i, 352 (Barrillon to Louis, 14 October 1680); i, 343 (Barrillon to Louis, 19 August 1680); Bod. Lib., Carte MSS 39, f. 107 (Reading to the earl of Arran, 2 February 1680); NA. PRO, 31/3/146 (Barrillon correspondence), f. 117; *HMC, Ormonde*, v. 459 (Francis Gwyn to Ormonde, 14 October 1670); *RPCS, third series*, vi, 565; Wodrow, *Sufferings*, iii 238. A second attempt was made to submit an indictment to a grand jury in November 1680. See Morrice, i, 280 (30 November 1680); Bod. Lib., Carte MSS 104, f. 54 (Sir Leoline Jenkins to Lord Middleton, 29 November 1680).

37 *LP*, iii, 191–2, 195, 196, 197–8, 198–9, 202–3, 211–2, 219–20; Fountainhall, *Historical Observes*, 75; *RPCS, third series*, vi, 431–2 (15 March – 8 April 1680), 454, 488 (5 July 1680); NRAS, 217, Moray Papers, box 7, no. 406 (letter duchess of Lauderdale to the earl of Moray, 6 April 1680), no. 471 (Letter Sir Andrew Forrester to the Earl of Moray, 6 April 1680), no. 585 (bishop [Paterson] to earl of Moray, 12 March 1680); Paterson, *Lauderdale*, 253.

38 W.N. Clarke (ed.), *A Collection of Letters Addressed by Prelates and Individuals of High Rank in Scotland and by Two Bishops of Soder to Sancroft, Archbishop of Canterbury* (Edinburgh, 1848), 8–9, 13–14; *RPCS, third series*, vi, 459–62 (revised instruction concerning indulged ministers, 10 June 1680).

39 For the texts see Wodrow, *Sufferings*, iii, 207–11, 212–13, 66–7, and also for Queensferry and Sanquhar, *A True and exact copy of a treasonable and bloody paper called, The fanaticks new-Covenant . . . together with their execrable declaration published at the cross of Sanquhair, . . .* (London and Edinburgh, 1680); [Alexander Shields], *A Hind Let Loose: Or, An Historical Representation of the Testimony of the Church of Scotland for the Interest of Christ; With the true State thereof in all its Periods* ([Edinburgh], 1687), 138–9; *RPCS, third series*, vi, 374, 539, 570–2; NRAS, 217, Moray Papers, box 7, no. 473 (Letter Sir Andrew Forrester to the earl of Moray, 20 April 1680), 476 (same to same, 6 May 1680); Mann, *Scottish Book Trade*, 172–3; Jackson, *Restoration Scotland*, 133–4; Harris, *Restoration*, 197–9.

40 Burnet, *History*, ii, 420–21; George Lockhart of Carnwath, *The Lockhart Papers: containing Memoirs and Commentaries Upon the Affairs of Scotland from 1702 to 1715*, 2 vols (London, 1817), 600; Fountainhall, *Historical Observes*, 7–8, 26–7 (November 1680 and January 1681); Fountainhall, *Historical Notices*, i, 331–3 (333 for quote, 11 October 1681; *RPCS, third series*, vi, 511 (29 July 1680), 573–5 (13 November 1680); NLS, MS 7009 Yester Papers, f. 68, 70; *A Hind Let Loose*, 195–7; Wodrow, *Sufferings*, iii, 181–3, 239, 249–62; Hay, *Enigma of James*, 24; Greaves, *Secrets of the Kingdom*, 69–75; I.B. Cowan, *The Scottish Covenanters, 1660–88* (London, 1976), 103–14.

41 Fountainhall, *Historical Observes*, 7–10; [James Stewart and James Stirling], *Naphtali, or the Wrestlings of the Church of Scotland for the Kingdom of Christ* ([Rotterdam], 1667), 157; Wodrow, *Sufferings*, iii, 251–5, iv, 412; *RPCS, third series*, xiii, 156–8; Macaulay, *History of*

England (London, 1855), i, 271, 498, 558; Lang, *George Mackenzie*, 194–7; Jackson, *Restoration Scotland*, 70–1; Mann, *Scottish Book Trade*, 58. In addition to the royal brothers, the Council at Whitehall consisted of the Earls of Moray, Middleton, Mar, Airlie, Ancram and Breadalbane, Drummond of Lundin as Treasurer-Depute, Mackenzie of Rosehaugh, the Lord Advocate, Richard Maitland of Gogar, the Justice Clerk, John Wedderburn of Gosford, and the English minister Sunderland. *RPCS, third series*, viii, 268–9 (22 October 1683).

42   Wodrow, *Sufferings,* iii, 310; Burnet, *History*, ii, 156; NLS, Wodrow MSS Quatro XXVI (xx), f. 208 (anonymous letter giving reasons for not taking the Test. c.1682); Wodrow MSS Quarto XXVIII, ff. 5v–6, 'Apologetical Declaratione of the trew Presbyterians of the Church of Scotland'; NRS, Papers of Scott of Harden, Lords Polwarth, Berwickshire GD157/1861 'The Act and Apologetick Declaration of the Presbyterians of the Church of Scotland'; Wodrow, *Sufferings*, iii, 362; 369–420, 420–82; [Shields], *A Hind Let Loose*, 143; Cowan, *Scottish Covenanters*, 110–11; Harris, *Restoration*, 360–4.

43   Wodrow, *Sufferings*, iii, 498–505; iv, 71–94, 277–8; *HMC, Buccleuch and Queensberry (Drumlanrig)*, i, 197–8 (Letter James to Queensberry, 26 October 1683); Fountainhall, *Historical Notices*, ii, 521, 510–22; *CSPD, 1683–4*, 65–7; *CSPD, 1684–5*, 55 'Additional Instructions to the Secret Committee of the Privy Council'; *ST*, x, 990–1046; *RPS*, A1685/4/1–38 (depositions and decreets in parliament (1685) concerning Rye House plotters); Harris, *Restoration*, 364–7; Greaves, *Secrets of the Kingdom*, 241–6;

44   *RPCS, third series*, vii, 409–10 (5 May 1682), 431 (15 May 1682), 434–6 (20 May 1682), 497–9 (3 August 1682); viii, 69–70 (1 March 1683), 133–8 (13 April 1683) (to meet in Stirling, Glasgow, Ayr, Dumfries, Jedburgh and Edinburgh); *Letters Illustrative of Public Affairs*, 107–111 ('Report to Privy Council Committee for Public Affairs concerning Galloway', Claverhouse, nd. 1683); *HMC, Buccleuch and Queensberry (Drumlanrig)*, i, 177 (letter James to Queensberry, 2 December 1682), 292 (letter Claverhouse to Queensberry, 3 May 1685, the 'shooting' of one John Brown who refused to take the abjuration oath); Wodrow, *Sufferings*, iv, 244–5; NRAS, 1275, Buccleuch and Queensberry, 120 (letter Tarbat to Queensberry, 25 October 1682).

45   *Letters Illustrative of Public Affairs,* 111–13 (report of Sirling circuit court, 6 June 1683); 128–130 (further report, 19 June 1683); 146 (letter Charles, earl of Middleton to Aberdeen, 21 July 1683); Wodrow, *Sufferings*, iv, 147–9. 160, 166–7, 182–7; *CSPD, 1684–5*, 219 (letter King Charles to Privy Council, 24 November 1684); *HMC, Buccleuch and Queensberry (Drumlanrig)*, i, 204 (letter James to Queensberry, 5 April 1684); 213 (minister in Galloway killed, letter James to Queensberry, 22 December 1684); 251–2 (Hamilton to Queensberry, 1 May [1684]); murdered king's guard, NRS, GD 406, Hamilton Papers (additional boxes), 483/11/2 (Letter Aberdeen to duke of Hamilton, 10 June, 1683); for enthusiasm for the robust work of the Glasgow circuit court see *HMC, Buccleuch and Queensberry (Drumlanrig)*, ii, 183–96 (letters John Drummond of Lundin [later Melfort] to Queensberry, 13 to 22 October 1684); NRAS, 1275, Buccleuch and Queensberry, 120 (letter Tarbat to Queensberry, 10 November 1684, *Apologetical Declaration* found at Linlithgow); Cowan, *Scottish Covenanters*, 116. For Hamilton and the Test see correspondence with James, concluding with James's optimistic statement 'knowing you to be truly my friend', NRS, GD406, 1/10582–5 (18 March, 30 March, 5 June and 17 June, 1682) and also NRS, RH3/163, 'Red Book', ii, 165–8.

46   *CSPD, 1683–4*, 111, 120; *1684–5*, xx, 52–3, 62, 200, 234; *RPCS, third series*, vi, 429, 521; ix, pp. xix, 32–5, 52, 154–9; *HMC, Buccleuch and Queensberry (Drumlanrig)*, i, 176–7,

177,177–8, 202, 204, 209, 211 (letters from James to Queensberry concerning military affairs, 24 November 1682 to 18 November 1684). For Claverhouse in London see NRS, Breadlalbane Muniments, GD112/39/135 (letter Claverhouse to Breadalbane, 23 March 1683); *HMC, Buccleuch and Queensberry (Drumlanrig)*, i, 275–81 (letters *Claverhouse* to Queensberry (9 March to 3 May 1683)); i, 186 (James to Queensberry, 3 April, 1683), 188 (same to same, 24 April and 1 May 1683), and Scott (ed.), 'Letters of John Graham of Claverhouse',186–206.

47   *RPCS, third series*, x, 32–3, 35–6 (wording of abjuration oath), 107 ('Instructions to the commissioners for the southerne and westerne shyres', 13 January 1685); xi, 26–7 (commission and instructions to Drummond, 1 April 1685); xiii, 123–4, 156–8; Wodrow, *Sufferings*, iv, 416–27, 428 ('the Presbyterian ministers address of thanks', 21 July 1687); Cowan, *Scottish Covenanters*, 125–8, 132; H. Macpherson, 'The Wigtown Martyrs' in *Records of the Scottish Church History Society* (1947), ix, 166–84.

48   Dalrymple, *Memoirs*, i, part1, Book 1, 18; NA. PRO 31/3, 152 (Barrillon correspondence), 4 May 1682; R. Hutton, 'The Triple-crowned Island' in L.K.J. Glassey (ed.), *The Reigns of Charles II and James VII and II* (New York, 1997), 79; Cowan, *Scottish Covenanters*, 113–14; McAlister, 'James VII and the Conduct of Scottish Politics', 138–41; Miller, *James II*, 108–9; Hay, *Enigma of James*, 2–8.

49   NRAS, 1275, Buccleuch and Queensberry, 120 (letter Tarbat to Queensberry, 6 October 1685).

50   *A True Narrative of the Reception of their Royal Highnesses at their Arrival in Scotland* (Edinburgh, London and Dublin, 1680), 1–4; Fountainhall, *Historical Observes*, 1–2; *Historical Selections*, 18–19; *Historical Notices*, i, 281; *RPCS, third series*, vi, 565; vii, 1, 4, 13–14, 23–4; NRS, GD157/1641 *A Proclamation Offering a Reward and Indemnity to such as shall discover the burning of Priestfield, 13 January 1681* (Edinburgh, 1681) and *A Proclamation Concerning the Students in the College of Edinburgh, 20 January 1681* (Edinburgh, 1681); [N.M.], *A Modest Apology for the Students of Edenburgh Burning the Pope December 1680 (sic), Humbly Rescuing the Actors from the Imputation of Disloyalty and Rebellion, with which they are charged in a letter* (London, 1681). The student protest took place on 26 December, Christmas being celebrated then with the 25th being a Sunday, McAlister, 'James VII and the Conduct of Scottish Politics', 42–44. For the birthday celebrations of May 1681 see *London Gazette*, no. 1623 (6–9 June 1681); Fountainhall, *Historical Observes*, 40; Harris *Restoration*, 340–1.

51   Fountainhall, *Historical Observes*, 49–51.

52   Mann, 'James VII: King of the Articles', 199, 202–3; *Historical Notices*, ii, 469–70; *HMC, Buccleuch and Queensberry (Drumlanrig)*, ii, 168–9 (letter Lundin to Queensberry, 24 November [1683]).

53   *RPCS, third series*, i, 1–4 (23 February, 1661), iv, 186–9 (19 May 1674), v, 6–9 (20 July 1676); i, 216, vi, 54, vii, 415. Tarbat was added to the Council in April 1662, was removed for involvement with John, first earl of Middleton, in the 'billeting affair' of 1662/3 but was reinstated in 1678. Tweeddale became a councillor in 1661 but was removed in 1674 after his political alliance with Lauderdale ended, and was readmitted in April 1682; *ODNB*, C. Kidd, 'George Mackenzie (1630–1714)': doi:10.1093/ref:odnb/17580; J. Young, 'John Hay (1626–1697)': doi:10.1093/ref:odnb/12726; Lee, *'Dearest Brother'*, 314.

54   *RPCS, third series*, vii, 259, 306; ix, 32–5 (14 July, 1684); xi, 12–14 (3 May, 1685); xii, 238, 140–3 (30 May, 1687); Wodrow, *Sufferings*, iii, 300–2; *HMC, Buccleuch and*

Queensberry (Drumlanrig), i, 212 (letter James to Queensberry, 8 December 1684); ii, 53 (letter Moray to Queensberry, 18 April 1685), 73 (same to same, 1 June 1685); 171–2 (Lundin to Queensberry, [1684/5]); NRAS, 217, Moray Papers, box 7, no. 610 (letter Melfort to Moray (? May, 1686); Fountainhall, *Historical Notices*, ii, 729; McAlister, 'James VII and the Conduct of Scottish Politics', 98–113; Linklater and Hesketh, *For King and Conscience*, 121–6.

55 Fountainhall, *Historical Observes*, 75; *LP*, iii, 202–3 (letter 'secret committee' to Lauderdale, 13 August 1680); Harris, *Restoration*, 335.

56 *LP*, iii, 83–5 (letter 'committee of conventicles' to Lauderdale, 6 July 1676); *RPCS third series*, v, 239 (6 September 1677); vi, 196 (20 September 1681); Brown, *Kingdom or Province*, 25–6. The 1681 committee consisted of the Earls of Mar, Glencairn, Perth, Queensberry and Balcarres, the Bishop of Edinburgh, Charles Maitland of Hatton, the Treasurer Depute, General Dalzell, Rosehaugh, the Lord Advocate, and Lundin. That of 1677 was intended for the vacation only but became permanent.

57 *CSPD, 1683–84*, 27 November 1683 (warrant, remit and instructions to the 'secret committee'); Fountainhall, *Historical Notices*, ii, 470; NRS, GD406/1/7515 (letter Hamilton to Arran, 12 November 1685), 406/1/6161 (letter Perth to Hamilton, [?] February 1687); HMC, *Buccleuch and Queensberry (Drumlanrig)*, ii, 26 (Moray to Queensberry, new secret committee 'first' discussed with James, 16 September 1683), 169 (Lundin to Queensberry, 24 November [1683]); i, 100 (James to secret committee, 8 May, 1685); i, 204–8 (James to Queensberry and secret committee, 22 July to 12 September 1684); *RPCS, third series*, xiii, xiv (6 October 1688); Harris, *Restoration*, 360, following Hutton, *Charles II*, 430–1.

58 HMC, *Dartmouth*, i, 48–9 (letter James to Legge, 23 January [1681]) (same to same, 25 January [1681]), 67 (same to same, 11 September 1681); *Life*, i, 626–31, 676–8, 699–700; *The copy of a Letter Sent from Scotland, To His Grace The Lord Archbishop of Canterbury* (Edinburgh, 1682); [William Bassett], *A Plea for Succession in Opposition to Popular Exclusion* (London, 1682), 2; *London Gazette*, no. 1643 (15–18 August, 1681), no. 1644 (18–22 August, 1681); Turner, *James II*, 197; Harris, *Restoration*, 251–2.

59 *Life*, i, 724–9; PRO 31/3, 150 (Barrillon correspondence), f. 5; HMC, *Dartmouth*, i, 72 (James to Legg, 21 and 22 November 1681); Dalrymple, *Memoirs*, i, Part 1, Book 1, 16–17; NRAS, 217, Moray Papers, box 7, no. 296 'An humble & loyall address to His Majesty from the Master, Governours & Assistants of the Scots Corporation in the Cities of London & Westminster agreed upon & signed 30th November, 1681'; Hutton, *Charles II*, 411–2.

60 Anon, *Some Historical Memories of the Life and Actions of his Royal Highness*, 76; *London Gazette*, no. 1703 (13–16 March, 1681/2); Luttrell, *Brief Relation of State Affairs*, i, 171; Harris, *Restoration*, 282–3.

61 Dalrymple, *Memoirs*, i, appendix, 372–7 (William to Jenkins, 26 July 1680 to 11 February 1681), Part 1, Book 1, appendix, 67–80 (Letters Sydney, Godolphin and Temple to William, all dated 28 June 1681; James to Barrillon, 28 July 1681); Morrice, i, 311 (4 August 1681).

62 See Hutton, *Charles II*, 408–11, for the best summary and note esp. sources ex fn. 24.

63 *Life*, i, 730–1; MacPherson (ed.), *Original papers*, i, 135–6; Browning (ed.), *Reresby*, 264–5; Burnet, *History*, ii, 326–7; Dalrymple, *Memoirs*, i, Part 1, Book 1, appendix, 128 (letter Earl of Dartmouth to Erasmus Lewis, 25 January 1683); 'Familiar Letters of Charles II and James, duke of York', 168 (letter James to Countess of Litchfield, 9 May 1682);

Morrice, i, 334 (11 May, 1682); Bod. Lib., Carte MSS 216, f. 14 (letter Francis Augier, earl of Longford to Arran, 13 May 1682); Turner, *James II*, 213–14; Callow, *Making of King James*, 233–7.

64   *RPCS, third series*, vii, 412–29; Fountainhall, *Historical Observes*, 89, 127–35; *HMC, Buccleuch and Queensberry (Drumlanrig)*, i, 170–8 (letter James to Queensberry, 22 July 1682–4 December 1682); ii, 102–5 (letter Lunin to Queensberry, 26 June 1682); NRAS, 217, Moray Papers, box 7, no.297 'Copy or draft of report of commissioners taking trial of the mint in Scotland, 4 April, 1682', no.726 (letter Queensberry to Moray, 13 July 1682), no. 730 (same to same, 26 August 1682); NRAS, 1275 Buccleuch and Queensberry, bundle 976 (letters from Richard Maitland, Lord Maitland to Queensberry, 29 September, 2 October, 4 October and 23 October 1684, emphasising support from James and Charles), volume 113, 'bishops' letters' (letter John Paterson, bishop of Edinburgh to Queensberry, 26 August 1682); Hutton, *Charles II*, 413–14, 430–31.

65   Smith, *History of the Modern British Isles*, 261–5; Hutton, *Charles II*, 431.

66   Fountainhall, *Historical Observes*, 68, 127–32, 134; *HMC, Buccleuch and Queensberry (Drumlanrig)*, ii, 14–17, 21–2, 24, 26–7, 30–8 (letters Moray to Queensberry, 8 July 1682–30 December 1684), 107–75 (letters Lundin to Queensberry, 26 July 1682–30 September 1684); NLS, Wodrow MSS Quarto, XXVII (xv), 'Some Arguments Against the 'Black Bond', ff. 97–105; *RPCS, third series*, viii, 349–9, 367; Burnet, *History*, ii, 418–19; Harris, *Restoration*, 360. This account conflicts with that of Hutton, *Charles II*, 430–1. There is little evidence of one secretary being in Edinburgh and the other in London on a consistent basis, if that was ever the plan. Moray had preferred William Hay of Drummelzier, son of Lord Hay of Yester, and a lieutenant general.

67   NA, SP 45, 12 *A Proclamation Signifying His Majesties Pleasure That all Men being in Office . . . shall so continue . . .* (London, 1685).

68   Fountainhall, *Historical Notices*, 622, 654, 712–3; *Historical Selections*, 237; Burnet, *Supplement*, 154, 170; Colquhoun, '"Issue of the late civill wars": James Duke of York and the Government of Scotland', 294, 302; HMC, *Buccleuch and Queensberry (Drumlanrig)*, ii, 52 (letter Moray to Queensberry, 14 April 1685), 86–7 (same to same, 14 July 1685), 83, 135–43 ('Answers by the duke of Queensberry to the libel given in to his Majesty against him by the Lord Melfort after the first session of parliament in April 1685'); NRS, GD 406/1/7521 (letter Hamilton to Arran, 28 November 1685), 1/9167 (letter [Melfort] to Hamilton, 19 December 1685), 1/9224 (letter Perth to [Hamilton], 26 November 1685); Turner, *James II*, 369; *RPCS, third series*, xi, 133, 173. Much of this account is based on the excellent summary in McAlister, 'James VII and the Conduct of Scottish Politics', 244–55, 224.

69   For general discussions of James and the Scottish Parliament see Mann, 'James VII: King of the Articles', 184–207; Mann, 'James VII as Unionist and Nationalist', 101–19; Mann, 'The Scottish Parliament and the First Jacobite', in *Living with Jacobitism: The Three Kingdoms and Beyond* (London, 2014).

70   BL, Add MSS Mackintosh Collections, 'Letters from the Extraordinary Ambassadors to the States General, 1685', 34508, f. 14–14v (letter Baron de Wasfenaer Duivenvoirde to the States General, 15 May 1685), for an outsider's view on how the Scottish Parliament was set up with the English one in mind; *CSPD, 1680–81*, 363; *RPS*, 1681/7/3; *LP*, iii, 223 (James to Lauderdale, 23 June 1681), 223–5 (reply, 4 July 1681); *RPS*, 1669/10/13; BL, Add MS 11252, f. 8 'Private Instructions from King Charles II to James, duke of York, High Commissioner in Scotland', 20 July 1681; NRAS, 1275, Buccleuch and Queensberry,

110, 20 July, 1681; MacIntosh, *Scottish Parliament*, 79–83, 90–2. For commissioners instructions see Mann, 'Inglorious Revolution', 134–40.

71 For the 1681 session see MacIntosh, *Scottish Parliament*, 188–202 and McAlister, 'James VII and the Conduct of Scottish Politics', 51–92.

72 NLS, Adv. MSS 31.6.15, Fountainhall's Judicial and Historical Collections, ff. 206–9; *RPS*, 1681/7/18, C1681/7/11–13, 1681/7/23, 1681/7/17; *London Gazette*, no. 1644 (18–22 August, 1681); NRS, Hamilton Papers, GD406, M1/298/8 (13 August 1681); Mann, 'James VII: King of the Articles', 195–6. See Harris, *Restoration*, 345–6 for a suggested analysis of the Succession Act though the relationship he poses with the 1567 Coronation Act is debatable.

73 Bod. Lib., MSS Eng. Hist. C.5237, ff. 21–2 (letter James to Ormonde, 13 September 1681).

74 *RPCS, third series*, vii, 323–4; 412–3; 554–5; viii, 37–9; 198–9; 269–70; 418–9; ix, 122–3; *HMC, Buccleuch and Queensberry (Drumlanrig)*, i, 194–6 (Letters James to Queensberry, 24 July and 9 August 1683); NRAS, 1275, Buccleuch and Queensberry, bundle 63 (royal warrant to William, duke of Hamilton, 6 January, 1685); Morrice, i, 450 (27 November 1684).

75 *RPS*, 1681/7/42; Harris, *Restoration*, 347.

76 'The method and manner of Ryding the Scottish Parliament' in *Miscellany of the Maitland Club*, iii, pt 1. (Edinburgh, 1842), 101–37, at 119–23; *RPCS, third* series, vii, 169–70; Fountainhall, *Historical Observes*, 45; *RPS*, 1681/7/4; A.J. Mann, 'Continuity and Change: the Culture of Ritual and Procession in the Parliament of Scotland', *Parliament, Estates and Representation*, 29 (2009), 151–2. For further discussion of the 'riding' see also Mann, 'The Scottish Parliaments: the Role of Ritual and Procession in the pre-1707 Parliament and the New Parliament of 1999' in E.Crewe and M.G.Müller (eds), *Rituals in Parliaments: Political, Anthropological and Historical Perspectives on Europe and the United States* (Frankfurt am Main, 2006), 135–58.

77 *Copies of Two Papers Written by the late King Charles II* (London, 1686); BL, Add. MSS 72887, Petty Papers, ff. 59–60, 60–61v, BL, Add. MSS 34508 Mackintosh Collections, ff. 31–2, 32–4 (Charles II's papers), 12–12v (letter Baron de Wasfenaer Duivenvoirde to the States General, 27 April (NS) 1685, describing king's evil); *An Account of What His Majesty Said at His First Coming to Council* (London, 1684/5); Bod. Lib., Carte MSS 71, ff. 423, 424, 420 *A Publication of royal authority of . . . James the Seventh, King of Scotland &c. [upon his Majesty's accession]* (Edinburgh , 1685); *HMC, Laing*, i, 417 (10 and 20 February, 1685); Fountainhall, *Historical Observes*, 147–8, 157; Turner, *James II*, 224–8 (Letter Barrillon to Louis, 6 February 1684/5), 252–3; *RPCS, third series*, x, 28–9 (6 November 1684), 133–5 (10 February, 1685), 154–6 (16 February, 1685), 195–6 (22 March 1685); NA, SP 31/1/92, 'The Form of the Proceeding to the Coronation of their Majesties King James the Second and Queen Mary' (23 April, 1685); Bod. Lib., Carte MSS 129 ff. 'The order of the king's coronation', 108–122v; *London Gazette*, 2013 (2–5 March 1684/5); Miller, *James II*, 120; Turner, *James II*, 256–7. Given his plan to make the Catholic Church as 'established' as the Church of England, James would later express regrets at the precise wording of his extempore statement. *Life*, ii, 4.

78 Charles James Fox, *A History of the Early Part of the Reign of James II . . . to which is added An Appendix* (London/Philadelphia, 1808), appendix xlviii–lvi (letter Barrillon to King Louis, 1 March, 1685); *Life*, ii, 10; J. Grant (ed.), *Seafield Correspondence from 1685 to 1708* (SHS, Edinburgh, 1912), 3–4 (letter George Leslie of Birdsbank to the Earl of Findlater,

28 April 1685); NRS, Papers of the Drummond Family, earls of Perth (Drummond Castle Papers), GD160/529/6 (letter James to Perth, 3 May 1685), 'it will be a good example to the English Parliament'.

79 Fountainhall, *Historical Observes*, 153. Latin motto: 'The world is fashioned according to the example of kings'; *HMC, Buccleuch and Queensberry (Drumlanrig)*, i, 90 (commission to Queensberry, 28 March 1685).

80 *HMC, Buccleuch and Queensberry (Drumlanrig)*, i, 90–3 (28 March 1685), 94 (15 April), 94 (21 April), 94–5 (29 April), 95 (4 May), 95 (12 May), 96 (14 May), 96 (25 May), 96–7 (25 May), 97 (25 May), 98 (25 May) and (10 June); *RPS*, 1685/4/15; 1681/7/17; 1685/4/84; Mann, 'James VII: King of the Articles', 193–5; NRAS, 1275, Buccleuch and Queensberry; 1153 (letter James to Queensberry, 24 April 1685); Mann, 'The Law of the Person', 192–3.

81 NRS, PA2/32, f. 151–151v; *RPS*, 1685/4/16 and *Seafield Correspondence*. 2–3 (Letter George Leslie to Findlater, 28 April, 1685); Mann, 'James VII: King of the Articles', 198; *RPS*, 1685/4/15, 4/23, 4/16; Mackenzie, *Vindication*, 23; [Shields], *Hind Let Loose*, 202; Wodrow, *Sufferings*, iv, 279–82; Fountainhall, *Historical Notices*, ii, 636–49; NRS, SP13/195, 'List of Persons accused of treason and other crimes before the next parliament' (3 March, 1685). For the entire record for 1685, see *RPS*, 1685/4/1–146, M1685/4/1–20, C1685/4/1 (minutes of the committee of the articles), A1685/4/1–38; *HMC, Buccleuch and Queensberry (Drumlanrig)*, i, 122–28; NRAS, 1275, Buccleuch and Queensberry; 1176, 1 'coppie minutes'. The minutes for the lords of the articles for the sessions of 1670, 1672 and 1673–4 are lost. The best secondary narrative is McAlister, 'James VII and the Conduct of Scottish Politics', 235–43.

82 [Shields], *Hind Let Loose*, 202; Wodrow, *Sufferings*, iv, 279–82; NRS, SP13/195, 'List of Persons accused of treason and other crimes before the next parliament' (3 March 1685). Tarbat was shocked that 'good Fletcher of Saltoun [was] brought to the stage', NRAS, 1275, Buccleuch and Queensberry, volume 120 (letter Tarbat to Queensberry, 20 September 1684); BL, Add. MSS Mackintosh Collections, 34508, 75v–76 (Letter Baron de Wasfenaer Duivenvoirde to the States General, 28 [NS] September 1685); *RPCS third series*, xi, 79, 122, 153, 164, 592–4.

83 NRS, PA2/ 32, f. 149v; *RPS*, 1685/4/9; *RPCS, third series*, xi, 12–14; R. Rait, 'Parliamentary Representation in Scotland V: the Lords of the Articles', *SHR*, 13 (1915), 77; Mann, 'James VII: King of the Articles', 193–5, 198–9, appendix 6.2, 206–7.

84 Dalrymple, *Memoirs*, ii, 22–4 (letters James to William, 22 May 1685, 17 June 1685, 3 July 1685); NA, PRO, SP8/3 (Letter James to William, 3 July 1685); Childs, *Army of James II*, 119–36; Fountainhall, *Historical Notices*, ii, 657; *RPCS, third series*, xi, 125; *HMC, Buccleuch and Queensberry (Drumlanrig)*, ii, 74–6 (letters Moray to Queensberry, 4 and 9 June, 1685); Ferguson (ed.), *Papers illustrating the History of the Scots Brigade*, i, 538; Nottingham University Library [NUL], Portland collection, PwA 1614 and 1615 (letter William to William Bentinck [later earl of Portland], 4 and 6 July 1685).

85 *HMC, Buccleuch and Queensberry (Drumlanrig)*, i, 103 (letter James to Queensberry, 25 May 1685); NRS, Papers of the Drummonds, GD160/529/7 (letter James to Perth, 10 May 1685), 8 (same to same, 18 May 1685), 9 (same to same, 1 June 1685), 10 (same to same, 4 June 1685), 11 (same to same, 20 June 1685); NRS, Stirling Home Drummond Moray of Abercairny, Miscellaneous Papers, royal letters GD24/5/59/4 (identical letter to 20 June above but dated 10 June and appears to be to 'lord commissioner' [Queensberry], not Perth); NLS, MS 7010 Yester Papers, 10 (letter Perth to earl of Tweeddale 15 May

1685), 11 (orders Dumbarton to Tweeddale, 31 May 1685), 12 (same to same, 12 June 1685), 13 (orders privy council (Perth and Tarbat) to Tweeddale, 17 June 1685); *Chronicles of Atholl and Tullibardine*, i (instructions from the earl of Perth to Atholl on Argyll rebellion, 23 June 1685), 250–4; Willock, *A Scots Earl*, 343–408.

86 *RPS*, 1685/4/146; *London Gazette*, no. 2036 (21–25 May, 1685); Cobbett (ed.), *Parliamentary History*, iv, 1351–4, 1357–8; ; Turner, *James II*, 266–302; Harris, *Revolution*, 71–3.

87 *CLC*, ii, 116–8 (cclxxxiv, 19 December 1686); Burnet, *James the Second* (Oxford, 1852), 63–5, 79, 99, 100–4, 113, 131, 139, 251; Fountainhall, *Historical Observes*, 222–3; BL, Add MSS. Mackintosh Collections 'Letters from the Extraordinary Ambassadors to the States General, 1685', 34508, ff. 92v, 95 (letter Van Citters to the States General, 27 [NS] November, 1685. D'Atta arrived 20[NS] November); Miller, *James II*, 146–7; Turner, *James II*, 290–1, 323–4, 326–8; Harris, *Revolution*, 88–9, 95–100, 195–6.

88 For an excellent summary see Harris, *Revolution*, 101–25; Speck, *James II*, 101–8.

89 E. Corp, 'Melfort: A Jacobite Connoisseur', *History Today*, 45 (1995), 41; *ODNB*, Corp, 'James Drummond (1648–1716)': doi:10.1093/ref:odnb/8070 and T.F Henderson and A.J. Mann, 'Alexander Stewart (bap.1634, d.1701)': doi:10.1093/ref:odnb/26455; Fountainhall, *Historical Observes*, 220–1, 240; Burnet, *James the Second*, 37: Burnet, *Supplement*, 154; *RPS*, 1686/4/3; Mann, 'James VII: King of the Articles', 199; Turner, *James II*, 369–70.

90 *RPCS, third series*, xi, 48–9, 212, 595–6, 603–4, xxii, xxviii, 15, 68, 83, 91–7; Fountainhall, *Historical Observes*, 227, 243–4; Fountainhall, *Historical Notices,* ii, 640, 644, 676–7, 700–1; NLS, Wodrow MSS Folio, XXXIII (cxx), 'King's letter regarding the tumult, 9 February 1686; NRS, GD160/529/16 6 (letter James to Perth, 10 February 1685); *Seafield Correspondence,* 16–18; Miller, *James II*, 214; Childs, *Army of James II*, 22, 30.

91 NRS, GD 406/1/7121, 6146–8 (Letters Hamilton to Earl of Arran, 10 and 23 February, 2 and 4 March 1686); Fountainhall, *Historical Notices,* ii, 736; Speck, *James II*, 92: Harris, *Revolution*, 154.

92 NRS, GD 406/1/6311 (letter Hamilton to Arran, 12 March 1686), 406/1/9184 (letter [Melfort to Hamilton], 23 March 1686), 406/1/7180 (letter [Hamilton to Arran], 4 May 1686), 406/1/6312 (letter [Hamilton to Arran], 17 May [1686]); NRAS, 217, Moray Papers, box 7, no. 738 (Letter Perth to Moray, 26 March 1686); no. 591 (letter Melfort to Moray, 20 April 1686), no. 590 (letter James to Moray, 8 May 1686).

93 NRAS, 217, Moray Papers, box 7, no. 299, 'Instructions to the earl of Moray, 12 April 1686'; no. 271, 272 (Instructions James to Moray, 19 April 1686), no. 591 (Letter Melfort to Moray, 20 April 1686), no. 592 (letter Melfort to Moray, 22 April 1686 (wrongly catalogued as 2 September).

94 *RPS*, 1686/4/6; *His Majesties Most Gracious Letter to the Parliament of Scotland* (Edinburgh, 1686); NRS, GD 406/1/7202 (Letter Hamilton to Arran, 6 May, 1686); Fountainhall, *Historical Notices,* ii, 720–1, 718–39; *HMC, Manuscripts of the Earls of Mar and Kellie* (London, 1904), 217–19; Mann, 'James VII: King of the Articles', 202. For the best summary of the 1686 session see McAlister, 'James VII and the Conduct of Scottish Politics', 280–305. The minutes of the Lords of the Articles and other committees are missing.

95 NRS, GD 406/1/7021 (letter [Hamilton] to Arran, 20 May 1686), 406/1/6312, 406/1/7182; NRAS, 217, Moray Papers, box 7, no. 613 (letter Melfort to Moray, 18 May 1696), 618 (same to same, 22 May 1686), 617 (same to same, 22 May 1686), no. 322

(draft address by Moray to parliament [?28 May 1689], no. 624 (letter Melfort to Moray, 3 June 1686), no. 295 (letter James to Moray, 3 June 1686); *HMC, Mar and Kellie*, 218–19; NRS, Dalhousie Muniments, GD 45/1/152 'Draft act permitting private exercise of Catholicism'; NLS, Wodrow MSS Folio, XXXIII (cxxvii), ff. 215–6, 'Draft act anent the penal statutes'; Wodrow, *Sufferings*, iv, 366–7; *RPS*, 1686/4/119 (adjourned to 17 August); *RPCS, third series*, xii, 372 (adjourned to 21 October) , 480 (dissolved 8 October); McAlister, 'James VII and the Conduct of Scottish Politics', 295, 301. The date of the vote before the whole house is problematic. Turner, using *HMC, Twelfth Report, Appendix Part VII, Manuscripts of S.D. Le Fleming* (London, 1890), 200, references a report, dated 3 June, concerning voting on a previous Thursday. McAlister opts for 27 May, the same date as the committee vote, but Parliament did not sit on this day. It sat on 28 May (a Friday), however. Unusually, Fountainhall does not help us. Turner, *James II*, 375; McAlister, 'James VII and the Conduct of Scottish Politics', 296.

96 NRAS, 217, Moray Papers, box 7, nos. 278, 281, 282, 275, 289, 275 (instructions James to Moray, 12, 22 May, 2, 10 June 1686), nos. 600, 601, 603, 604, 605, 608, 609, 612, 613, 619, 621, 624 625 626, 627 (letters Melfort to Moray, 1, 4, 5, 8, 13, 15, 17, 18, 24, 27, May, 3 6, 10 June), no. 604 (letter Melfort to Moray, 8 May 1696), no. 610 (same to same, [?15] May), no. 594–5 (same to same, [?10 June] 1686), no. 628 (same to same, 12 June 1696); Mann, 'James VII: King of the Articles', 195.

97 NRAS, 217, Moray Papers, box 7, no. 616 (letter Melfort to Moray, 20 May 1686); Dalrymple, *Memoirs*, ii, appendix to Books 3 and 4, 110.

98 NRAS, 217, Moray Papers, box 7, nos. 620 and 621 (letters Melfort to Moray, 24 and 27 May 1686); Dalrymple, *Memoirs*, ii, part 1, appendix to Book 5, 107–10; NLS, Wodrow MSS Quarto, XXVII (xxiii), f. 64 'The princes [Prince of Orange's] farewell to the States, Oct, 13 1688' (William's declaration on his invasion of Britain) and 'Fagel's answer to the prince in name of the States'; Smith, *History of the Modern British Isles*, 281.

99 Burnet, *James the Second*, 155–6, 186–7, 196–202; Dalrymple, *Memoirs*, ii, part. 1, Book 2, 29; Turner, *James II*, 348–55, 412–15; Miller, *James II*, 183–4, 190–5; Harris, *Revolution*, 184–5.

100 There is a debate about the size of the standing army and how these figures are presented; estimates vary. Pincus states that James had 9,000 troops at the start of his reign which increased to 40,000 (excluding Scots and Irish troops) at the close, but this had not been a gradual increase. The English army expanded to c.20, 000 because of the Monmouth rebellion and stayed at that level until October 1688 when it was increased to 35,000–40,000. In addition, many of the troops were training or on garrison duties. The 53,000 listed in the state papers includes 3,000 Scots and nearly 9,000 Irish as per November 1688. See Pincus, *1688*, 144; Childs, *Army of James II*, 174–6, 184; Harris, *Revolution*, 274–5; *CSPD, 1687–9*, no. 2124, 'list of the king's army' [?23 November 1688]; NRS, PRO, SP8/2, pt 2, ff. 99–100.

101 *Life*, ii, 89; *CLC*, ii, 175; *ST*, xii, 239; *London Gazette*, no. 2354 (7–11 June, 1688); Morrice, ii, 259–60, 267–8; W. E. Buckley (ed.), *Memoirs of Thomas, Earl of Ailesbury*, 2 vols, Roxburghe Club, 122 (Westminster, 1890), 170; Burnet, *James the Second*, 119, 122–3, 254–6, 359–60; Turner, *James II*, 316–20; Miller, *James II*, 170–2, 185–6; Harris, *Revolution*, 203, 260–9.

102 Burnet, *Supplement*, 528–9 (letter Burnet to Admiral Arthur Herbert, [nd] September/October 1688); *CSPD, 1687–9*, 309, 320–1; *ST*, xii, 489–92; *CLC*, ii, 190–6; *London Gazette*, nos. 2386–8 (27 September–8 October); Ailesbury,

Memoirs, i, 181–2; Burnet, *James the Second*, 357–8; Turner, *James II*, 417–22; Harris, *Revolution*, 276–8.

103 *Life*, ii, 188–90, 220–27, 643–7; MacPherson (ed.), *Original papers*, i , 281–4; Ailesbury, *Memoirs*, i, 188–9; Burnet, *James the Second*, 376–83; Browning (ed.), *Reresby,* 534–6; Luttrell, *Brief Relation of State Affairs,* i, 479; NA, SP 31/4/200, 'Letters of George Prince of Denmark and Lord Churchill to the king declaring that they have absconded [November 1688]'; Childs, *Army of James II*, 182–96; Miller, *James II*, 201–3; Harris, *Revolution*, 283–4.

104 BL, 4478 B, Birch Miscellanea, 6, 'Extracts from & Transcripts of original Letters of K. James II, and his Queen and the Princess Anne of Denmark to the Princess of Orange, afterwards Queen Mary'; 1686–1688, ff. 46–61; Correspondence James and Mary, ff. 46–61 (27 January 1686 to 9 October 1688, quote at f. 50, 9 October 1688); ff. 53–61, letters Anne to Mary, Princess of Orange (31 January 1688 to 22 June 1688, quotes at ff. 56v–59 (20 March 1688), ff. 59v–60 (18 June 1688), and ff. 60–60v (22 June 1688); letters Queen Mary to Princess of Orange, 51v–52v (31 July to 5 October 1688, quote at 51v (31 July 1688)); ff. 61–66v, 'Questions sent by the Princess of Orange (18) to the Princess Anne of Denmark July 21, 1688', with the later answered.

105 NRS, SP31/4/244, *A Memorial of the Protestants of the Church of England, presented to their Royal Highnesses the Prince and Princess of Orange* (London, [June/July] 1688); SP 31/4/160–187 'Report of extraordinary council meeting to prepare a case for the legitimacy of the birth of the prince', 22 October 1688; *CSPD, 1687–9*, 226, 327; Prince William, *Declaration of His Highness William . . . Prince of Orange, etc. of the Reasons Inducing Him, To Appear in Arms for Preserving of the Protestant Religion and for Restoring the Laws and Liberties of the Ancient Kingdome of Scotland* (The Hague, 1688); *Life*, ii, 191–201.

106 Throughout much of Europe the birth was treated more positively. See NA, SP 77/55 Letter Book of Sir Richard Bulstrode, 1686–88, ff. 444–6 (letter from the abbot of the Benedictines in Brussels, 19 June 1688) or f. 446 (letter from Francois, Prince of Nassau, 4 July 1688 (NS)).

107 *Life*, ii, 233–4, 246–7; Browning (ed.), *Reresby,* 536; *HMC, Stuart Manuscripts*, i (London, 1902), 35 and RA SP/MAIN/1/23, 'Lettre de la reyne Dangleterre Ecrite du Calais au Roy de france' (11 December 1688).

108 *CLC*, ii, 208–11, 219–23, 230; *Life*, ii, 237–42, 249–56, 262; NUL, Portland collection, PwA 2274 and 2275 (letter Halifax, Godolphin and Nottingham to William, 8 December, 1688); Ailesbury, *Memoirs*, i, 201–2, 208, 214–15; Burnet, *James the Second*, 389–92, 395–7; Browning (ed.), *Reresby,* 539–40; *HMC, Dartmouth*, i, 236 (letter Sir Henry Shere to Dartmouth, 17 December 1688); NRS, Papers of the Montgomery Family, earls of Eglinton, GD3/10/3/9, 'Copy letters King James to the general of his army, and from Feversham to prince of Orange' (?10 December 1688, wrongly dated 2 December); Turner, *James II*, 433–5, 444–9; Miller, *James II*, 205–8. Sunderland fled to The Netherlands not to France.

109 *CLC*, ii, 226–30, 232–4; Burnet, *James the Second*, 409–10, 417–18; *Life*, ii, 264–7, 270–2; Ailesbury, *Memoirs*, i, 218, 222–5; Browning (ed.), *Reresby,* 540–1; *HMC, Hamilton*, 175; King James II, *His Majestie's Reasons for Withdrawing Himself from Rochester* ([London], 1688); Turner, *James II*, 449–55; Middleton, *Life of Middleton*, 124–8; Linklater and Hesketh, *For King and Conscience*, 148–9; Callow, *King in Exile*, 10–23: R. Beddard (ed.), *Kingdom without a King: Journal of the Provisional Government in the Revolution of 1688* (Oxford,1988), 62–4.

110   Browning (ed.), *Reresby*, 518–20; Childs, *The Army of James II*, 182–96; Linklater and Hesketh, *For King and Conscience*, 150–1.

111   I.B. Cowan, 'The Reluctant Revolutionaries: Scotland in 1688', in E. Cruickshanks (ed.), *By Force or Default? The Revolution of 1688–1689* (Edinburgh, 1989), 65–81; B.P. Lenman, 'The Poverty of Political Theory in the Scottish Revolution of 1688–90' in L.G. Schwoerer (ed.), *The Revolution of 1688–89* (Cambridge, 1992), 244–59; B.P. Lenman, 'The Scottish nobility and the revolution of 1688–1690', in R. Beddard (ed.), *The Revolutions of 1688* (1991), 137–62.

112   Miller, *Popery and Politics*, Appendix 3, 269–272, 240–46; Harris, *Revolution*, 182–236; Pincus, *1688*, 143–78.

113   *RPCS, third series*, xii, 435 (21 August, 1686), xiii, xviii; xlviii; Fountainhall, *Historical Notices*, ii, 814, 856–7, 867; RA SP/MAIN/1/22 (letter Perth to Cardinal Howard, 3 February 1688); M. Glozier, 'The Earl of Melfort, the Court Catholic Party and the Foundation of the Order of the Thistle, 1687', *SHR*, 69 (2000), 233–8; Gifford et al. *Buildings of Scotland: Edinburgh*, 149–50. The eight original members of the order were Perth, Gordon, Atholl, Hamilton, Seaforth, Melfort, Dumbarton and Moray.

114   NA, SP8/1, part 2, 254–5, 'Copie of the list of gratuitous pensions signed at Whitehall the 31st October, 1685. With additional pensions since' (1685–88), ff. 255–255v; *Life*, ii, 635–6.

115   AUL, GB 3380, SCA, Historical Archives, BL1.109, 27 (Letter to Perth from ten priests, Gordon Castle, 13 June 1688), BL1.98, 24 (Letter David Burnet to Charles Whyeford, 29 September 1687), BL1.106, 12 (letter Perth to Whyeford, 8 March 1687); B.M. Halloran, *The Scots College Paris, 1603–1792* (Edinburgh, 1997), 58–63; M. Dilworth, 'The Scottish Mission in 1688–1689', *Innes Review*, 20, 1 (1969), 68–79.

116   Hopkins, *Glencoe*, 25, 105–6; Brown, *Kingdom or Province*, 165; D. Maclean, 'Roman Catholicism in Scotland in the Reign of Charles II', *Records of the Scottish Church History Society*, 3 (1929), 46, 50–2; D. Szechi, 'Defending the True Faith: Kirk, State and Catholic Missioners in Scotland', *Catholic History Review*, 82, 3 (1996), 399; J. Darrah, 'The Catholic Population of Scotland since the Year 1680', *Innes Review*, 4, 1 (1953), 51–2, 58.

117   *Papers of Devotion*, 1–4 (August 1694); *RPCS, third series*, xii, 194, 204–5, 253, 435; xiii, ix; Wodrow, *Sufferings*, iv, 371–2, 443–4; Fountainhall, *Historical Notices*, ii, 764, 816; Mann, *Scottish Book Trade*, 119, 132–3, 163–91, 256–7 (for the list of titles); W. Cowan, 'The Holyrood Press, 1686–1688', *Edinburgh Bibliographical Transactions*, 6 (Edinburgh, 1904), 83–100; Harris, *Revolution*, 151–3.

118   NUL, Portland collection, PwA 2129 (letter James Johnston to [?William Bentick] 23 January 1688), 2141 (same to ?same, 16 February 1688) and 2275; NLS, Wodrow MSS, Octavo xxx, ff. 37–53; G. Gardner, *The Scottish Exiled Community in the Netherlands, 1660–1690* (East Linton, 2004), 161–75; Turner, *James II*, 352–3.

119   N. Japikse (ed.), *Correspondentie van Willem III en van Hans Willem Bentinck* ('S-Gravenhage, 1928), ii, 13–15 (Letter Patrick Hume of Polwarth to Prince William, 22 April 1687'); Dalrymple, *Memoirs*, ii, part 1, Book 5, 21–2; NA, SP 8/2, part 2, 109–112 ('report on Scottish affairs' nd 1688); Greaves, *Secrets of the Kingdom*, 323–4; Gardner, *Scottish Exiled Community*, 179–92; Harris, *Revolution*, 368.

120   Dalrymple, *Memoirs*, ii, part 1, Book 5, 21–2; *ODNB*, J.R. Young, John Dalrymple (1648–1707): doi: 10.1093/ref: odnb/7052; Young, James Douglas (1662–1711): doi: 10.1093/ref/7897.

121   *RPCS, third series*, xii, 454, 491–3, 511, 514, 524–6, 540–3, 552; xiii, vii, xiv, xv, xviii, xxv; Fountainhall, *Historical Notices*, ii, 727, 755, 759–60, 763–4, 773, 776, 779, 792; Japikse

(ed.), *Correspondentie van Willem III*, ii, 15–21 (Patrick Hume of Polwarth, 'Memorial Upon the Edict in Scotland, 12 February 1687'); Brown and Mann, 'Introdcution' in Brown and Mann (eds), *Parliament and Politics in Scotland, 1567–1707*, 37–8. The burghs subject to some level of interference in 1686 and 1687 were Aberdeen, Anstruther (Easter and Wester), Arbroath, Ayr, Banff, Burntisland, Culross, Cupar, Dumbarton, Dumfries, Dunbar, Dundee, Dunfermline, Dysart, Edinburgh, Elgin, Glasgow, Haddington, Irvine, Inverkeithing, Inverurie, Kinghorn, Kirkcaldy, Kirkwall, Linlithgow, Peebles, Perth, Pittenweem, Queensferry, Rothesay, Rutherglen, St Andrews, Stirling, Wick and Wigtown. In some cases only one royal nominee was pressed, at others the whole council. By the Revolution forty-two royal burghs had been affected to a greater or lesser degree.

122 NRS, PA7/25/22/10 (signed commission for Linlithgowshire [West Lothian], 4 October, 1688). Reference from Dr Alan MacDonald; Young (ed.), *Burgh and Shire Commissioners*, i, 206, ii, 528. It seems Scots were much more willing revolutionaries than even recent revisionism suggests.

123 BL, 34510, Mackintosh Collections, 'Letters from the Embassador Van Citters to the States General, 1687', 111 (16 April 1688); NRS, RH3/163, 'Letters to and from the duke and duchess of Hamilton, 'Red Book', ii, 189 (letter James to Hamilton, 11 February 1688), 190 (letter Hamilton to James, 25 February 1688); *HMC, Hamilton*, 174–5; NUL, Portland collection, PwA 2120 (letter James Johnston to [?William Bentick], 21 December 1687); Fountainhall, *Historical Notices*, ii, 708, 772.

124 Colin Lindsay, Earl of Balcarres, *Memoirs Touching the Revolution in Scotland, MDCLXXXVIII–MDCXC* (Bannatyne Club, Edinburgh, 1841), 12, 15–18; *Chronicles of Atholl and Tullibardine*, i, 269–71; *Life*, ii, 336–9; *RPCS*, third series, xiii, liv; AUL, SCA, BL, 109, 22 (letter David Burnet to Charles Whyeford, 1 November 1688), 24 (same to same, 27 November), 27 (same to same, 30 November); NLS, Wodrow MSS Folio, XXVI, 4, clxi, ' Letter signed HC, unaddressed, relating story of late Monday night, when apprentices and others rifled Abbey church and were fired on by Captain Wallace. Edin.' (12 December, 1688); Mann, *Scottish Book Trade*, 132–3, 184.

125 Browning (ed.), *Reresby*, 542; Morrice, ii, 395; Dalrymple, *Memoirs*, ii, part 1, Book 7, 265–7; Balcarres, *Memoirs*, 21–2; NRS, Miscellaneous small collections of family, business and other papers, Fearne of Nigg and Picalzean, Ross-shire, GD1/576/19, 'A true account of the Transactions of Scots Affairs, 1688'; NA, SP 31/4/236, 'His Highness the Prince of Orange his Speech to the Scots Lords and Gentlemen with their address and his Highness his answer. With a true account of what past at their meeting in the Council-Chamber at Whitehall (7–14 January 1688/9); *A Speech . . . to the Scotch Nobility and Gentry . . . on the Eight of January 1689* ([London], 1689); *CSPD, 1687–9*, 392, no. 2141; Harris, *Revolution*, 379–80; Smith, *History of the Modern British Isles*, 287–9.

CHAPTER 5

1 E.R. Campana di Caveli, *Les Derniers Stuarts à Saint–Germain en Laye*, 2 vols (Paris, 1871), ii, 504; M. Hail, *Queen Mary of Modena: Her Life and Letters* (London, 1905), 226–8; E. Asse (ed.), *Memoires de Mme. de la Fayette* (Paris, 1890), 230; Turner, *James II*, 458–9; Callow, *King in Exile*, 46–7. Haile claims Razzini's words were spoken by Abbé Atto Melani writing to the Tuscan Secretary of State, 7 February 1689, but similar thoughts were expressed by other diplomatic witnesses. Haile, *Queen Mary*, 239.

2 Gregg, 'France, Rome and the exiled Stuarts, 1689–1713' in Corp (ed.), *Court in Exile*,

21–2; *ODNB*, P. Hopkins, Kenneth Mackenzie (bap.1661, d.1701): doi:10.1093/ref:odnb/17593. For a count of the Scots in James's court at Saint-Germain see E. Corp, 'Scottish People at the Exiled Jacobite Courts', *The Stewarts*, 22, 1 (2004), 40–4.

3 *Life*, ii, 329; [Anon], *A Full and True Account of the Landing and Reception of the late King James at Kinsale* (1689), 1–2; Campana, *Les Derniers Stuarts*, ii, 509–11; Gregg, 'France, Rome and the Exiled Stuarts', 22–3; Harris, *Revolution*, 426–7; Turner, *James II*, 462–5.

4 J.T.Gilbert (ed.), *A Jacobite Narrative of the War in Ireland* (Dublin, 1892, revised 1971), 79–80; George Walker, *A True Account of the Siege of Derry* (1689), 34–7; NRS, SP13/203 (29 June 1689) 'Speech of James to the Irish Parliament'; Richard Doherty, *The Williamite War in Ireland* (Dublin, 1998), 37; Harris, *Revolution*, 427–8, 438–46; Miller, *James II*, 226–8; H. Murtagh, 'The War in Ireland, 1689–91' in W.A. Maguire (ed.), *Kings in Conflict: The Revolutionary War in Ireland and its Aftermath 1689–1750* (Belfast, 1990), 61–92.

5 Campana, *Les Derniers Stuarts*, ii, 524–5; C. Rousett, *Histoire de Louvois et de son administration politique et militaire depuis la paix de Nimège* (Paris, 1862–3), iv, 206–7 (d'Avaux to Louvois, 10 July 1698 (NS); Turner, *James II*, 473; Gregg, 'France, Rome and the Exiled Stuarts', 24–9.

6 J. Hogan (ed.), *Négociations de M. Le Comte d'Avaux en Irelande, 1689–1690* (Dublin, 1934), 446 (letter d'Avaux to Colbert de Croissy), 475 (letter d'Avaux to Louvois); Miller, *James II*, 228–9; Turner, *James II*, 485–7.

7 Haile, *Queen Mary*, 267 (letter Luazun to marquis de Seigneley, 4 July 1690); Gregg, 'France, Rome and the Exiled Stuarts', 25–6; Turner, *James II*, 488–90.

8 Gilbert (ed.), *Jacobite Narrative*, 95–102; Grant (ed.), *Seafield* Correspondence, 63–4 (letter James Ogilvie to Earl of Findlater, 22 August 1690); Callow, *King in Exile*, 129–48; Doherty, *The Williamite War*, 109–16; P.B. Ellis, *The Boyne Water. The Battle of the Boyne* (London, 1976), *passim*; P. Lenihan, *Battle of the Boyne* (Stround, 2003), *passim*; Miller, *James II*, 231–33.

9 Gilbert (ed.), *Jacobite Narrative*, 167–81, 298–308; Murtagh 'War in Ireland', 88–9; Harris, *Revolution*, 448–50; Callow, *King in Exile*, 179–80.

10 Haile, *Queen Mary*, 254 (letter Mary to Gordon, 21 May 1689); E. W.M. Balfour Melville (ed.), *An Account of the Proceedings of the Estates of Scotland, 1689–1690*, 2 vols (Edinburgh 1954–5), i, 2–4, 7; Balcarres, *Memoirs*, 23–6; RPS, 1689/3/5, 9–12, 30; NRS, Papers of Gordon Family, GD44/40/2/3/7 (warrant of convention of estates to earls of Tweeddale and Lothian to instruct Gordon to remove from Edinburgh Castle in 24 hours); Linklater and Hesketh, *For King and Conscience*, 158–9, 164.

11 *HMC, Manuscripts of the duke of Buccleuch and Queensberry (Montagu House)*, ii (London, 1903), 38–9 (letter James to Balcarres, Dublin, 29 March 1689); J. MacKnight (ed.), [J. Drummond of Balhaldie], *Memoirs of Sir Ewan Cameron of Locheill* (Maitland Club. Edinburgh, 1842), 233–4; Hopkins, *Glencoe*, 125–6.

12 W. Fraser (ed.), *The Melvilles Earls of Melville and the Leslies Earls of Leven*, 3 vols (Edinburgh, 1890), ii, 33–4 (letter James to Cannon, 1 July 1689); NRS, Papers of the Leslie family, earls of Leven and Melville, GD26/11/170 (commissions for Cannon's regiment, 17 May 1689); J.M. Hog, P.F. Tytler and A. Urquhart (eds), Hugh Mackay, *Memoirs of the War Carried on in Scotland, 1689–1691* (Edinburgh, 1833), 45–7; Hopkins, *Glencoe*, 154–5; Linklater and Hesketh, *For King and Conscience*, 198–205.

13 MacPherson (ed.), *Original papers*, i, 369–72; Scott (ed.), 'Letters of John Graham of Claverhouse', 253–6 (Dundee to Lord Murray, 19 July 1689); Mackay, *Memoirs*, 46–61;

Memoirs of Cameron of Locheill, 258–71; *Chronicles of Atholl and Tullibardine*, i, 303 (letter Lord James Murray to Lord Murray, 29 July 1689); Hopkins, *Glencoe*, 156–60 (the best account); Linklater and Hesketh, *For King and Conscience*, 206–24.

14 His reputation was great but he did not rally support as Jacobites hoped. See Glozier, *Scottish Soldiers in France*, 226–7.

15 *Chronicles of Atholl and Tullibardine*, i, 306; Anon, *The Exact Narrative of the Conflict at Dunkeld* (London, 1689), 1–3; Mackay, *Memoirs*, 70–1; Hopkins, *Glencoe*, 183–9.

16 *HMC, Le Fleming*, 273 (newsletter of Seaforth's landing and Berwick expected, 7 June 1690); NRS, Papers of Leven and Melville GD26/8/117 (letter Cannon to Melfort, stating desperate need for supplies and money, [?]1690); *Melvilles and Leslies*, ii, 151 (Livingstone to Mackay, [May 1690]); AUL, SCA, BL, Box Y, 63 ('An Acct for the affaires of Scotland', 10 June 1690); Anon, *A True and real Account of the defeat of General Buchan* (London, 1690); Mackay, *Memoirs*, 93–102; *London Gazette*, no. 2556 (8–12 May 1690); Hopkins, *Glencoe*, 215–18, 233–5, 243–5.

17 J. Gordon (ed.), *Highland Papers Illustrative of the Political Condition of the Highlands in Scotland, 1689–1696* (Maitland Club, 1845), 3–83 (5 February 1691 to 3 May 1692), 99–119 (20 June 1695, report of commission); *RPS*, A1695/5/4, 1695/5/160, 5/174; RA, SP/M 18, 1, 28 (letter James to Major General Buchan, 12 December 1691); Dalrymple, *Memoirs*, ii, 217–20; NRS, Breadalbane Muniments, GD112/43/18, 6 ('articles between Breadalbane and the highlanders at Achallader, 30 June 1691'); NRS, Papers of the Earls of Airlie, GD16/52/12 30 June, 1691 ('Copy Engagement by Major-General Buchan and Brigadier Sir George Barclay, officers of King James's forces in Scotland, consenting to forbearance, but with copy of bond sworn by Glengerrie and other highland chiefs, Achallader, 30 June 1691'); NRS, Papers of the Gordon Family, dukes of Gordon GD44/40/2/3/12 ('Copy act for a cease-fire signed by John 1st e of Breadalbane, Achallader', 30 June 1691); NRS, Yule Collection GD90/2/140 (Breadalbane's report on negotiations, [nd] 1692); Hopkins, *Glencoe*, 276–9, 301, 308–39; Riley, *King William and the Scottish Politicians*, 94–7.

18 RA SP/M/ 18/104-105 ('Order for the Prince of Wales to wear the star & garter, 19 Ap. 1692' followed by 'The like order for the Duke of Powis & E of Melfort', 19 Ap. 1692'); *Life*, ii, 479–92, 619–42 ('Advice to his Son'); BL Add. MS 10118, ff. 299–303; NLS, MS 14266, 'Journal of David Nairne, 1655–1708' (NS) f. 50v (2 June 1692) (Melfort and David Nairne sent to apologise to Louis); NA, SP 89/17, part 2, 360 (James to Louis, nd 'J'en suis inconsolable parce qu'elle regarde vottre majestie par le desavantage qui vient d'arriver a votre flotte'); Callow, *King in Exile*, 192–5; Gregg, 'France, Rome and the exiled Stuarts', 34–5; J. Childs, 'The Abortive Invasion of 1692' in E. Cruikshanks and E. Corp (eds), *The Stuart Court in Exile and the Jacobites* (London, 1995), 61–72; Middleton, *Earl of Middleton*, 134–5; P. Aubery, *The Defeat of James Stuart's Armada, 1692* (Leicester, 1979), *passim*.

19 RA SP/M/18/106 (letter James to Major General Buchan, May 1692), RA SP/M/18/107–9 (letters to Lord Keith to deliver up Slains, Lord Errol Dunnottar and other letters to Queensberry, Arran, and the earl of Aberdeen). Some of these letters may never have reached their destinations. Steele, *Proclamations*, ii, 445–6; Bod. Lib., Carte MSS 181, 476; AUL, SCA, SM2/27/, 21 'Ane list of such gentlemen in the Highlands of Scotland as may render good service to his majesty' [nd. but appears 1692]; Hopkins, *Glencoe*, 355.

20 MacPherson (ed.), *Original papers*, i, 425–30, 430–1, 431–2, 433–40 (various drafts of

revised declaration); NLS, MS 14266, 'Nairne Journal' (NS) f. 50v (13 April 1693); *Life*, ii, 498, 501; Gregg, 'France, Rome and the Exiled Stuarts', 38–42.

21 Anon, *His Majesties Most Gratious Declaration to all his Loving Subjects* (Saint-Germain-en-Laye, 1693), 1–3; *Life*, ii, 501–10; Bod. Lib., Carte MSS 256, 'Letters of Middleton, secretary of state, 1693–95, Saint-Germain', f. 48; Callow, *King in Exile*, 246–8. For dispersal of the declaration see NUL, Portland collection, PwA 1408 and 1409 (letters Sir John Trenchard to the earl of Portland, 23 May and 9 June 1693).

22 BL, Add. MS 37661, ff. 75–75v (letter Melfort to Captain Middleton, 26 September 1692) from 'Letterbox of Melfort, 22 June to 31 December'; RA SP/M/18/130 (letter James to Captain Middleton, 19 March 1694), RA SP/M/18/127 (letter same to same, 21 August 1693), RA SP/M/18/128 (orders to Major Middleton, 19 March 1694); NLS, MS 14266, 'Nairne Journal' (NS) f. 49 (1 April 1693); *ODNB*, B.L.H. Horn, George Gordon (b. in or before 1649, d.1716): doi:10.1093/ref:odnb/11038.

23 NLS, MS 14266, 'Nairne Journal' (NS) f. 67v (15 January 1694) and (Louis visits St Germain on hearing of Mary's death, 16 January 1694).

24 *Life*, ii, 561–71; AUL, SCA, BL, 1/172/16 (letter Walter Innes to Lewis Innes, 29 June 1684); MacPherson (ed.), *Original papers*, i, 561–4; Acton (ed.), 'Letters of James the Second to the Abbot of La Trappe' *Miscellanies of the Philobiblon Society*, 14 (1872–76), 47–8, 53–4, 63–4; Haile, *Queen Mary*, 308, 311–13; Gregg 'France, Rome and the Exiled Stuarts, 1689–1713', 47–52. For the manifesto see NUL, Portland collection, PwA 664 (letter earl of Portland to Richard Hill, 16/26 February, 1697); Japikse (ed.), *Correspondentie van Willem III en van Hans Willem Bentinck*, ii, no. 203, 227; NUL, Portland collection PwA 1138 (Copy of manifesto, 8 June 1697); PwV, 67/44, copy of manifesto in French (8 June 1697); and also NRS, Hamilton Papers GD406, M9/220, the same; NLS, MS 14266, 'Journal of David Nairne' (NS) ff. 106–111v (27 February to 3 May 1696 (NS)), 117v (8 September 1696, Nairne to write 'memoire for the court of France dissuading the peace with the Prince of Orange'), 119 (8 October 1696), 130v (11 July 1697); Callow, *King in Exile*, 273–79, 286–94.

25 BL, Add MS 37660 ff. 37–40 (letter Melfort to Queen Mary, 3 January 1690), ff. 106–7 (same to same, 13 February 1690) from 'Letterbook of Lord Melfort', 10 December 1689 to 2 March 1690; BL, Lansdowne MSS 11638A–C, 'Earl of Melfort Letters and Memorials Dispatched at Rome, 8 March to 3 June 1690, 6 June to 26 August 1690, 26 August to 13 December 1690'; Bod.Lib. Carte MSS 181, ff. 362–3 (instructions from Queen Mary to Melfort on his mission to Rome, October 1689); *ODNB*, E. Corp, John Drummond (1649–1714), doi:10.1093/ref:odnb/8077.

26 BL, Add. MS 38144, ff. 3v–4 (letter James to Pope Alexander, 26 November 1689) from 'Papers relating to negotiations between James II and Pope Alexander VIII, 1689–90', ff. 2–31; C. Nordmann, 'Louis XIV and the Jacobites' in R. Hutton (ed.), *Louis XIV and Europe* (London, 1976), 86–8; RA SP/MAIN/1/59 (letter James to Cardinal Howard, 15 January 1691); NLS, MS 14266, 'Journal of David Nairne (NS) ff. 71v–72v (28 February to 10 March 1695); Bod. Lib., Carte MSS 209 Letters from the Earl of Perth [in Rome], ff. 298 'Instructions, 9 May 1695), 300 (letter to Nairne expressing little hope of help from Pope, 7 June 1695), 323–323v (address to Pope, July 1695); E. Corp, James Drummond (1648–1716): doi:10.1093/ref:odnb/8070.

27 Wodrow, *Sufferings*, iv, 477–92; [Sir George Mackenzie of Rosehaugh and George Mackenzie, Viscount Tarbat], *A Memorial for His Highness the Prince of Orange in Relation to the Affairs of Scotland* (Edinburgh, 1689); *RPS*, 1689/3/16; NLS, Yester Papers 7026,

ff. 94–5, 7035, f. 167; Morrice, ii, 440, 471–2; NLS, Wodrow MSS Quarto, XXXVIII, ff. 124v, 128; Riley, *King William and the Scottish Politicians*, 1–10, 49–53. In early January 1689 Scottish Episcopalians feared the game was up. Bowle (ed.), *Diary of John Evelyn*, 366 (7 January 1689).

28 *Proceedings of the Estates of Scotland*, ii, 295–6; NRS, PA7, 25/58/10, 2 (commission to Dysart) ex. D.J. Patrick, 'Unconventional Procedure: Scottish Electoral Politics after the Revolution' in Brown and Mann (eds), *Parliament and Politics in Scotland, 1567–1707*, 212–13.

29 NLS, Wodrow MSS Octavo XXX, f. 58v; *Leven and Melville Papers*, 125, 'Tarbat's Memorial in Relation to the Church' ([nd] June 1689); Balcarres, *Memoirs*, 24; *RPS*, 1689/3/2 (sederunt), *RPS*, 1689/3/6, 13, 14, 22, 23, 41, 44, 49, 51, 66, 97, 113, 134, 136, 225 (controverted election decisions 15 March to 24 May 1695); Patrick, 'Unconventional Procedure', 214–40, and for those in London and their and parliamentary backgrounds see 242–4 and Riley, *King William and the Scottish Politicians*, 165–78; Harris, *Revolution*, 390. For a more detailed account of the election and aftermath see Patrick, 'People and Parliament in Scotland', PhD thesis, chapters 3 and 4.

30 *Proceedings of the Estates of Scotland*, i, 1; *RPS*, 1689/3/27 (commission to Leven); Balcarres, *Memoirs*, 24, 31; Morrice, ii, 509–10; [John Sage], *The Case of the Present Afflicted Clergy in Scotland Truly Repres*ented ([Edinburgh], 1690); Harris, *Revolution*, 376–7, 389–90.

31 The English account of proceedings and Dalyrmple give Hamilton's majority as 40, Harris that it was 15. *Proceedings of the Estates of Scotland*, i, 1; Dalrymple *Memoirs*, ii, Part I, Book 8, 301–2; Balcarres, *Memoirs*, 25; Harris, *Revolution*, 388.

32 *His Highness [William] the Prince of Orange his Speech to the Scots Lords and Gentlemen, with their Address and His Highness his Answer* ([London],1689); J. Dalrymple, *Memoirs*, ii, Book 7, 265; Wodrow, *Sufferings*, iv, 476; *RPS*, 1689/3/16, 18, 19; Balcarres, *Memoirs*, 28.

33 *Proceedings of the Estates of Scotland*, i, 16–17; *RPS*, 1689/3/64 (committee formed), 1689/3/94 (Resolution to declare the throne vacant); Jackson, *Restoration Scotland*, 193–4; Harris, *Revolution*, 390.

34 *RPS*, 1689/3/108 (Claim of Right), 3/121 and 3/161 (Articles of Grievance), 3/131 (coronation oath), 3/162 (request convention to be a parliament); *Proceedings of the Estates of Scotland*, i, 85–9; *London Gazette*, no. 2453 (13–16 May 1689); Morrice, ii, 555; NRS, Earls of Leven and Melville, GD26/13/35 'Malversationes' [nd, 1689] of King James, used as basis for Claim of Right; J.R. Young, 'The Scottish Parliament and the Covenanting Heritage of Constitutional Reform', in A.I. Macinnes and J.Ohlmeyer (eds), *The Stuart Kingdoms in the Seventeenth Century* (Dublin, 2002), 226–40; Harris, *Revolution*, 392–404 (an excellent summary). For 1640/41 constitutional measures see *RPS*, 1640/6/27, 39 and 1641/8/55, 215.

35 *HMC, Hamilton*, 178–9 (intercepted letters to Jacobites dated 29 and 30 March, 1689); NRS, SP13/202 (letter James to Viscount Dundee, 17 May 1689); Scott (ed.), 'Letters of John Graham of Claverhouse', 239 (Letter Claverhouse to John Macleod of Macleod, 23 June 1689). Jackson mistakenly believes that James's letter refers to the Edinburgh convention, see Jackson, *Restoration Scotland*, 195.

36 G. Donaldson, *James V-James VII* (Edinburgh, 1990), 70, 164–51; 'Marie de Guise and the Three Estates, 1554–1558' in Brown and Tanner (eds), *Parliament and Politics in Scotland, 1286–1567*, 179–202; I.B. Cowan, 'The Marian Civil War 1567–1573', in N. MacDougall (ed.), *Scotland and War AD79–1918* (Edinburgh, 1991), 95–112.

37 Bod.Lib. Carte MSS 181, ff. 298–9 (letter Dundee to Melfort, 28 June 1689).

38 J. Halliday, 'The Club and the Revolution in Scotland, 1689–90', *SHR*, 45 (1966), 143–59; Riley, *King William and the Scottish Politicians*, 30–1, 39–41.

39 NRS, Papers of the Leslie Family, Earls of Leven and Melville, Correspondence and General Papers, GD26/13/45 (letter on behalf of Lord Shrewsbury to Lord Melville, 29 January 1690) plus confession of Annandale (not dated, but August 1690); GD26/8/91, Jacobite Papers (March 1690); GD26/8/94 (Letter, unsigned, dated 30 May 1690, indicating nature of plot and implicating Annandale, Ross and Skelmorlie, as well as the earl of Arran); *Life*, ii, 425–7; BL, Lansdowne 1163A, Earl of Melfort's Letters and Memoirs Despatched at Rome ('Memorial concerning affairs in Scotland sent to the Queen', 18 April 1690), 73v–76; (letter by Melfort to Queen, 23 April 1690), 79v–80v; Balcarres, *Memoirs*, 51–63; NRS, Leven and Melville, GD26/8/115 (copy declaration (no date but clearly 1690) by the 'noblemen, chieftains of clans and others who at present appear . . . in arms for our rightfull and lawfull sovereign King James'). The 'protection of Protestantism' and claim that Melville had become another Lauderdale links this to Montgomery.

40 *RPS*, 1690/4/12, 4/13, 4/22; W. L. Melville (ed.), *Leven and Melville Papers. Letters and State Papers Chiefly Addressed to George Earl of Melville, Secretary of State for Scotland 1689–91* (Edinburgh, 1842), 447–9, 453–6, 459–63; NUL, Portland collection, PwA 859 (no date), 860 (16 September 1690), and 2358 (12 August 1690), concerning confessions of conspirators before Queen Mary.

41 NRS, GD26/8/127 (Letter to the earl of Melville on the events at James's court at Saint-Germain, 30 August 1691); *RPS*, 1690/4/161; BL, Add MS 37661, ff. 1v–2 (letter Melfort to Montgomery, 4 July 1692) , ff. 150v–1 (letter Melfort to Montgomery, 1 December 1692); NRS, Hamilton Papers, GD 406, M9/235/1–4, 'Memoranda concerning the alleged contact by Lord Belhaven and the Duke of Hamilton with the exiled court at St Germain', 9–26 May 1702; P. Hopkins, 'Sir James Montgomery of Skelmorlie' in Cruikshanks and Corp (eds), *The Stuart Court in Exile*, 39–59; Young (ed.), *Shire and Burgh Commissioners*, ii, 508.

42 [Macky], *A View of the Court of St. Germain from the Year 1690–1695, with an Account of the Entertainment Protestants meet with there* (London, 1696), and republished in *Memoirs of the Secret Service of J. Macky* (London, 1733). For Prior, see for example *HMC, Manuscripts of the Marquess of Bath*, iii (Hereford, 1908), 285 (letter Prior to James Vernon, 8 November 1698). For negotiations and Portland's frustration at being unable to get access to Louis, or even hunt, because of James presence at the French court, see NUL, Portland collection, PwA 1761 (William to Portland, 8 January 1698), 1762 (same to same, 8 January 1698), 1768 (Portland to William, 18 February 1698), 1770 (same to same, 22 February 1698), 1771 (William to Portland, 23 February 1698), 1774 (same to same, 3 March 1698), 1776 (Portland to William, 7 March 1698), 1777 (William to Portland, 12 March 1698), 1801 (Portland to William, 4 May 1698), 1803 (William to Portland, 12 May 1698), 1806 (same to same, 22 May 1698), 1809 (Portland to William, 9 June 1698); Japikse (ed.), *Correspondentie van Willem III en van Hans Willem Bentinck*, i, 227–50, 298–301, 303–5, 323–5, 331–4.

43 C.E. Lart (ed.), *The Parochial Registers of Saint Germain-en-Laye: Jacobite Extracts of Birth, Marriages and Deaths, volume one, 1689–1702* (London, 1910), 128–9; NLS, MS 14266, 'Journal of David Nairne' (NS) ff. 43 (28 June 1692), 112v (30 May 1696). Note that the journal is not continuous and has gaps when Nairne was in Ireland and Rome with Melfort or away from court on family business. This David Nairn[e] is not to be confused

with the Sir David Nairn, under-secretary to Lord Melville in the 1690s. Mann, 'Inglorious revolution', 121–44.

44 Corp, 'Scottish People at the Exiled Jacobite Courts', 40–1; E. Corp, 'The royal household under James II, 1690–1701', in Corp (ed.), *Court in Exile*, 104–35, esp. 105–6.

45 NLS, MS 14266, 'Journal of David Nairne' (NS) ff. 81v (20 and 28 June 1695), 123 (30 December 1696), 129v (7 and 16 June 1697), 140–1 (20 and 28 June 1698), 141v (8 August 1698), 144v (22 November 1698); E. Corp, 'The Court as a Centre of Italian Music', in Corp (ed.), *Court in Exile,* 202–5; Cruickshanks and Corp (eds), *Stuart Court in Exile*, xv; E. Corp, 'The Jacobite Chapel Royal at Saint Germain-en-Laye', *Recusant History,* 23 (1997), 528–42.

46 NLS, MS 14266, 'Journal of David Nairne' (NS) ff. 54–54v (23 June and 8 July 1694); NRS, Papers of the Drummond Family, GD160/527/29 (receipt for jewels and pictures, 11 March 1689) and 13/2 (inventory dated 15 July 1693); BL, Add. MS 19254, ff. 79–81; 'Letters of James the Second to the Abbot of La Trappe', 9; *Life*, ii, 412–13; Haile, *Queen Mary*, 517–20 (inventory dated 26 September 1715) ; E. Corp, 'The Portraits of the Stuarts and their Courtiers' in Corp (ed.), *Court in Exile*, 180–91, 197–201; E. Corp, *The King over the Water: Portraits of the Stuarts in Exile after 1689* (Edinburgh, 2001), 33–45 (a beautiful production); Cruickshanks and Corp (eds), *Stuart Court in Exile*, xv–xvii; Callow, *King in Exile*, 168–9, 233–7.

47 NLS, MS 14266, 'Journal of David Nairne', for Fontainebleau (NS) ff. 59v (23 to 24 September 1694, returned early due to death of Francesco, duke of Modena, Mary's brother), 119–v (10 to 26 October 1696), 133–v (24 September to 8 October 1697), 163 (28 September to 12 October 1700), and references for other destinations are numerous. E. Corp, 'The Stuarts and the Court of France' in Corp (ed.), *Court in Exile*, 166–9. Corp uses details from Nairne as well as the journal of Phillipe de Coucillon, marquis de Dangeau, to fill gaps. See Dangeau, *Journal*, E. Soulié and L. Dussieux (eds), 19 vols (Paris, 1854–60).

48 B. St John and J.B. Perkins (eds), *The Memoirs of the Duke of Saint-Simon on the Reign of Louis XIV and the Regency*, 2 vols (New York, 1936), i, 167–71; *Life*, ii, 588; *HMC, Stuart Manuscripts*, i, 74; NLS, MS 14266, 'Journal of David Nairne' (NS), ff. 73 (17 March 1695), 75v (12 April 1695), 126 (7 March 1697), 139v (6 June 1698), 143 (8 September 1698), 150 (9 June 1699), 155 (18 and19 December 1699), 158 (29 April 1700); RA SP/M/18/114-115 ('List of [Scottish] Offrs subsisted at La hogue, 1692'); G. Rowlands 'An Army in Exile: Louis XIV and the Irish Forces of James II in France,' *Royal Stuart Paper* 60 (2001), 17–18 ; Callow, *King in Exile*, 184, 298–301, 356–7.

49 RA SP/M/18/246 , 'Rules for the Family of Our Dearest son The Prince of Wales' (19 July, 1696); NRA(S), 3253, Dunmore Papers, RH4/195/1, box 1 (1650–1959) microfilms (general series), No. 24, 4 May 1685. 'Abstract of what belongs to the groomes of his Majesties bedchamber towards performance of their duties according to the king's orders signed by his Majesty'; RA, SP 2/10, 'Rules for General Officers', 1–8; NLS, MS 14266, 'Journal of David Nairne' (NS) ff. 78v (18 May 1695), 100 (1 January 1696), 114v (18 July 1696), 115 (28 July 1696), 125v (26 January 1697); Oman, *Mary of Modena*, 176; B. Bevan, *King James the Third of England: a study of kingship in exile* (London, 1967), 30.

50 NLS, MS 14266, 'Journal of David Nairne' (NS) ff. 82 (30 June 1695), 112v (2 June 1696), 128v (14 May 1697), 4 July 1698), 150c (29 June 1699), 158v (17 May 1700); G. Scott, 'The Court as a Centre of Catholicism' in Corp (ed.), *Court In Exile*, 251–3; Callow, *King in Exile*, 301, 312–25.

51 NLS, MS 14266, 'Journal of David Nairne' (NS), ff. 139v (21 May 1698), 159v (2 and 15 June 1700); E. Corp, 'The Château-Vieux de Saint-Germain' in Corp (ed.), *Court in Exile*, 78–9.

52 AUL, SCA, BL, 2/37/7 (letter Innes to John Irvine, [?] 1698); NLS, MS 14266, 'Journal of David Nairne' (NS) James to Scots College ff. 74v (20 March 1695), 96 (19 November 1695), 127 (2 April 1697), 128 (4 March 1697), 152v (31 August 1699), 153 (14 September 1699), for the memoirs note especially ff. 146 (8 January 1699), 152–152v (22 and 27 August 1699), 172 (12 August 1701); Holloran, *The Scots College*, 81–2 (although the 1698 date for the bequest conflicts with Nairne's journal); RA SP/M/18/290 'Warrant charging Mr Inese with the custody of his ma[jesties] orig[inal] Memoires in order to be preservd in the Archives of the Scotch Colledge of Paris 24 March 1701'; J.F. McMillan, 'The Innes Brothers and the Scots College, Paris' in Cruickshanks and Corp (eds), *Stuart Court in Exile* , 94. Nairne set about his task by checking the accuracy of James's notes against biographies of the Prince de Condé and Cardinal Mazarin. In 1696 James had given an edited copy of his military memoirs of the 1650s to Bishop Bouillon for his biography of Turenne and the original manuscript had been tidied in the 1660s by Anne, duchess of York. See Callow, *Making of King James*, 2–7; Miller, *James II*, 242–45; E. Gregg, 'New Light on the Authorship of the Life of James II', *EHR*, 109 (1993), 947–65.

53 Stevenson (ed.), *The Letters of Madame*, i, 97; M. Kroll (ed.), *Letters of Liselotte: Elisabeth Charlotte, Princess Palatine and Duchess of Orleans* (London, 1970), 57; NLS, MS 14266, 'Journal of David Nairne' (NS) ff. 162 (26 August 1700), 154v (13 December 1699); NRS, Papers of the Drummond Family, GD160/529 /41 (letter James to Perth from Fontainebleau concerning stag hunting, 28 September 1699); Turner, *James II*, 458; Callow, *King in Exile*, 63, 208–9. Hunting was the sport of princes and King William also hunted when on campaign. See NA, SP 101/63, no. 124 (16/26 August 1697) and no. 367 (1/11 October 1697) with Elector of Bavaria and Prince Vandemont.

54 NRS, CH12/12/1546 Records of the Episcopal Church of Scotland, Episcopal Chest, Anon, *King James the Second, His Last Expressions and Dying Words* (printed on silk, Paris, 1701); NLS, MS 14266, 'Journal of David Nairne' (NS) ff. 145–6 (27 December 1698 and 4 January 1699), 167 (4 and 11 March 1701), 167v (29 March 1701), 169v (7 June 1701), 171v–173v (10 July to 16 September 1701, quote at 173); Callow, *King in Exile*, 368–78; Miller, *James II*, 239–40.

CONCLUSION

1 NLS, MS 14266, 'Journal of David Nairne' (NS) ff. 173v (16 and 17 September); BL, Add. MS 10118, 'A course and rough first draught of the History of England's late most Holy and most glorious Royal Confessor & Defender of the true Faith, King James II', ff. 409v–410 (description of the tomb); E. Corp, 'The Last Years of James II, 1690–1701', *History Today*, 51, 9 (2001), 25.

2 *Life*, ii, 619–42; *The Late King James, His Advice to His Son, Written in His own Hand and Found in his Cabinet After his Death (*London, 1703); BL, Add. MS 'A course and rough first draught of the History of . . . King James II'; [Anon], *The Life of James II. Late King of England* (London, 1702); [David Jones], *The Life of James II. Late King of England – Containing An Account of his Birth, Education, Religion and Enterprises both at home and abroad – In Peace and War* (London, 1702); [Anon], *The Memoires of King James II*

– Containing an Account of the Transactions of the Last Twelve Years of His Life: with the circumstances of his death. Translated from the French Original (London, 1702); G. Scott, 'Sacredness of Majesty: the English Benedictines and the Cult of King James II', *Royal Stuart Papers*, 23 (1984), 2–3, 5–8.

3   F. Madan (ed.), *Stuart Papers relating chiefly to Queen Mary of Modena and the Exiled Court of King James II*, 2 vols (Roxburghe Club, London, 1889), ii, 514–33, at 517–18 and 523–4 (French accounts of miracles; translations by Dr Mike Rapport); BL, Add. MS 20311, Papers of Cardinal Gualterio, I, ff. 8–15; Scott, 'Sacredness of Majesty', 3–5, 9–10.

4   *Life*, ii, 622–32; *Papers of Devotion*, 1–2, 19, 26 (August 1694), 61, 73 (1696), 115–24 (July 1697); Bod. Lib., Carte MSS 180, ff. 61–3 'A collection of several pious meditations of our Holy King writ in his own hand' (c. July 1698); Mann, 'James VII as Unionist and Nationalist', 106–7. The passage on smallpox and early dangers in his devotional writings seems to be from the Exclusion Crisis, not, as Speck claims, from 1667. *Papers of Devotion*, 107–9 (nd, ?1679); Speck, *James II*, 27.

5   Middleton, *Earl of Middleton*, 139–70; Jones, *Charles Middleton*, 255–72; Ferguson, *Scotland's Relations with England*, 161–5; Miller, *James II*, 126, 235; E. Corp, 'James II and Toleration: The Years in Exile at Saint Germain-en-Laye', *Royal Stuart Paper*, 51 (London, 1997); J. Miller, 'James II and Toleration' in Cruikshanks (ed.), *By Force of By Default? The Revolution of 1688–1689* (Edinburgh, 1989), 8–27 and Szechi, *The Jacobites: Britain and Europe*, 128.

6   Miller, *James II*, 240.

7   Ailesbury, *Memoirs*, i, 224.

8   Hogan (ed.), *Négociations en Irelande*, 23, 26; NLS, Yester Papers MS 7011, f. 56 (letter Sir James Hay to Tweeddale, 14 July 1688); Young (ed.), *Shire and Burgh Commissioners*, i, 334.

9   *Life*, ii, 621; Mackenzie, *Jus Regium: or the Just and Solid Foundations of Monarchy in General*; Rose, *Godly Kingship in Restoration England: The Politics of the Royal Supremacy, 1660–1688* (Cambridge, 2011), 229–32. For an alternative view see Pincus, *1688*, 118–22.

10   Mann, 'James VII as Unionist and Nationalist', 108–19.

11   Archives Nationales (Paris), J.677, no. 6; NRS, SP7/1; N. Macdougall, *An Antidote to the English: The Auld Alliance, 1295–1560* (East Linton, 2001), 25–7; Halloran, *The Scots College Paris*, 80, 181; D. McRoberts, 'The Scottish Catholic Archives, 1560–1978', *Innes Review*, 28, 2 (autumn, 1977), 72; NLS, MS 14266, 'Journal of David Nairne' (NS) f. 112v (3 June 1696); S. Boardman, *The Early Stewart Kings: Robert II and Robert III, 1371–1406* (East Linton, 1996), 20–2.

12   RA SP/M/18/250 'His majties promise to settle a fund in france of 100lb sterlin yearly rent to be payd to the Scots College of Paris, six months after his ma[jesties] restoration, 8 May 1697' (NS); *Life*, ii, 635; Bod. Lib., MSS Eng. e. 3454, 66–76b 'An Anonymous Treatise to a Catholic King of Great Britain, c.1710'.

13   Morrice, ii, 375 (10 December 1688, quoting Sir Robert Howard).

14   Bod. Lib., Carte MSS 180, f. 56 'A Short Relation of the Life and Death of James the Second, King of England etc, written by his majesties confessor The Reverend Father Sanders'(1703); Kroll (ed.), *Letters of Liselotte*, 57 (20 October 1690, Fontainebleau); *Life*, ii, 12; Ashley, *James II*, 255.

Select Bibliography

MANUSCRIPTS

Bodleian Library
Carte Manuscripts
Clarendon Manuscripts
English Historical Manuscripts

British Library
Add. MS 4478B, Birch Miscellanea
Add. MS 10118
Add. MS 11252, Autograph Letters of Charles I
Add. MS 17017, Letters of James, duke of York
Add. MS 18447, Copies of letters from the Duke of York to George Legge, earl of Dartmouth
Add. MS 18958
Add. MS 19254, Transcripts of letters of James Drummond, earl of Perth
Add. MS 20311, Papers of Cardinal Gualterio
Add. MS 20731
Add. MS 21483, Autograph letters to James II and others 1669–1688
Add. MS 23114
Add. MS 23119
Add. MSS 23136–23248, Lauderdale Papers, c. 1630–81
Add. MS 25124
Add. MS 28085, Papers Relating to Ireland
Add. MS 28747
Add. MS 29571
Add. MS 32681, Correspondence of Henry Sydney
Add. MS 33573
Add. MS 34507–34512, Mackintosh Collection (letters from ambassadors to the States General. 1685–88)
Add. MS 35125, Lauderdale Papers, Supplementary
Add. MS 37660, Letter Book of Lord Melfort (December 1689–March 1690)
Add. MS 37661, Letter Book of Lord Melfort (22 June to 31 December 1692)

Add. MS 38144, Papers Relating to negotiations between James II and Pope Alexander VIII (1689–90)

Add. MSS 39187, 39200, 39202, Mackenzie Papers

Add. MS 72887, Sir William Petty

Edgerton Manuscripts, 2542, 2543

Lansdowne Manuscripts, 1163A–C, Earl of Melfort's Letters and Memoirs despatched at Rome (March 1690–December 1690)

Sloane Manuscripts 629, 1009, 2753

Stowe Manuscripts 191, 199, 30

National Archives

PRO 31/5, Transcripts of the French Ambassador's Despatches (Baschet)

SP 8, State Papers, Letters James to Mostly Prince of Orange (1674–86) (King William's Chest)

SP 31, 1–5, Secretaries of State Domestic Papers (1685–88)

SP 77, State Papers Foreign, Flanders

SP 94, Letter Book of Alexander Stanhope (1686–88)

SP 101, Secretary of State: State Papers Foreign (1678–99)

Scottish National Library

Advocates manuscripts

   Adv. MSS 31.6.15, Fountainhall's Judicial and Historical Collections

Manuscript Collection

   MS 2512, Papers of Charles Kirkpatrick Sharpe

   MS 3134–8, Yule Collection

   MS 3424–27, Dalrymple Collection

   MS 7001, Yester Papers

   MS 7003, Yester Papers

   MS 7004, Yester Papers

   MS 7008, Yester Papers

   MS 7009, Yester Papers

   MS 7010, Yester Papers

   MS 7011, Yester Papers

   MS 7023, Yester Papers

   MS 7025, Yester Papers

   MS 7026, Yester Papers

   MS 7102, Royal Letters

   MS 14266, 'Journal of David Nairne, 1655–1708'

   MS 14492, Yester Papers

Wodrow Manuscripts

   Folio XXVI; XXXI; XXXIII

   Quatro XXVI; XXVII; XXXVIII

   Octavo XXX

National Records of Scotland

Church Records

   CH/1/1/11, 'The results of the consultations of the Ministers of Edinburgh and some other Brethren of the Ministerie, 1688'

CH12/12/1546, Records of the Episcopal Church of Scotland, Episcopal Chest

Exchequer Records

E73/38, Exchequer Records, Customs Accounts, 1680–1

Gifts and Deposits

GD 1, Miscellaneous small collections. Fearne of Nigg and Picalzean, Ross-shire

GD 3, Papers of the Montgomery Family, earls of Eglinton

GD 6, Biel Muniments

GD 16, Papers of the earls of Airlie

GD 18, Clerk of Penicuik Papers

GD 25, Stirling Home Drummond Moray of Abercairny, Miscellaneous Papers

GD 26, Papers of the Leslie family, earls of Leven and Melville

GD 44, Papers of Gordon Family

GD 73, Papers of Hay Family of Belton

GD 90, Yule Collection

GD 103, Papers of the Society of Antiquaries of Scotland

GD 112, Beadalbane Muniments

GD 124, Papers of the Earls of Mar and Kellie

GD 157, Papers of the Scott Family of Harden, Lords Polwarth

GD 160, Papers of the Drummond Family, earls of Perth

GD 220, Montrose Muniments

GD 224, Buccleuch Muniments

GD 305, Cromartie Muniments

GD 406, Hamilton Papers, M1

GD 406, Papers of the Dukes of Hamilton (and additional material M1, M9, L1)

Parliamentary and Council Papers

PA 2, Parliamentary Records

PA 7/9–12, Supplementary Parliamentary Papers, 1661–89

PA 7/22, Supplementary Parliamentary Papers, Addenda, 1661–78

PA 11/8, Committee of Estates

PA 12/5, minutes of committee of estates

PC 8/7, Register of the Commissioners for Pacifying the Highlands, 1682–86

State Papers

SP 4, State Papers

SP 7, State Papers

SP 13, State Papers

Register House

RH1, Miscellaneous Transcripts

RH3/163, Correspondence of the Dukes of Hamilton (microfilm)

RH 9, Miscellaneous Papers

RH 14, Proclamations

RH 15, Miscellaneous Papers, Gordon of Carnoustie

RH 18, Miscellaneous Publications

National Register of Archives (Scotland)

NRAS 217, Papers of the Stuart Family, earls of Moray

NRAS 1275, Montagu Scott Douglas Family, dukes of Buccleuch and Queensberry

NRAS 3253, Dunmore Papers [RH4/195/1]

Royal Archives, Windsor
SP/M Stuart Papers

Dr William's Library
Roger Morrice Entring Books: 3 volumes (April 1677–April 1691)

Scottish Catholic Archives, Aberdeen University (formerly Edinburgh) (*GB 3380*)
Blair Letters (1680–1700)
Scottish Mission

Edinburgh University Library, Edinburgh
La.III.354, Lauderdale Correspondence, 1657–98

Nottingham University Archives
PwA 141-2840, Portland Collection (1688–1694)

John Rylands Library, Manchester University
English Manuscripts

Archives des Affaires étrangères, La Courneuve, Paris
Correspondance Politique Angleterre

Archives Nationales, Paris
J.677

PRINTED PRIMARY SOURCES

Ackerman, J.Y. (ed.), *Letters of Roundhead Officers written from Scotland and chiefly addressed to Captain Adam Baynes, July MDCL–June MDCLX* (Bannatyne Club, Edinburgh, 1856)

Acton, Lord (ed.), 'Letters of James the Second to the Abbot of La Trappe' in *Miscellanies of the Philobiblon Society*, 14 (1872–76)

Addison, L. *A Discourse of Tangier under the Government of the Earl of Teviot* (1685)

Airy, Osmund (ed.), *The Essex Papers* (Camden Society, London, 1890)

Almack, E. (ed.), *Eikon Basilike, Or, The King's Book* (London, 1903)

Anon, *An Account of What His Majesty Said at His First Coming to Council* (London, 1684/5)

Anon, *Coronation of Charles the Second, King of Scotland, England, France and Ireland, as it was acted and done at Scone* (Aberdeen, 1651)

Anon, *The Exact Narrative of the Conflict at Dunkeld* (London, 1689)

Anon, *A Full and True Account of the Landing and Reception of the late King James at Kinsale* (1689)

Anon, *The Life of James II. Late King of England* (London, 1702)

Anon, *The Memoires of King James II – Containing an Account of the Transactions of the Last Twelve Years of His Life: with the circumstances of his death. Translated from the French Original* (London, 1702)

Anon, *Papers from the Scottish Quarters, containing the substance of two votes made by the Estates at Edinburgh at their general meeting this present Septemb. 1646* (London, 1646)

Anon, *Reasons for the Indictment of the Duke of York* (London, 1680)

Anon, *The Scotch-Mist Cleared Up. To prevent Englishmen being wet to the skin. Being a true Account of the Proceedings against Archibald Earl of Argyle, for High-Treason* ([London], 1681)

Anon, *A Short View of the Life and Actions of the Most Illustrious James Duke of York* (London, 1660)

Anon, *Some Historical Memoires of the Life and Actions of his Royal Highness . . . James, Duke of York and Albany . . . from his Birth, Anno 1633 to this Present Year, 1682* (London, 1683)

Arthur, H. (ed.), 'Some Familiar Letters of Charles II and James, Duke of York, addressed to their Daughter and Niece, the Countess of Litchfield', *Archaeologica*, second series, 58, 1 (Society of Antiquaries, 1902)

Asse, E. (ed.), *Memoires de Mme. de la Fayette* (Paris, 1890)

Balfour, Sir James, *The Historical Works of Sir James Balfour of Denmilne and Kinnaird*, 4 vols, Haig, J. (ed.) (Edinburgh, 1825)

Balfour Melville, E.W.M. (ed.), *An Account of the Proceedings of the Estates of Scotland, 1689–1690*, 2 vols (Edinburgh, 1954–5)

Balfour Paul, J. (ed.), *The Scots Peerage*, 8 vols (Edinburgh, 1904)

[Barclay, Robert], *Advertisement to all Trades-men, Husbandmen, Servants and others who are willing to Transport themselves unto the Province of New-East-Jersy in America* (Edinburgh, 1684)

Barron, D.G. (ed.), *In Defence of the Regalia, 1651–2: being selections from the family papers of the Ogilvies of Barras* (London, 1910)

Bathurst, B. (ed.), *Letters of Two Queens* (London, 1924)

Batten, Sir William, *A True Relation of what past betweene the Fleet his Highness the Prince of Wales, and that under the Command of the Earle of Warwick* (1649)

Bayne, P. (ed.), *Documents Relating to the Settlement of the Church of England* (London, 1862)

Bell, R. (ed.), *Memorials of the Civil War*, 2 vols (London, 1849)

Birch, T. (ed.), *The State Papers of John Thurloe*, 7 vols (London, 1742)

Bowle J. (ed.), *The Diary of John Evelyn* (Oxford, 1983)

Bray, W. (ed.), *The Diary and Correspondence of John Evelyn*, 4 vols (London, 1862–3)

Braybooke, P. (ed.), *The Autobiography of Sir John Bramston* (Camden Society, London, 1845)

Browning, A. (ed.), *Memoirs of Sir John Reresby* (Glasgow, 1936)

Browning, A. (ed.), *English Historical Documents 1660–1714* (London, 1953)

Bryant, A. (ed.), *The Letters, Speeches and Declarations of King Charles II* (London, 1935)

Buckley, W.E. (ed.), *Memoirs of Thomas, Earl of Ailesbury*, 2 vols, Roxburghe Club, 122 (Westminster, 1890)

Buisson, M. De, *La Vie du Vicomte de Turenne* (Cologne, 1687)

[Burnet, Gilbert], *Some Reflections On His Majestie's Proclamation of the 12th of February for a Toleration in Scotland* ([Amsterdam], 1687)

Burnet, Gilbert, *Bishop Burnet's History of the Reign of King James the Second* (Oxford, 1852)

Campana di Caveli, E.R., *Les Derniers Stuarts à Saint-Germain en Laye*, 2 vols (Paris, 1871)

Carlyle, T. (ed.), *Oliver Cromwell's Letters and Speeches*, 4 vols (Leipzig, 1861)

Carte, T. (ed.), *A Collection of Original Letters Concerning the Affairs of England from the Year 1641 to 1660 found among the Duke of Ormonde's Papers*, 2 vols (London, 1739)

Carte, T. *The Life of James Duke of Ormonde*, 6 vols (Oxford, 1851)

Cary, H. (ed.), *Memorials of the Great Civil War, 1646–52: Edited from the Original Letters in the Bodleian Library*, 2 vols (London, 1842)

Clark, A. (ed.), *The Life and Times of Anthony Wood, Antiquary, of Oxford, 1632–1695, described by himself,* 5 vols (Oxford, 1894)

Clarke, W.N. (ed.), *A Collection of Letters Addressed by Prelates and Individuals of High Rank in Scotland and by Two Bishops of Soder to Sancroft, Archbishop of Canterbury* (Edinburgh, 1848)

A Congratulatory Epithalamium, or Speech on the Arrival of Her RH, and Happy Marriage to the most illustrious Prince James, Duke of York (London, 1673)

Cooper, W.D. (ed.), *Saville Correspondence* (London, 1858)

Davies, G. (ed.), King James, *Papers of Devotion of James II* (Oxford, 1924)

The Diary of Mr John Lamont of Newton, 1649–1671 (Maitland Club, Edinburgh, 1830)

Dunn, J. (ed.), *Letters Illustrative of Public Affairs in Scotland addressed by contemporary Statesmen to George, Earl of Aberdeen, Lord Chancellor of Scotland, 1681–1684* (Spalding Club, Aberdeen, 1851)

[Eccles, William], *An Historical Account of the Rights and Privileges of the Royal College of Surgeons* (Edinburgh, 1707)

Ferguson, J. (ed.), *Papers Illustrating the History of the Scots Brigade in the Service of the United Netherlands, 1572–1782,* 3 vols (SHS, Edinburgh, 1899)

Firth, C.H. (ed.), *Clarke Papers,* 4 vols (Camden Society, London, 1891–1901)

Firth, C.H. (ed.), Edmond Ludlow, *Memoirs,* 2 vols (Oxford, 1894)

Firth, C.H. (ed.), *Scotland and the Commonwealth* (SHS, Edinburgh, 1895)

Firth, C.H. (ed.), *Scotland Under the Protectorate: Letters and Papers Relating to the Military Government of Scotland from January 1654 to June 1659* (SHS, Edinburgh, 1899)

Fotheringham, J.G. (ed.), *The Diplomatic Correspondence of Jean De Montereul and the Brothers De Bellievre, French Ambassadors in England and Scotland, 1645–48,* 2 vols (SHS, Edinburgh, 1898)

Fox, Charles James, *A History of the Early Part of the Reign of James II . . . to which is added An Appendix* (London/Philadelphia, 1808)

Foxcroft, H.C. (ed.), *A Supplement to Burnet's History of My Own Time* (Oxford, 1902)

Fraser, W. (ed.), *The Scotts of Buccleuch,* 2 vols (Edinburgh, 1878)

Fraser, W. (ed.), *The Melvilles, Earls of Melville and the Leslies, Earls of Leven,* 3 vols (Edinburgh, 1890)

[French, Nicholas], *A Narrative of the Settlement and Sale of Ireland* (Louvain, 1668)

Gardiner, S.R. (ed.), *The Hamilton Papers* (Camden Society, London, 1880)

Gardiner, S.R. (ed.), *Charles the Second and Scotland in 1650* (SHS, Edinburgh, 1894)

Gilbert, J.T. (ed.), *A Jacobite Narrative of the War in Ireland* (Dublin, 1892, revised 1971)

Gordon, J. (ed.), *Highland Papers Illustrative of the Political Condition of the Highlands in Scotland, 1689–1696* (Maitland Club, 1845)

Gordon of Ruthven, P., *A Abridegment of Britane's Distemper* (Spalding Club, 1844)

Grant, J. (ed.), *Seafield Correspondence from 1685 to 1708* (SHS, Edinburgh, 1912)

Grey, A. (ed.), *Debates in the House of Commons 1667–94,* 10 vols (London, 1763)

Hail, M. *Queen Mary of Modena: Her Life and Letters* (London, 1905)

Hay, M.V. (ed.), *The Blair Papers, 1603–1660* (London, 1929)

HMC, Eleventh Report, Appendix, Part VI, Manuscripts of the Dukes of Hamilton (London, 1887)

HMC, Eleventh Report, Part V, Manuscripts of the earl of Dartmouth, i (London, 1887)

HMC, Fifteenth Report, Appendix II, Hodgkin (London, 1897)

HMC, Fifteenth Report, Appendix, Part VIII, Manuscripts of the duke of Buccleuch and Queensberry (Drumlanrig), 2 vols (London, 1897, 1903)

HMC, Fifth Report (London, 1878)

HMC, Fourteenth Report, Manuscripts of Marquess of Ormonde, New Series, I-V (London, 1895–1908)

HMC, Laing Manuscripts at the University of Edinburgh, i (London, 1914)

HMC, Manuscripts of the duke of Buccleuch and Queensberry (Montagu House), ii (London, 1903)

HMC, Manuscripts of the Earls of Mar and Kellie (London, 1904)

HMC, Manuscripts of the Marquess of Bath, iii (Hereford, 1908)

HMC, Seventh Report, appendix (London, 1879)

HMC, Sixth Report (London, 1877)

HMC, Stuart Manuscripts, i (London, 1902)

HMC, Thirteenth Report, Appendix, Part 1, Manuscripts of the duke of Portland (London, 1891)

HMC, Twelfth Report, Appendix Part VII, Manuscripts of S.D. Le Fleming (London, 1890)

HMC, Twelfth Report, Appendix, Part V, Manuscripts of His Grace the Duke of Rutland (London, 1889)

HMC, Twelfth Report, Appendix, Part VIII, Manuscripts of the Duke of Athole (London, 1891)

Hogan, J. (ed.), *Négociations de M. Le Comte d'Avaux en Irelande, 1689–1690* (Dublin, 1934)

Huddleston, Richard, *A Short and Plain Way to the Faith and Church* (London, 1688)

Hyde, Anne, *A Copy of a Paper written by the late Dutchess of York* (London, 1686)

Hyde, Edward, *The Life of Edward, Earl of Clarendon*, 3 vols (Oxford, 1827)

King James, *His Majesties Most Gratious Declaration to all his Loving Subjects* (Saint-Germain-en-Laye, 1693)

King James, *The Late King James, His Advice to His Son, Written in His own Hand and Found in his Cabinet After his Death* (London, 1703)

Japikse, N. (ed.), *Correspondentie van Willem III en van Hans Willem Bentinck*, 2 vols ('S-Gravenhage, 1928)

John, duke of Atholl (ed.), *Chronicles of the Atholl and Tullibardine Families*, 5 vols (Edinburgh, 1908)

[Jones, David], *The Life of James II. Late King of England –Containing An Account of his Birth, Education, Religion and Enterprises both at Home and Abroad – In Peace and War* (London, 1702)

Jusserand, J.J., *A French Ambassador at the Court of Charles II* (London, 1892)

Kenyon, J.P. (ed.), *Halifax: Complete Works* (Harmondsworth, 1969)

Kirkton, James, *The Secret and True History of the Church of Scotland from the Restoration to the Year 1678* (Bannatyne Club, Edinburgh, 1817)

Kroll, M. (ed.), *Letters of Liselotte: Elisabeth Charlotte, Princess Palatine and Duchess of Orleans* (London, 1970)

Laing, D. (ed.), Baillie, Robert, *The Letters and Journals of Robert Baillie*, 3 vols (Bannatyne Club, Edinburgh, 1841–2)

Laing, D. (ed.), *Correspondence of Sir Robert Kerr, first Earl of Ancrum, and his son William, third Earl of Lothian*, 2 vols (Edinburgh, 1875)

Lart, C.E. (ed.), *The Parochial Registers of Saint Germain-en-Laye: Jacobite Extracts of Birth, Marriages and Deaths, volume one, 1689–1702* (London, 1910)

Latham, R. (ed.), *Samuel Pepys: The Shorter Pepys* (London, 1987)

Latham, R. and Matthews, W. (eds), *The Diary of Samuel Pepys*, 11 vols (London, 1970–83; repr. 1995 and 2000)

Lauder, Sir John of Fountainhall, *The Decisions of the Lords of Council and Session from June 6th 1678 to July 30th 1712*, 2 vols (Edinburgh, 1759–61)

Lauder, Sir John of Fountainhall, *Historical Selections from the Manuscripts of Sir John Lauder of*

Fountainhall, Volume First, Historical Observations, 1680–1686 (Bannatyne Club, Edinburgh, 1837)

Lauder, Sir John of Fountainhall, *Historical Notices of Scottish Affairs Selected from the Manuscripts of Sir John Lauder of Fountainhall*, 2 vols (Edinburgh, 1848)

Lauder, Sir John of Fountainhall, *Journals 1665–1676* (SHS, Edinburgh, 1900)

Lauders, A. et al. (eds), *Statutes of the Realm*, 12 vols (London, 1810–25)

Lindsay, Colin, Earl of Balcarres, *Memoirs Touching the Revolution in Scotland, MDCLXXXVIII–MDCXC* (Bannatyne Club, Edinburgh, 1841)

Lockhart of Carnwath, George, *The Lockhart Papers: containing Memoirs and Commentaries Upon the Affairs of Scotland from 1702 to 1715*, 2 vols (London, 1817)

Loftis, J. (ed.), *The Memoirs of Anne, Lady Halkett and Ann, Lady Fanshawe* (Oxford, 1979)

London Gazette nos 1464 to 2558

Loftis, J. and Hardacre, P.H. (eds), John Bampfield, *Colonel Joseph Bampfield's Apology* (London, 1993)

Lower, William (trans.), *A Relation in the Form of Journal of the Voiage and Residence which the most mighty Prince Charles the II King of Great Britain, &c. hath made in Holland, from the 25 of May, to the 2 of June, 1660* (The Hague, 1660)

Luttrell, Narcissus, *Brief Relation of State Affairs, 1678–1714* (Oxford, 1857)

[Macky], *A View of the Court of St. Germain from the Year 1690–1695, with an Account of the Entertainment Protestants meet with there* (London, 1696), and republished in *Memoirs of the Secret Service of J. Macky* (London, 1733)

[Marvell, A.], *An Account of the Growth of Popery and Arbitrary Government in England* (Amsterdam, 1677)

Macinnes, A.I., Harper, M.D. and Fryer, L.G. (eds), *Scotland and the Americas, c.1650–c.1939:A Documentary Source Book* (SHS, Edinburgh, 2002)

Mackay, Hugh, *Memoirs of the War Carried on in Scotland, 1689–1691* (Edinburgh, 1833),

Mackenzie, Sir George, *A Vindication of His Majesties Government, & Iudicatures, in Scotland; From some Aspersions thrown on them by scandalous Pamphlets, and News-books: and especially, with Relation to the late Earl of Argiles Process* (Edinburgh, 1683)

Mackenzie, Sir George, *Jus regium, or, The Just and Solid Foundations of Monarchy in general, and more especially of the Monarchy of Scotland* (Edinburgh, 1684)

Mackenzie, Sir George, *Memoirs of the Affairs of Scotland from the Restoration of King Charles II* (Edinburgh, 1821)

[Mackenzie, Sir George and Mackenzie, George Viscount Tarbat], *A Memorial for His Highness the Prince of Orange in Relation to the Affairs of Scotland* (Edinburgh, 1689)

MacKnight, J. (ed.), [J. Drummond of Balhaldie], *Memoirs of Sir Ewan Cameron of Locheill* (Maitland Club. Edinburgh, 1842)

Macleod, W. (ed.), *Journal of the Hon. John Erskine of Carnock, 1683–1687* (SHS, Edinburgh, 1893)

MacPherson, J. (ed.), *Original Papers . . . and Life of James II*, 3 vols (London, 1775),

Macray, W.D. (ed.), *The Ruthven Correspondence: letters and papers of Patrick Ruthven, Earl of Forth and Brentford, and of his family: A.D. 1615–A.D. 1662; with an appendix of papers relating to Sir John Urry* (Oxford, 1868)

Madan, F. (ed.), *Stuart Papers relating chiefly to Queen Mary of Modena and the Exiled Court of King James II,* 2 vols (Roxburghe Club, London, 1889)

Magalotti, L., *Lorenzo Magalotti at the Court of Charles II. His Relazione d'Inghilterra of 1668* (Waterloo, Canada, 1980)

Mahaffy, R.P. (ed.), *Calendar of State Papers Relating to Ireland, 1660–70*, 4 vols (London, 1905–10)

Maidment, J. (ed.), *Argyll Papers, 1640–1723* (Edinburgh, 1834)

Maidment, J. (ed.), *The Remains of Sir Robert Sibbald, containing his autobiography, memoirs of the Royal College of Physicians, a portion of his literary correspondence, and an account of his MSS* (Edinburgh, 1833–37)

Maidment, J. (ed.), *The Spottiswoode Miscellany: A collection of original papers, illustrative chiefly of the civill and ecclesiastical history of Scotland* (Edinburgh, 1844)

Meikle, H.W. (ed.), *The Correspondence of the Scots Commissioners in London* (Edinburgh, 1917)

Melville, W.L. (ed.), *Leven and Melville Papers. Letters and State Papers Chiefly Addressed to George Earl of Melville, Secretary of State for Scotland 1689–91* (Edinburgh, 1842)

Memoirs of Mademoiselle de Montpensier, 3 vols (London, 1848)

Mercurius Politicus 1651–1660

Mignet, F.A.M., *Négociations relatives à la succession d'Espagne*, 4 vols (1835–42)

Miscellanea aulica: or, a collection of state-treatises, never before publish'd. Containing, Letters by K. Charles and K. James II. in their Exile. (London, 1702)

Mowat, S. and Richards, E.J., *High Court of Admiralty Records, 1627–1750* (Edinburgh, 2005), CD-Rom

[N.M.], *A Modest Apology for the Students of Edenburgh Burning the Pope December 1680 (sic), Humbly Rescuing the Actors from the Imputation of Disloyalty and Rebellion, with which they are charged in a letter* (London, 1681)

Nalson, J., *A True Copy of the Journal of the High Court of Justice for the Trial of King Charles I* (London, 1684)

Napier, M. (ed.), *Memorials of Montrose and his Times*, 2 vols (Maitland Club, 1848–50)

Nicoll, John, *A Diary of Public Transactions and other Occurrences Chiefly in Scotland, from January 1650 to June 1667* (Edinburgh, 1836)

Norrington, R. (ed.), *Dearest Minette: The Letters between Charles II and his Sister Henrietta, the Duchesse d'Orleans* (London, 1996)

Ornsby, G. (ed.), *The Correspondence of John Cosin, Lord Bishop of Durham, together with other papers illustrative of his life and times*, 2 vols (Durham, 1868–72)

Paton, H.M. (ed.), 'Letters from John, Earl of Lauderdale and others, to Sir John Gilmour, President of the Session' in *SHS, Miscellany, V* (Edinburgh, 1933)

Paton, H.M. (ed.), 'Letters from John, Second Earl of Lauderdale, to John, Second Earl of Tweeddale, and Others' in *SHS, Miscellany, VI* (Edinburgh, 1939)

Peterkin, A. (ed.), *Records of the Kirk of Scotland, Containing the Acts and Proceedings of the General Assemblies* (1838)

'Philanax Verax', *A Letter to His Royal Highness the Duke of York touching his Revolt from, or Return to the Protestant Religion (London, 1681)*

Poems on Affairs of State, from the Reign of K. James the First, to this present year 1703, I (London, 1703)

Powell, J.R. and Timings, E.K. (eds), *Documents Relating to the Civil War, 1642–1648* (London, 1963)

A Proclamation Concerning the Students in the College of Edinburgh, 20 January 1681 (Edinburgh, 1681)

A Proclamation Offering a Reward and Indemnity to such as shall discover the Burning of Priestfield, 13 January 1681 (Edinburgh, 1681)

A Proclamation Signifying His Majesties Pleasure That all Men being in Office . . . shall so continue . . . (London, 1685)

A Publication of Royal Authority of . . . James the Seventh, King of Scotland &c. [upon his Majesty's Accession] (Edinburgh, 1685)

Ramsay, A.M., *The History of Henri de la Tour d'Auvergne*, 2 vols (London, 1735)

Registrum Magni Sigilli Regum Scotorum: Register of the Great Seal of Scotland, xi (1660–68)

The Right Honourable the Earl of Arlington's Letters (1664–1674) (London, 1701)

Rousett, C., *Histoire de Louvois et de son administration politique et militaire depuis la paix de Nimège* (Paris, 1862–3)

[Sage, John], *The Case of the Present Afflicted Clergy in Scotland Truly Represented* ([Edinburgh], 1690)

Scott, A.M. (ed.), 'Letters of John Graham of Claverhouse', *SHS, Miscellany, XI* (Edinburgh, 1990)

Scott, Sir Walter (ed.), A. Hamilton, *Memoirs of Count Grammont* (London, 1902)

Sells, A. L. (ed.), King James, *The Memoirs of James II: His Campaigns as Duke of York, 1652–1660* (Bloomington, 1962)

Selly, G. H. (trans.), *The Memoirs of La Grande Mademoiselle* (New York, 1928)

[Shields, Alexander], *A Hind Let Loose: Or, An Historical Representation of the Testimony of the Church of Scotland for the Interest of Christ; With the true State thereof in all its Periods* ([Edinburgh], 1687)

Some further matters of fact relating to the administration of Affairs in Scotland under the Duke of Lauderdale offered to His Majesties Consideration in Obedience to his Royal Command (?Edinburgh, 1679)

Spalding, John, *Memorialls of the Trubles in Scotland and in England, 1624–1645*, 2 vols (Spalding Club, Aberdeen, 1850–1)

St John, B. and Perkins, J.B. (eds), *The Memoirs of the Duke of Saint-Simon on the Reign of Louis XIV and the Regency*, 2 vols (New York, 1936)

The State Letters of Henry, Earl of Clarendon, 2 vols (Oxford, 1763)

Steele, R., *A Bibliography of Royal Proclamations*, 3 vols in 2 (New York, 1967)

Stevenson, G.S. (ed.), *The Letters of Madame. The Correspondence of Elizabeth-Charlotte of Bavaria, Princess Palatine, Duchess of Orleans*, 2 vols (London, 1924)

[Stewart, James and Stirling, James], *Naphtali, or the Wrestlings of the Church of Scotland for the Kingdom of Christ* ([Rotterdam], 1667)

Stuart J. (ed.), *The Miscellany of the Spalding Club*, volume iii (Gordon Letters) (Aberdeen, 1846)

Sylvester, M. (ed.), R. Baxter, *Reliquiae Baxterianae, Or Mr Richard Baxter's Narrative of the Most Memorable Passages of his Life and Times* (London, 1696)

Terry, C.S. (ed.), *The Cromwellian Union: papers relating to the negotiations for an incorporating union between England and Scotland 1651–1652, with an appendix relating to the negotiations in 1670* (SHS, Edinburgh, 1902)

Thomson, T. (ed.), Turner, Sir James, *Memoirs of His Own Life and Times* (Edinburgh, 1829)

A True and Exact Copy of a Treasonable and Bloody Paper [of Queensferry] . . . Together with the Execrable Declaration [of Sanquhar] (Edinburgh, 1680)

A True and Exact Relation of his Royal Highness' Progress Upon the 3rd, 4th and 5th February Instant (Edinburgh, 1681)

A True Narrative of the Reception of their Royal Highnesses at their Arrival in Scotland (Edinburgh, London and Dublin, 1680)

Turner, Sir James, *Pallas Armata: Military Essayes of the Ancient Grecian, Roman, and Modern Art of War, written in the years 1670 and 1671* (London, 1683)

Verney, M.M. (ed.), *Memoirs of the Verney Family*, 4 vols (London, 1899)

Walker, Edward, *Historical Discourses upon Several Occasions* (London, 1705)

Warner, G.F. (ed.), *The Nicholas Papers*, 4 vols (London, 1886–1920)

Wishart, George, *The History of the Kings Majesties Affaires in Scotland under the conduct of the most Honourable James, Marques of Montrose, Earl of Kincardin, &c., and generall governour of the kingdome, in the years 1644, 1645, & 1646.* (Amsterdam, 1649)

Wood, M. (ed.), *Extracts from the Records of the Burgh of Edinburgh, 1626 to 1641* (Edinburgh, 1927)

Wood, M. (ed.), *Extracts from the Records of the Burgh of Edinburgh, 1665 to 1680* (Edinburgh, 1950)

Young, M.D. (ed.), *The Parliament of Scotland: Burgh and Shire Commissioners*, 2 vols (Edinburgh, 1993)

SECONDARY PRINTED TEXTS

Ashley, M., *James II* (London, 1977)

Balfour, V., *Henry Bennet, Earl of Arlington, Secretary of State to Charles II* (Oxford, 1914)

Becket, T.J.C., *The Making of Modern Ireland 1603–1923* (London, 2008, ex 1981 edition)

Belloc, H., *James The Second* (London, 1928)

Berenger, J., *Turenne* (Paris, 1987)

Brown, K.M., *Kingdom or Province? Scotland and the Regal Union, 1603–1715* (Basingstoke, 1993)

Brown, K.M. and Mann, A.J. (eds), *The History of the Scottish Parliament, volume 2: Parliament and Politics in Scotland, 1567–1707* (Edinburgh, 2005)

Buckroyd, J., *Church and State in Scotland, 1660–1681* (Edinburgh, 1980)

Buckroyd, J., *The Life of James Sharp, Archbishop of St Andrews, 1618–1679* (Edinburgh, 1987)

Callow, J., *The Making of King James: The Formative Years of a Fallen King* (Stroud, 2000)

Callow, J., *King in Exile. James II: Warrior, King and Saint, 1689–1701* (Stroud, 2004)

Carlton, C., *Charles I: the Personal Monarchy* (London, 1995)

Cartwright, J.M. (Ady), *Madame, A Life of Henrietta, Daughter of Charles I, and Duchess of Orleans* (London, 1900)

Childs, J., *The Army of Charles II* (London, 1976)

Childs, J., *The Army of James II and the Glorious Revolution* (Manchester, 1980)

Clarke, A., *Prelude to Restoration in Ireland: The End of the Commonwealth, 1659–1660* (Cambridge, 1999)

Corp, E., 'James II and Toleration: The Years in Exile at Saint-Germain-en-Laye', *Royal Stuart Papers*, 51 (London, 1997)

Corp, E., *The King over the Water: Portraits of the Stuarts in Exile after 1689* (Edinburgh, 2001)

Corp, E., 'Scottish People at the Exiled Jacobite Courts', *The Stewarts*, 22, 1 (Edinburgh, 2004)

Corp, E. (ed.) (with contributions from E. Gregg, H. Erskine-Hill and G. Scott), *A Court in Exile: The Stuarts in France, 1689–1718* (Cambridge, 2004)

Cowan, E.J., *Montrose: for Covenant and King* (Edinburgh, 1995)

Cowan, I.B., *The Scottish Covenanters 1660–88* (London, 1976)

Cowan, I.B., 'The Reluctant Revolutionaries: Scotland in 1688', in E. Cruickshanks (ed.), *By Force or Default? The Revolution of 1688–1689* (Edinburgh, 1989), 65–81

Cruickshanks, E. (ed.), *The Stuart Courts* (Stroud, 2000)

Cruickshanks, E. and Corp, E. (eds), *The Stuart Court in Exile and the Jacobites* (London, 1995)

Dalton, C., *The Scots Army 1661–1688, with memoirs of the commander-in-chiefs* (London and Edinburgh, 1909)

Delpech, J., *The Life and Times of the Duchess of Portsmouth* (London, 1953)

Dennehy, C.A. (ed.), *Restoration Ireland* (Farnham, 2008)

Devine, T.M., *Scotland's Empire, 1600–1815* (London, 2003)

Doherty, R., *The Williamite War in Ireland* (Dublin, 1998)

Donaldson, G., *James V–James VII* (Edinburgh, 1978)

Dow, F.D., *Cromwellian Scotland* (Edinburgh, 1979, reprinted 1999)

Ellis, P.B., *The Boyne Water. The Battle of the Boyne* (London, 1976)

Fea, A., *James II and his Wives* (London, 1908),

Ferguson, W., *Scotland 1689 to the Present* (Edinburgh, 1978)

Ferguson, W., *Scotland's Relations with England: A Survey to 1707* (Edinburgh, 1977, reprinted 1994)

Fitzpatrick, B., *Seventeenth-Century Ireland: The War of Religions* (Basingstoke, 1988),

Fraser, A., *King Charles II* (London, 1979, 1993, reprinted 2002)

Gardner, G., *The Scottish Exiled Community in the Netherlands, 1660–1690* (East Linton, 2004),

Glassey, L.K.J. (ed.), *The Reigns of Charles II and James VII & II* (Basingstoke, 1997)

Glozier, M., *Scottish Soldiers in France in the Reign of the Sun King: Nursery of Men of Honour* (Leiden, 2004)

Goodare, J., *The Government of Scotland, 1560–1625* (Oxford, 2004)

Gordon, R., *A Genealogical History of the Earldom of Sutherland* (Edinburgh, 1813)

Graham, E.J., *A Maritime History of Scotland, 1650–1790* (East Linton, 2002)

Graham, J.M. (ed.), *Annals and Correspondence of Viscount and the First and Second Earls of Stair,* 2 vols (Edinburgh, 1875)

Grainger, J.D., *Cromwell Against the Scots: The Last Anglo-Scottish War, 1650–1652* (East Linton, 1997)

Greaves, R.L., *Secrets of the Kingdom: British Radicals from the Popish Plot to the Revolution of 1688–89* (Stanford, 1992)

Haley, K.H.D., *The First Earl of Shaftesbury* (Oxford, 1968),

Halloran, B.M., *The Scots College Paris, 1603–1792* (Edinburgh, 1997)

Harris, T., *Restoration, Charles II and his Kingdoms, 1660–1685* (London, 2005)

Harris, T., *Revolution, The Great Crisis of the British Monarchy, 1685–1720* (London, 2006)

Harris, T. and Taylor, S. (eds), *The Final Crisis of the Stuart Monarchy: The Revolutions of 1688–91 in the British, American and European Context* (Woodbridge, 2013)

Hartman, C.H., *Charles II and Madame* (London, 1934)

Hay, M.V., *The Enigma of James II* (London, 1938)

Hopkins, P., *Glencoe and the End of the Highland War* (Edinburgh, 1990)

Hutton, R., *The Restoration: A Political and Religious History of England and Wales, 1658–1667* (Oxford, 1986, reprinted 2001)

Hutton, R., *Charles II: King of England, Scotland and Ireland* (Oxford, 1989)

Hutton, R. (ed.), *Louis XIV and Europe* (London. 1976)

Hutton, R. and Pincus, S. (eds), *A Nation Transformed: England after the Restoration* (Cambridge, 2001, reprinted 2011)

Insh, G.P., *Scottish Colonial Schemes* (Glasgow, 1922)

Jackson, C., *Restoration Scotland, 1660–1690: Royalist Politics, Religion and Ideas* (Woodbridge, 2003)

Jones, G.H., *Charles Middleton: The Life and Times of a Restoration Politician* (Chicago, 1967)

Kennedy, A.D., *Governing Gaeldom: The Scottish Highlands and the Restoration State, 1660–1688* (Leiden, 2014)

Landsman, N.C., *Scotland and its First American Colony, 1683–1765* (Princeton, NJ, 1985)

Lang, A., *Sir George Mackenzie, King's Advocate, of Rosehaugh: his Life and Times, 1636(?)–1691* (London, 1909)

Lee, M., Jr, *The 'Inevitable' Union and Other Essays on Early Modern Scotland* (East Linton, 2003)

Lee, M., Jr, *'Dearest Brother': Lauderdale, Tweeddale and Scottish Politics 1660–1674* (Edinburgh, 2010)

Lee, M., Jr, *The Cabal* (Urbana, 1965)

Lenihan, P., *Battle of the Boyne* (Stround, 2003)

Lenman, B.P., *The Jacobite Risings in Britain 1689–1746* (London, 1980)

Lenman, B.P., 'The Scottish Nobility and the Revolution of 1688–1690', in R. Beddard (ed.), *The Revolutions of 1688* (Oxford, 1991), 137–62

Lenman, B.P., 'The Poverty of Political Theory in the Scottish Revolution of 1688–90' in L.G. Schwoerer (ed.), *The Revolution of 1688–89* (Cambridge, 1992), 244–59

Lingard, J., *History of England* (London, 1855)

Linklater, M. and Hesketh, C., *For King and Conscience: John Graham of Claverhouse, Viscount Dundee (1648–1689)* (London, 1989)

Lonqueville, T., *The Adventures of King James II of England* (London, 1904)

Lonqueville, T., *Marshal Turenne* (London, 1907)

Macaulay, T.B., *The History of England* (1848–61, Harmondsworth, 1979)

Macinnes, A.I., *Charles I and the Making of the Covenanting Movement 1625–1641* (Edinburgh, 1991)

Macinnes, A.I., *Clanship, Commerce and the House of Stuart, 1603–1788* (East Linton, 1996)

Macinnes, A.I., *The British Revolution, 1629–1660* (Basingstoke, 2005)

Macinnes, A.I., *Union and Empire: The Making of the United Kingdom in 1707* (Cambridge, 2007)

MacIntosh, G.H., *The Scottish Parliament under Charles II, 1660–1685* (Edinburgh, 2007)

Maguire W.A. (ed.), *Kings in Conflict: The Revolutionary War in Ireland and its Aftermath 1689–1750* (Belfast, 1990)

Mann, A.J., *The Scottish Book Trade 1500 to 1720: Print Commerce and Print Control in Early Modern Scotland* (East Linton, 2000)

Mann, A.J., 'Inglorious Revolution: Administrative Muddle and Constitutional Change in the Scottish Parliament of William and Mary', *Parliamentary History*, 22, pt 2 (2003), 134–40

Mann, A.J., 'The Scottish Parliaments: the Role of Ritual and Procession in the pre-1707 Parliament and the New Parliament of 1999' in E.Crewe and M.G.Müller (eds), *Rituals in Parliaments: Political, Anthropological and Historical Perspectives on Europe and the United States* (Frankfurt am Main, 2006)

Mann, A.J., 'Continuity and Change: the Culture of Ritual and Procession in the Parliament of Scotland', *Parliament, Estates and Representation*, 29 (2009), 151–2.

Mann, A.J., 'The Law of the Person: Parliament and Social Control' in K.M. Brown and A.R. MacDonald (eds), *Parliament in Context, 1235–1707* (Edinburgh, 2010)

Mann, A.J., 'James VII as Unionist and Nationalist: A Monarch's View of the Scottish Parliament Through his Writings', *Parliaments, Estates and Representation*, 33, 2 (2013), 101–19

Marshall, R.K., *The Days of Duchess Anne: Life in the Household of the Duchess of Hamilton, 1656–1716* (London, 1973)

Masters, B., *The Mistresses of Charles II* (London, 1997)

Middleton, D., *The Life of Charles 2nd earl of Middleton* (London, 1957)

Miller, J., *Popery and Politics in England, 1660–1688* (Cambridge, 1973, reprinted 2008)

Miller, J., *James II: A Study in Kingship* (London,1978; reissued 1989 and 2000)

Miller, J., *The Glorious Revolution* (London, 1997)

Miller, J., *The Stuarts* (London, 2004)

Mullett, M., *James II and English Politics 1678–1688* (London, 1994)

Murdoch, S. (ed.), *Scotland and the Thirty Years' War* (Leiden, 2001)

Murdoch, S. and Mackillop, A. (eds), *Fighting for Identity: Scottish Military Experience c.1550–1900* (Leiden, 2002)

Ollard, R., *The Image of the King* (London, 1979)

Ollard, R., *The Escape of Charles II after the Battle of Worcester* (London, 1986)

Oman, C., *Mary of Modena* (London, 1962)

Paterson, R.C., *A Land Afflicted: Scotland and the Covenanter Wars, 1638–1690* (Edinburgh, 1998)

Paterson, R.C., *King Lauderdale, The Corruption of Power* (Edinburgh, 2003)

Pincus, S., 'The European Catholic Context of the Revolution of 1688–89: Gallicanism, Innocent XI, and Catholic Opposition' in A.I. Macinnes and A.H. Williamson (eds), *Shaping the Stuart World 1603–1714* (Leiden, 2006)

Pincus, S., *1688: The First Modern Revolution* (Yale, 2009)

Riley, P.W.J., *King William and the Scottish Politicians* (Edinburgh, 1979)

Robert, R., *Chartered Companies: Their Role in the Development of Overseas Trade* (London, 1969)

Rose, J., *Godly Kingship in Restoration England: The Politics of the Royal Supremacy, 1660–1688* (Cambridge, 2011)

Scott, G., 'Sacredness of Majesty: the English Benedictines and the Cult of King James II', *Royal Stuart Papers*, 23 (1984)

Seaward, P., *The Restoration, 1669–1688* (Basingstoke, 1991)

Sharpe, K., *Rebuilding Rule 1660–1714: The Restoration and Revolution Monarchy* (London, 2013)

Smith, D.L., *A History of the Modern British Isles, 1603–1707: The Double Crown* (Oxford, 1998)

Sowerby, M., *Making Toleration. The Repealers and the Glorious Revolution* (Cambridge, MA, 2013)

Speck, W.A., *Reluctant Revolutionaries* (Oxford, 1988)

Speck, W.A., *James II: Profiles in Power* (London, 2002)

Spurlock, R.S., *Cromwell and Scotland: Conquest and Religion 1650–1660* (Edinburgh, 2007)

Stevenson, D., *The Scottish Revolution, 1637–44: The Triumph of the Covenanters* (Edinburgh, 1973, reprinted 2003)

Stevenson, D., *Revolution and Counter Revolution in Scotland, 1644–51* (Edinburgh, 1977, reprinted 2003)

Szechi, D., *The Jacobites: Britain and Europe 1688–1788* (Manchester, 1994)

Szechi, D., *George Lockhart of Carnwath, 1689–1727* (East Linton, 2002)

Testa, E.E., *James II – Bigot or Saint?* (Lewis, 1987)

Trevelyan, G.M., *The English Revolution* (London, 1936)

Trevor, M., *The Shadow of a Crown. The Life Story of James II of England and VII of Scotland* (London, 1988)

Turner, F.C., *James II* (London, 1948)

Underdown, D., *Royalist Conspiracy in England 1649–1600* (New Haven, 1960)

Wedgewood, C.V., *The Trial of Charles I* (London, 1964)

Wedgewood, C.V., *The King's Peace 1637–1641* (London, 1983)

Wedgewood, C.V., *The King's War 1641–1647* (London, 1983)

Whatley, C.A. & Patrick, D.J., *The Scots and the Union* (Edinburgh, 2006)

Willcock, J., *A Scots Earl in Covenanting Times: Being the Life and Times of Archibald, 9th Earl of Argyll (1629–1685)* (Edinburgh, 1907)

Wilson, D., *All the King's Women: Love, sex and politics in the life of Charles II* (London, 2004)

Wilson, C.T., *James The Second and the Duke of Berwick* (London, 1876)

Young, J.R., *The Scottish Parliament 1639–1661: A Political and Constitutional Analysis* (Edinburgh, 1996)

Young, J.R., 'The Scottish Parliament and the Covenanting Heritage of Constitutional Reform', in A.I. Macinnes and J.Ohlmeyer (eds), *The Stuart Kingdoms in the Seventeenth Century* (Dublin, 2002)

THESES

Colquhoun, K.M., '"Issue of the late civill wars": James, Duke of York and the Government of Scotland, 1679–1689' (University of Illinois at Urbana-Champaign, PhD thesis, 1993)

Kennedy, A.D., 'The Civic Government of the Scottish Highlands During the Restoration, 1660–1688' (University of Stirling, PhD thesis, 2011)

Lee, R. A., 'Government and Politics in Scotland, 1661–1681' (University of Glasgow, PhD thesis, 1995)

Lennox, R. W., 'Lauderdale and Scotland: A Study in Restoration Politics and Administration' (University of Columbia, PhD thesis, 1977)

MacIntosh, G.H., 'The Scottish Parliament in the Restoration Era, 1660–1681' (University of St Andrews, PhD thesis, 2002)

McAlister, K.F., 'James VII and the Conduct of Scottish Politics, c.1679–c.1686' (University of Strathclyde, PhD thesis, 2003).

Patrick, D.J., 'People and Parliament in Scotland 1689–1702' (University of St Andrews, PhD thesis, 2002)

Scally, J., 'The Political Career of James, Third Marquis and First Duke of Hamilton (1606–1649), to 1643' (University of Cambridge, PhD thesis, 1992)

Index